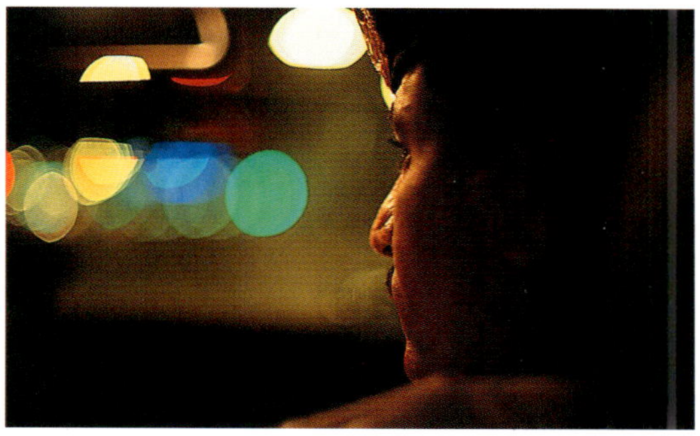

KATARINA PREMFORS

DUBAI 24 HOURS

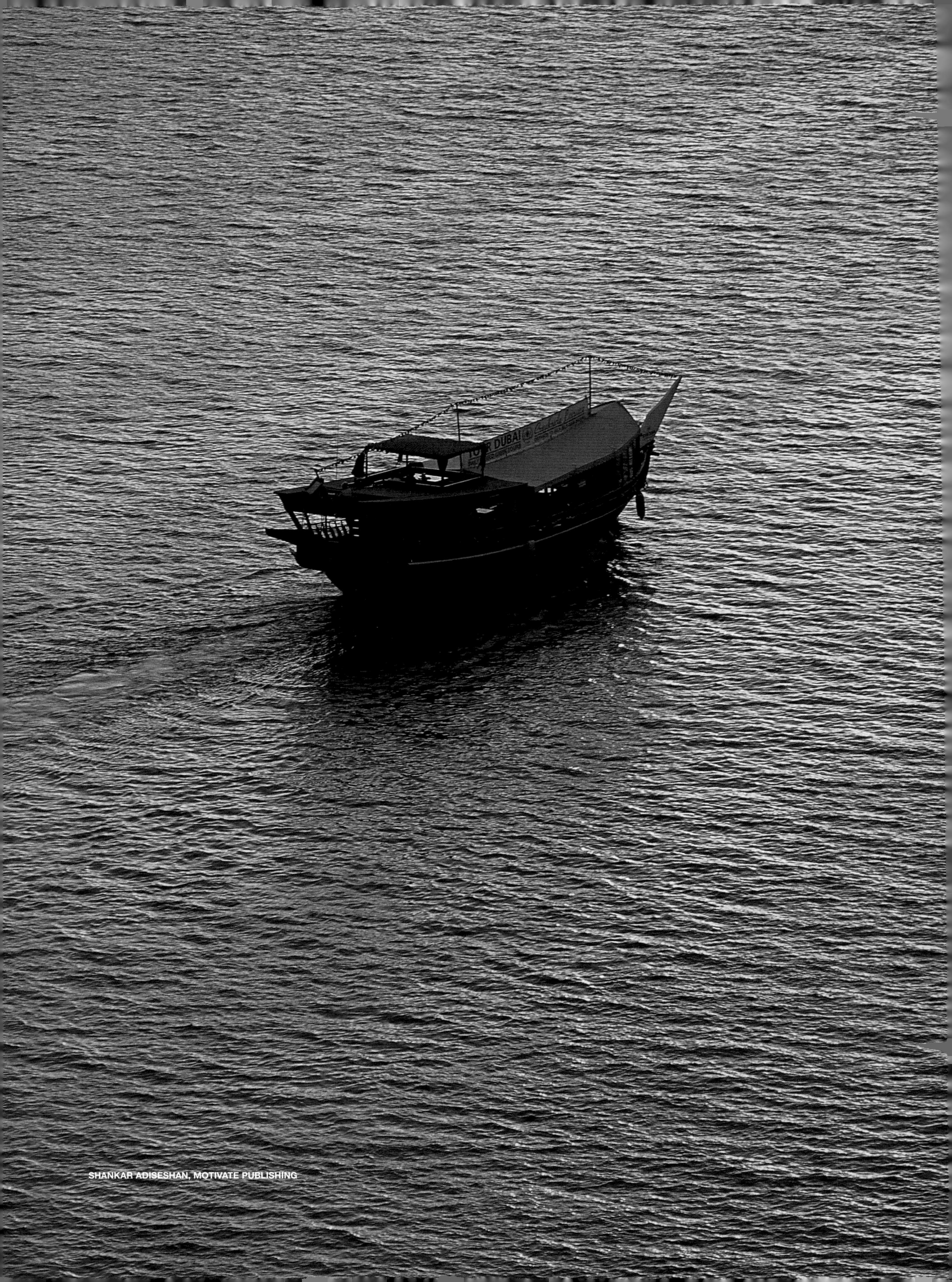

SHANKAR ADISESHAN, MOTIVATE PUBLISHING

DUBAI 24 HOURS

As experienced by a team of Dubai's
leading photographers

Written by
Michael Tobias

alarabiya productions FZLLC

MOTIVATE
PUBLISHING

DUBAI 2003
UNITED ARAB EMIRATES

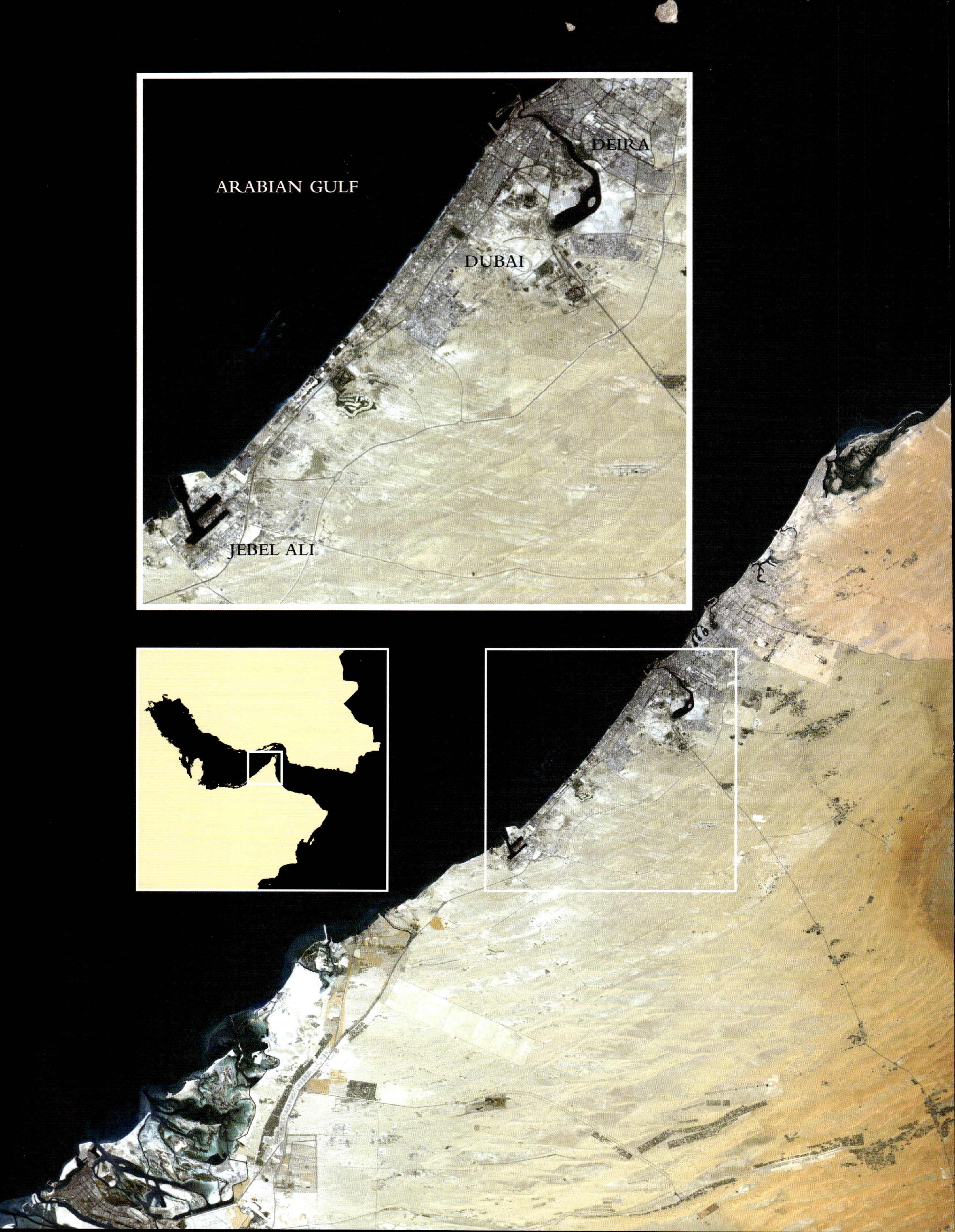
ARABIAN GULF
DEIRA
DUBAI
JEBEL ALI

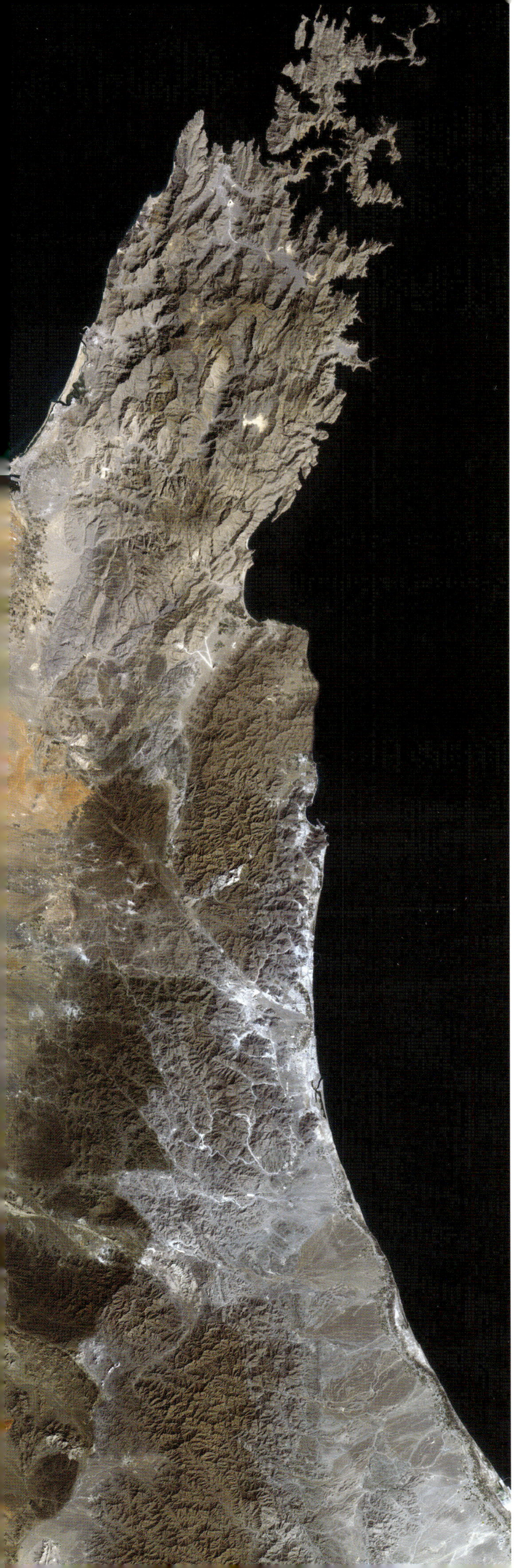

SATTELITE IMAGE OF UAE SUPPLIED BY DUBAI MUNICIPALITY, GIS CENTRE/SPACE IMAGING

Published by
Alarabiya Productions and Motivate Publishing
Dubai: PO Box 2331, Dubai, UAE
Tel: (+971) 4 282 4060, fax: (+971) 4 282 0428
e-mail: books@motivate.co.ae www.booksarabia.com

Abu Dhabi: PO Box 43072, Abu Dhabi, UAE
Tel: (+971) 2 627 1666, fax: (+971) 2 627 1566

London: Acre House, 11/15 William Road, London NW1 3ER
e-mail: motivateuk@motivate.co.ae

Directors: Obaid Humaid Al Tayer and Ian Fairservice

Written by Michael Tobias
Edited by David Steele
Book research by Tariq Syed
Editorial Assistant: Zelda Pinto
Alarabiya editorial co-ordinator: Naji Kitmitto

Design: Fred Dittlau and Johnson Machado

The *Dubai 24 hours* project was produced by Alarabiya Productions in collaboration with Dubai 2003.
Executive Producer: Ramzi Rassi

ISBN: 1 86063 153 3

British Library Cataloguing-in-Publication Data
A catalogue record for this book is available from the British Library

Printed and bound in the UAE by Emirates Printing Press, Dubai

◄ THIS SATELLITE IMAGE OF DUBAI AND THE northern United Arab Emirates is a composite of four separate photos taken during 2001 and 2002.

FOREWORD

THE UNITED ARAB EMIRATES IS acclaimed as a country that aims high and achieves its goals. At the same time, its residents work relentlessly to make this happen and, in doing so, accomplish their personal ambitions.

This is particularly apparent in the city of Dubai. By the time our current, far-reaching projects and visions are completed, we'll have the infrastructure to excel as a world-class city. Even more, Dubai will be a metropolis that sets an example to the rest of the world while providing unique opportunities for people to come in contact with each other with new technologies, innovations, ideas and applications.

We've travelled far and fast on this road to the future and are proud that we've achieved our aims without losing our unique identity and culture. These will continue to be just as important as the past, present and future live peacefully together side-by-side, each drawing strength from the other.

The eyes of the world are firmly focused on Dubai at present and we should grasp this extraordinary opportunity to promote the city and its vision.

Dubai 24 hours does just this. It graphically reflects the nature and diversity of this human experience and the environment in which Dubai has progressed – and continues to achieve distinctions and cultivate excellence.

The sands of time will show this strength. Our eyes are set on the future and there should be no hesitation in saying the future is already here. . . .

HH Sheikh Hamdan bin Rashid Al Maktoum
Deputy Ruler of Dubai, UAE Minister of Finance and Industry,
Chairman, Dubai 2003 Steering Committee

PREFACE

A GLITTERING, MULTINATIONAL BEACON WITHIN AN equally beckoning desert, Dubai announces its generous intentions to the world. Its bejeweled horizons, towering skyline, warm coastal waters and rugged interior frame the city and surrounding emirate of the same name.

Therein simmers a lovely invitation. Her honour, religious tolerance and rich incitements have scored internationally, setting a high standard for commerce, art, technology and the fusion of cultures within the region.

But these are surface observations, obtainable at a glance. Beneath the polished veneers, human lives of fascinating intensity embrace a modern truth. Not simply of the recent onset of an enormous revenue stream, advantages of location and resources which Dubai shares with some of the other half-dozen emirates, but, rather, of an irrepressible excitement that all who venture here are likely to fall prey to.

The excitement stems from the founding fathers, the sheikhs themselves – Sheikh Rashid bin Saeed Al Maktoum and his sons, who dreamt of a commercial entrepôt, took calculated risks, and steadily exhibited the vigour and sheer willpower to implement those dreams.

It was not for the sheer acquisition of wealth alone, but to demonstrate what has since come to be seen as a remarkable and rather egalitarian experiment, in the desert, whose benefits to the populace are manifest everywhere.

This hub of technology and trade also exhibits a passion for wildlife and adventure. Species have been saved, such as the Arabian oryx after which the 25-square kilometre sanctuary, Al Maha, has been named. Within five years this one ecological quadrant will constitute more than 4.6 per cent of the entire emirate.

Other reserves have been created as well, reflecting a deep environmentalist ethic whose patronage and influence is consistent with the tenor of modernity shaping the hierarchies of power, the bastions of scientific research and the very force of positive social change that calls Dubai home. Which is not to ignore various ecological challenges facing the emirates, such as four-wheel drives unintentionally undermining subtle dune biodiversity, but these are

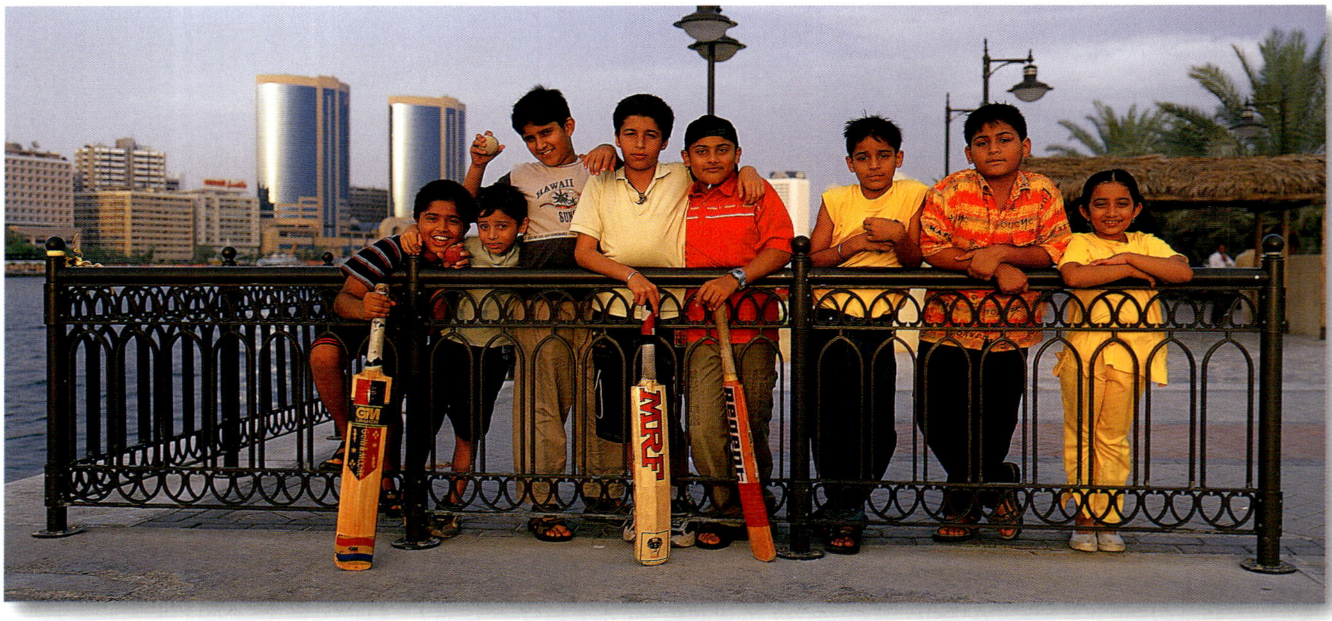

DARIUSH ZANDI

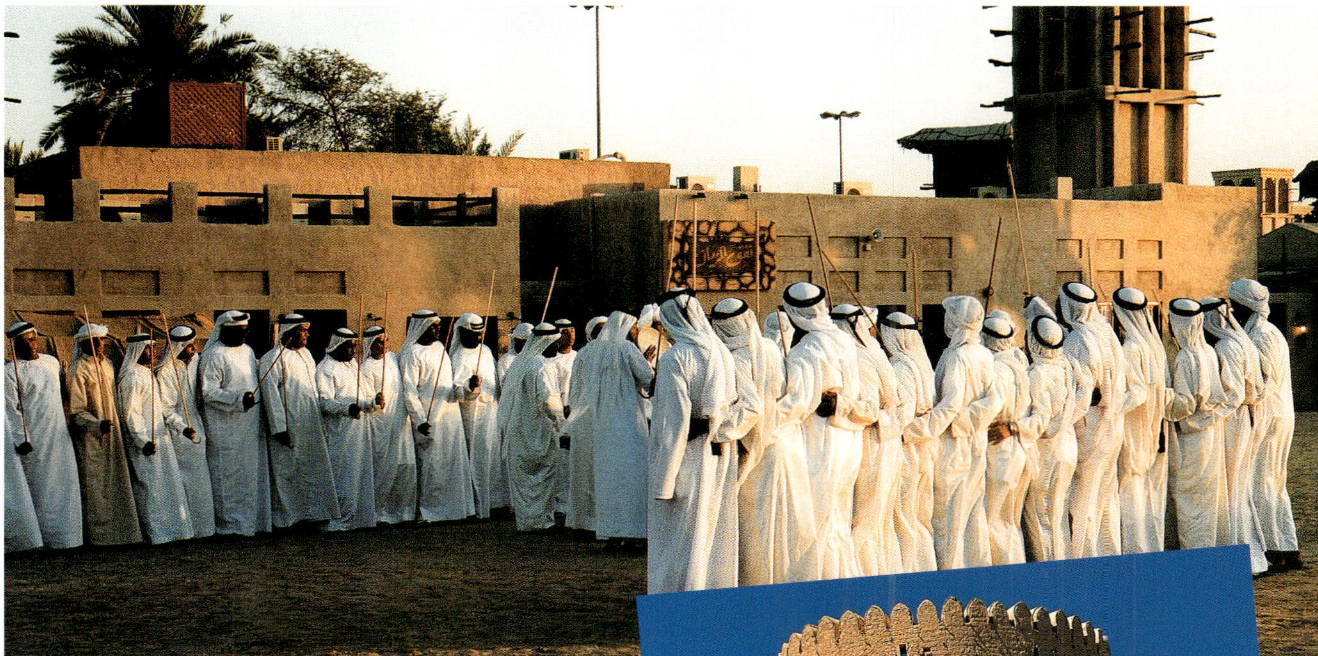

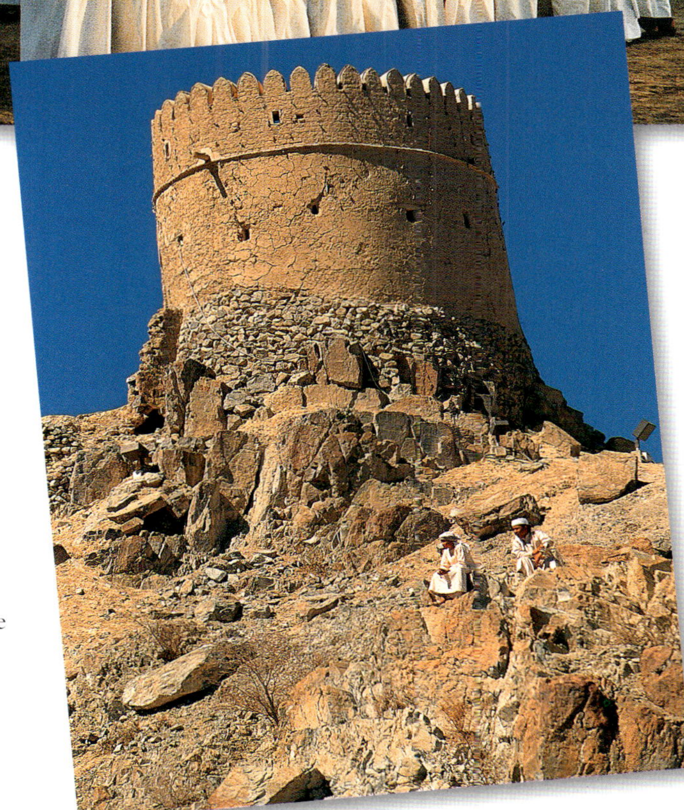

challenges inherent to rapid progress in every country of the world.

The city and environs teem with a subtle robustness that in many ways distinguishes it from the rest of the Middle East – because it is peaceful and intends to stay that way. There is a local Islamic sobriety, to be sure. Yet, a large percentage of the population has come from elsewhere, received warmly into this society with ideals, ethnic customs and sensibilities that have merged into a true melting pot where individualism, anecdote and eccentricity are treasured, and fine journalism and satire are admired more than ever before.

Scientists, Malayalam-speaking taxi drivers, photographers from Europe or Lebanon, Bangladeshi merchants, indigenous nomads and their camels, fishermen, and Wall Street analysts mingle in charming alleyways alive with countless working languages and customs – and where the night life, cuisine, gold jewellery and cultural wares are exceptional. Where globalisation has not smothered a beguiling history. And for all that, the city – with its skyscrapers and freeways – remains immaculate and its policemen actually smile.

Dubai 24 hours is not intended to be a comprehensive exposé, but more the haiku; a poetic glimpse of a deep and enduring world that is unpredictable and refreshing. This has been achieved with support from his HH General Sheikh Mohammed bin Rashid Al Maktoum, Crown Prince of Dubai and UAE Defence Minister, Alarabiya Productions and the many photographers and filmmakers who were brought on board, all of whom embody the same rare hybrid passions which make this city, and the emirates, so appealing.

THE MAKING OF *DUBAI 24* HOURS

THE PROJECT WAS, FROM THE OUTSET, TO BE AN EVENT; a collaboration of filmmakers, photographers, graphic designers, writers, musicians and the vast collective of subjects themselves within Dubai. The challenge: to sweep the emirate with an artistic ambition that would mirror the energies, passions and many faces of a dream locale, sharpening the focus and galvanising the vast range of talent into a story. And then, to give loft to that story, so that the dream would become a familiar reality – and that which was familiar would suddenly speak in a new way.

A local audience might feel new access, see novel perspectives, while an international audience would be introduced to a world utterly unknown to them. Exotic, ancient, fast-moving, lovely and driven by a compelling and fascinating future. . . .

That future would begin with Dubai 2003, the Annual Meetings of the Board of Governors of the World Bank Group and the International Monetary Fund, held in September: a convergence of financial forces from all round the world and its embrace by an entire multicultural hub of technology, art, science, finance and history.

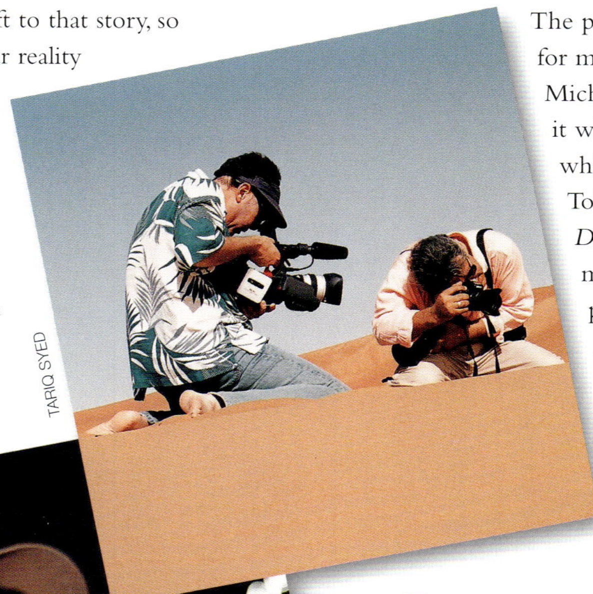

TARIQ SYED

The project was in development for many years. Writer/Director Michael Tobias had first discussed it with Producer Tariq Syed while they were completing Tobias' feature documentary *A Day in the Life of India* in the mid-1990s. Syed later presented the idea to Alarabiya and its Executive Producer, Ramzi Rassi. The rest is history.

With the persistent support of Alarabiya's

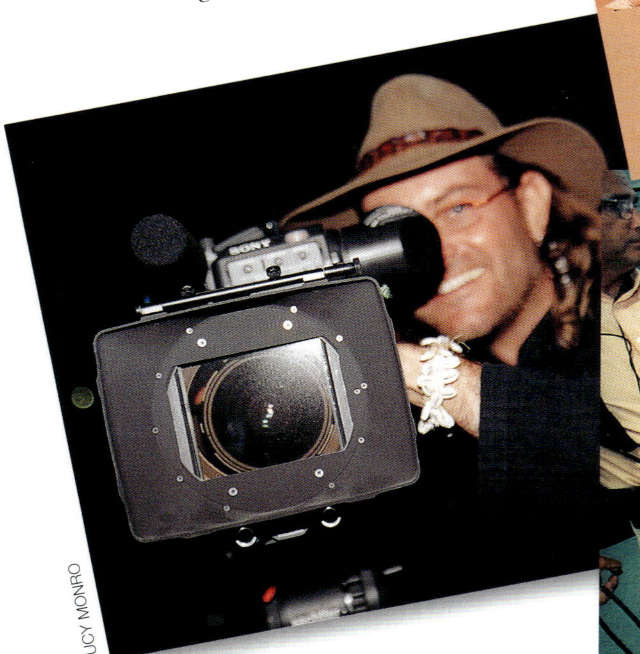

LUCY MONRO

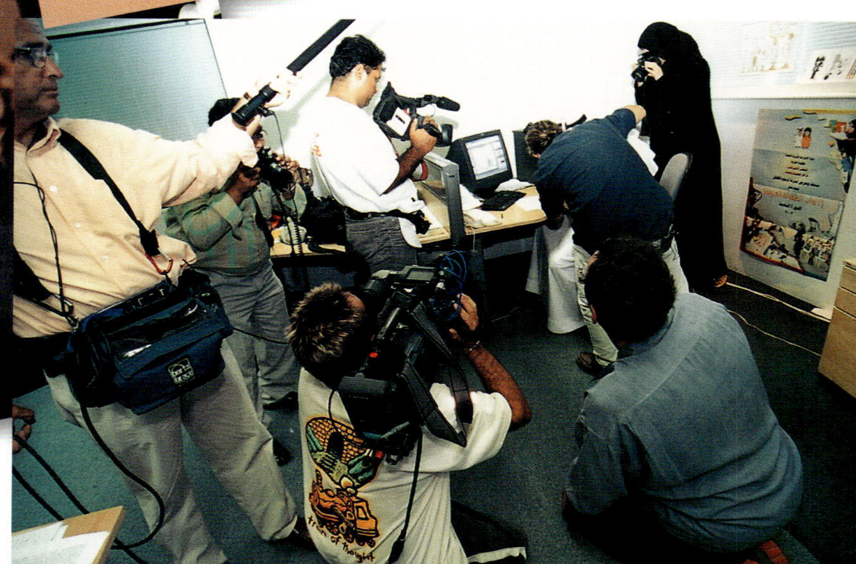

LUCY MONRO

Managing Director, Nasib Bitar, the project also enjoyed the backing of Dubai 2003, as well as that of HH Sheikh Mohammed Bin Rashid Al Maktoum, Crown Prince of Dubai and UAE Minster of Defence.

And then the actual logistics poured down like an avalanche. Timing was everything. The multiple formats, the mix of personalities and the selection of sequences had to be story-boarded, researched and choreographed. Time of day, transport, permissions, sensitivities, where to push the envelope, how to convey deep historical roots, contemporary dynamisms and the confluence of so many international customs within a metaphorically whole 24-hour time-frame. These were the mind-boggling challenges tackled by Ramzi Rassi and his team.

Tobias had directed films in nearly 50 countries but never in the UAE. It had to be shot before mid-May, he realised, prior to the threshold of 40 degrees Centigrade, when even the early morning heat would destroy any chance of capturing the magical hour of lighting.

He wanted to film inside a home, with a local family, with women unveiled.

"Impossible," came the customary response. But to this newcomer, anything was possible and, indeed, after some enquiries, the feasibility of a noon-day meal amongst three generations under one roof materialised. As did countless other seemingly impossible sequences.

But would the film teams be able to work with the photographers? Would they slow each other down? Would the distractions of multiple lenses wreak havoc on the set? All of these questions were unknown in this region. Indeed, *Dubai 24 hours* was a unique event in the country – and one that would capture the imagination of journalists and wire services throughout the Middle East. The idea was simple: follow the pulse, the dreams, the many realities, the living colours of a single emirate from before dawn until after midnight. And

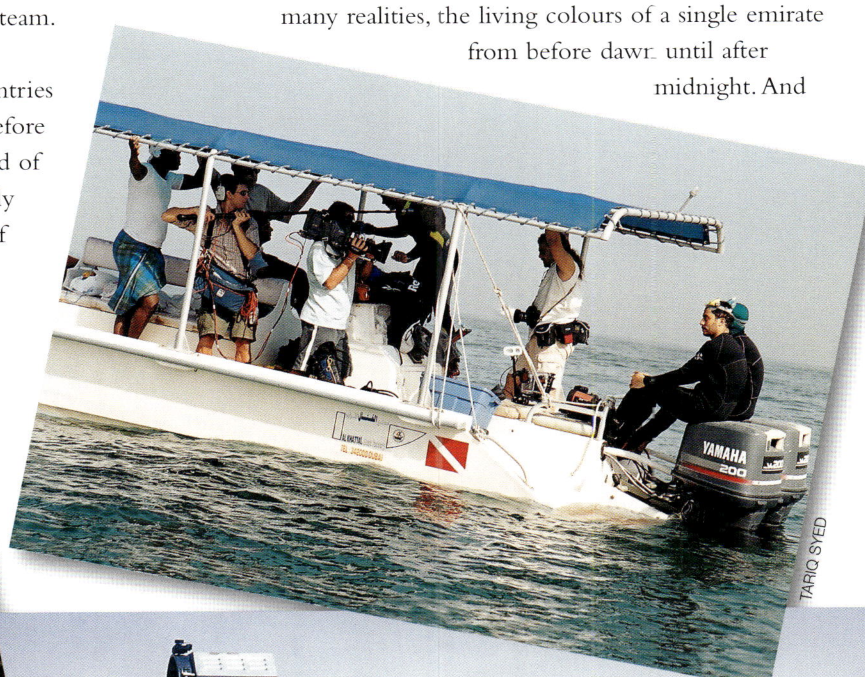

TARIQ SYED

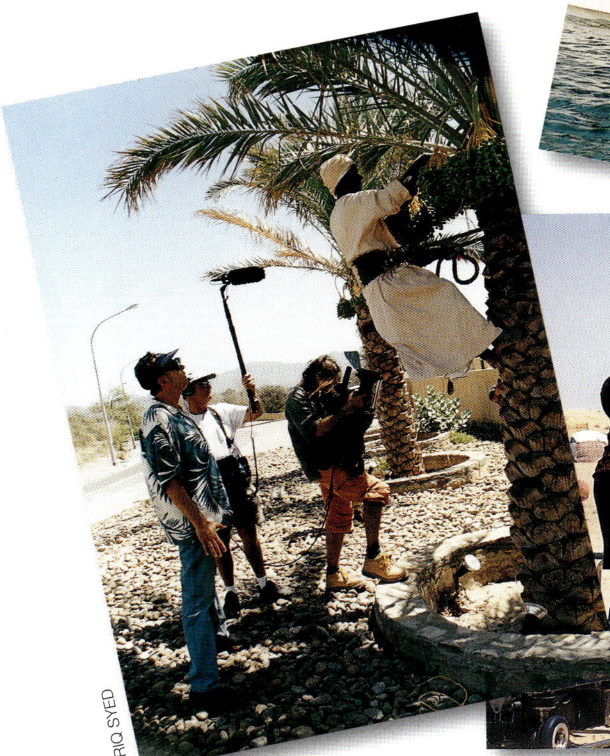

TARIQ SYED

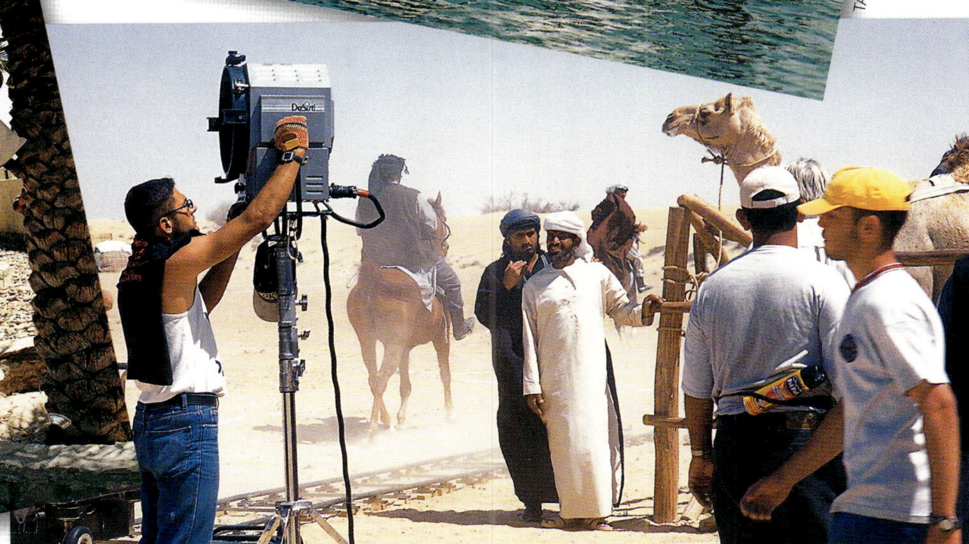

KATARINA PREMFORS

capture that phantasm of multiple worlds in both a feature-length film and a coffee-table book, with an accompanying DVD and CD. A music track both classical and modern, tinged with the fusion of elements characteristic of the region; elements that reveal the rich history beneath the shiny skyscrapers and delve inside the economic miracle that transformed a small fishing community into the 'Hong Kong' of the modern Gulf.

Animation Arts was entrusted with the segment research and filming. In mid April, Managing Director, Shehab Mahmoud, turned his company's offices into a battle zone and lined up video and audio technicians Craig Secker, Peter Davies, Ron Bagnulo, Mark Schofield, more than a dozen great photographers and a fantastic team of researchers and field producers. In all, there were nearly 100 people – all working at a fast tempo, ideas flashing like wildfires, to capture a vivid reality. More than 70 locations were filmed.

The post-production team was capped by famed British/Lebanese film editor, Hussein Younis, who was flown in for several months. Rajtaru Videosonics amply supported with huge off-line and online video storage, special effects, color corrections and editing using state-of-the-art Smoke technology. Mathew Faddy from Barry Kirsch Sound Studio painstakingly worked on audio tracks, music and sound FX track-laying and final mix. At Alarabiya, transcribers, researchers and technicians worked round the clock to meet a seemingly impossible deadline.

The book was published by Motivate, under the editorial guidance of David Steele, ably assisted by Zelda Pinto and Art Director Johnson Machado. A team of researchers, designers and printers worked through weekends and national holidays choosing photographs and checking details, facts and the underlying emotional truth of a complex emirate before putting the book to bed.

The goal: to reveal the grand appetite for life that characterises Dubai. *Dubai 24 hours* is the expression of a large team of eyes and discussions. The balance pays no heed to any special interests but, rather, grows naturally out of the consensus of those who love the place and her people.

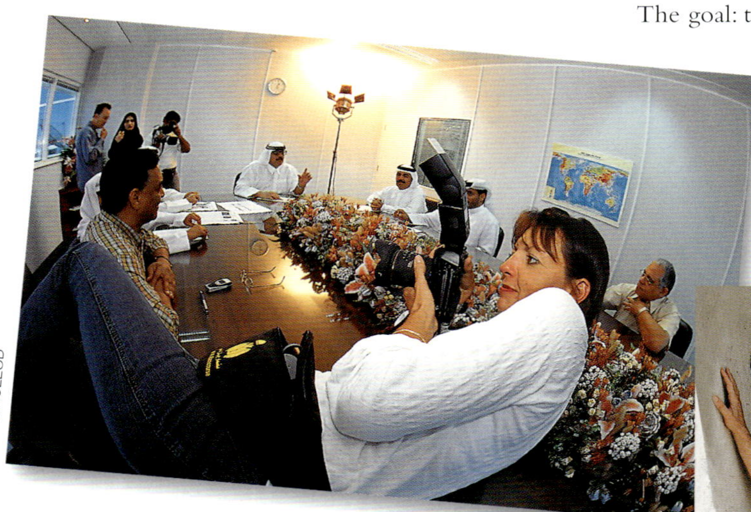

PAUL MACLEOD

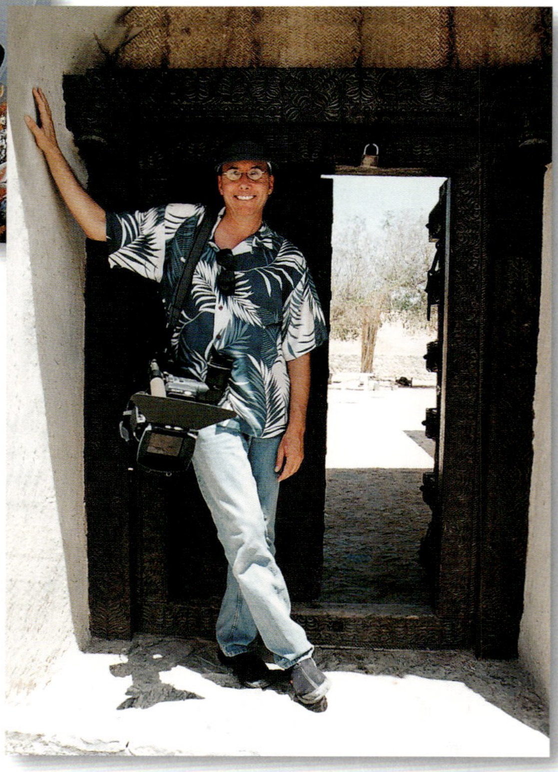

TARIQ SYED

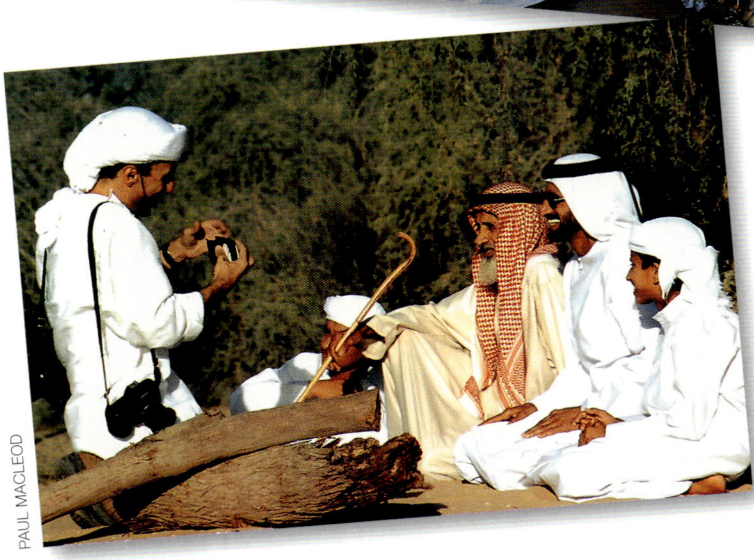

PAUL MACLEOD

Introduction

The concept for this book emerged by way of an innocent desire to capture a portrait . . . a lady before her mirror. Reflections catapulting thought into a myriad of layers that intimated suggestion and charged each nuance according to the particular passion and bent of the photographers themselves. We never viewed the book – or the feature documentary that shares its title – as a journalistic endeavour but as the reappraisal which human nature undergoes when given the opportunity to be openly introspective. To play with form and color and explore the values of light which necessarily mask and – in turn – reveal deeper hues and realities of any geographical moment.

Here, in Dubai, the wide traverse and countless travails of life have offered us a metaphor that is fitting for the 21st century. If the tone of the book seems oddly or consistently optimistic, it's because that is what was discovered here.

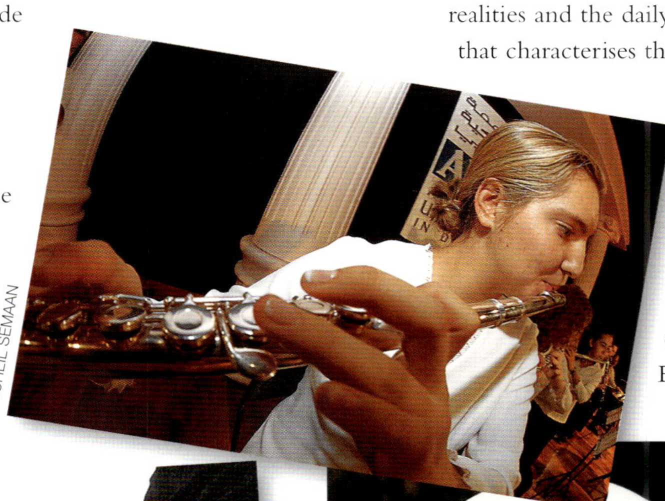
SOUHEIL SEMAAN

In early May 2003, a team of more than 100 individuals, from a dozen countries, most – if not all of them – living in Dubai, assembled to capture reflections and to reacquaint themselves with familiar sites and individuals, communities and landscapes that always appear new to the eye when studied in the light of tomorrow's dawn.

The hope for merging a new faith in the powers of humanity, with the strength of renewal which is nature – nature that is loved and cherished – infused the excitement which drove this project.

Dubai 24 hours is not a literal fixation, but the raw material for a primeval cycle that lives through rituals, physical realities and the daily exercise of imagination that characterises the human communities at the heart of this book.

A dozen photographers were given 50 assignments to cover, to immerse themselves in, to roam freely through. While Dubai, at first blush, might seem limited in scope when compared with China or the European Union, the overpowering

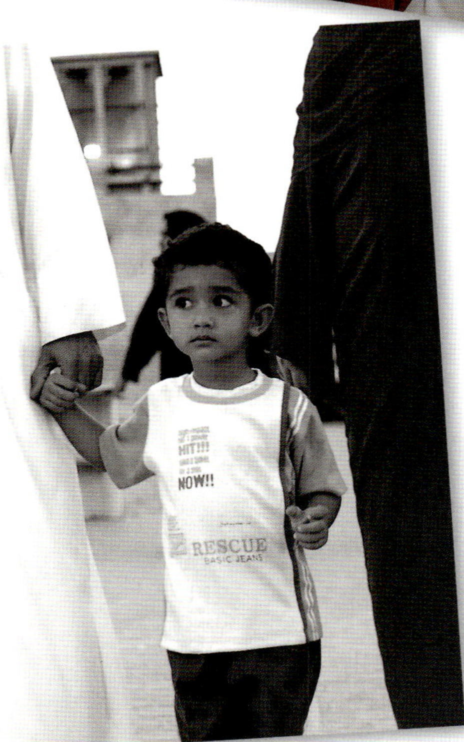

ALIYA AL SHAMSI

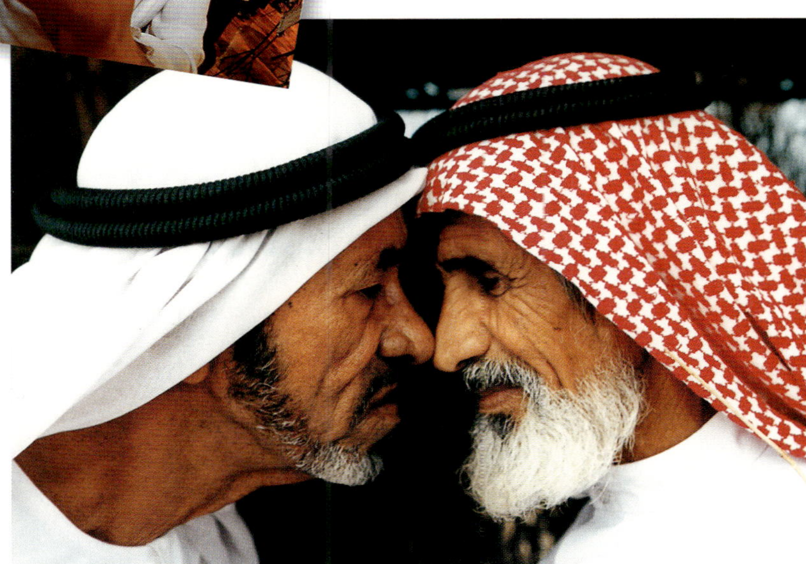
RAMESH SHUKLA

scale, promise and difficulties of its portraiture soon became apparent, as the variety of potential subject matter loomed large and destinations grew into worlds-within-worlds.

We expected this, a certain photographic triage that goes with the territory. But we did not expect the multitudinous burden of *so* many rich avenues to explore all at once.

Falcons competed with camels, camels with horses, horses with the people who rode them. A single stall in the gold souk burst forth with a dozen visitors in a single hour, each one with a wild tale to tell and a flashing smile to understand.

Sadness and joy demand a form of reconciliation, balance, understatement . . . while the sheer exuberance of life cannot be stinted upon. So that the task of penetrating the veils of a place as complex and intermingling as Dubai was, ultimately, one of difficult editorial choices from beginning to end.

All of the more than a million people who make Dubai their home were candidates for inclusion in this book, along with the natural surroundings that are their exquisite heritage. Regrettably, only the most modest sampling could make it into these pages. From early morning until night, the artists gathered together for this project carried their cameras and sought to find meaning wherever it particularly struck them. Still photographers and film crews worked together. In all, they filmed 80 hours of footage and exposed more than 8,000 still images – for more than a month, not just one 24-hour stretch. But the metaphor *is* intentional: the goal was always to reveal the grand appetite for life that characterises Dubai.

That passion, of course, necessarily reflects its authorial predilections. Because this is the expression of a large team of eyes and discussions, the balance pays no heed to any special interests but, rather, grows naturally out of the consensus of those who love the place and her people.

We knew we wanted poetry, actual poetry, which plays so powerful a role in the political and emotional history of the emirates. Love, as expressed between husband and wife, grandparents, parents and their children, and between friends, came to us in the guises of the rich social landscape and diverse, stable family life that is at the heart of Dubai's safety net, her humanity. The natural landscape surrounded us. And everywhere the city itself tempted a thousand and one expeditions.

The role of Islam, and its open embrace of other faiths and ideas, was clearly a unique opportunity to explore how, in an era dominated by the clash of stereotypes, superpowers and the tragedies of war, the UAE embraces a vastly different alternative – the paths of education, tolerance, innovation and peace.

But how to illustrate this? What images could be sought which faithfully secured the truism of this *modus operandi*

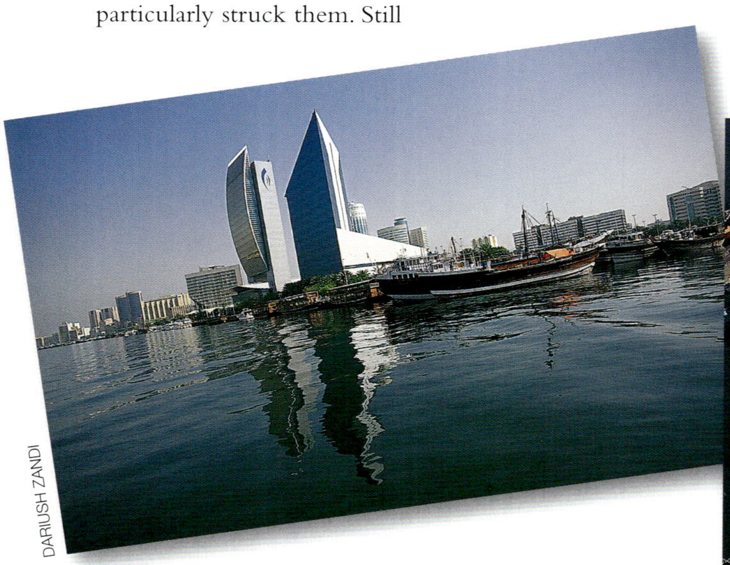

DARIUSH ZANDI

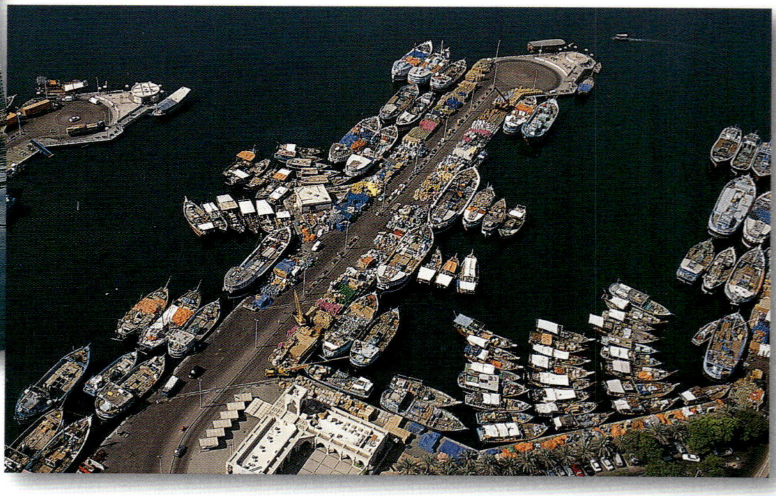

SHANKAR ADISESHAN, MOTIVATE PUBLISHING

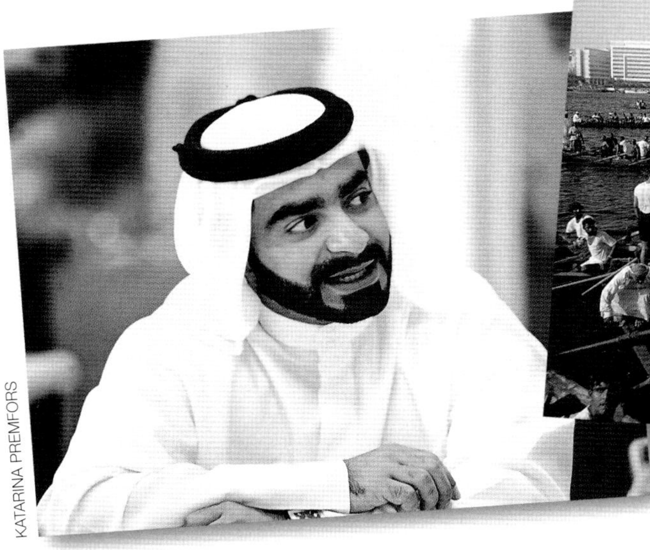
KATARINA PREMFORS

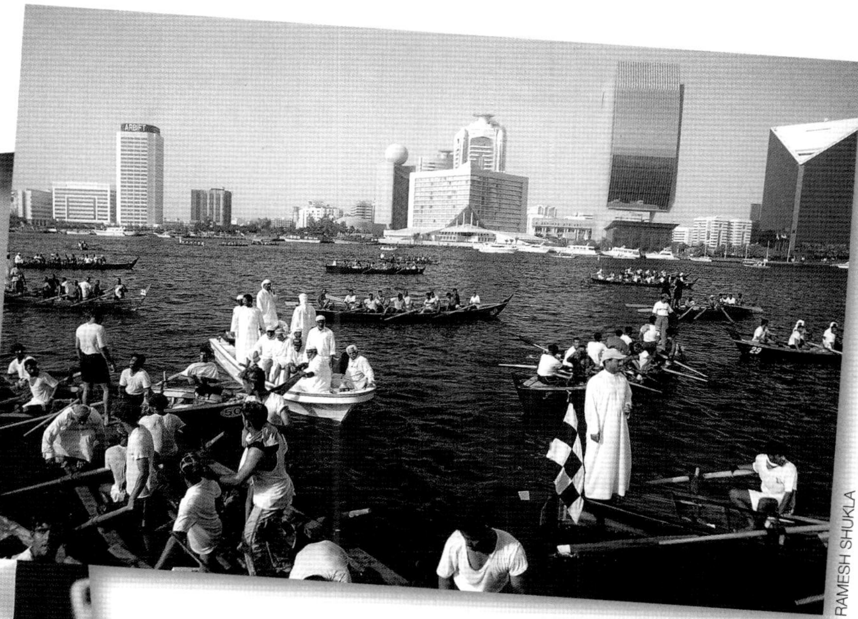
RAMESH SHUKLA

that is Dubai, its power base and her citizenry? We leave that question, and its myriad of answers and implications, to you – the reader, who will browse through these pages – and, we trust, reflect on the sincere energies that went into assembling them.

Politically, the United Arab Emirates, including Dubai, is little more than 30 years old, though her heritage is ancient. Dubai's own international airport welcomes more than 100 airlines and 22-million visitors each year, yet less than 19 per cent of the resident population are actually Emirati.

Her structural realities are, not surprisingly, novel, and correspondingly open to original ideas and experimentation, whether in the realm of engineering, the arts, ecological restoration, or entertainment. Upon visiting Dubai's Media City, former US President Bill Clinton referred to its incredible innovativeness, intimating the sheer enormity and intelligence of the project's ambition.

In our interview with the young Sheikha Lubna Al Qasimi, a member of the Ruling Family of Sharjah (an emirate bordering Dubai), now CEO of a half-billion dollar e-commerce company, she spoke freely of her desire, when a student at a university in northern California, to live with an American family, and of her admiration for DH Lawrence and George Orwell. She also described herself as not just a person of the United Arab Emirates, but a "world person".

The Sheikha – and so many other outstanding individuals like her, who the crews of *Dubai 24 hours* had the pleasure to meet – defies outside expectations of the modern Islamic woman; of an Arabic locale, and of the whole Middle East. And she does even more than that: with grace and ease she smartly characterises the internal mechanisms for resolving what many have presumed to be irreconcilable differences of cultures and mindsets.

Indeed, Dubai is more than a metaphor of the modern and open Islamic world. It is a working, successful model for how cultures can share and grow together, transcending bias and thereby achieving mutual enrichment.

Islam, dating from the time of the Prophet Mohammed (PBUH) in the early seventh century, means, literally, "turning to God". In the case of the more than one-billion Muslims on the planet, that translates into "turning to Mecca" five times each day to pray (*salat*), preferably at a nearby mosque.

In Dubai, you might discover a beautifully lit mosque next door to a 70-storey, five-star hotel, a BMW dealership, an Internet café, or a church. These juxtapositions are commonplace now in this part of the world. But, despite the entrepreneurial garb and curious admixtures, a quintessential spirit remains undiluted. There's no perfect name for it, but it's there nonetheless, quietly inhabiting this region of the UAE, fixed firmly in the hours of Dubai, tantalising all those who would seek to know her. Like a poem that you want to read over and over again. Never tiring of the beauty, or the sunrise.

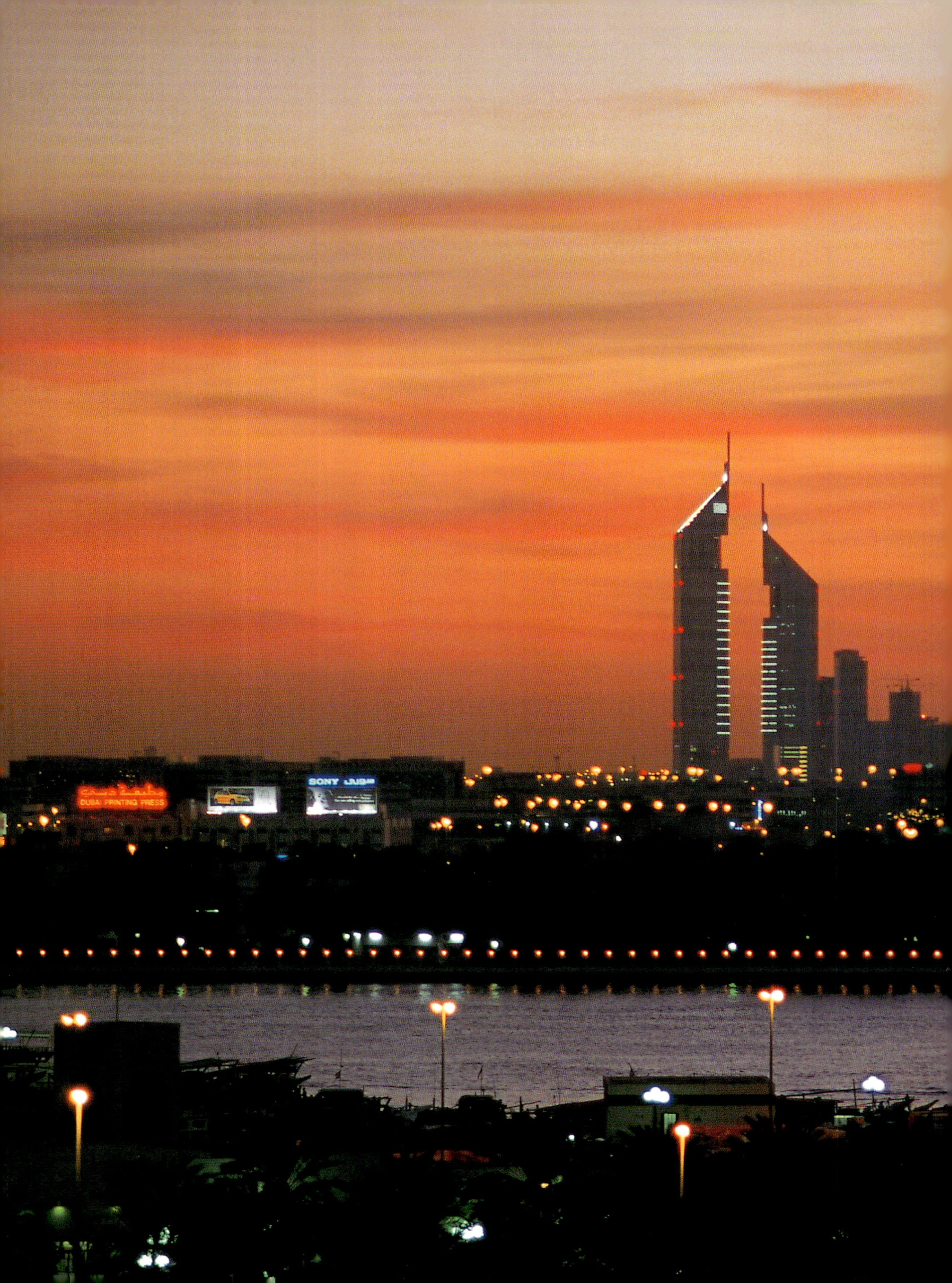
مطبعة دبي
DUBAI PRINTING PRESS
SONY سوني

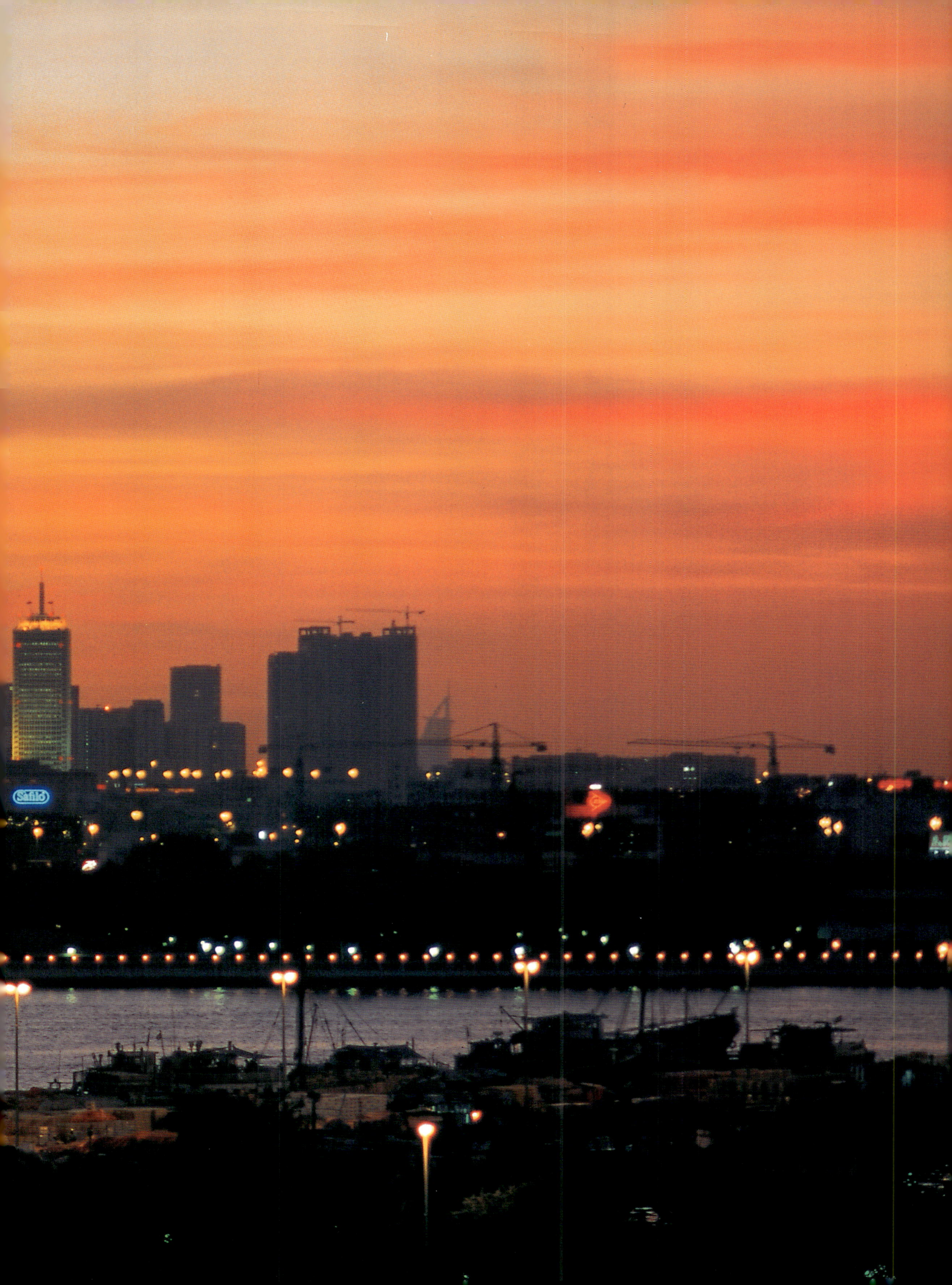
Safilo

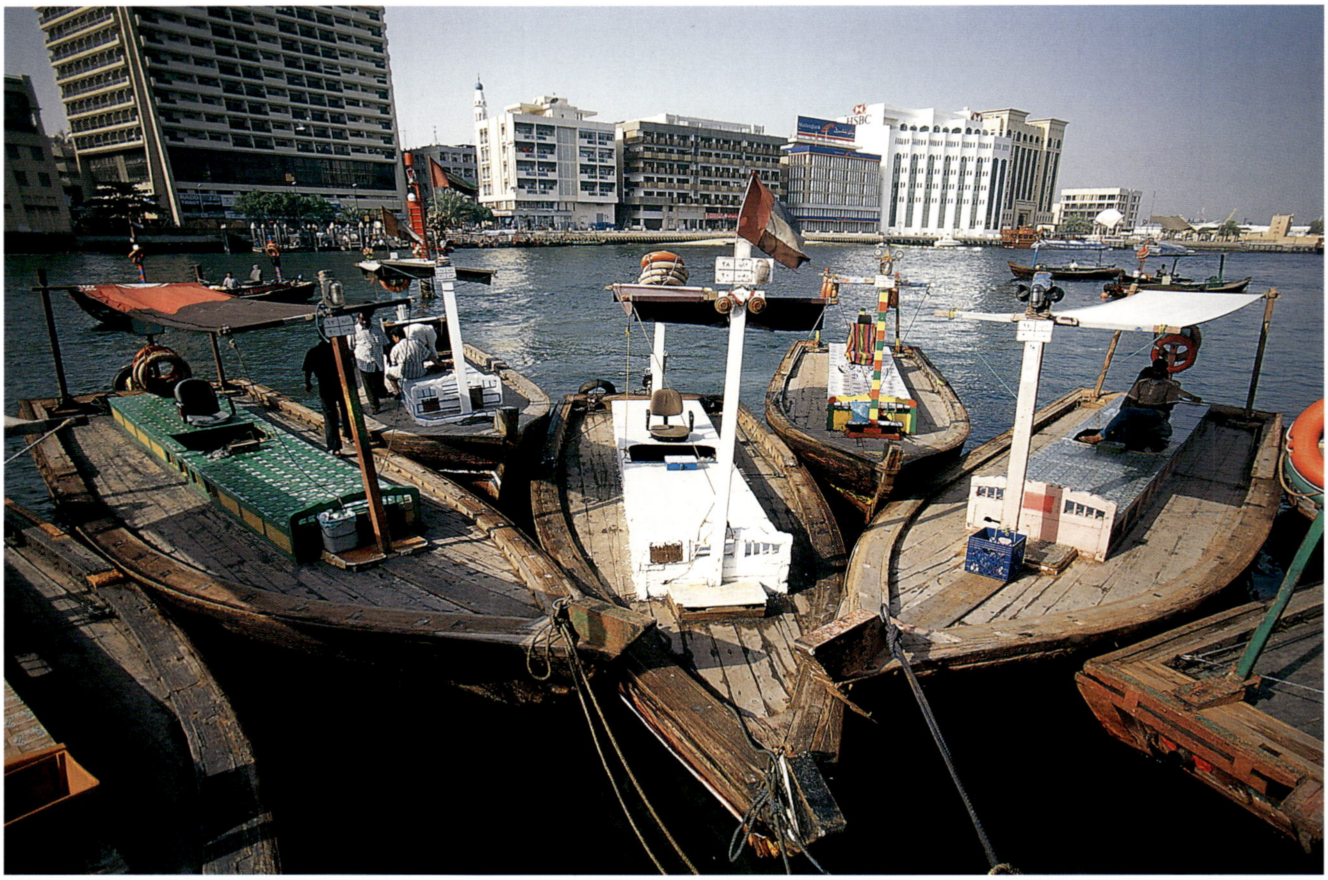

◀◀ DUBAI LIVES BY RULES THAT CANNOT BE KNOWN from the outside. Its infrastructure, history and way of life involve so much more than mere oil, which has only been crucial to Dubai's development since the late 1960s. Yet, as far back as 1830, a branch of the Bani Yas tribe from an oasis named Liwa settled here, led by the Maktoum family, who still rule the emirate today. In 1971 the British (who had increasingly been involved in the area since the 19th century) left, providing every incentive for Dubai to join forces with Abu Dhabi, Sharjah, Ajman, Umm al-Qaiwain, Fujairah and finally Ra's al-Khaimah. The result was the United Arab Emirates. The Dubai of today is a testimony to the late Ruler, His Highness Sheikh Rashid bin Saeed Al Maktoum, whose legacy continues under the leadership of the present Ruler, HH Sheikh Maktoum bin Rashid Al Maktoum, ably assisted by his brothers, Their Highnesses Sheikh Hamdan bin Rashid Al Maktoum, Deputy Ruler of Dubai and UAE Minister of Finance and Industry; and General Sheikh Mohammed bin Rashid Al Maktoum, Crown Prince of Dubai and UAE Minister of Defence. The names may be daunting to some outsiders (*bin* for 'son of', *bint* for 'daughter of' – followed by the last name of the child's father, *Al* for 'the family of'), but in this friendly city, its customs are as informal, open and inviting as any city in the world. *Photo by Dariush Zandi.*

▲ ▶ *ABRAS* – OR WATER TAXIS – ON DUBAI'S MAIN artery, the Creek. During the last century the Creek was used as a means of streamlining both the flow of goods and profits, aided by the absence of stifling import tariffs. With the resulting mercantile fever, Dubai evolved into an import/export hub, the precursor of today's free-zone concept that sets the city spectacularly apart from most other commercial centres in the world. The *abras* are still used by commuters, who pay a trifle to journey across memory lane. *Photos by Dariush Zandi.*

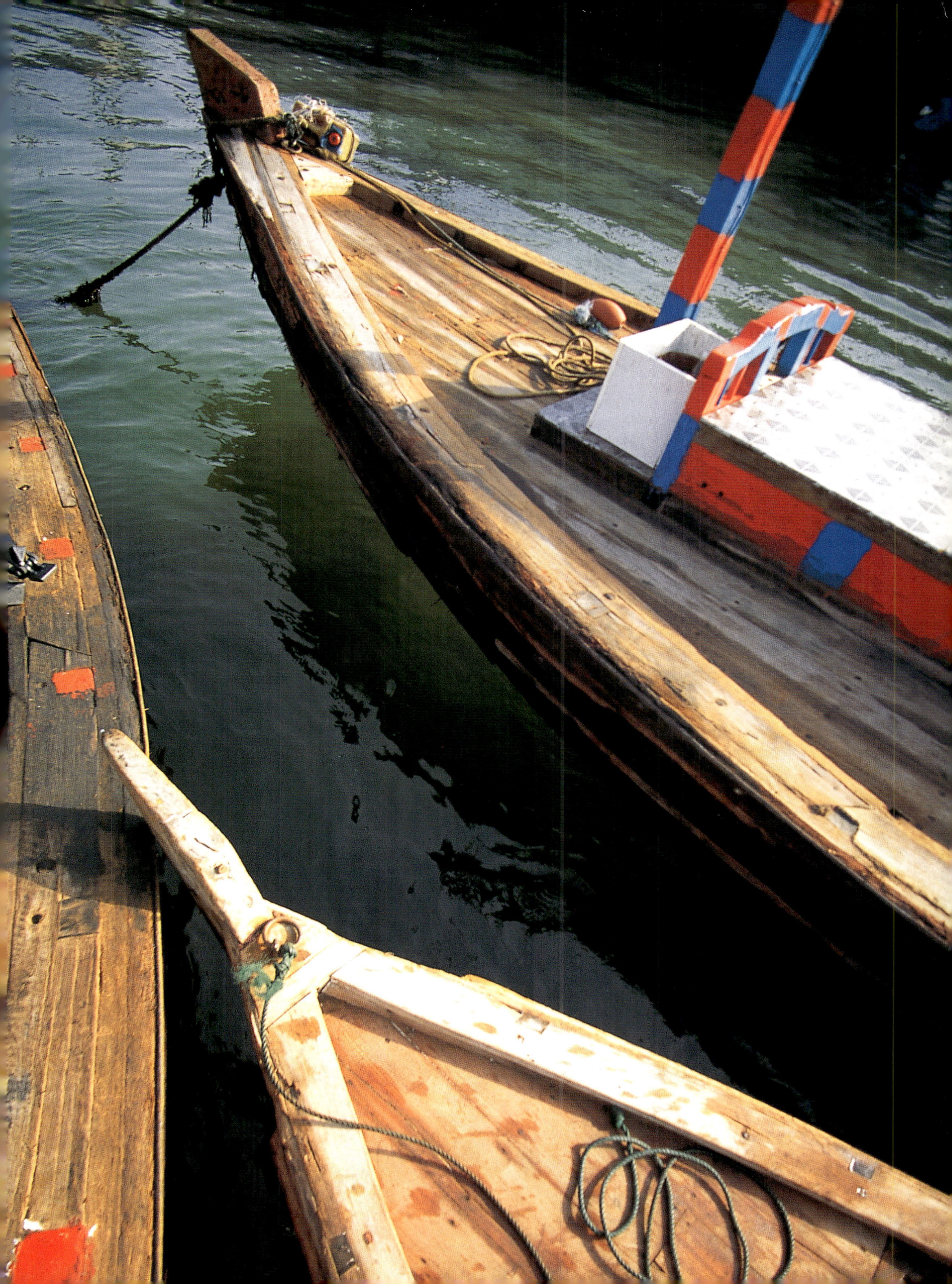

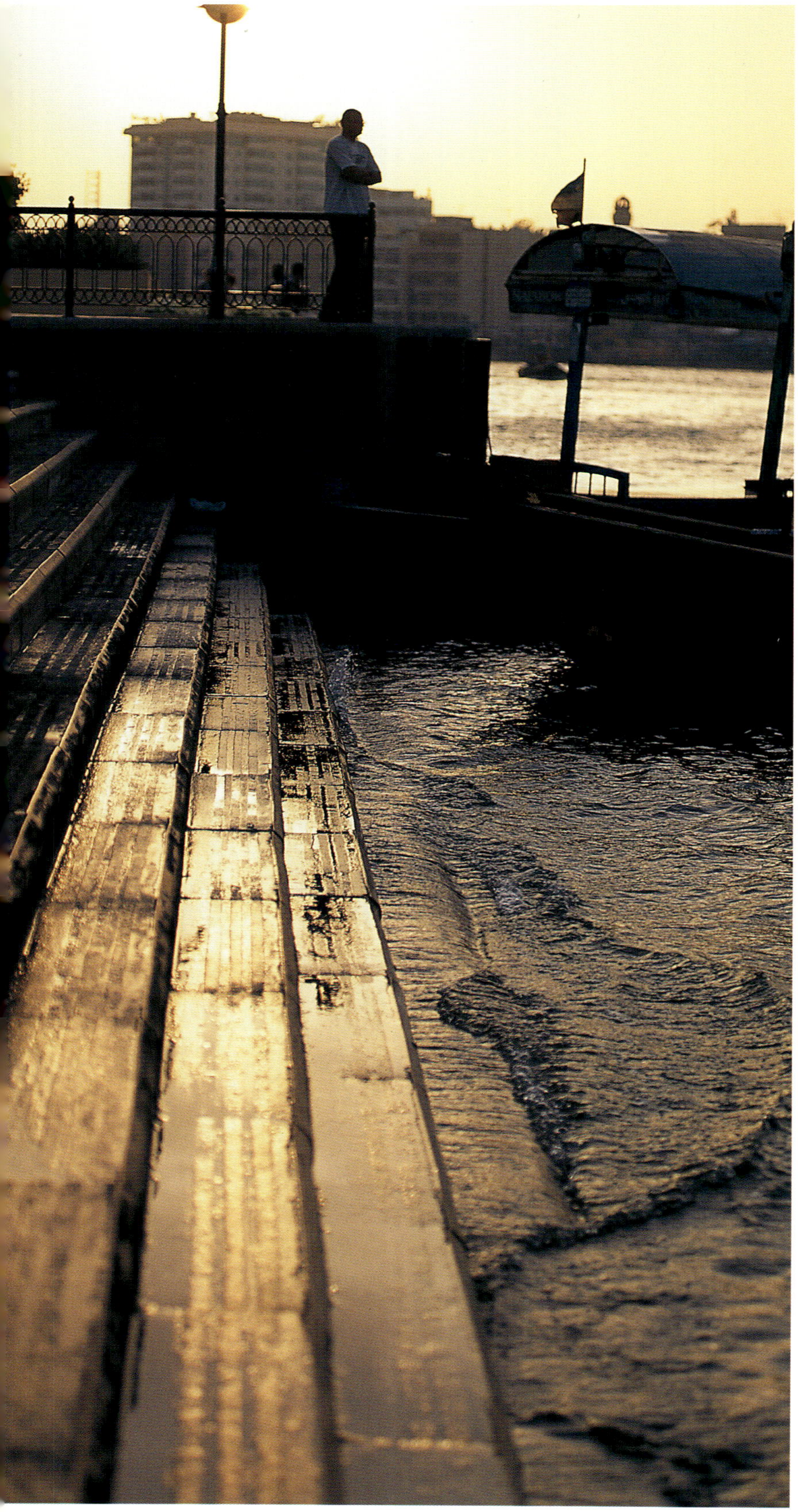

◀ In the late 1950s, the Creek was beginning to silt and Sheikh Rashid arranged the finance to have it dredged and to construct breakwaters at its mouth. Then, during the 1960s, he had it narrowed to facilitate a faster flow of tidal water – which scoured the bed and helped to keep it free of silt – while valuable land was also reclaimed. In 1963, Al Maktoum Bridge was completed, uniting Deira and Dubai. These efforts helped facilitate a technological and financial renaissance within the city, as ships bearing 500 tonnes were now able to ply the inner waterways, with cargoes from all over the world. While more than 700,000 tonnes of goods for export and re-export pass through the Creek each year, the trade is largely confined to wooden boats, in keeping with the sailing dhows of yesteryear, when trade was carried on with countries from India to East Africa. *Photo by Dariush Zandi.*

▶ Mariners from far afield motor to and from Dubai in dhows, harking back to the days of their forefathers (above). *Photo by Paul MacLeod.* Even the most mundane and back-wrenching labour of workers on the Creek, in the right light, becomes a painter's palette of color and flair (below). *Photo by Dariush Zandi.*

▶▶ Dubai's two bridges, and the banks of the Creek, are interesting places to observe and photograph colourful dhows, pleasure cruisers and *abras*. *Photo by Dariush Zandi.*

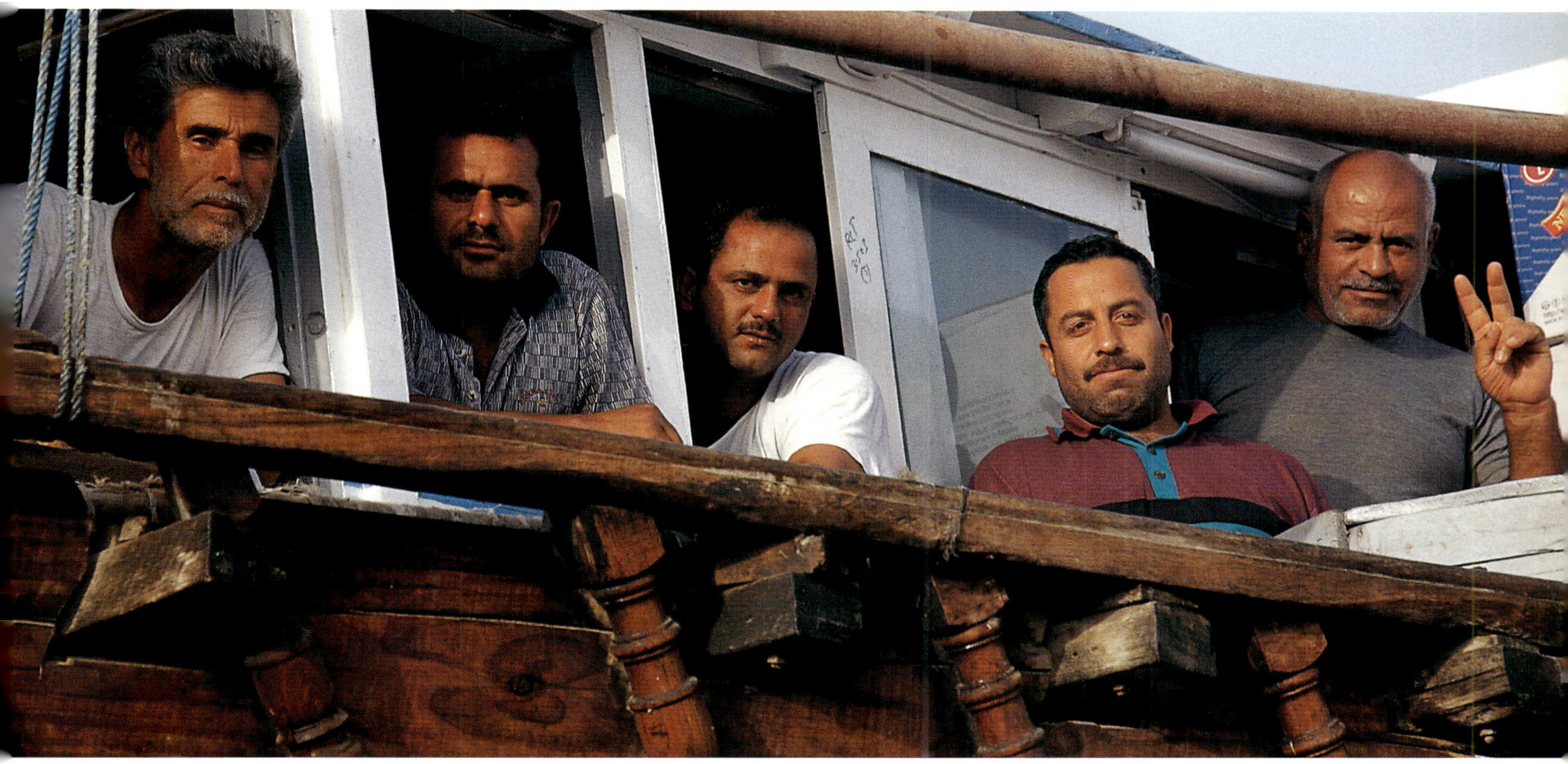

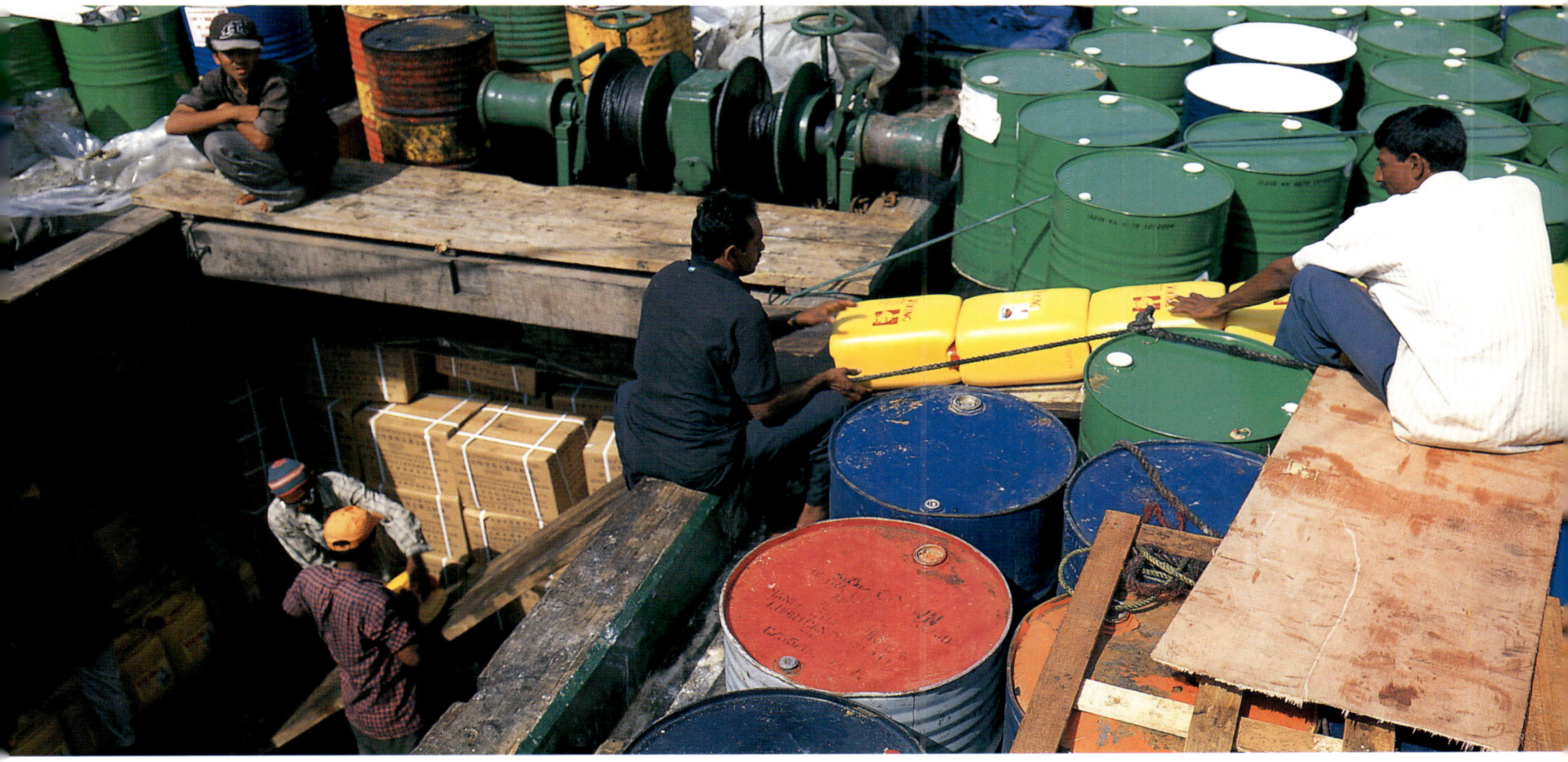

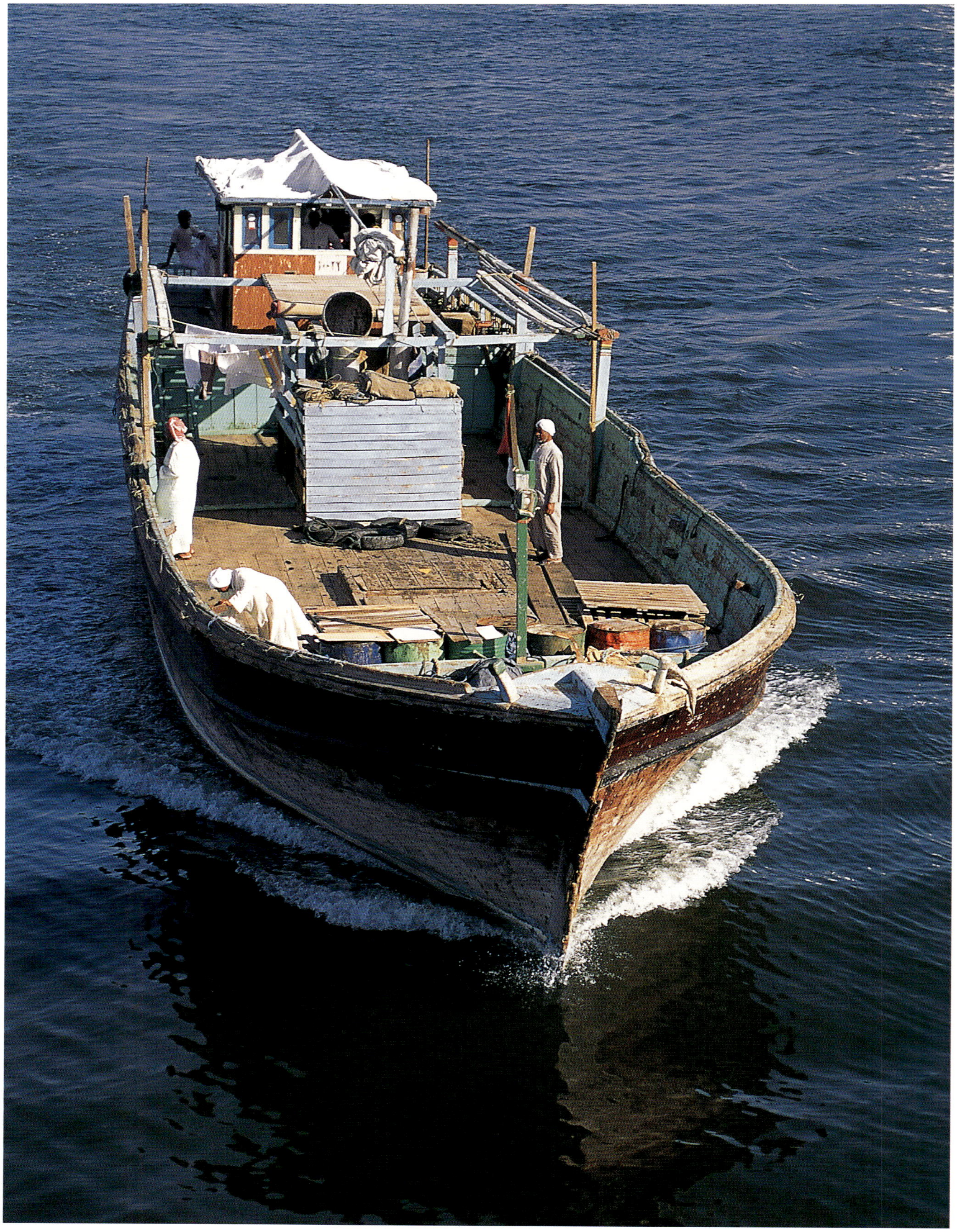

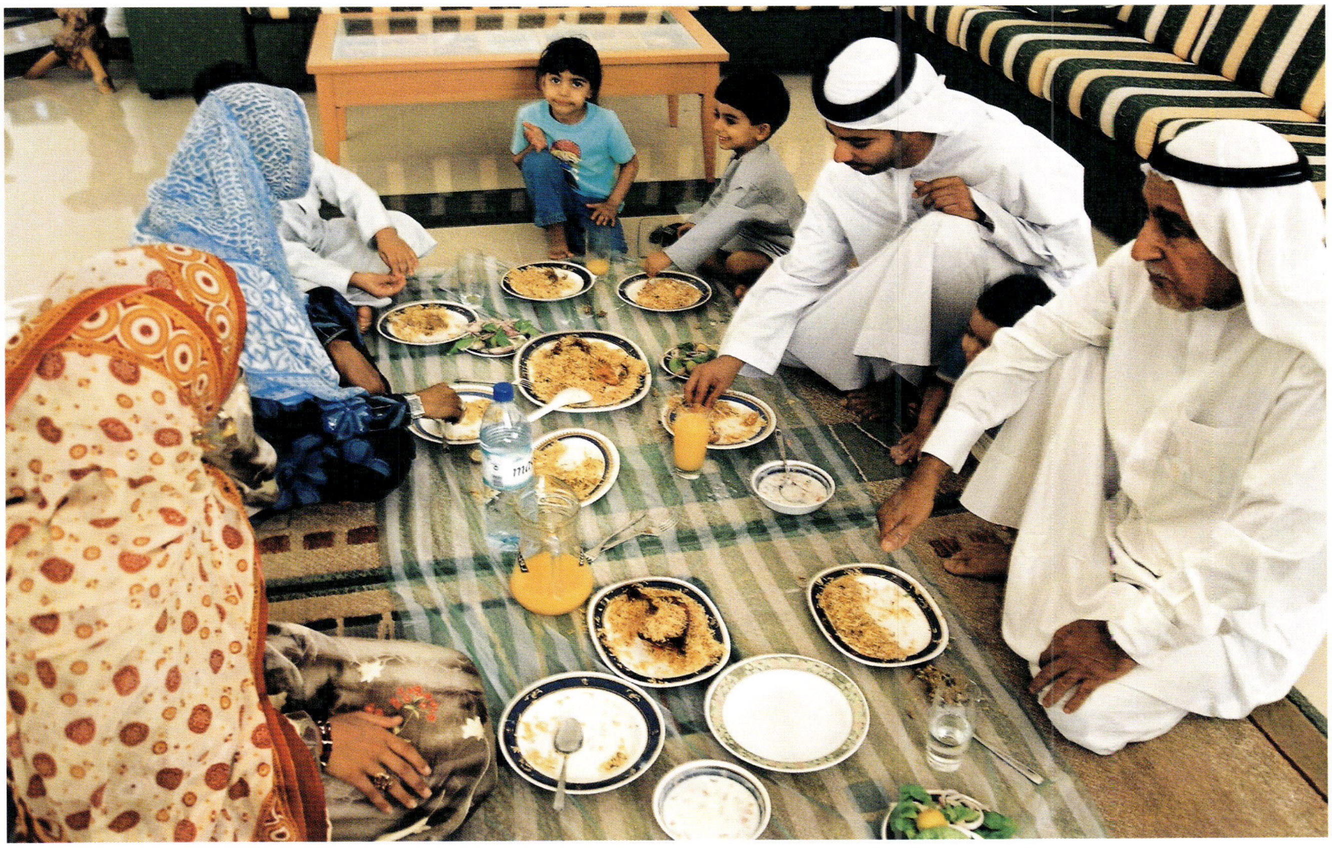

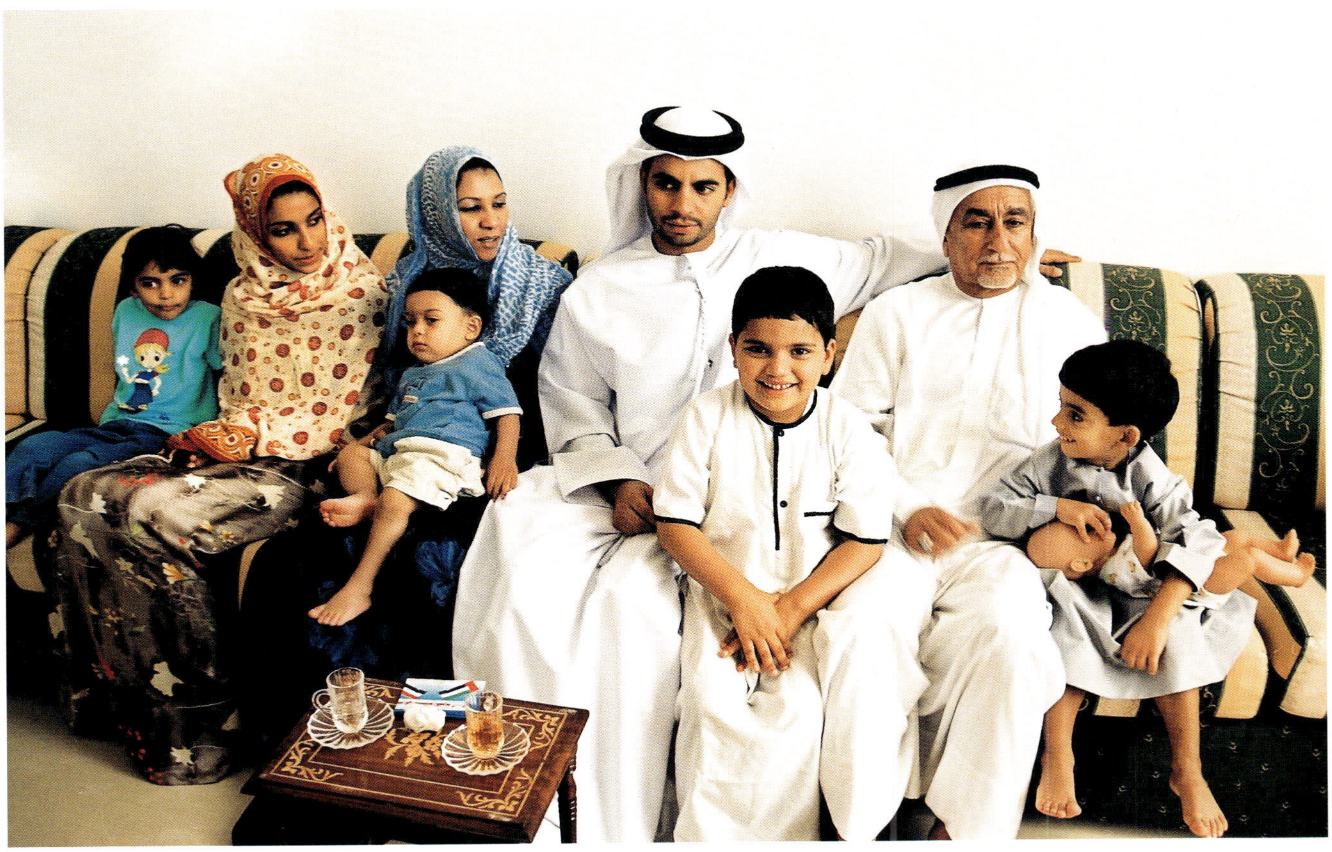

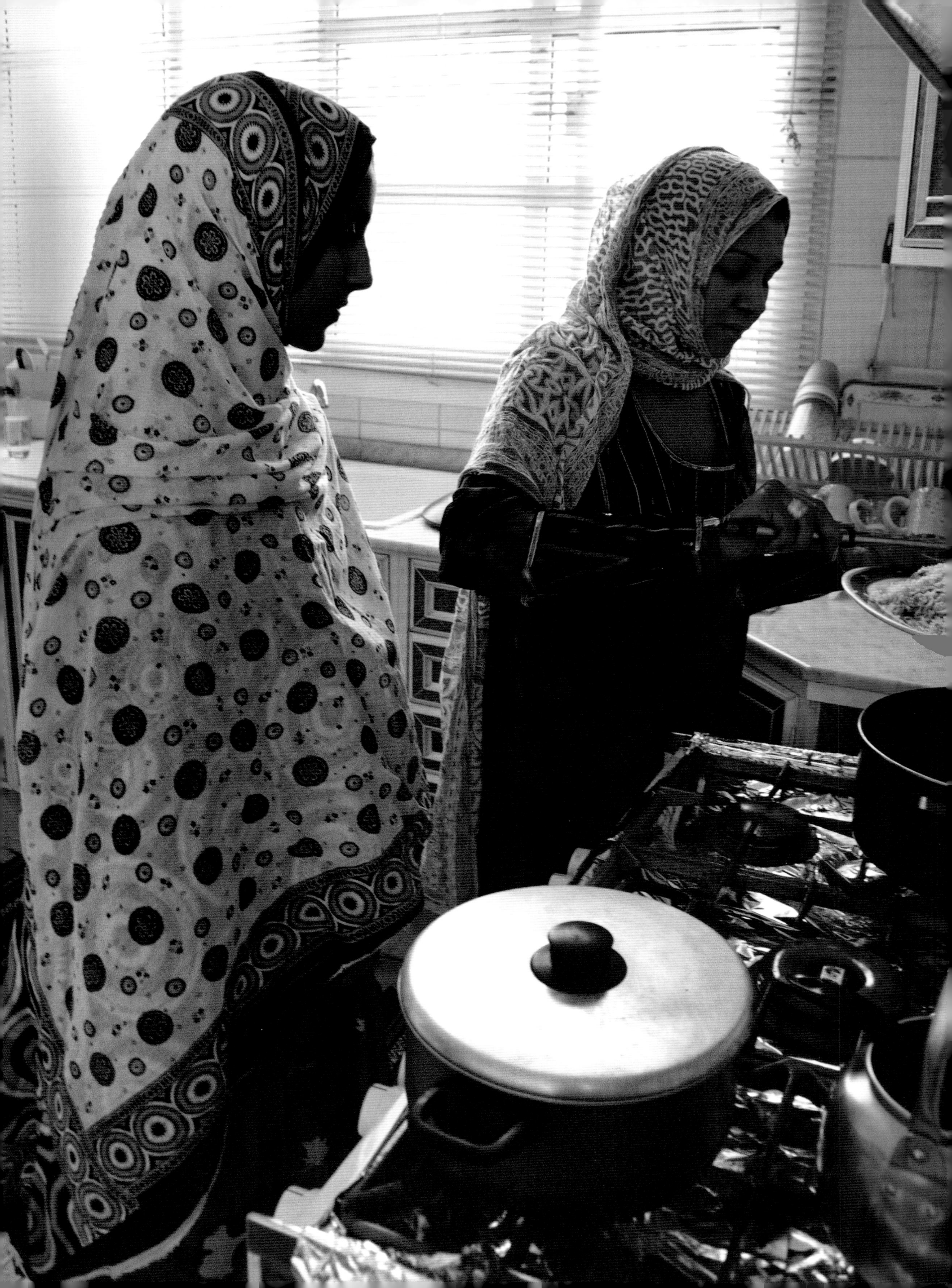

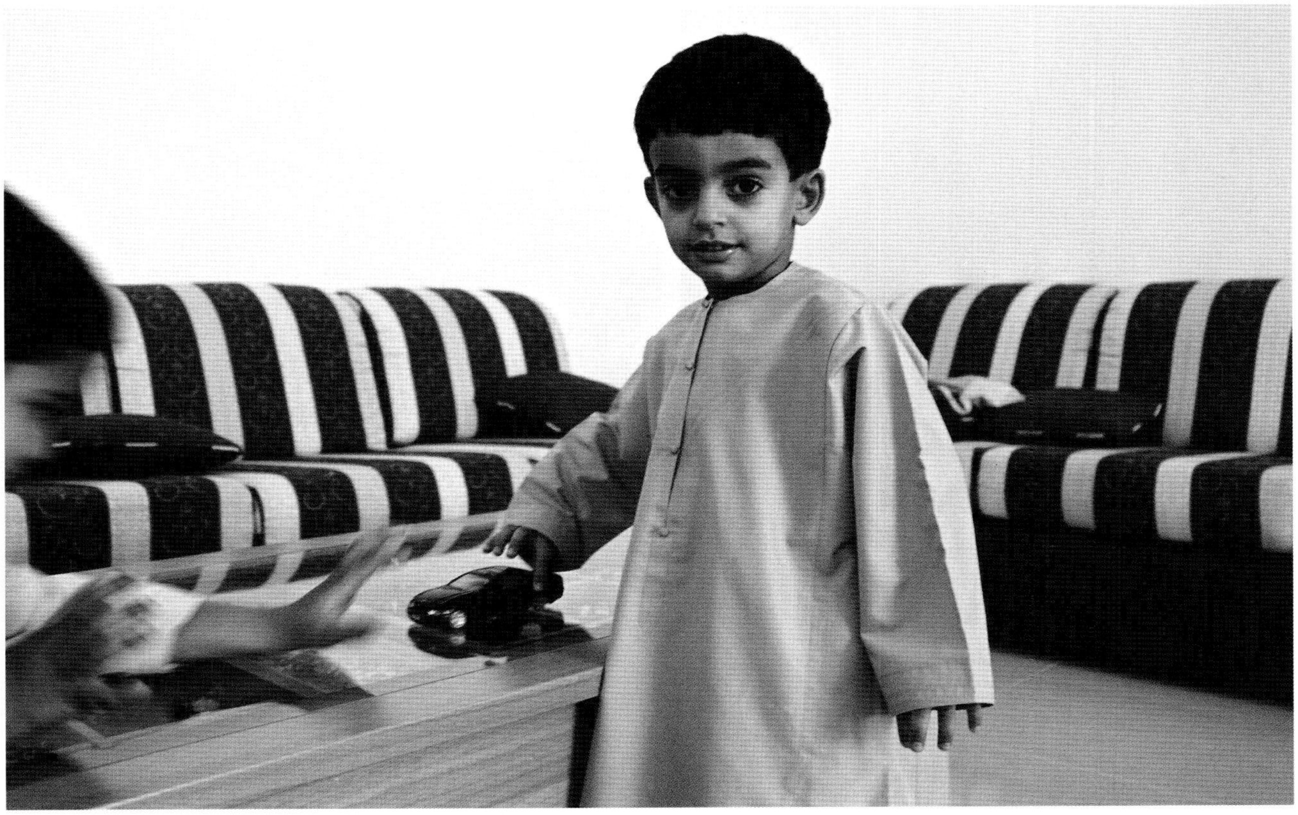

◄◄ Having just driven home from mid-day prayer at their local mosque, the Adnan Mohammed Al Marzooqi family enjoy their lunch together. They sit in the traditional manner on the floor, enjoying a meal of rice and lamb. After this culinary repast the family enjoy time together – and a refreshing cup of mint tea.

◄ Adnan's wife, Iman Fazal, and their daughter, Bushra, preparing a meal in their kitchen. Bushra, aged 16, aspires to be a television news commentator. The women of the family, unveiling their faces to male strangers (members of the film and photographic crews invited to the home) were, in fact, embodying a quite modern characteristic, a cultural transition, not entirely predictable even in contemporary Dubai.

▲ Four year old Khalifa plays with his brother, Nasser Khalid. Full of energy, and not being allowed outside in the summer heat, Khalifa performed somersaults on the couch during lunch. . . . *Photos by Alia Al Shamsi.*

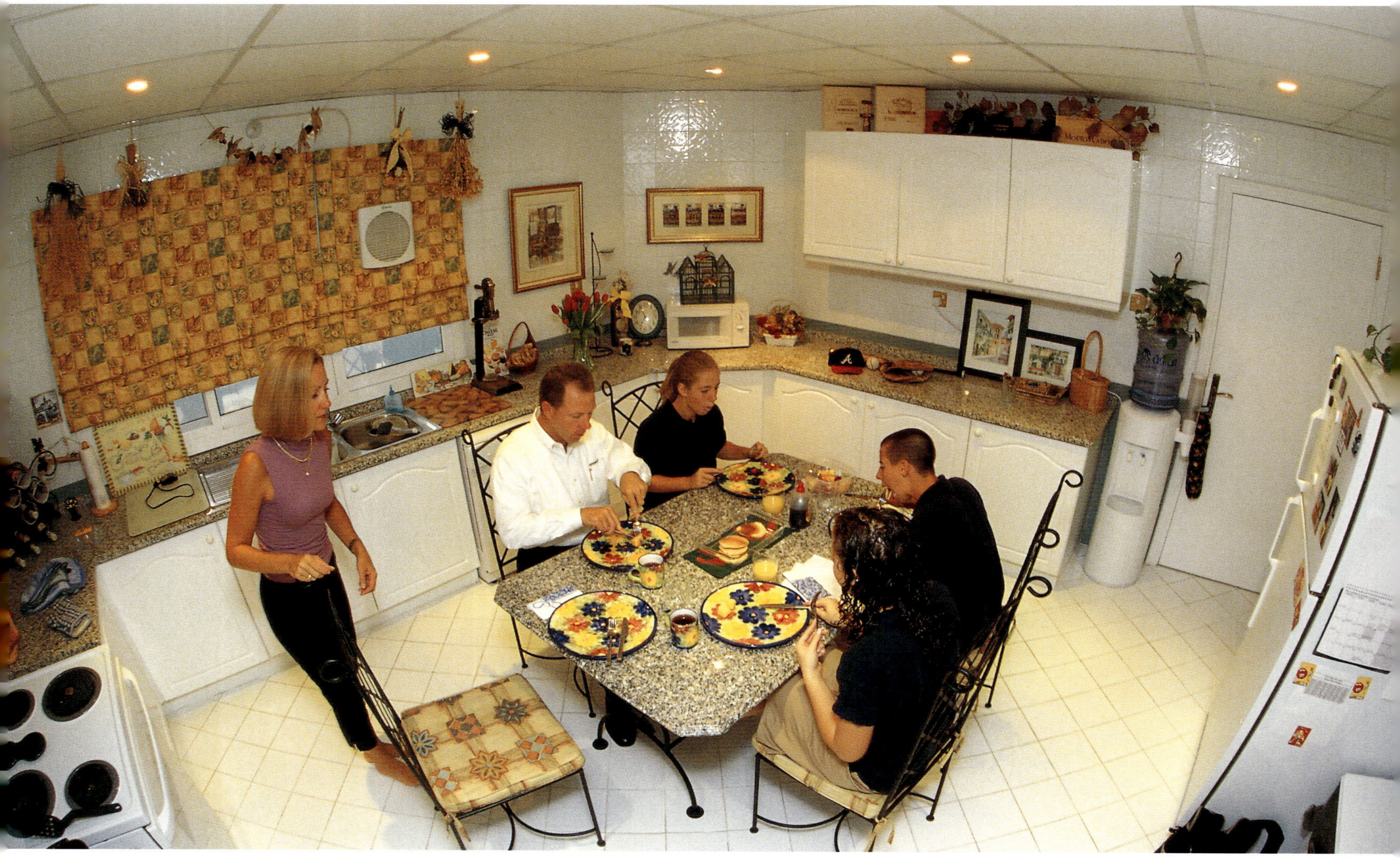

▲ An American family who've lived in Dubai for four years take breakfast together. Mike, the father, works for the Caterpillar Company and will walk their dog before watching his elder son, Ryan, play for a local baseball team. The number of Westerners who make Dubai their home has risen to tens of thousands.

▶ Hoping for a home run in the sand, Ryan faces the pitcher (above). Mother Doreen with her 16-year old daughter, Shannon: Shannon will eventually return to the United States where she hopes to pursue studies in accounting (below). *Photos by Souheil Semaan.*

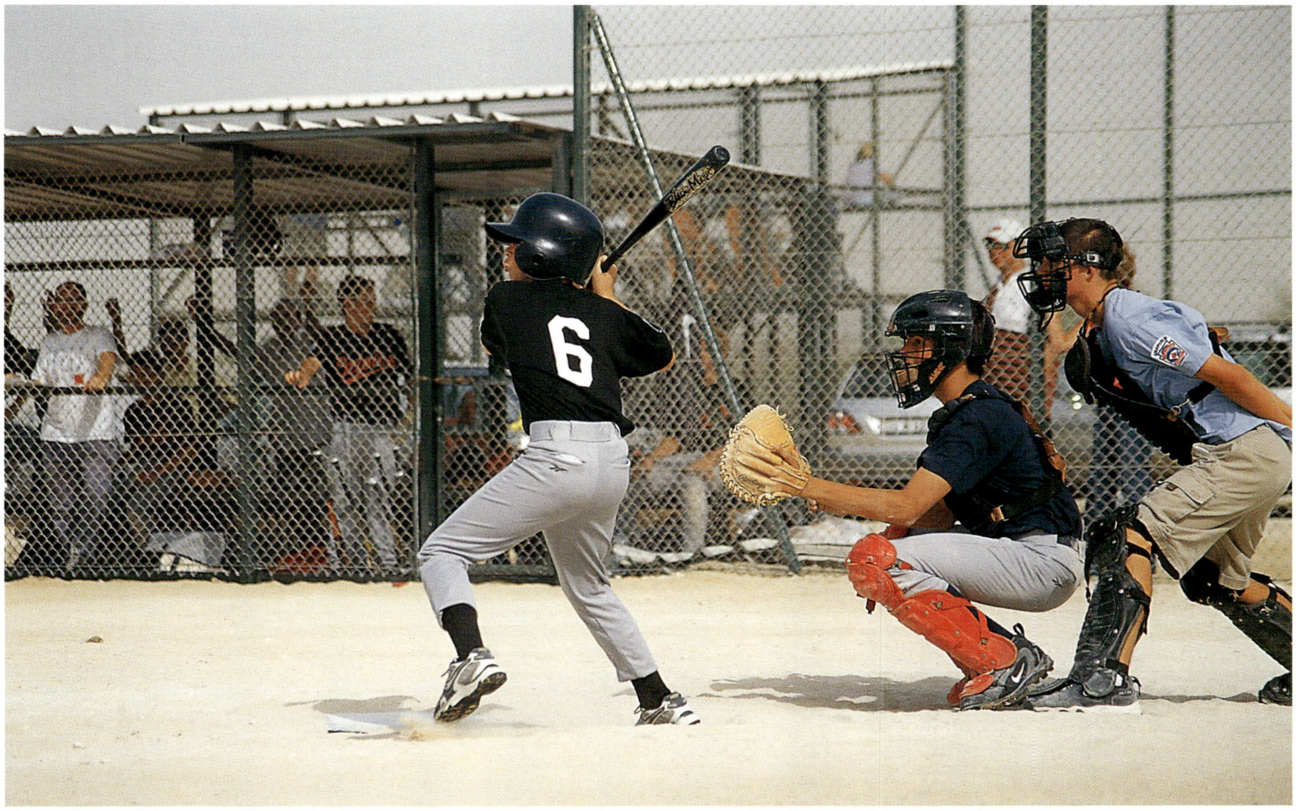
6

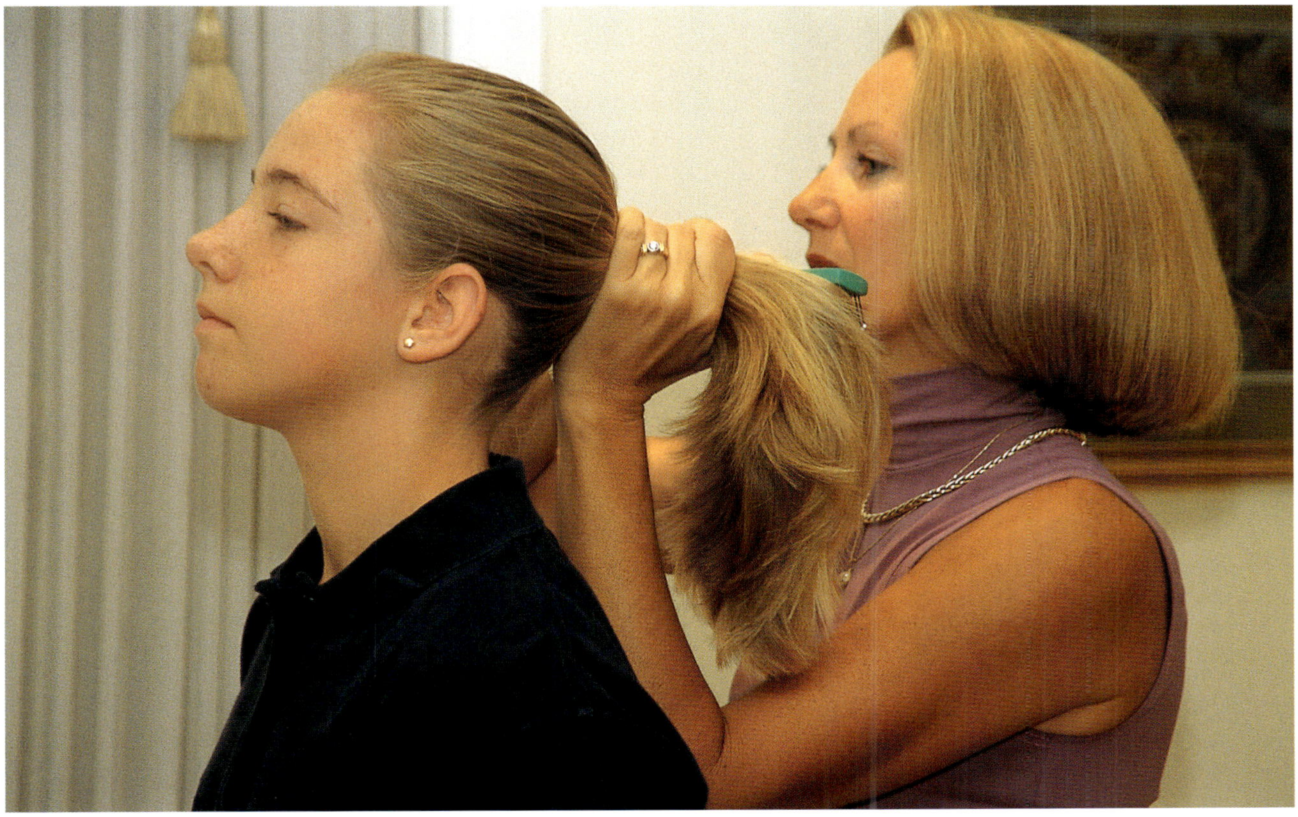

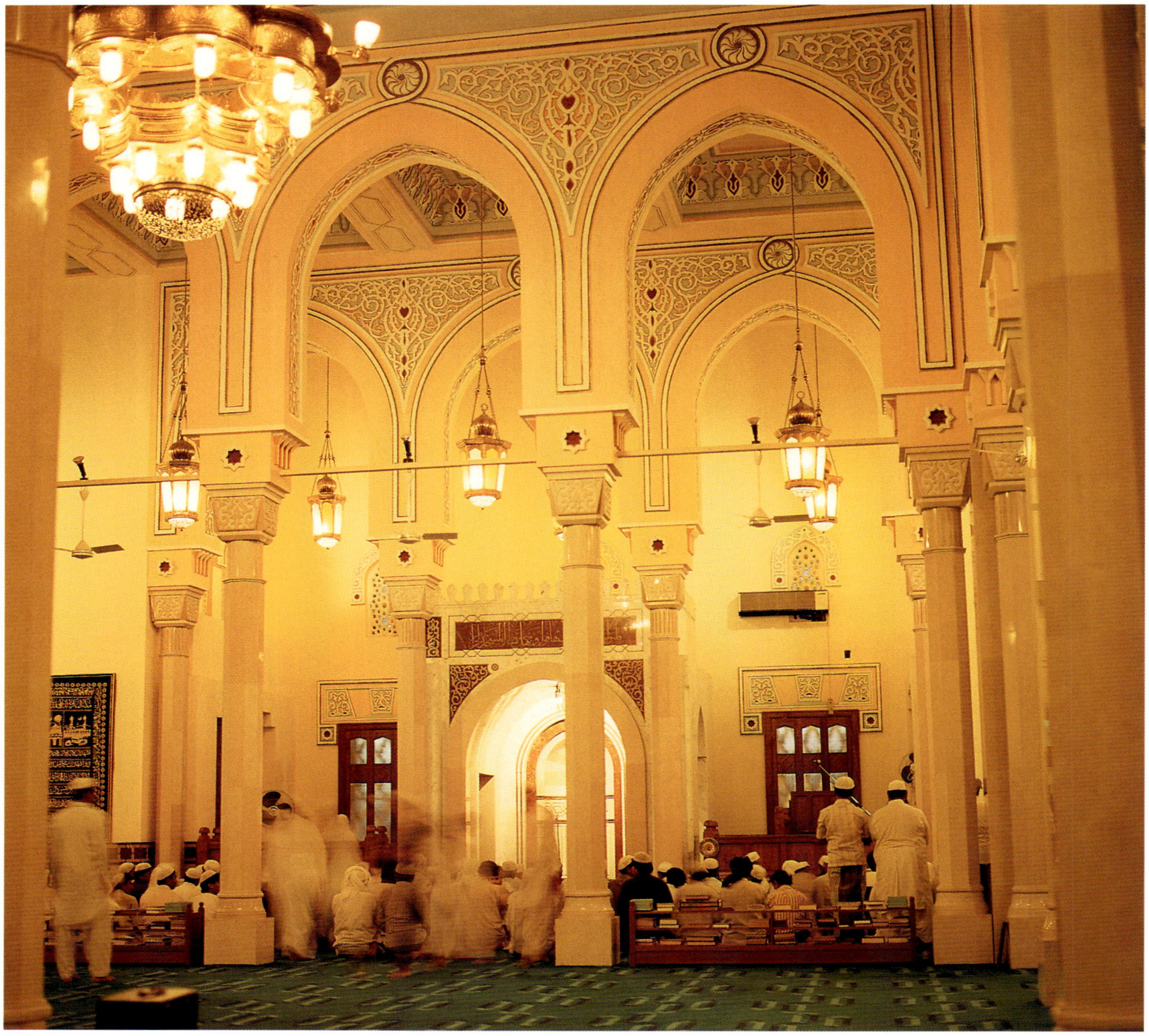

▲ ▶ Mosques are central to the whole edifice of Islamic devotion. Modern minarets, fitted with loud-speakers, transmit the call to worship by the muezzin five times each day, a nearly hypnotic musical prayer which is universally recognised. Friday is the special holy day to Muslims. Not all Muslims go to a mosque to pray. Many simply kneel on a prayer mat wherever they may be, facing towards Mecca, ever reminded that they must adhere to the principles of Faith, Prayer, Fasting, Charity and Pilgrimage. There is a plan in Dubai to provide a mosque within every quarter mile of the city, so that residents can go to pray without having to walk too far in the heat. The mosque interior (above) is that of the Jumeirah Mosque – whose minarets provide a striking contrast with Emirates Towers in the background (right). *Photos by Dariush Zandi (above) and Karel Kita, Motivate Publishing (right).*

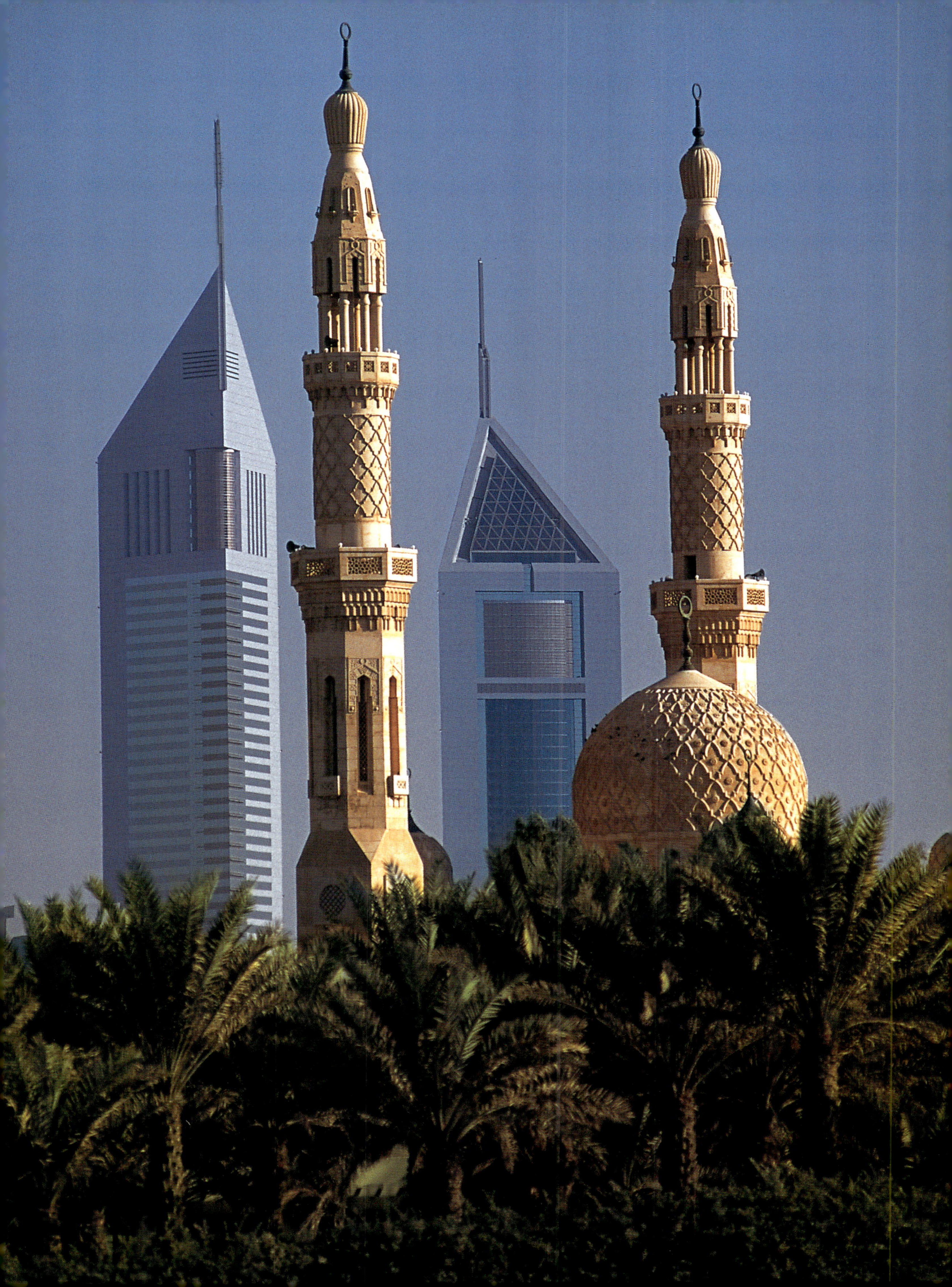

▲ SOME 60 MAGAZINES, NEWSPAPERS AND JOURNALS, ARE published in Dubai in Arabic, English, Malayalam, Urdu and even Persian. Foreign newspapers, especially British and Asian, are also readily available in bookshops and supermarkets. One of the local Arabic newspapers is *Al Bayan*. Here, Sami Al Riyami, Managing Editor of Economic Affairs for the newspaper, meets with his colleague, Fadeela Al Mueini, head of the paper's educational section. *Photo by Paul MacLeod.*

▶ PICTURED AT HIS POST, CARTOONIST HAIDAR Mohammed conjures up a satirical take on some aspect of Dubai life for *Al Bayan*. His tasteful teases may seize upon a father who's lost count of children and uses a roll-call at dinner, or the expat who doesn't know the difference between a telephone card and an ID card. Arabic humor is contagious and Haidar Mohammed is richly infected with it (above). Pictured below is Dhaen Shahin, the Deputy Editor in Chief, at an editorial meeting. *Photos by Lucy Monro.*

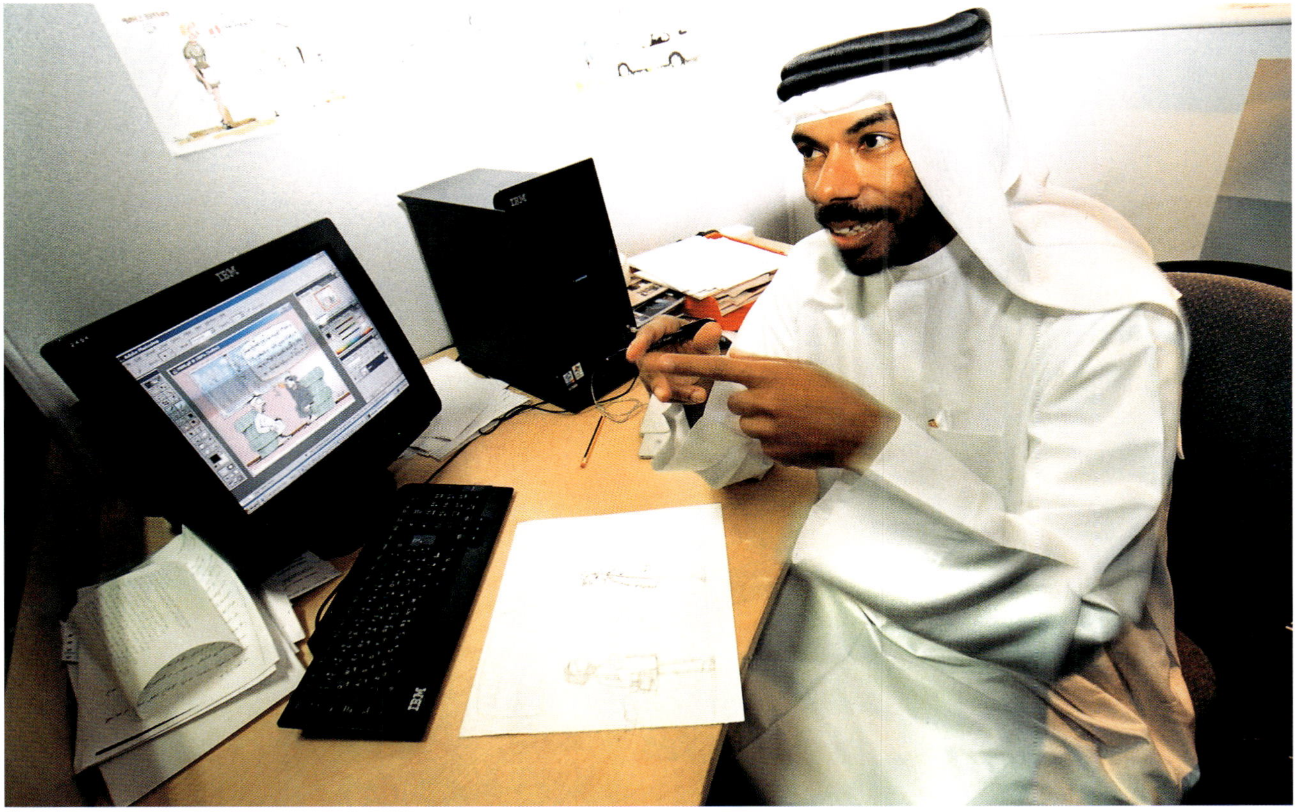

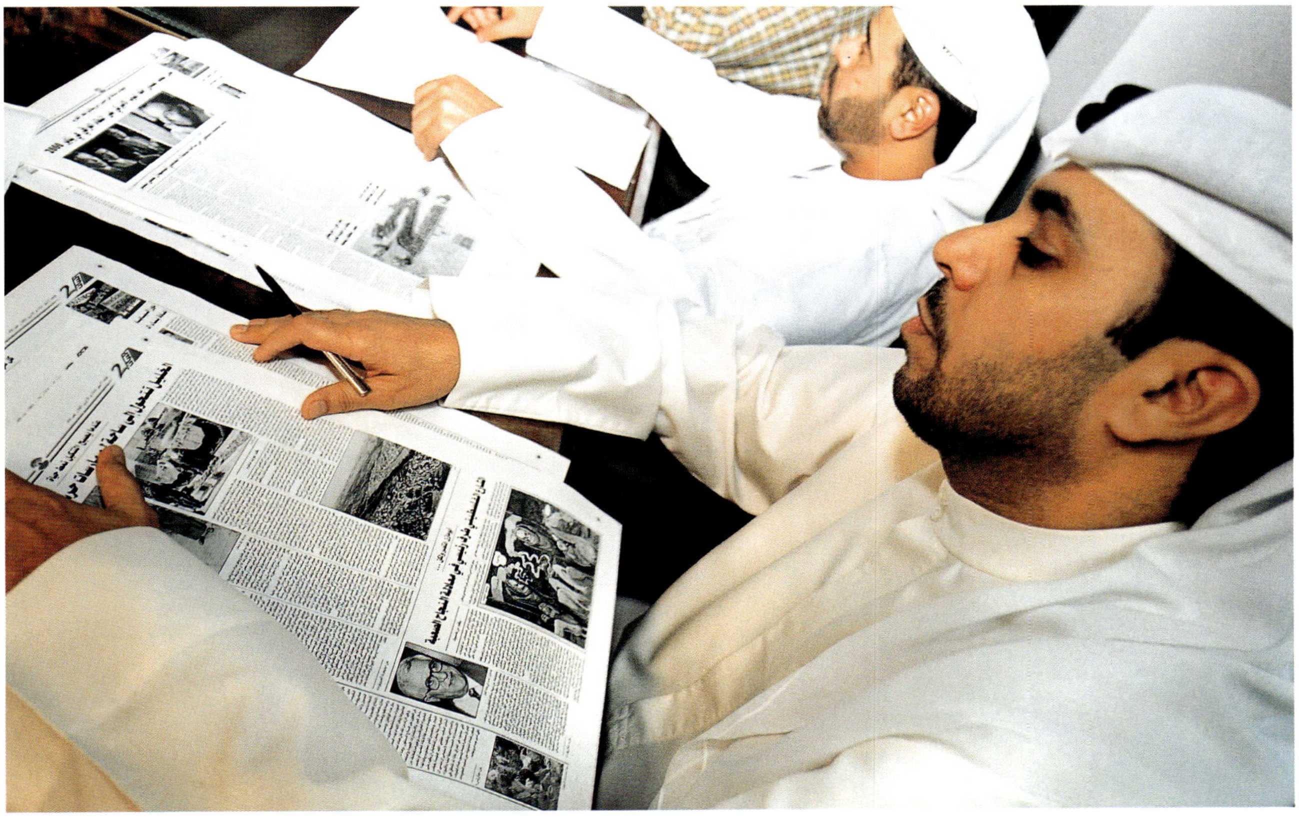

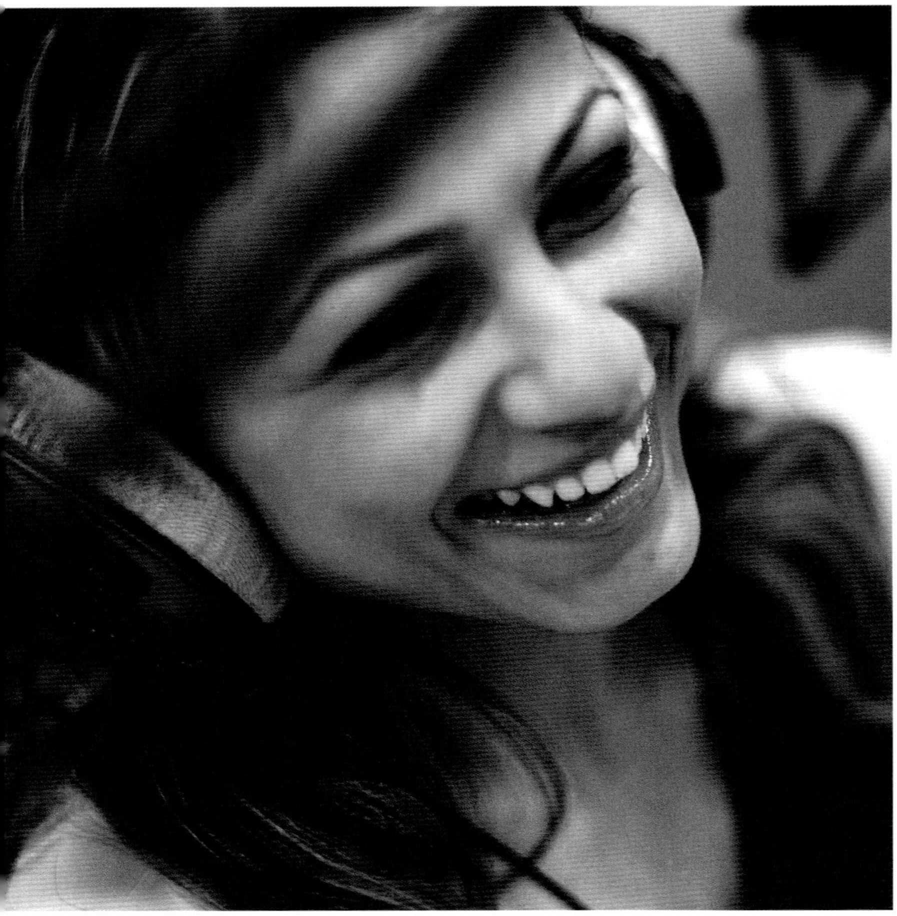

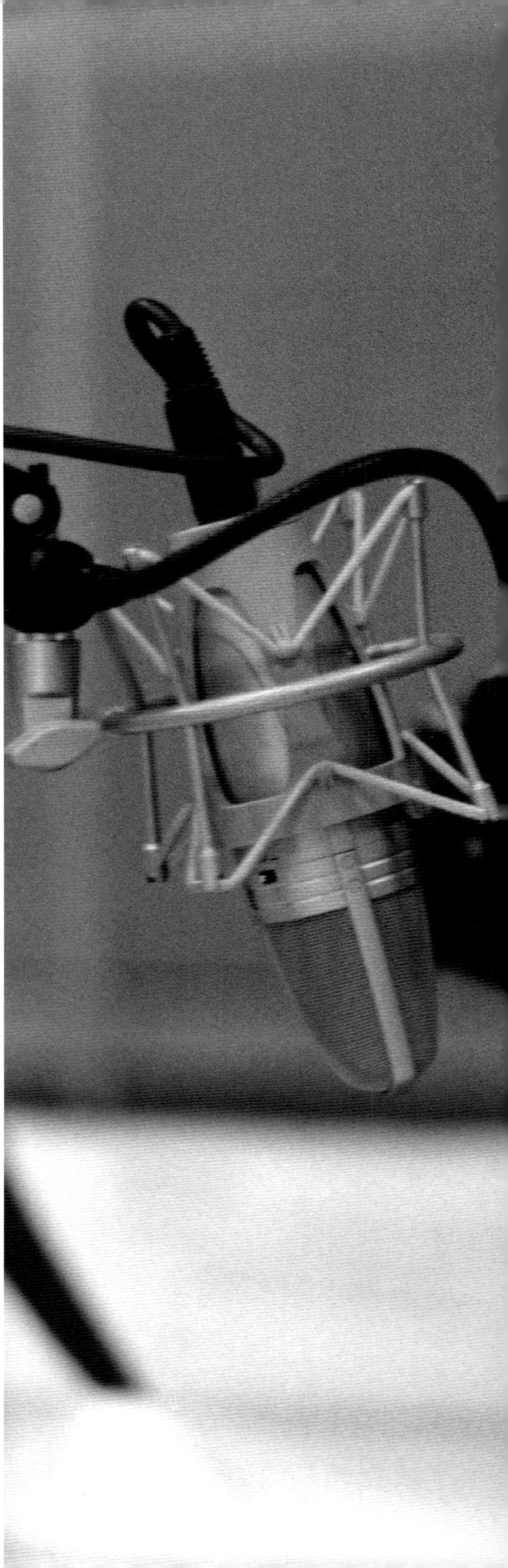

▲ ▶ WHETHER IN ARABIC, ENGLISH OR HINDI, RADIO music channels, daily chat shows, and nonstop in-depth reportage has conquered the news junkies and pop-culture addicts who – like anywhere else in the world – populate every living room, vehicle and Walkman throughout the city. Entertainment at its easiest, the presenters are celebrities in their own right and guide and tease the pulse of the big city and desert communities alike. One such presenter is Egyptian Mahira Abdul Aziz, who broadcasts on 98.9 FM – Alarabiya FM (ARN) (above); another is Indian presenter Tia Singh. You, too, can find her on City Radio 101.6 FM (right). *Photos by Katarina Premfors.*

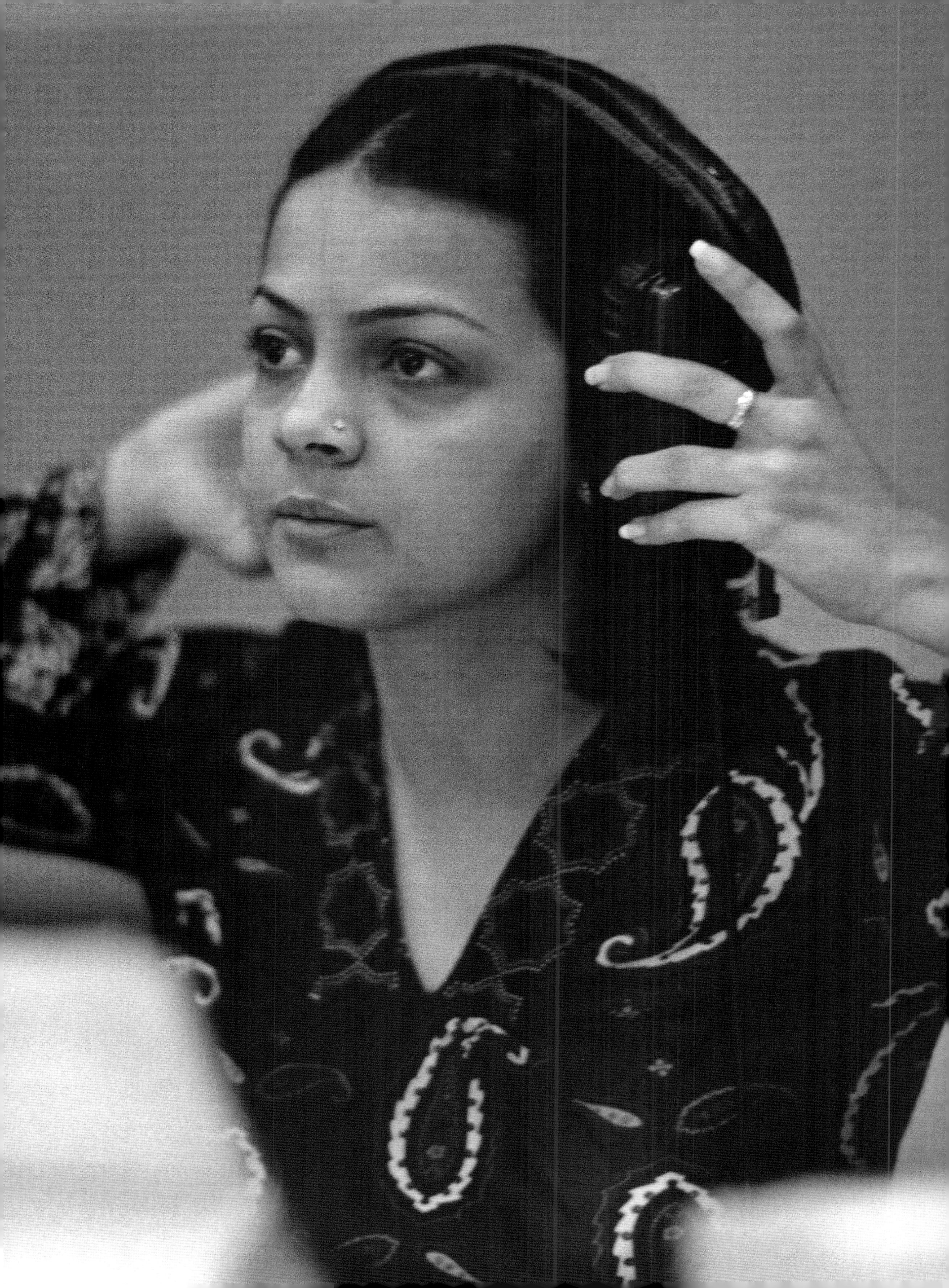

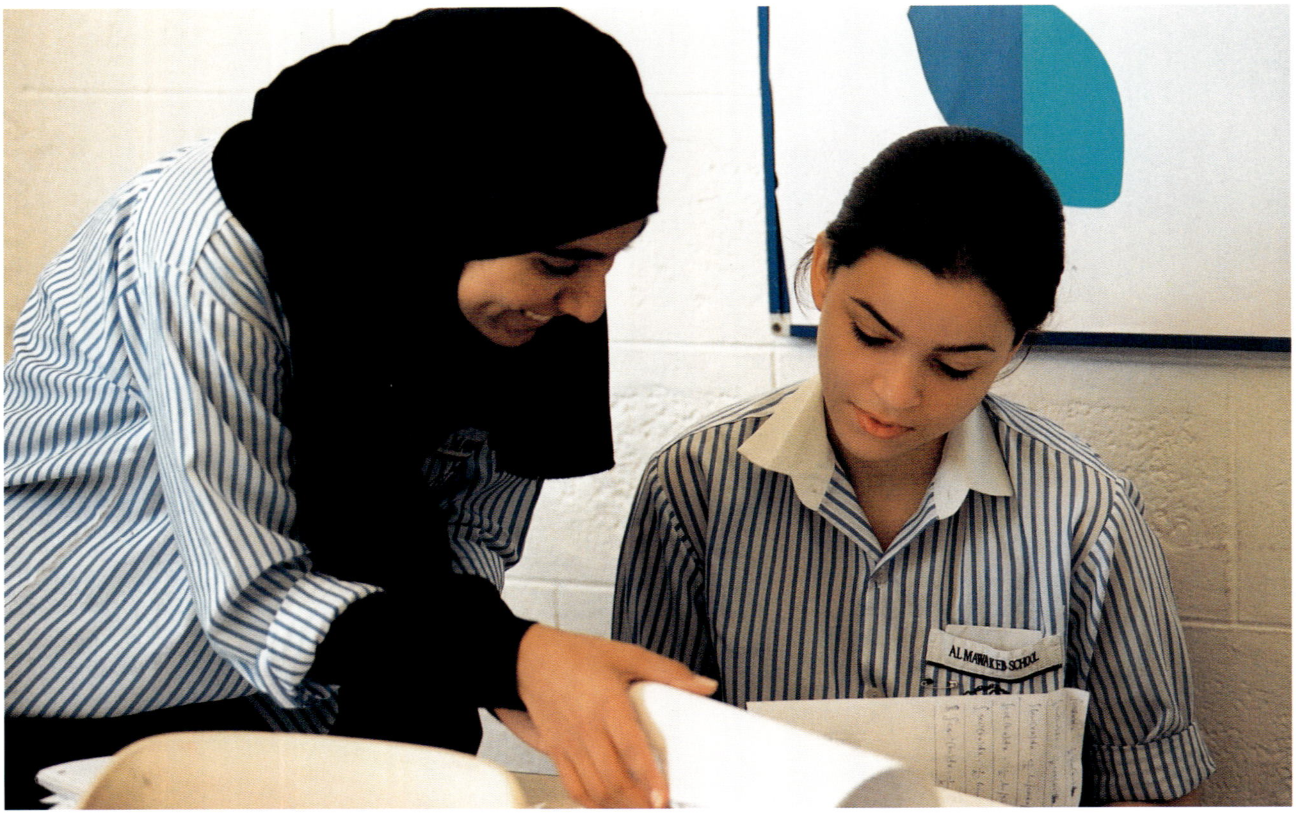
AL MAWAKEB SCHOOL

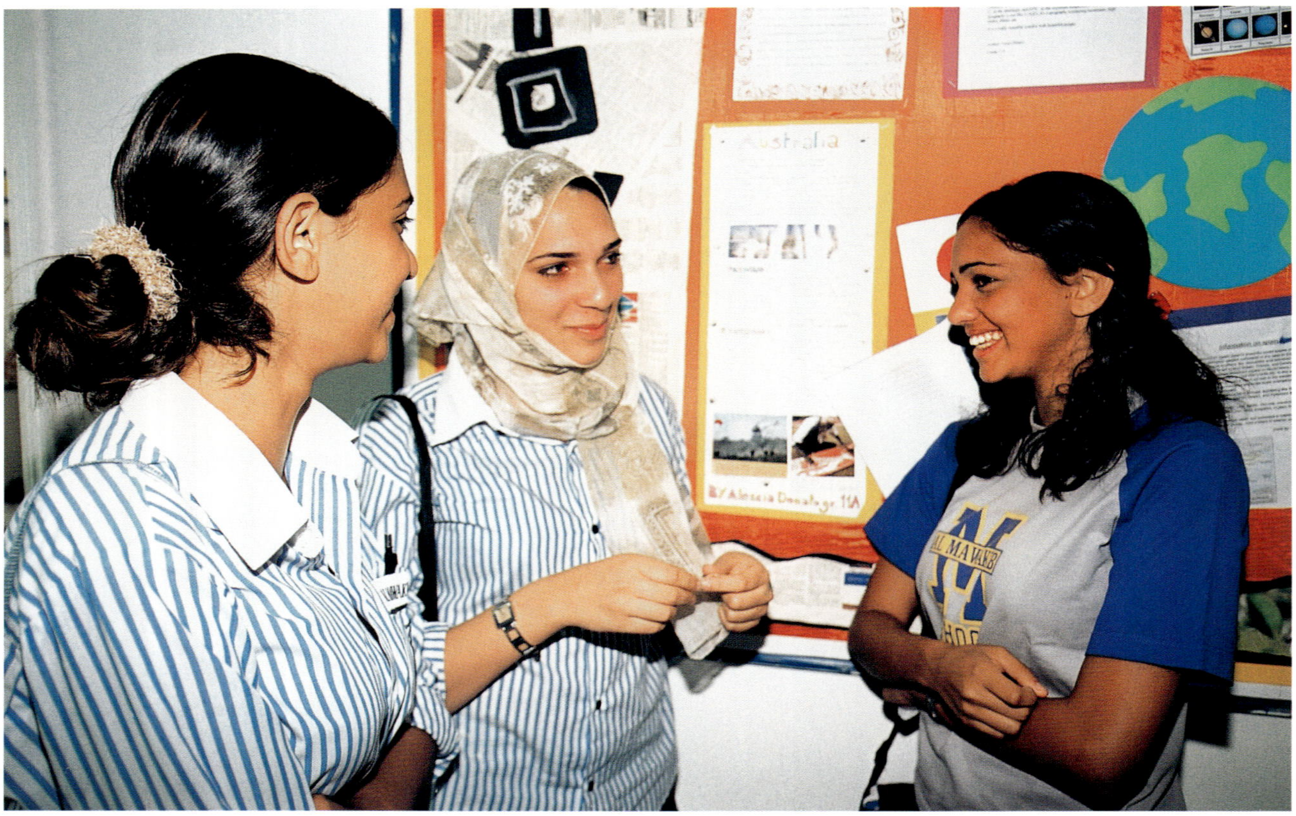
Australia

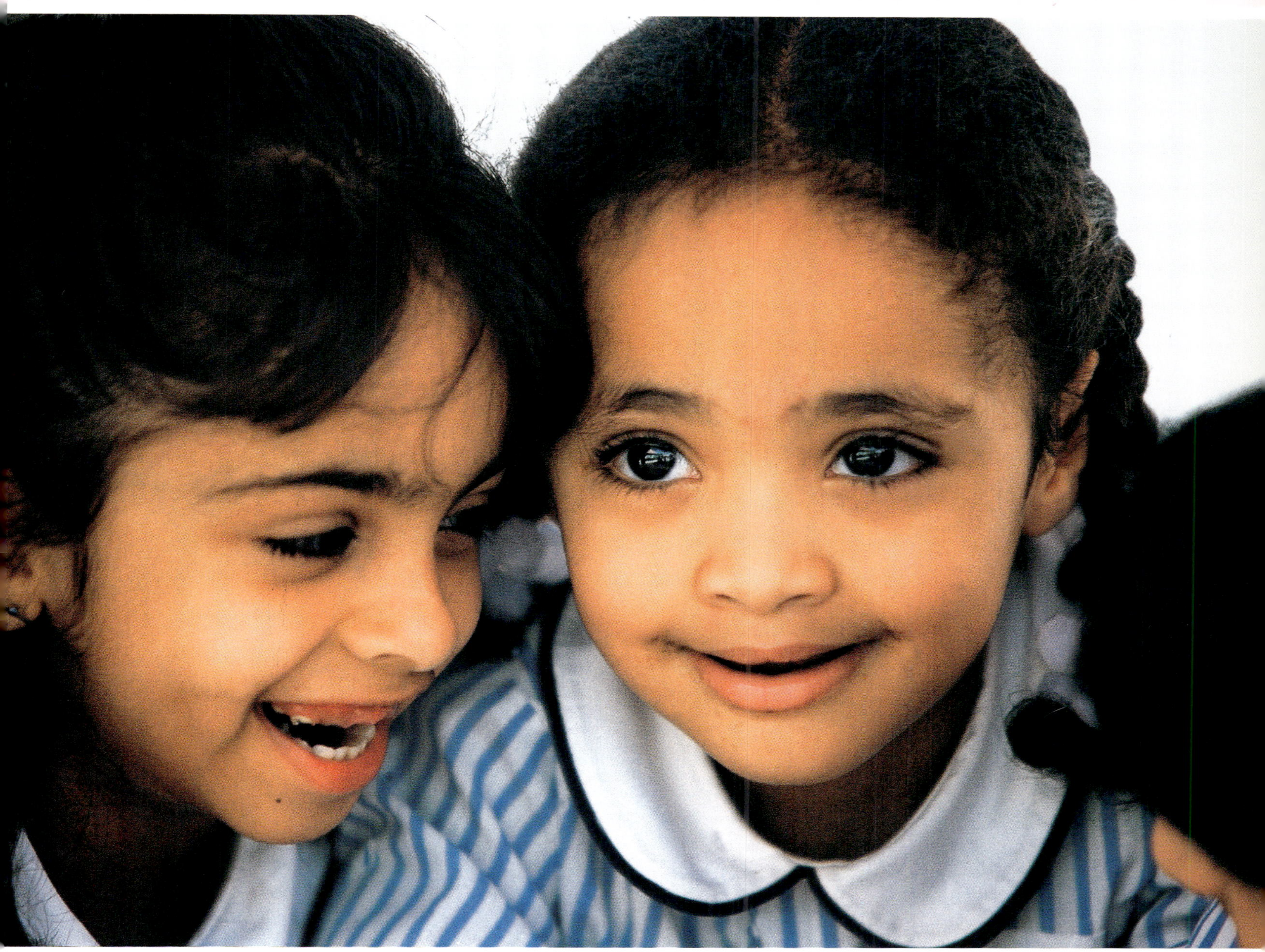

◄ ▲ *Dubai 24 hours* still photographer, Alia Al Shamsi, an alumnus of Al Mawakeb School, visited the school three years after graduating. It was a moment of joy and nostalgia for her, and an emotional reunion. *Photos by Lucy Monro.*

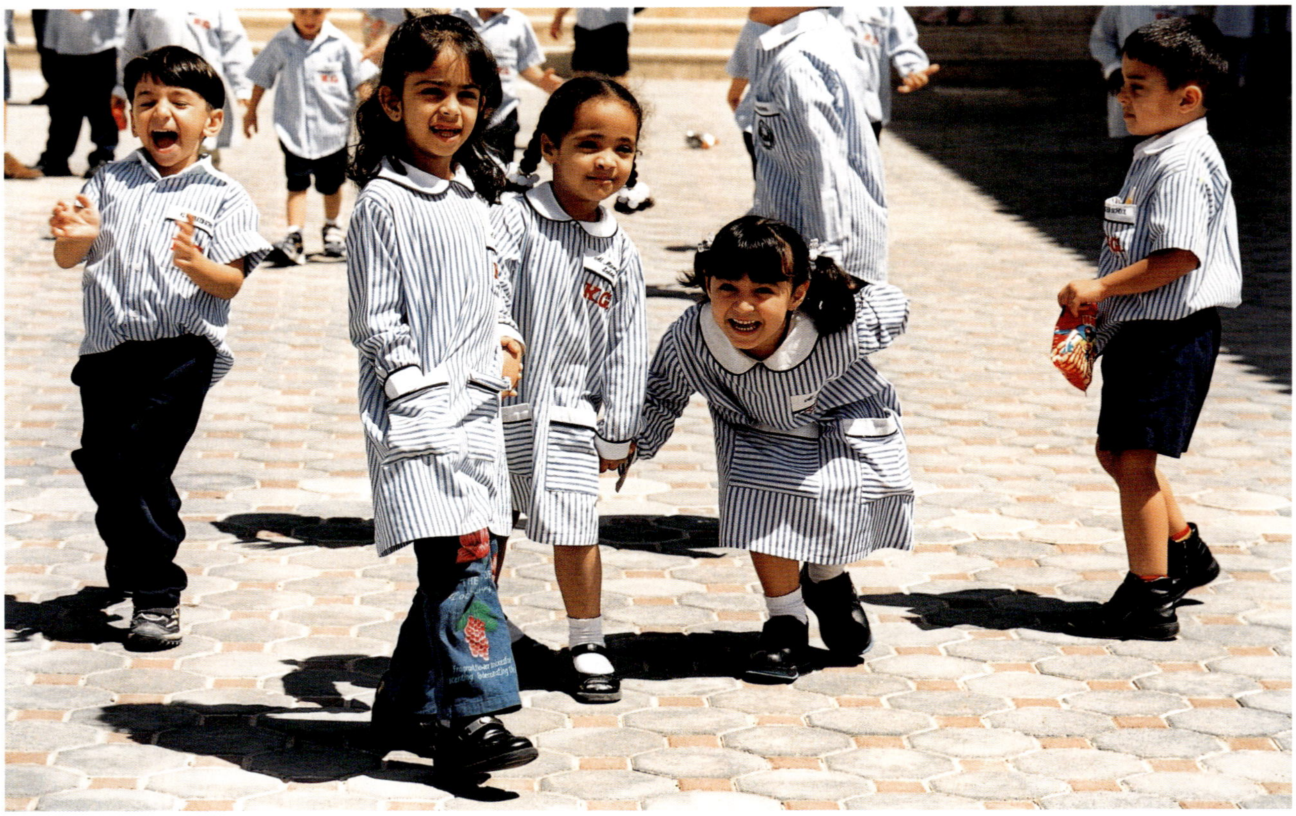

▲ ▶ There's a comprehensive network of government schools throughout the emirate, providing free primary and secondary education to UAE nationals. The Ministry of Education runs 34 boys' schools, 32 girls' schools and 10 kindergartens, working to an Arabic curriculum. There are also 22 evening schools and 27 private institutes for adults. For expatriate families, there are 79 private schools offering education of a high standard to the curriculum requirements of the UK, USA and a number of others including Italy, Japan, Iran, India and Pakistan. Arabic and English are usually the main languages of instruction, but other languages are used as necessary. *Photos by Lucy Monro.*

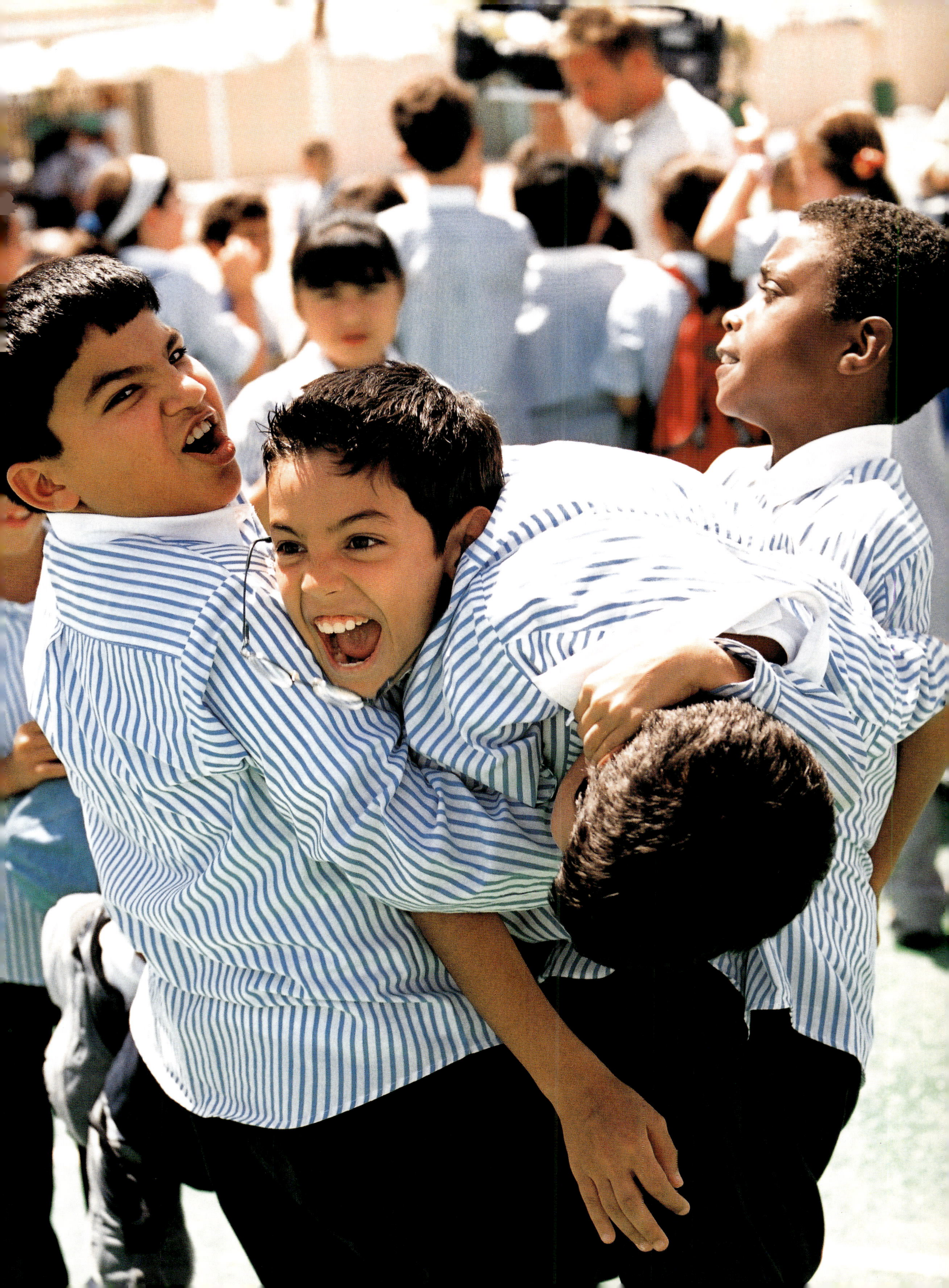

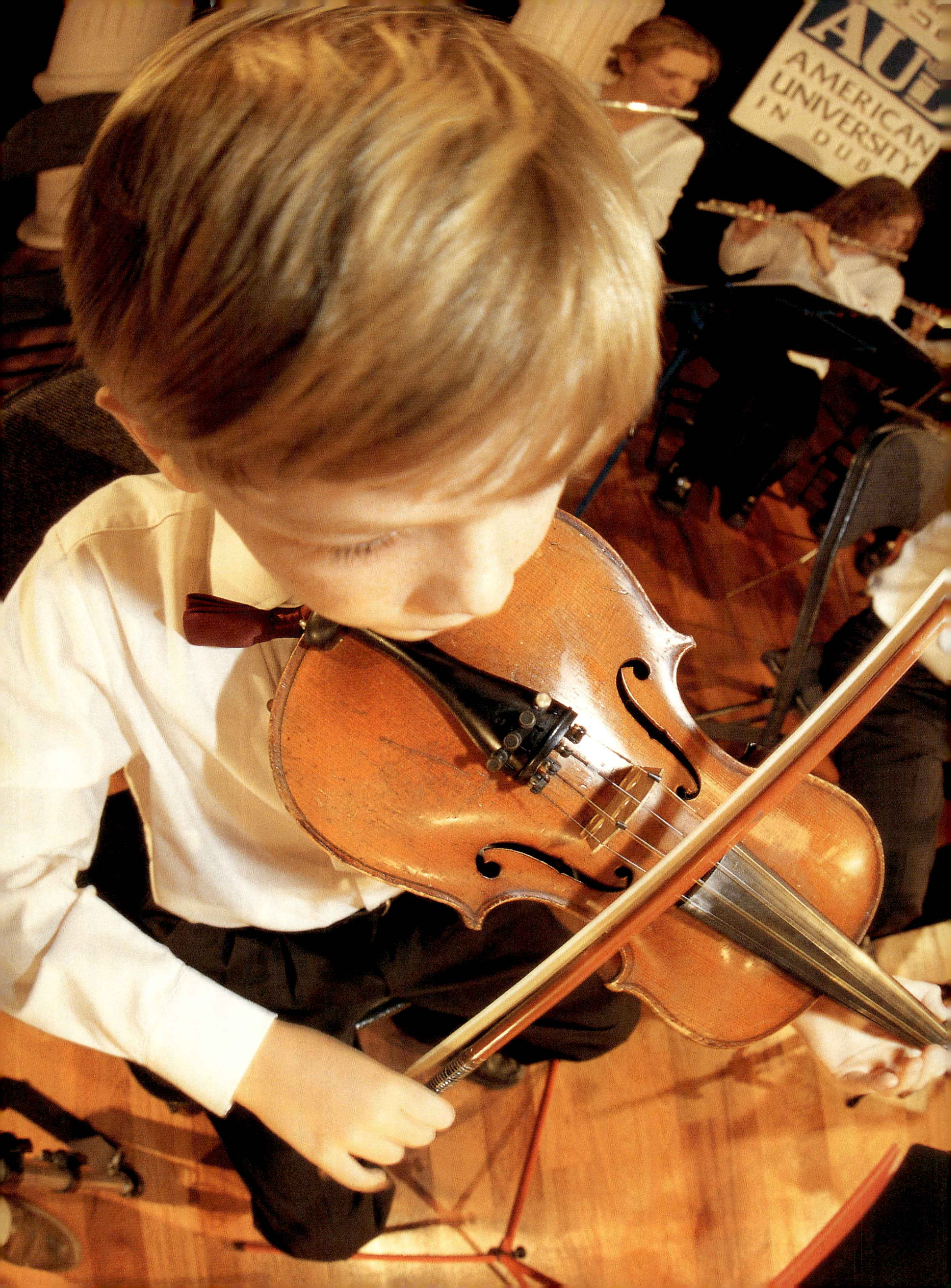
AUD
AMERICAN
UNIVERSITY

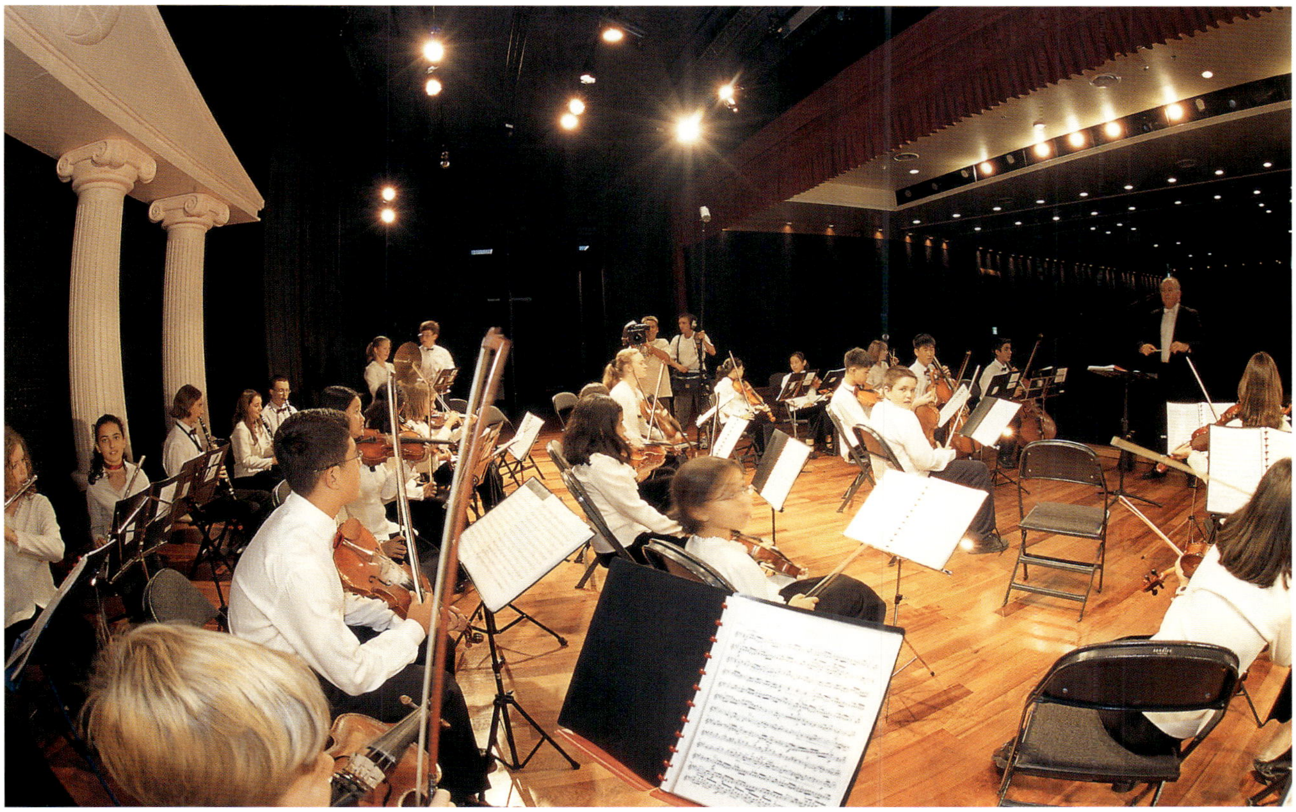

▲ ◀ THE EMIRATES CHILDREN'S SYMPHONY ORCHESTRA was formed in 1993 under the tutelage of conductor Riad Qudsi. Members range in age from seven to 15 and bring their own musical passions from a dozen countries – the USA, Korea, France, Ireland, Syria, Russia, New Zealand and others. Maestro Qudsi came from the cultural hub of Syria, Aleppo, and graduated from the Prague Conservatoire in 1974. His musical productions, world tours and sheer passion for humanitarian projects using music has endeared him to his many protégés and devotees throughout Dubai (above). Young Ben, from England, concentrates as he performs the UAE National Anthem on violin (left). *Photos by Souheil Semaan.*

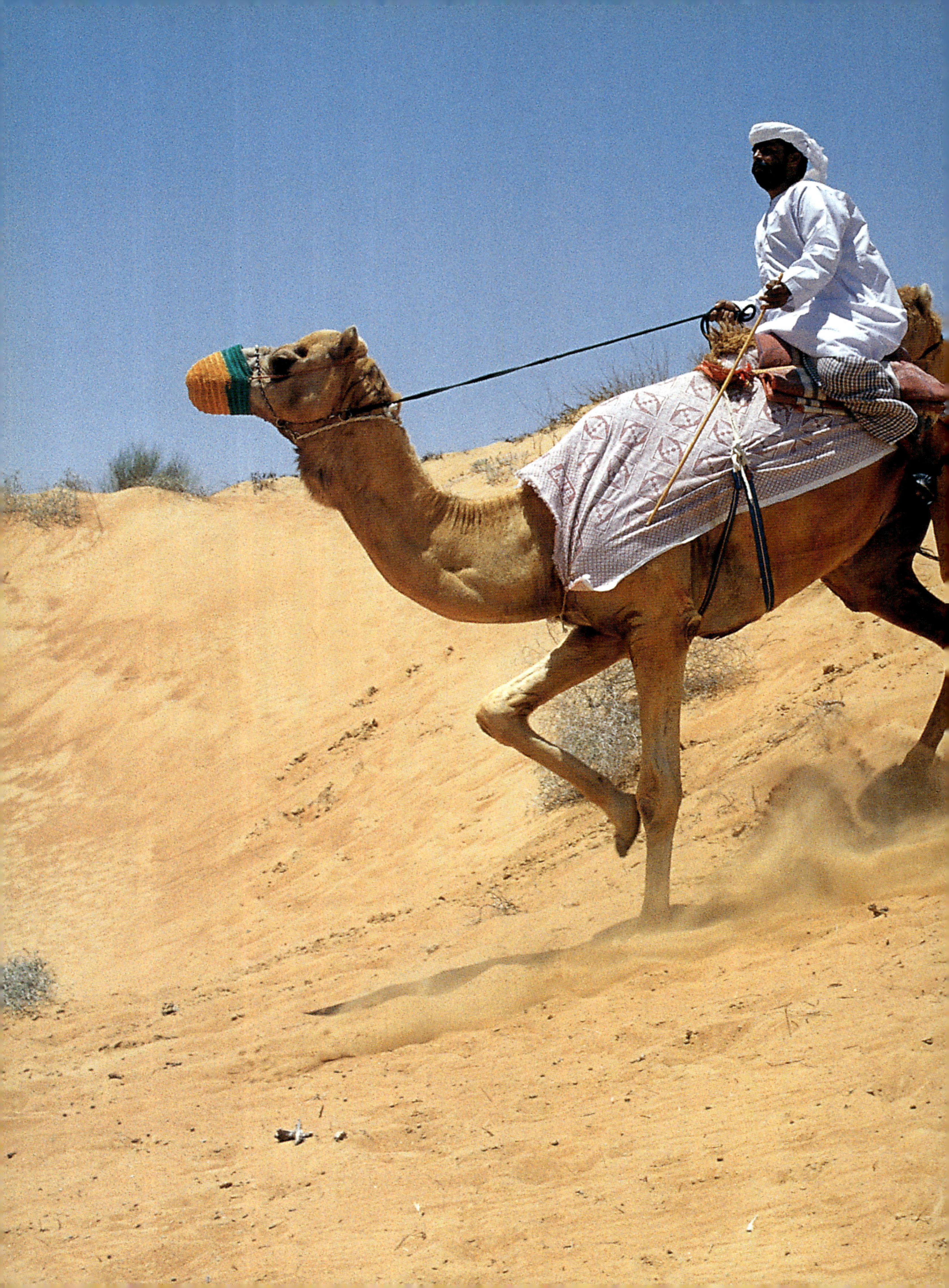

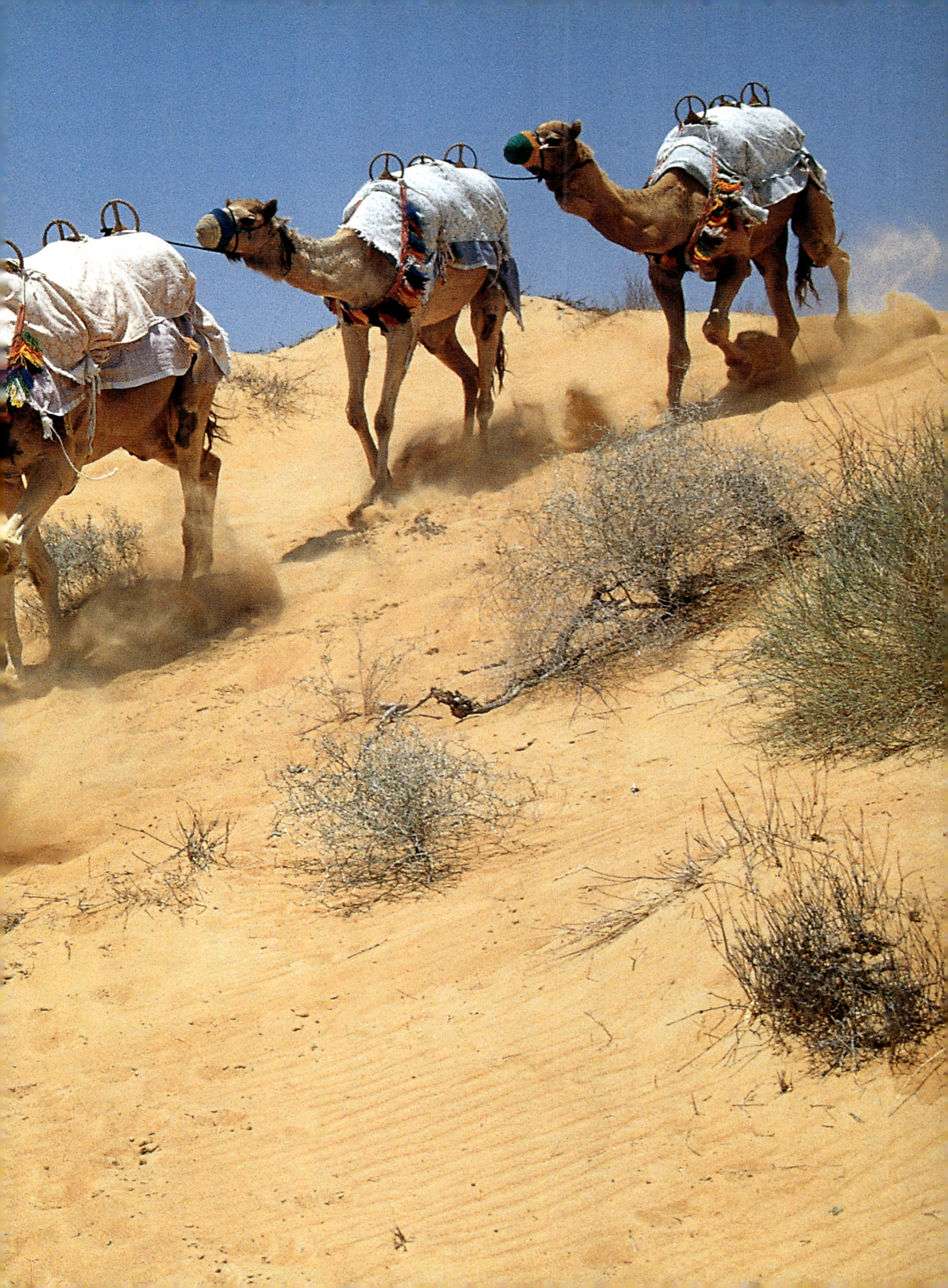

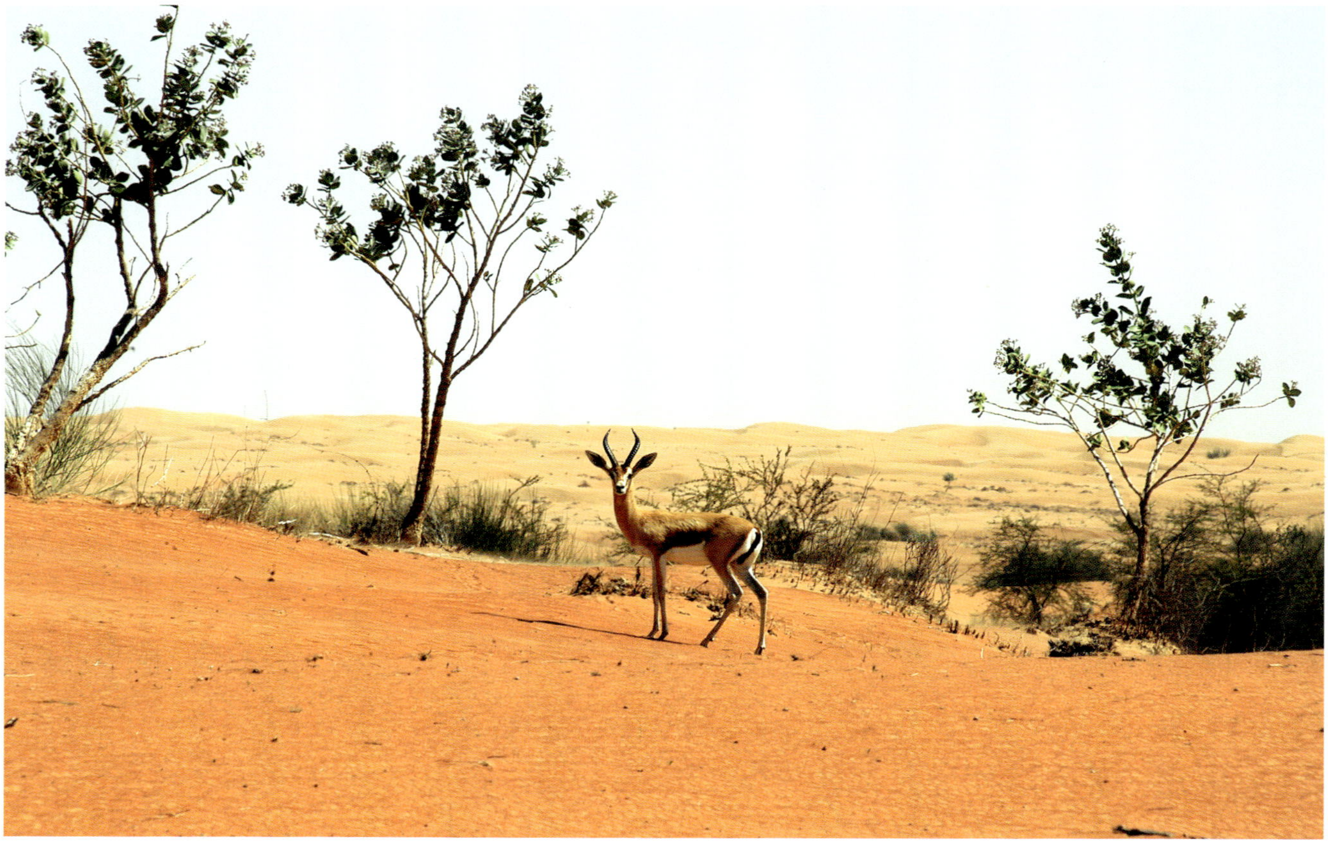

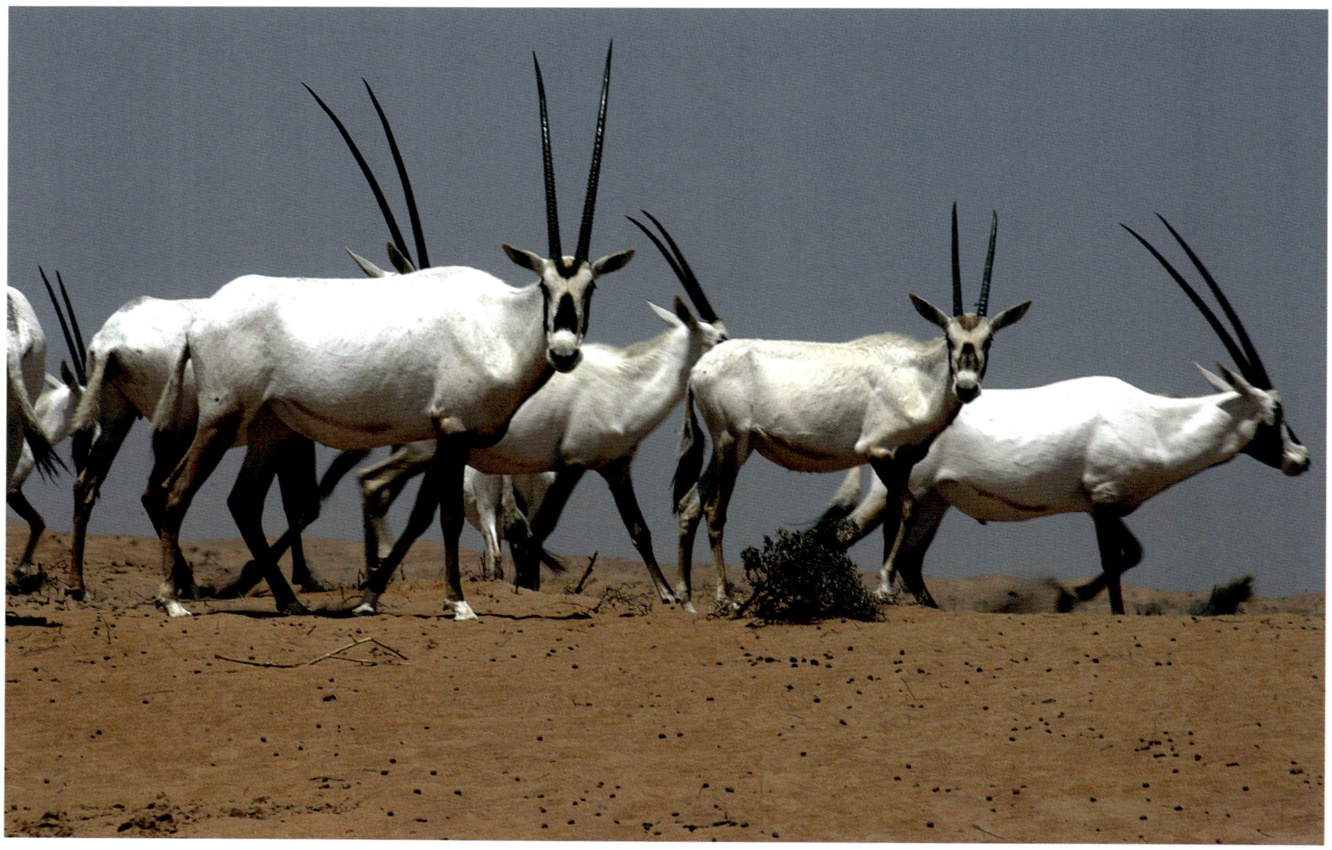

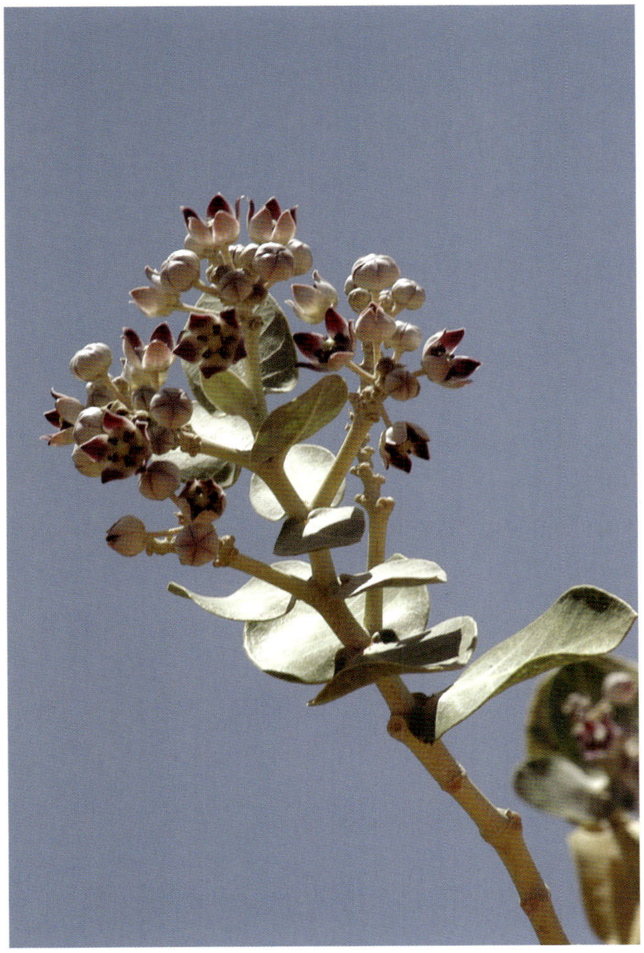

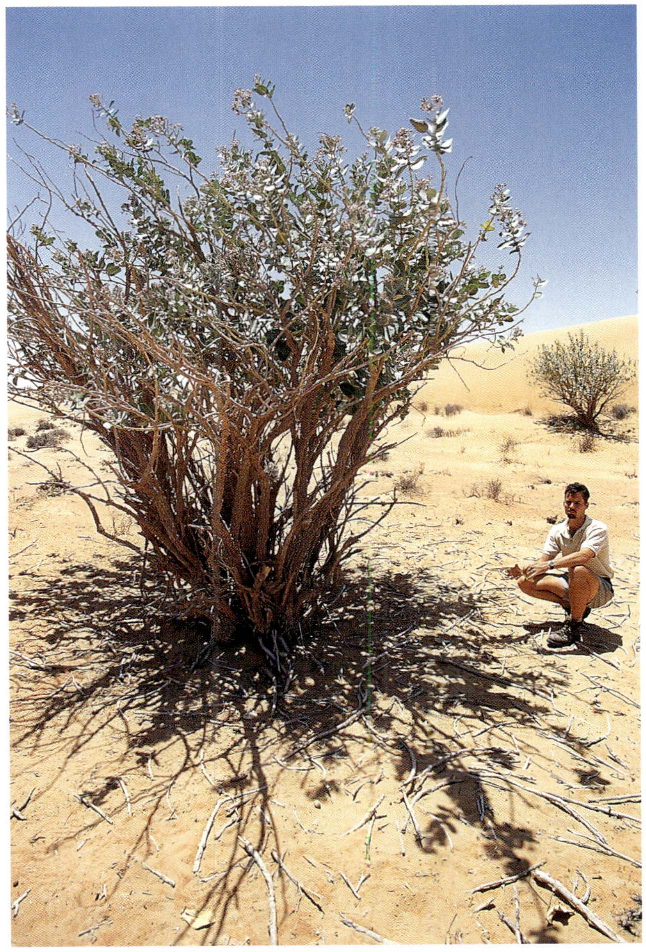

◀◀ A GROUP OF CAMELS AT THE AL MAHA DESERT Resort, 40 minutes southwest of Dubai city, established to restore the desert to its striking biodiversity. It is here, in the transitional desert zone between Africa and Asia, beneath the Hajar Mountains, that a globally unique mix of species and avian migrations occur. There are three species of gazelle, Arabian and scimitar-horned oryx, two indigenous wild-cat species, reptiles and more than 60 plant species. Tony Williams, the South African General Manager of Al Maha, along with his staff, hope to see this reserve pay for itself and its conservation work accomplished. With more than 150,000 ecotourists visiting Dubai each year, its chances of success are certainly encouraging.

◀ A MALE DAMANI GAZELLE, STANDING IN FRONT OF three Sodom's apples (*Calotropis procera*), gazes at the photographer (left top). Trees found at Al Maha include salam (*Acacia tortilis*), ghaf (*Prosopsis cineraria*) and sidr (*Ziziphus spina-christa*). The Arabian oryx (*Oryx leucoryx*), of which more than 5,000 survive today in their countries of origin (Oman, the UAE, Saudi Arabia, Bahrain, Qatar, Syria and Jordan). In the mid-1960s, the species was verging on extinction, with less than 500 remaining. Genetic breeding and carefully planned conservation efforts such as those at Al Maha Desert Resort, have brought this heraldic creature back to life (left bottom).

▲ RESERVE OFFICER, GREG SIMKINS, SITS IN THE SHADE OF a Sodom's Apple (right), a hardy desert shrub with a beautiful waxy flower (left).

▶▶ DUBAI IS SANDWICHED BETWEEN THE ARABIAN GULF and a sea of dunes. The Hajar Mountains, the backbone of Arabia, lie further inland. *Photos by Dariush Zandi.*

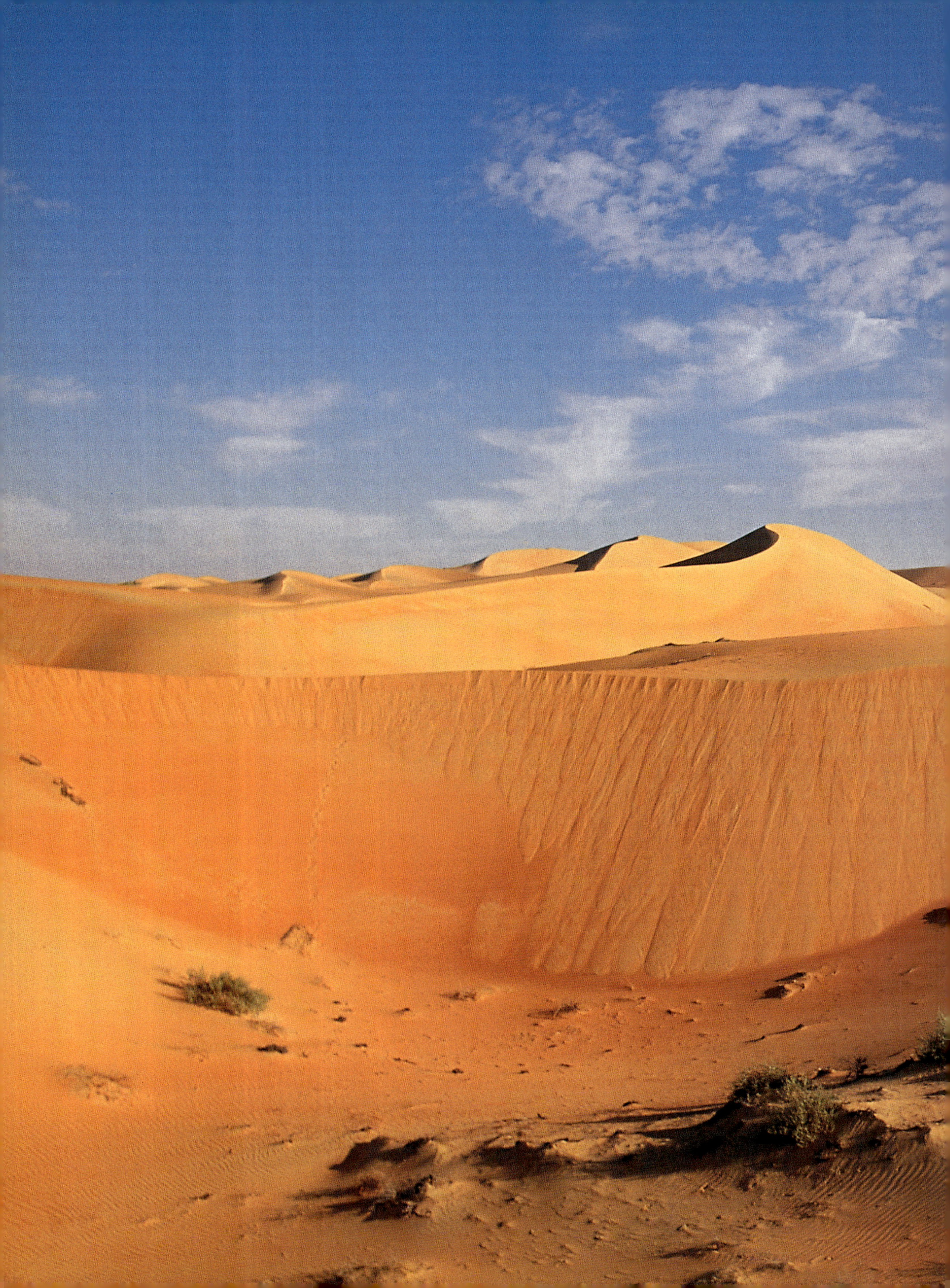

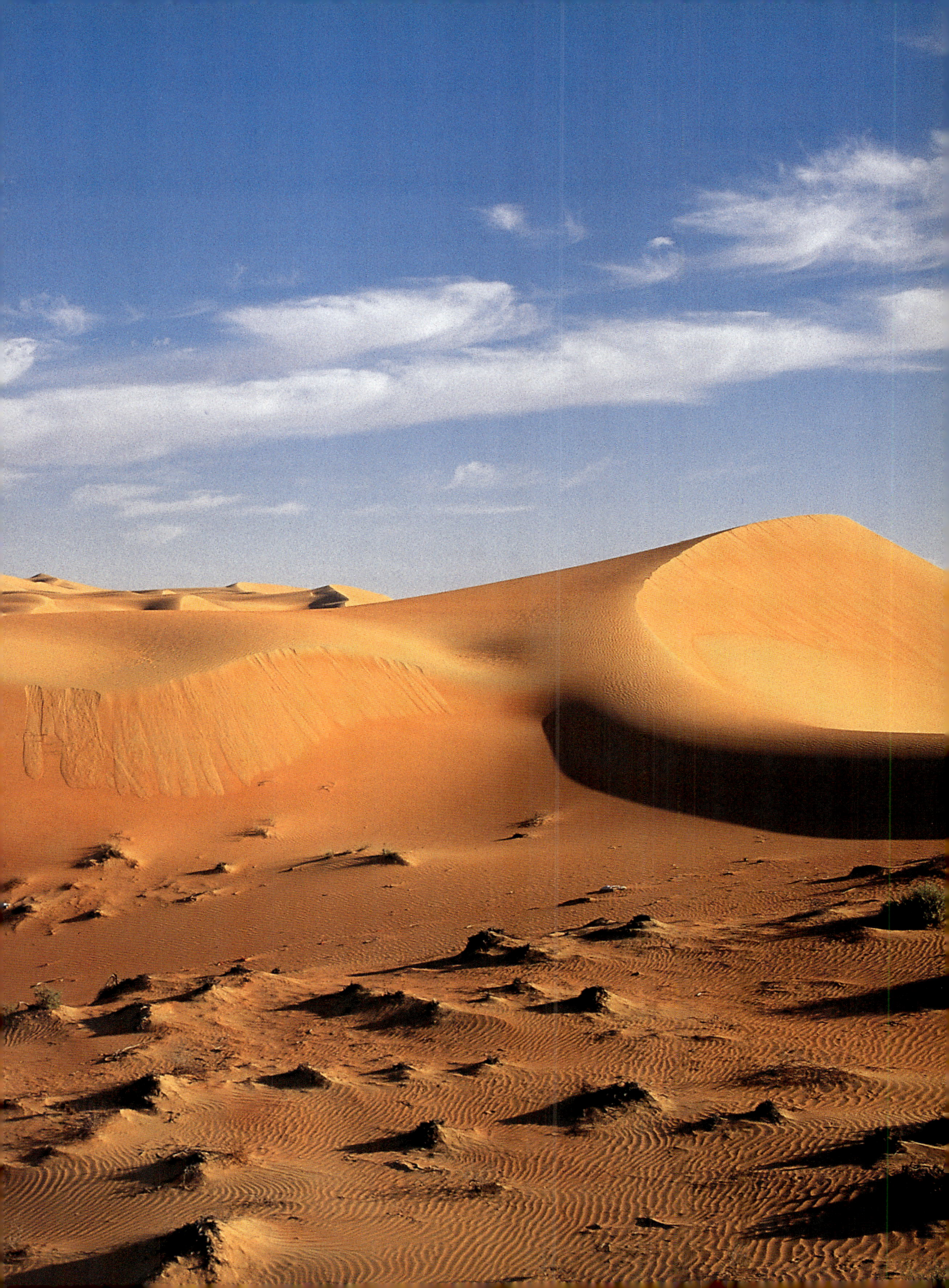

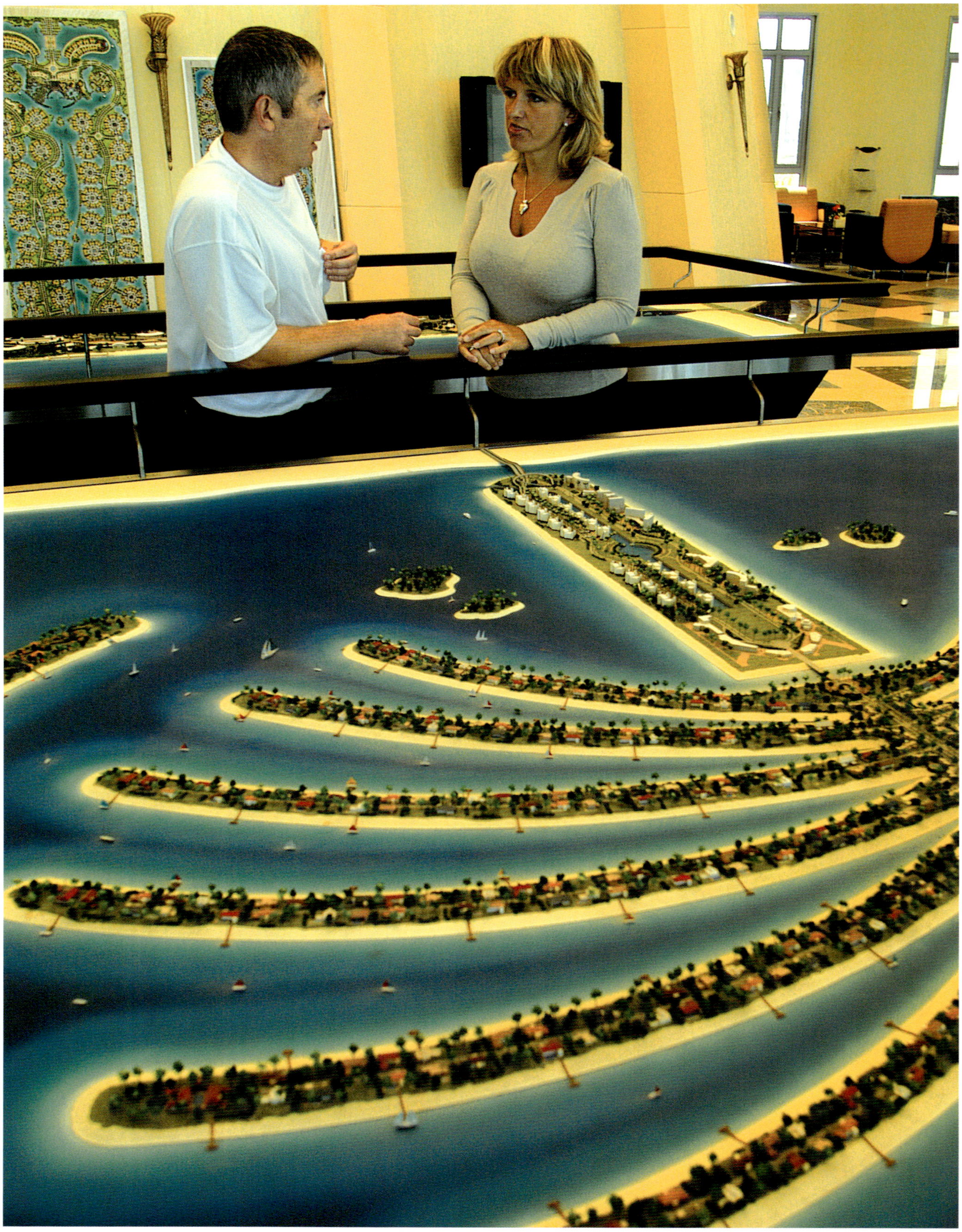

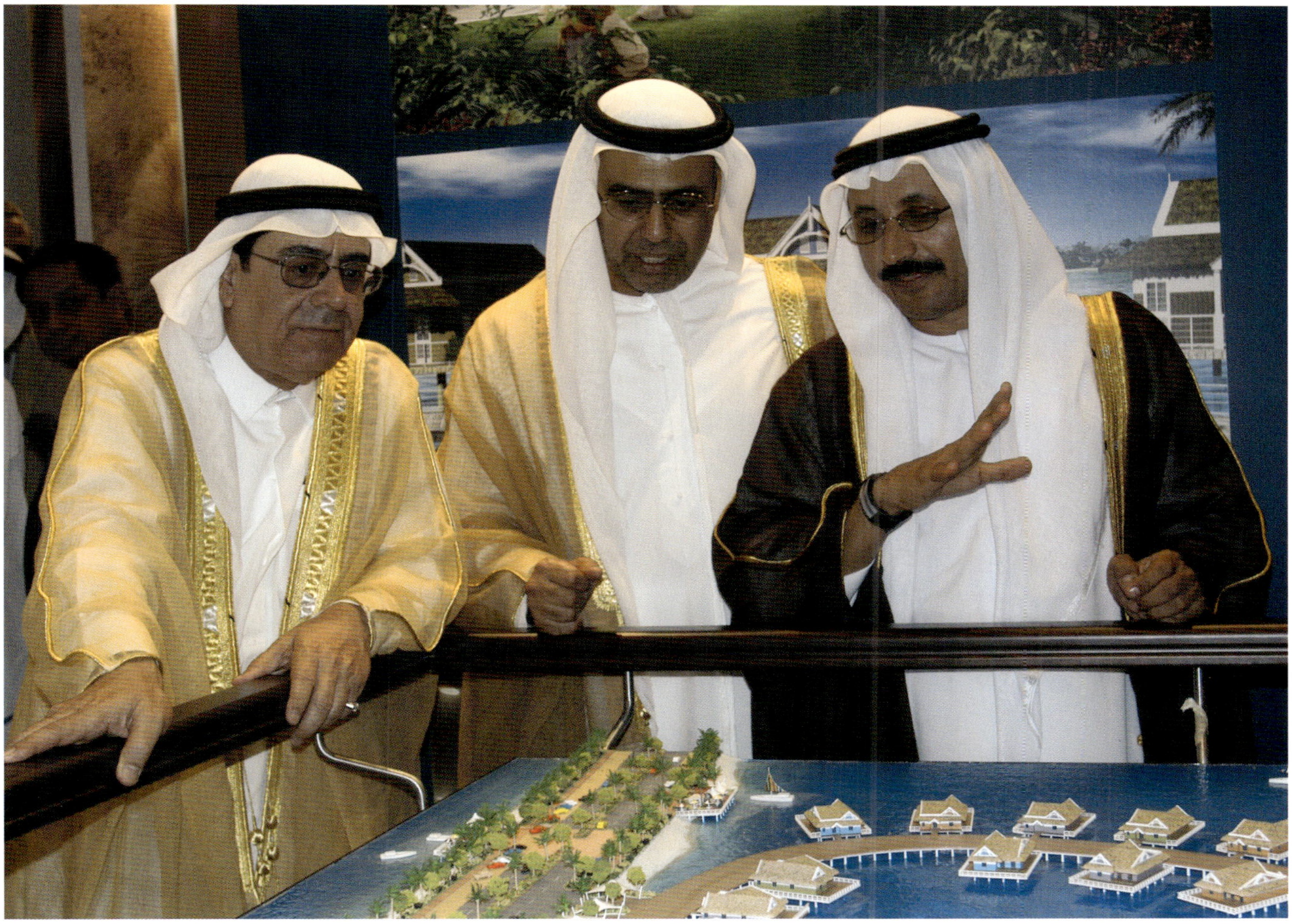

◄ The Palm project – the creation of two man-made islands – is Dubai's most ambitious endeavour yet and has been referred to as 'The Eighth Wonder of the World'. When complete, the islands will be visible from space and will add 120 kilometres to the emirate's coastline.

▲ Sultan bin Sulayem, Chief Executive of Dubai's Ports, Customs and Free Zone Corporation (PCFZ), and of Palm Developers, discusses a model of one of The Palm islands with leading Dubai businessmen Obaid Humaid Al Tayer, (President of the Dubai Chamber of Commerce and Industry) and Abdul Jalil Yousuf Darwish (Vice Chairman and Executive Director of HSBC Bank Middle East and treasurer of the Dubai Chamber of Commerce and Industry). Sultan bin Sulayem is recognised as one of the most astute businessmen in Dubai and, among other duties, is Chairman of Tejari.com (see pages 78/79) and the property company Nakheel. *Photos by Samar S Jodha.*

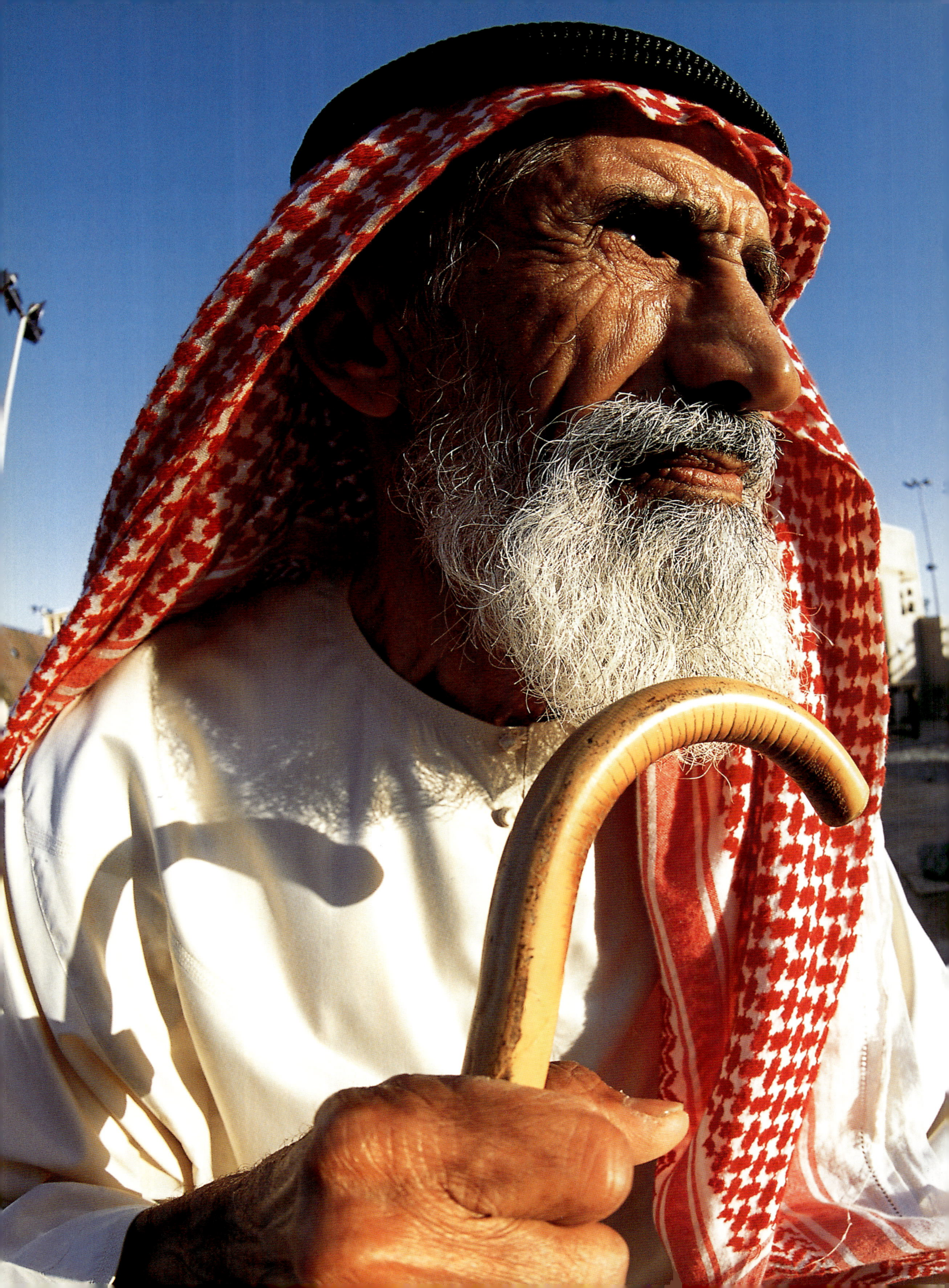

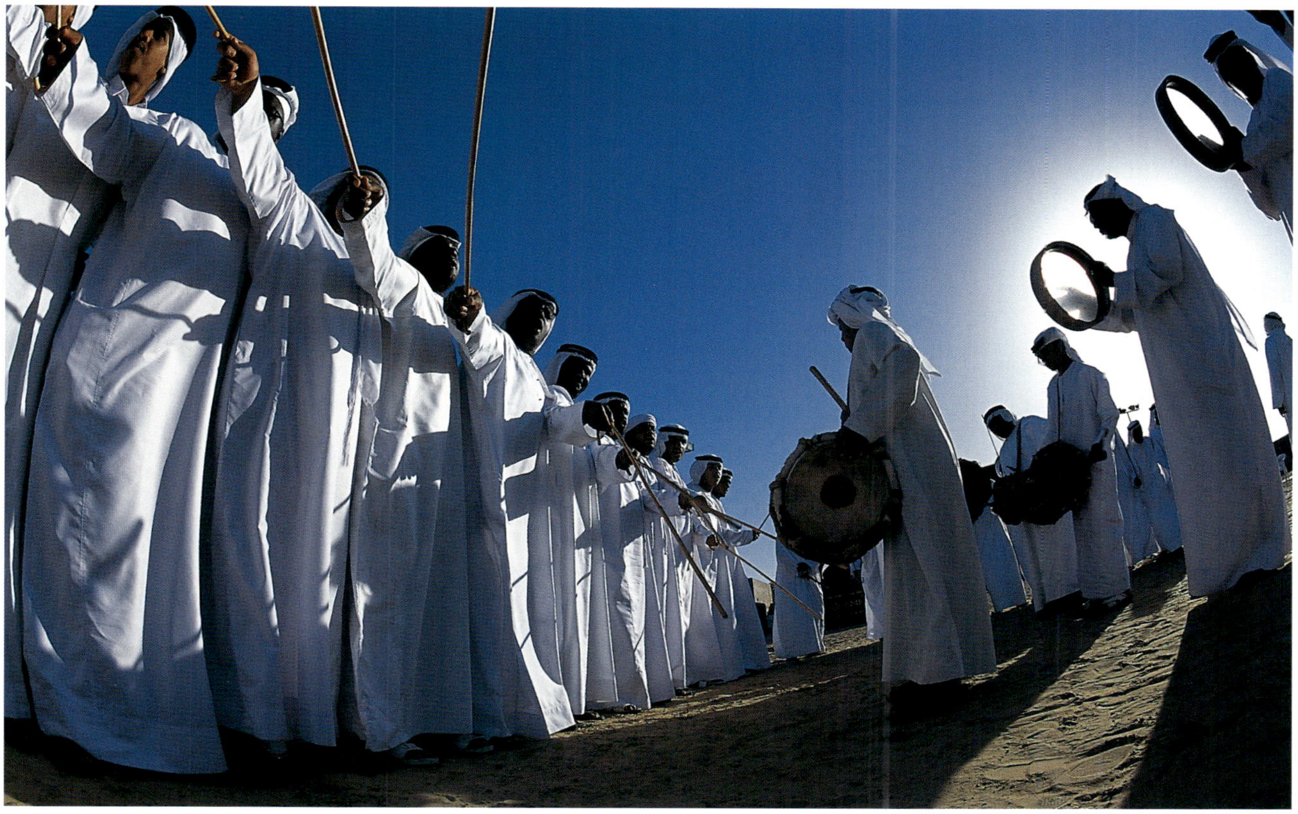

◀ THE VENERABLE HUMAID ALI ALREZI, A BEDOUIN AND poet (see pages 122/123), is also one of the familiar faces at Dubai's Heritage Village, situated in the Shindagha area not far from the mouth of the Creek.

▲ A DANCE GROUP OF EMIRATIS PERFORM *AYALA*, A traditional Gulf dance, at the Heritage Village. Swords, rifles, camel sticks, tambourines and drums are used during dances marking various celebrations. *Photos by Joe Sassine.*

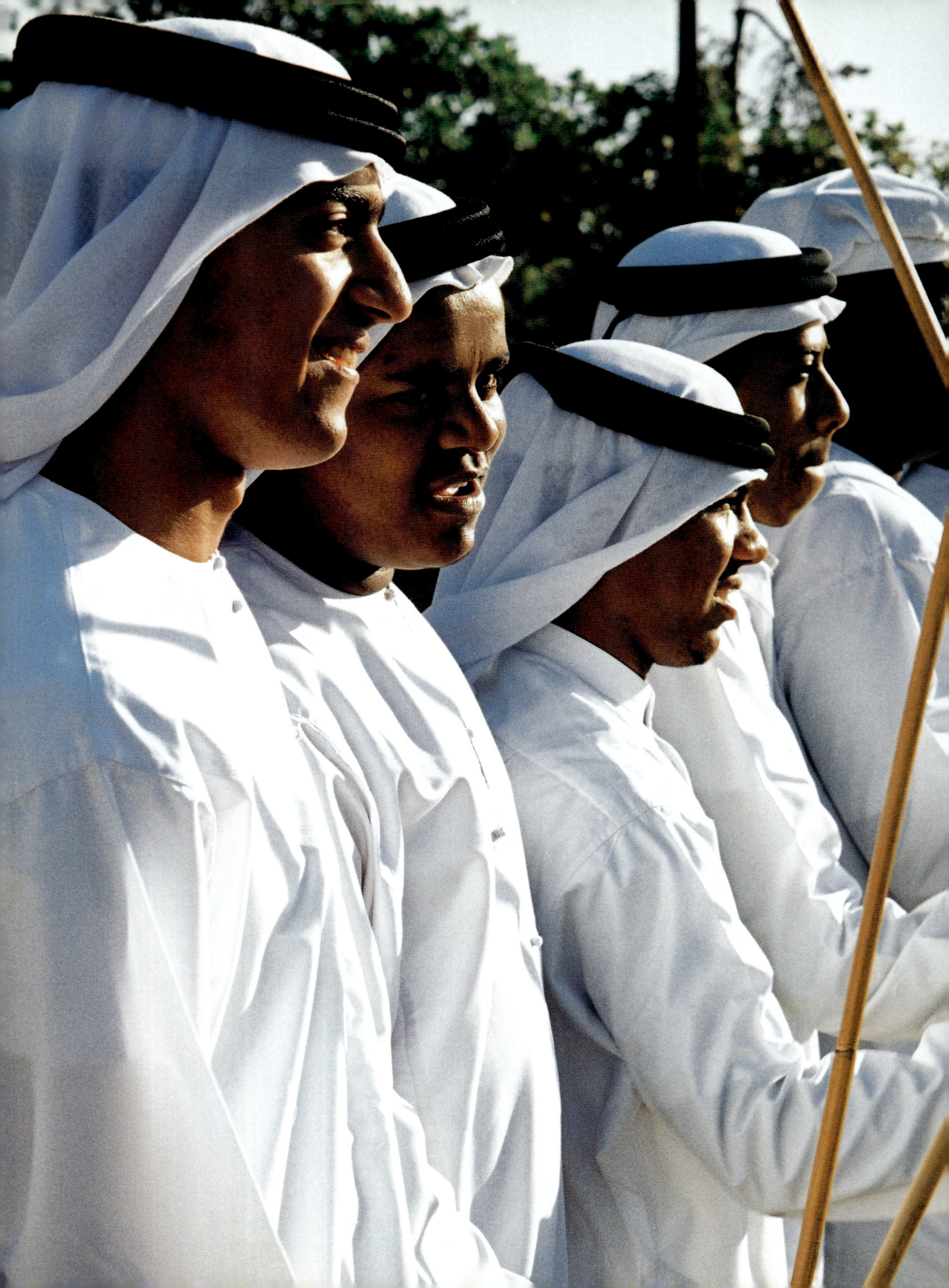

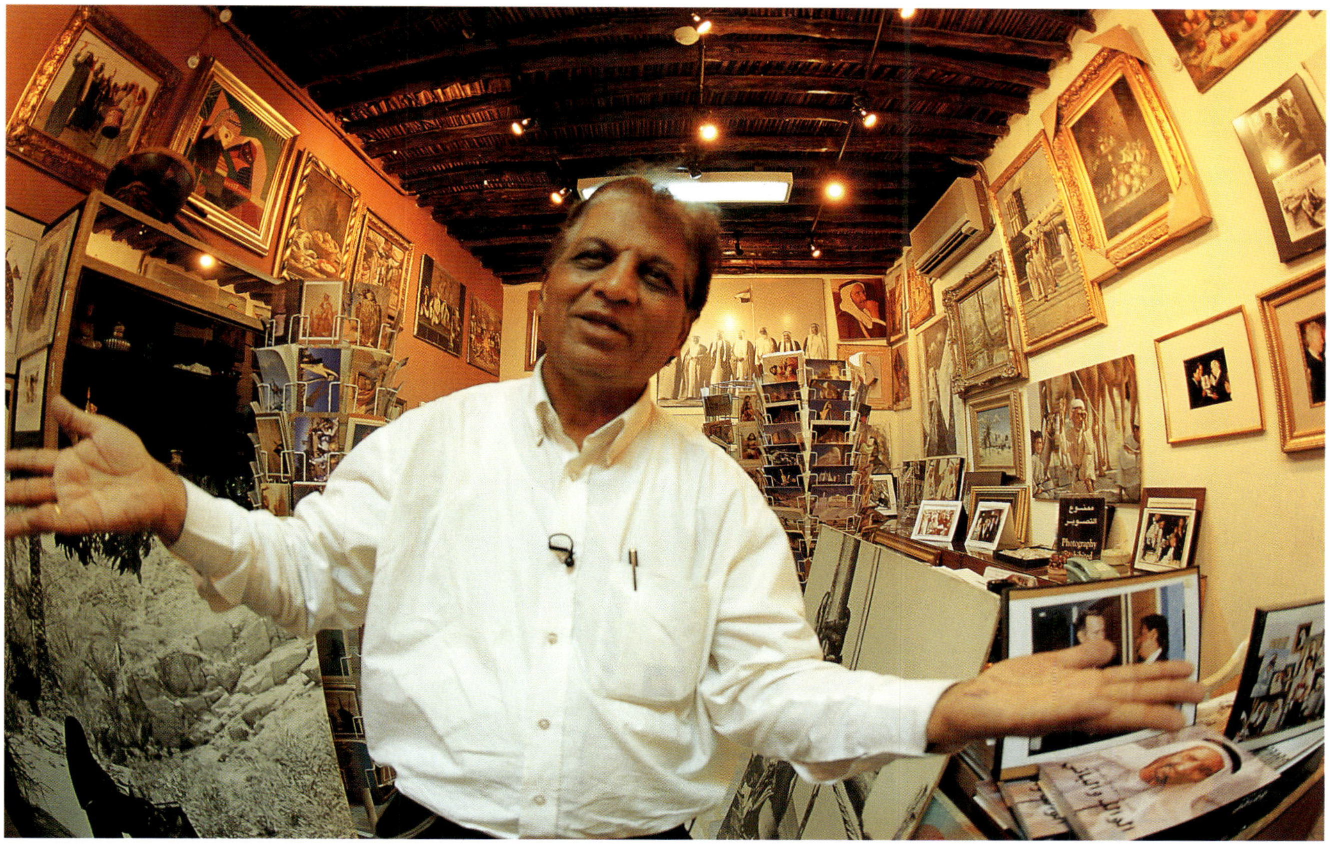

◄ DUBAI'S DANCE AND CULTURE GROUPS ATTRACT PEOPLE of all ages and are especially popular at weddings, festivals and other special occasions. Here, some young men enjoy a dance known as *Al Ardah*. *Photo by Asma Hamad Al Shamsi.*

▲ PICTURED IN ONE OF HIS ART GALLERIES, THE PROLIFIC Ramesh Shukla arrived in Dubai more than 40 years ago, on assignment from India, his place of birth. He immediately fell in love with Dubai, and managed to photograph the creation of the United Arab Emirates in 1971. Since that time, his wonderful photographs and books of sheikhs and commoners have gained him international fame. In evoking the spirit of the people, the diverse communities and those special moments of bygone eras, Shukla, perhaps more than any artist in the emirates, has chronicled the pace of change and the psyche of a country. *Photo by Joe Sassine.*

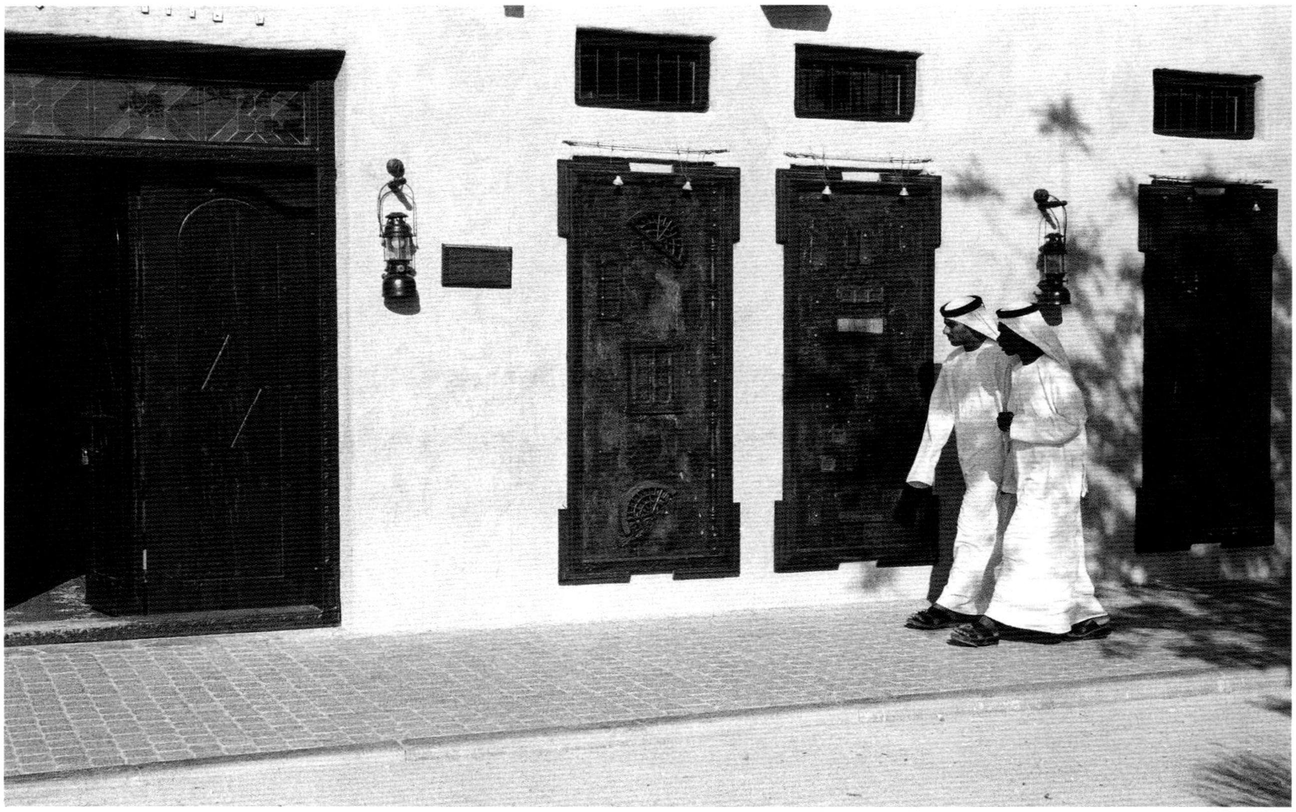

▲ LOCALS STROLL PAST TRADITIONAL WOODEN CARVED doors at the absorbing Heritage Village.

▶ A BRIGHT-EYED YOUNG WOMAN PEERS FROM HER traditional *shaylah* (headdress) and from beneath her *abaya*, the black robe which has become a considerable fashion statement for women, categorically refuting the notion that such apparel is the male partner's idea of restricting visual access to the female. Indeed, Islamic women borrowed this style from Christian aristocracy in Medieval times, when the more delicate gender found it particularly attractive. *Photos by Alia Al Shamsi.*

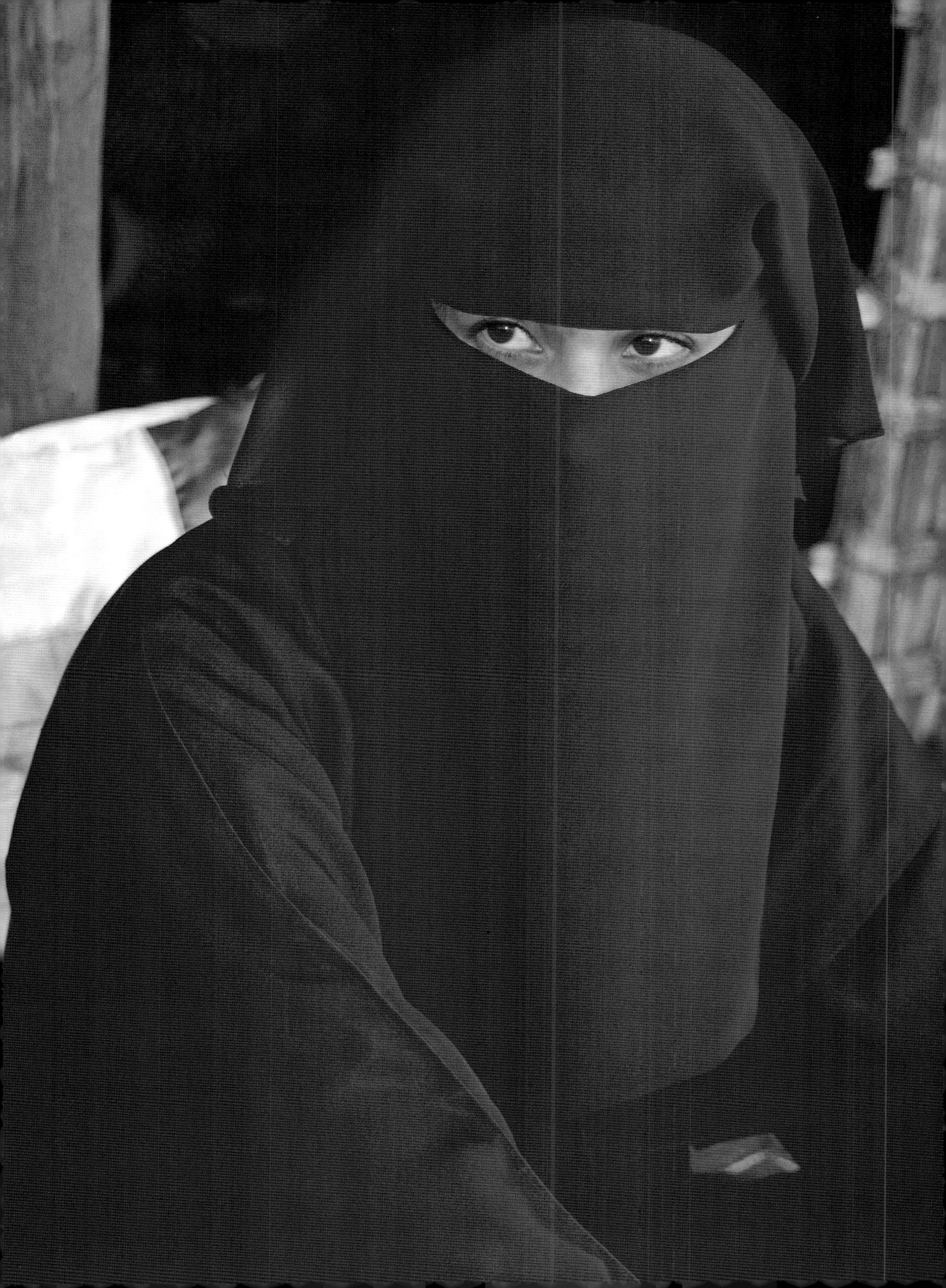

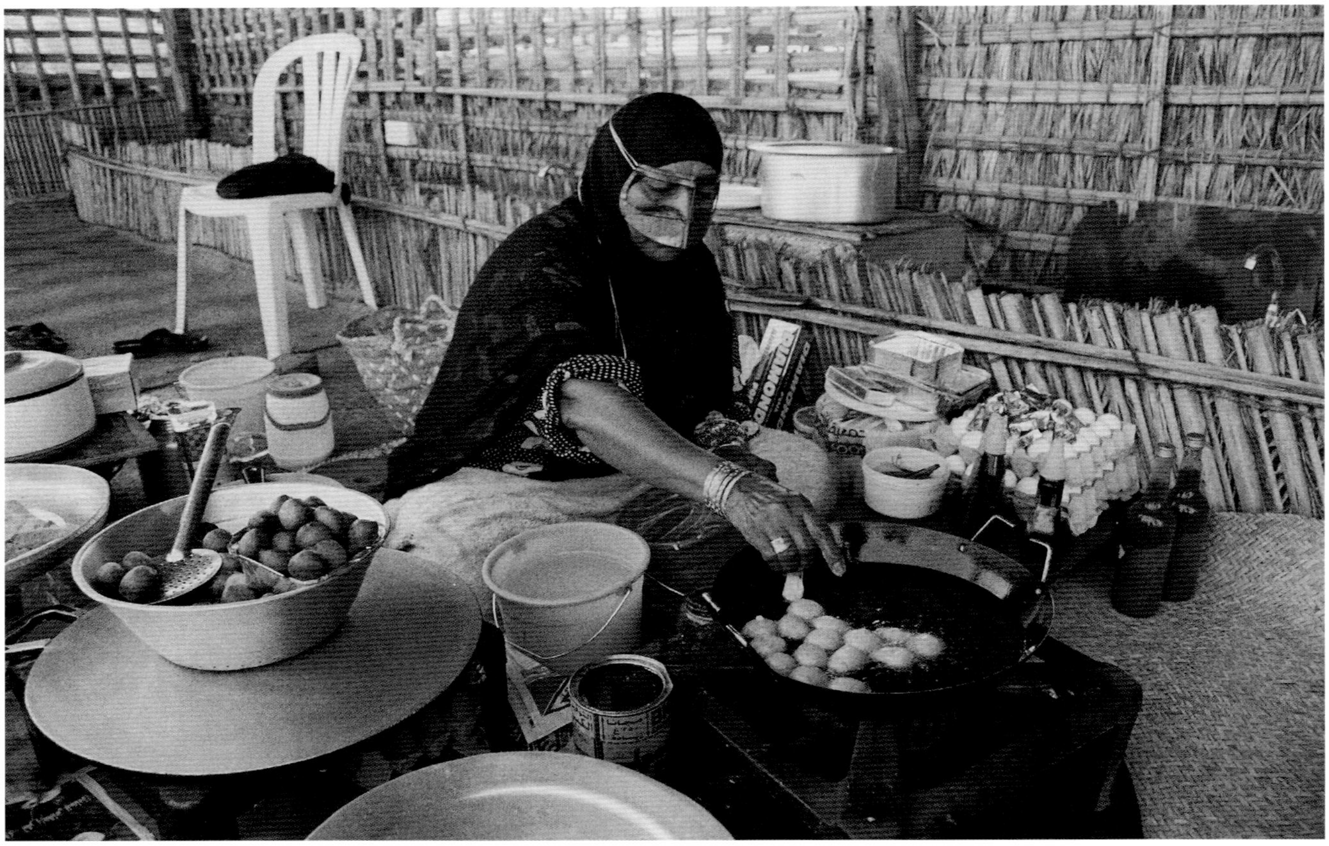

▲ ▶ THESE WOMEN, FRYING SNACKS AND WEAVING A pillow, at the Heritage Village, are each wearing a traditional *burga* – a stiff material face mask that covers the eyebrows, nose and mouth. *Photos by Alia Al Shamsi.*

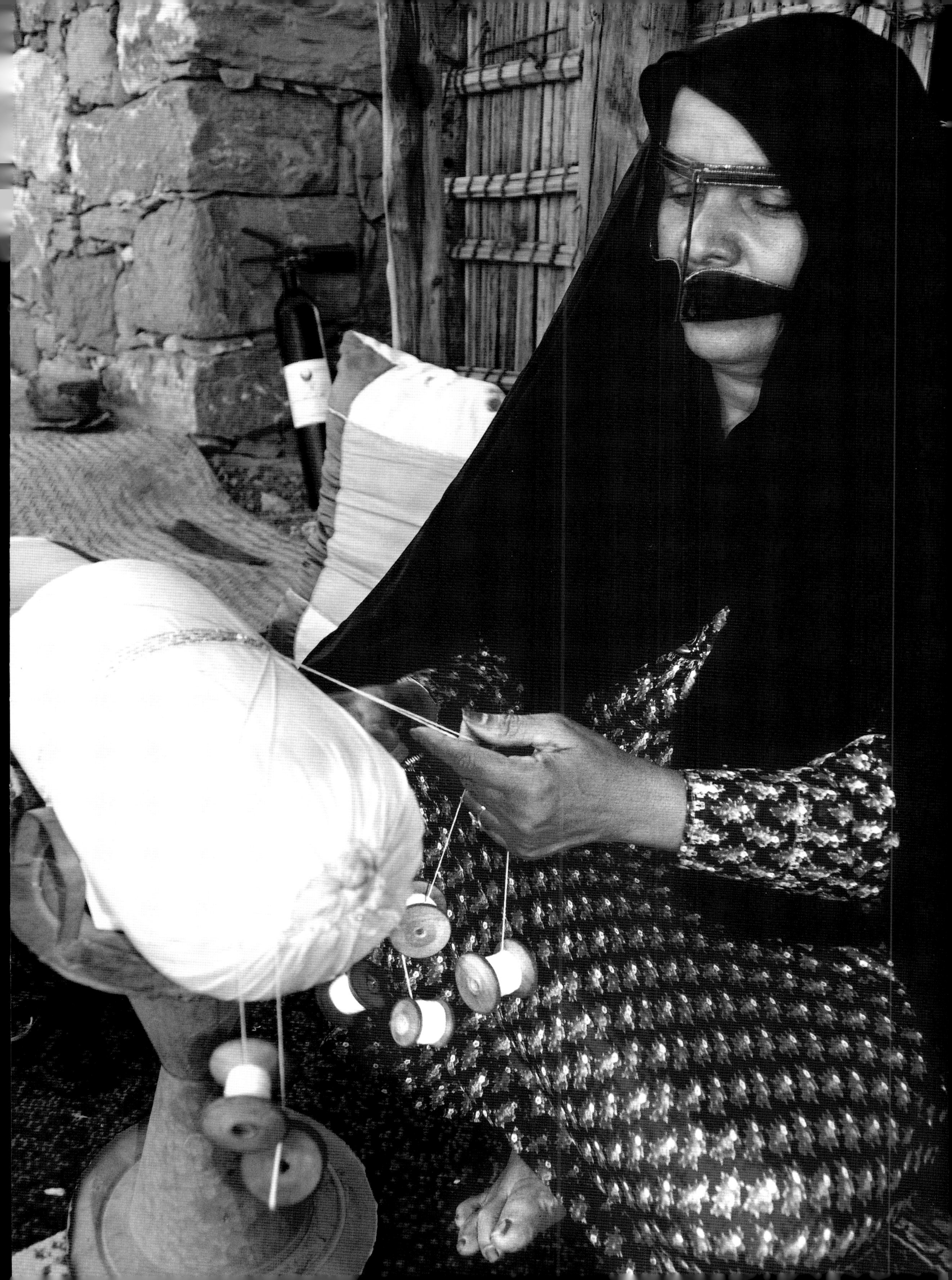

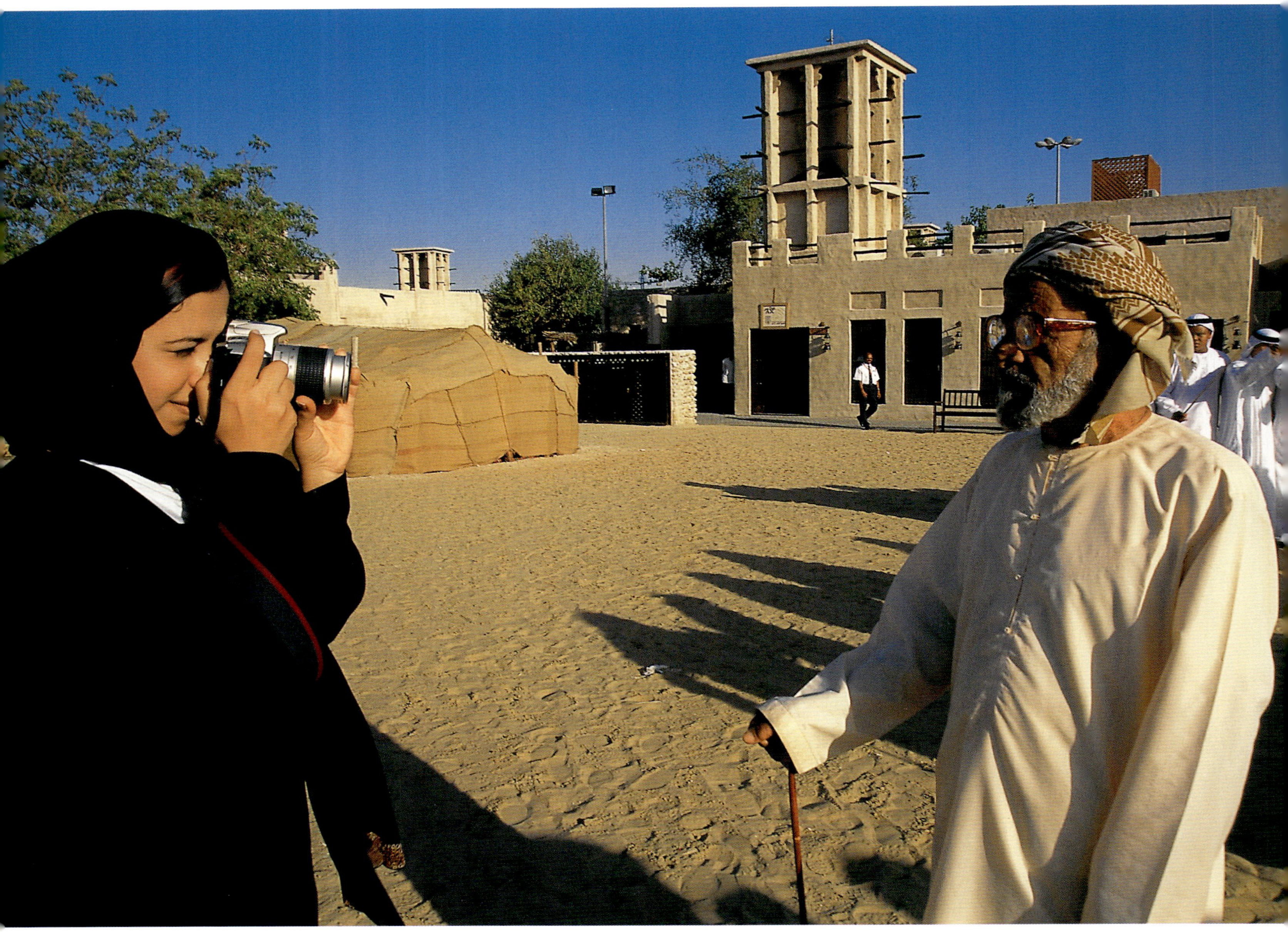

▲ Dressed in the typical clothes of an Arab woman, Alia al Shamsi, one of the youngest crew members of the *Dubai 24 hours* team of still photographers, conjures a special moment with a local character at the Heritage Village.

▶ At the Heritage Village, locals muse and gossip before the famed wind-towers whose distinct mark on the city revisits the time when Emirati architecture was influenced by Persian design. *Photos by Ramesh Shukla.*

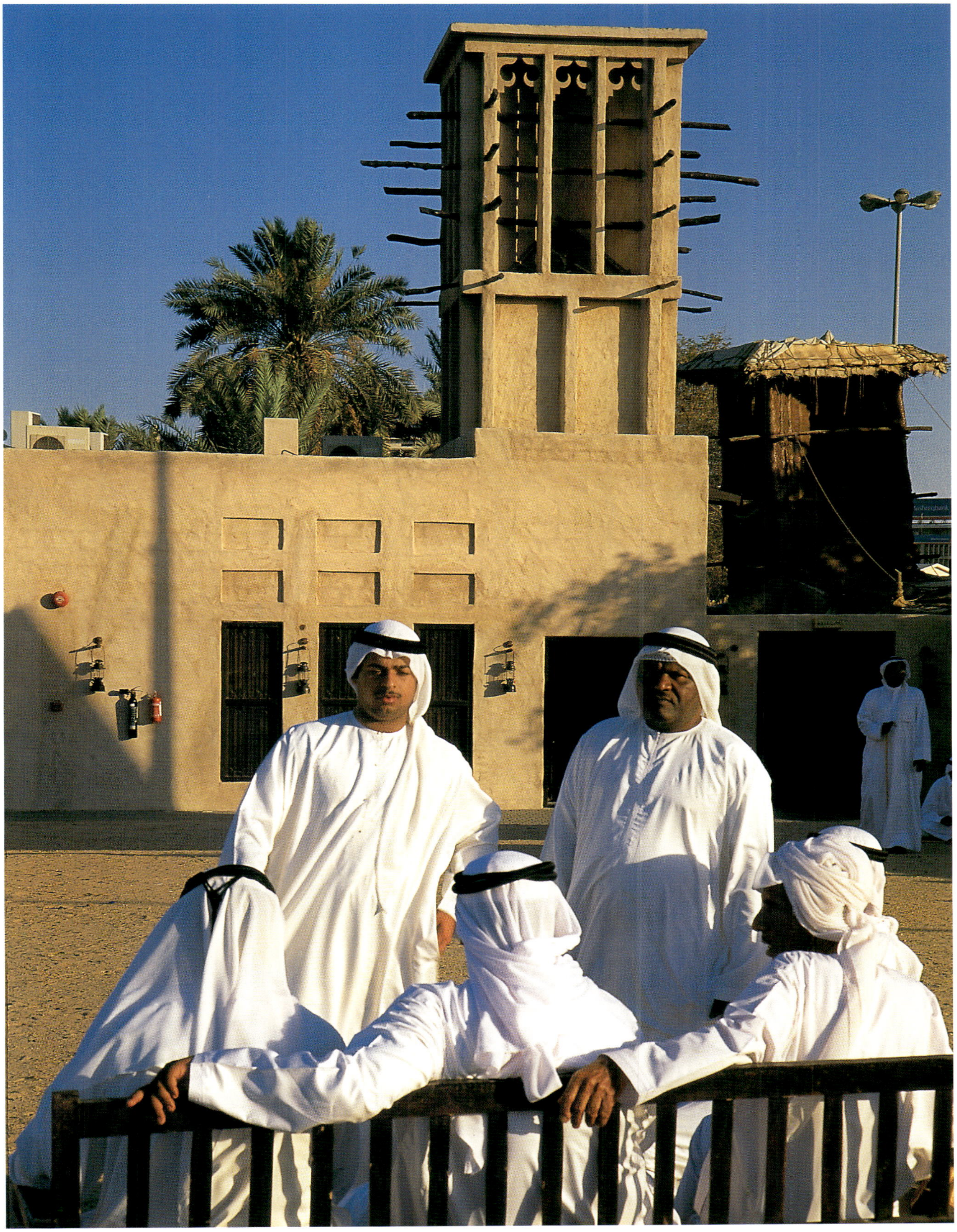

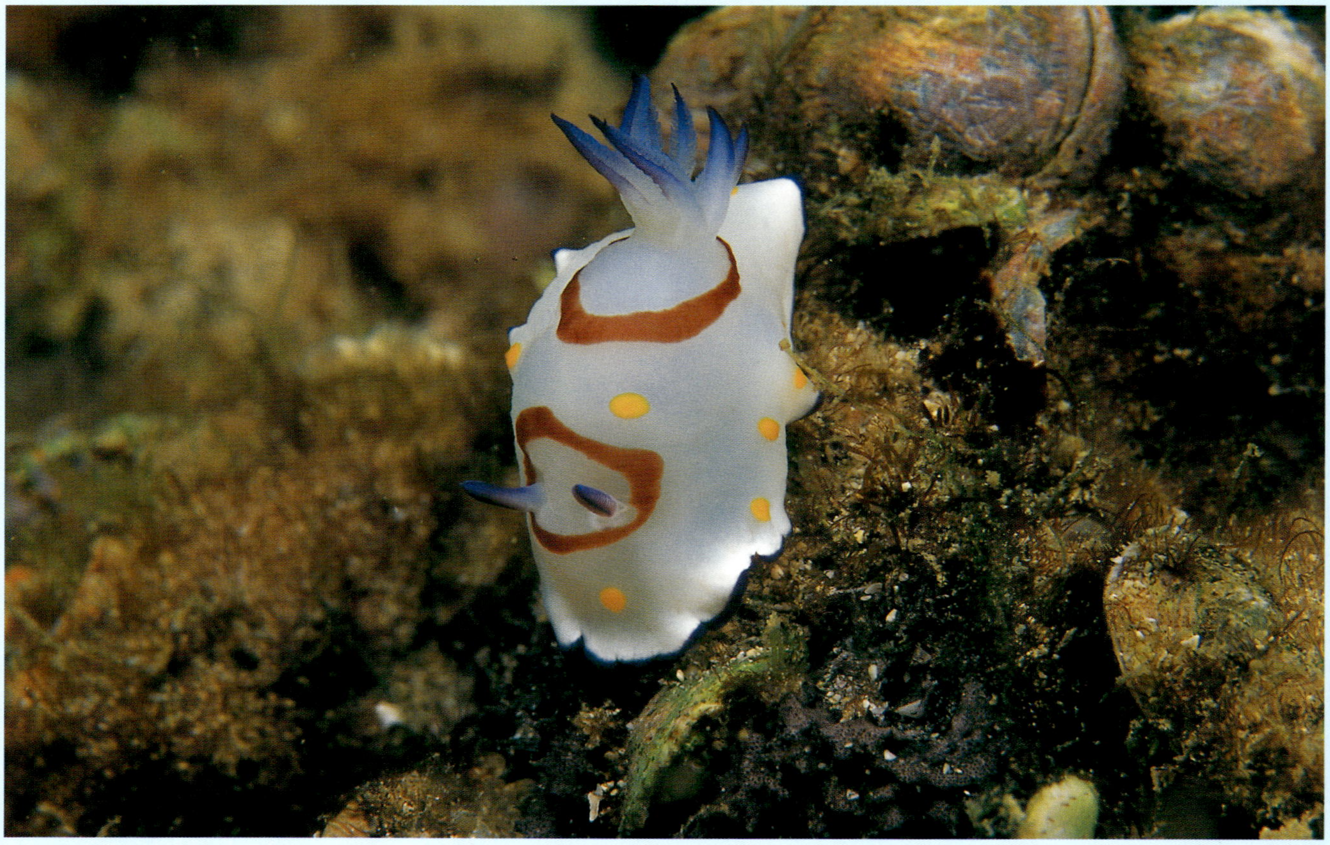

▲ Beyond the UAE's 1,318 kilometres of coastline, more than 500 known species of fish make their home. The world's largest fish – the whale shark – can occasionally be seen feeding on plankton and rare dugongs (the mammals some ancient mariners thought were mermaids) also occur together with four, possibly five, species of turtle which venture on to some of the nearly 300 offshore islands to lay their eggs. This diminutive creature, however, is not a fish or a mammal but a flatworm, feeding in the Arabian Gulf's shallow waters, usually no more than 30 metres deep. *Photo by Nasser Al Shaiba.*

▶ Off the coast of Dubai, renowned marine biologist Nasser Al Shaiba prepares to photograph bottom-dwellers with his underwater camera. *Photo by Souheil Semaan.*

▶▶ Pearl oysters occur along the Gulf's shallow banks and more than 20,000 divers were harvesting them a century ago. In Dubai, 335 dhows were once devoted to the industry but now there are none – with recession, the Second World War and the Japanese cultured pearl having changed the face of the industry. *Photos by Souheil Semaan (left and right bottom) and Tariq Al Sharief (right top).*

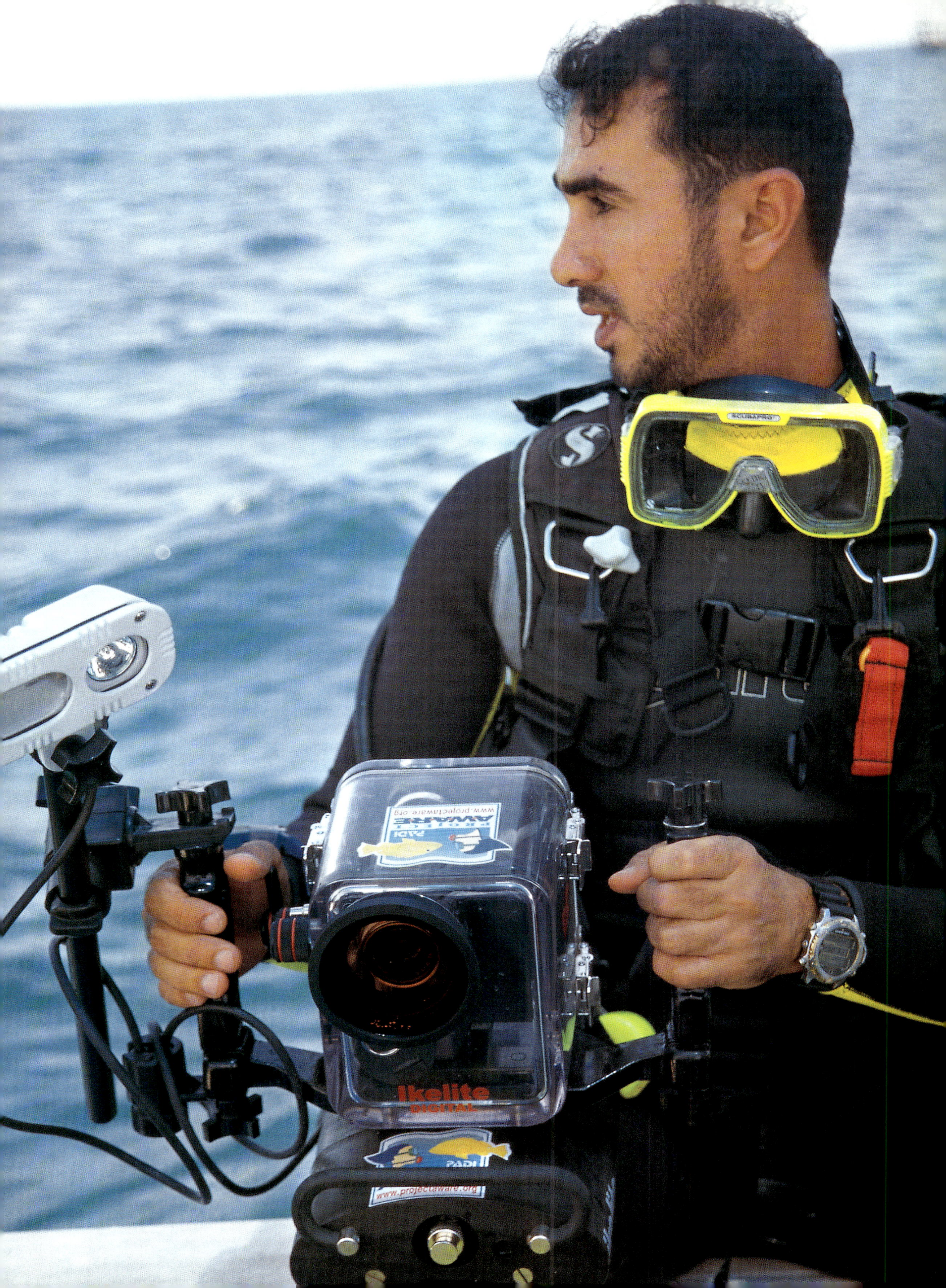
SCUBAPRO
Ikelite
DIGITAL
PADI
www.projectaware.org

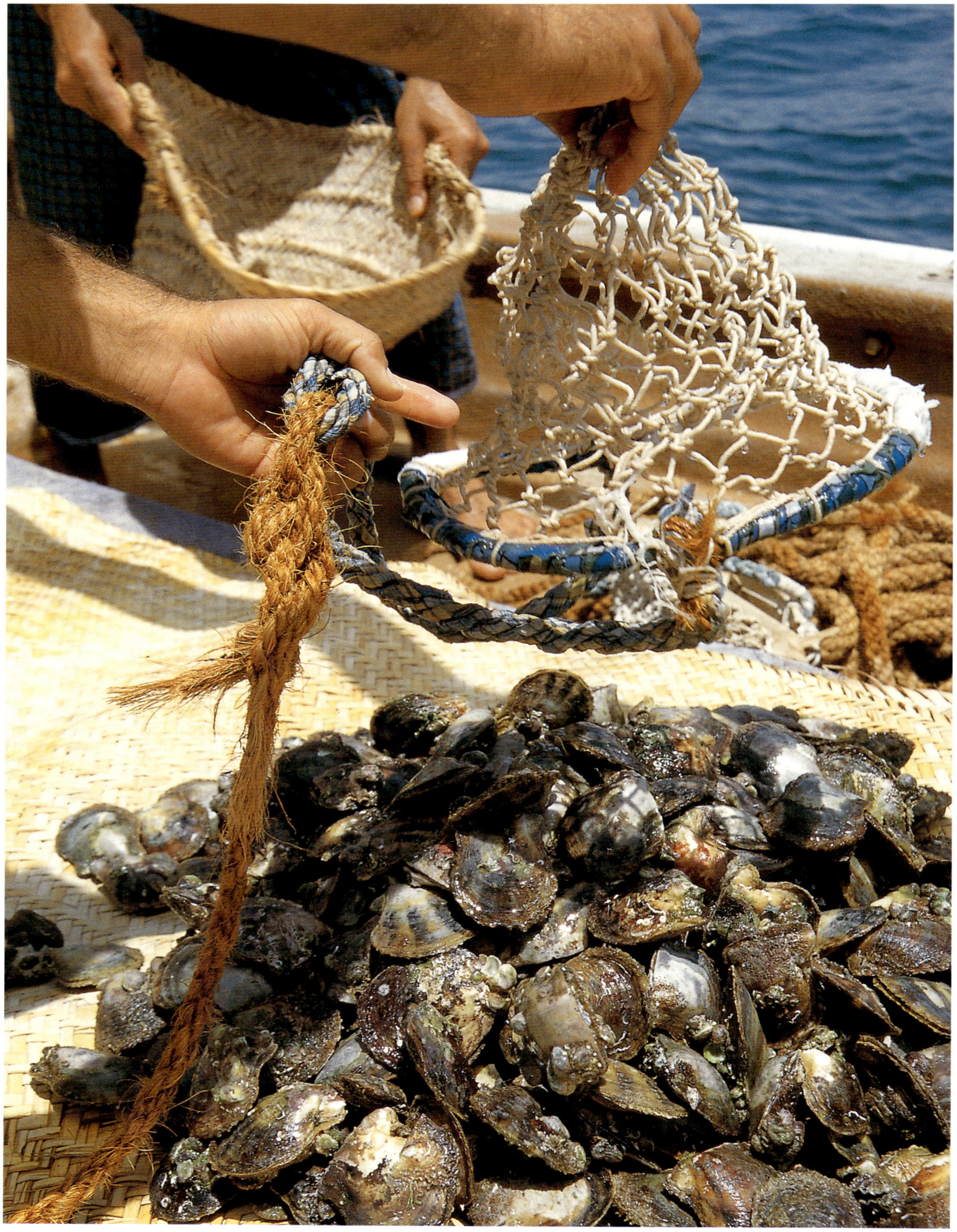

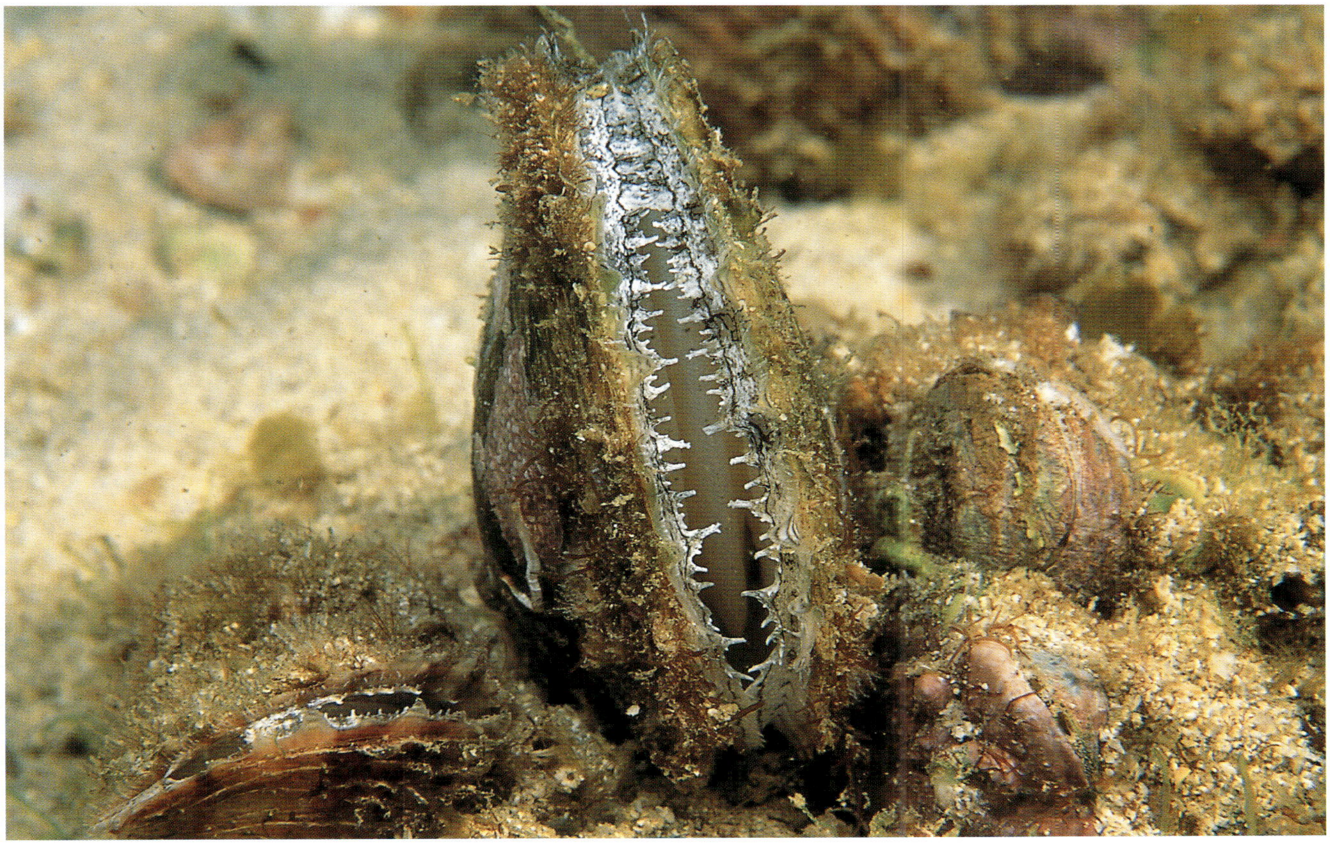

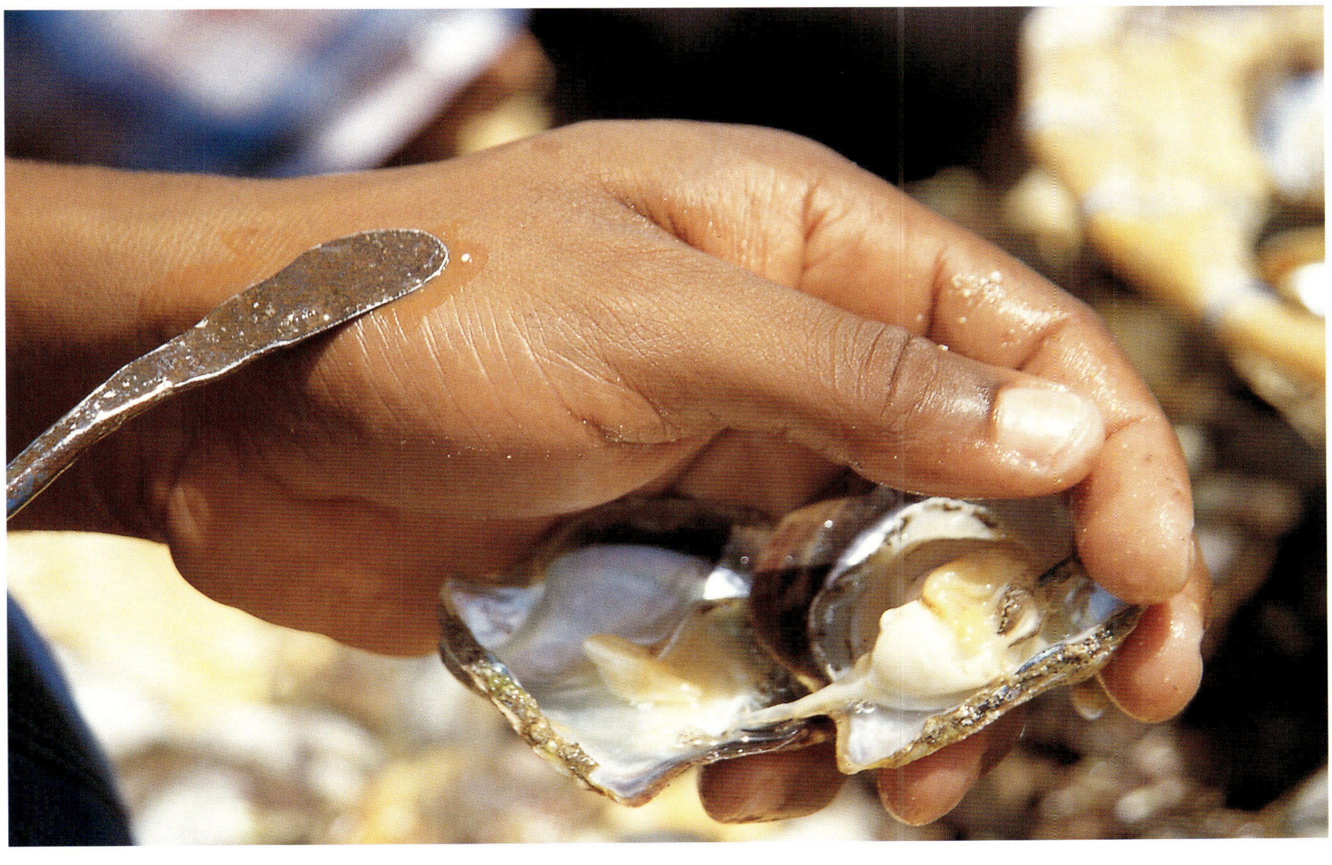

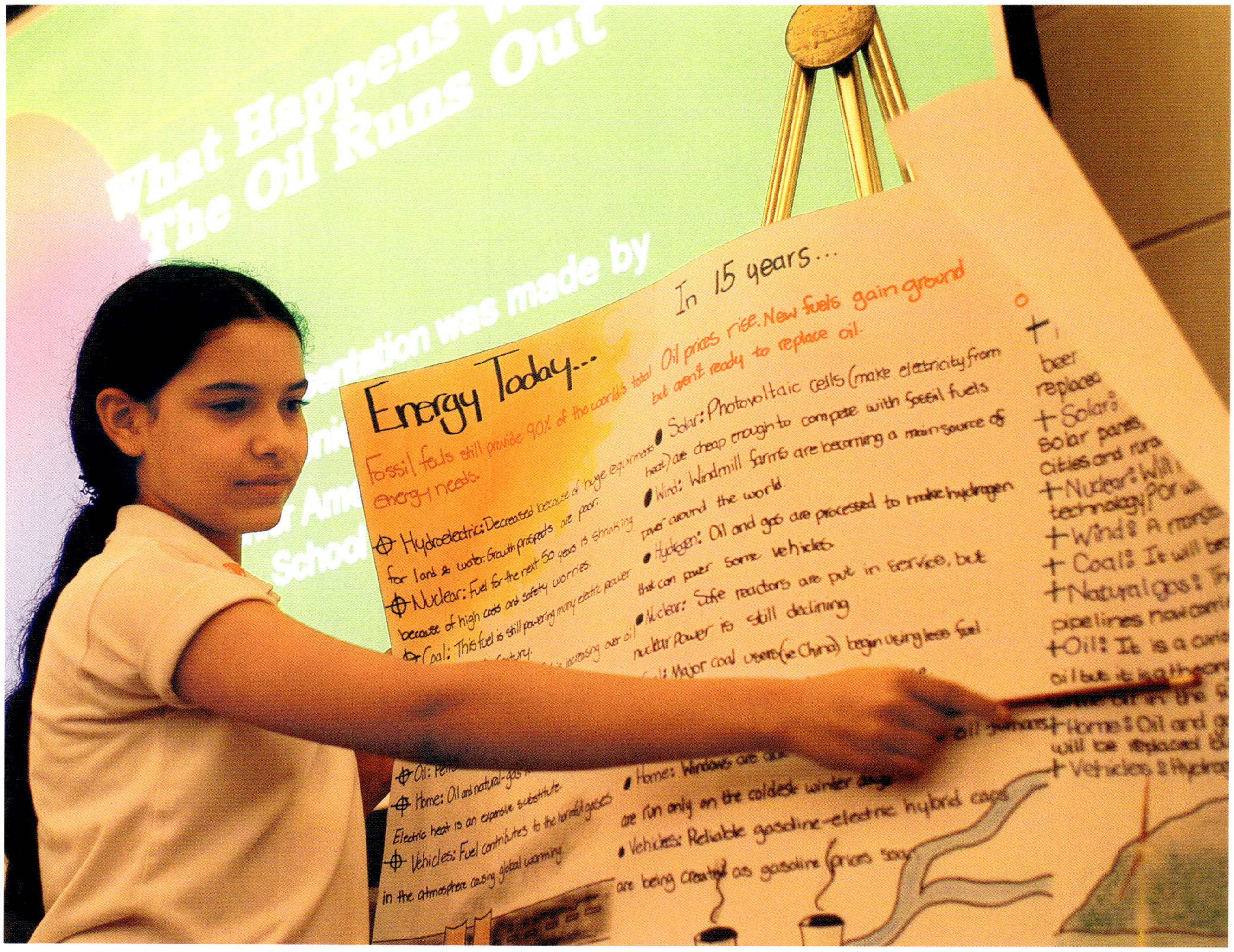

▲ ▶ Not a day passes without environmental issues surfacing in the media of the emirates. Here, at a hotel in Dubai, students from throughout the federation gather as part of the Emirates Environment Group to present speeches on everything from biodiversity conservation to the most recent projections for the petroleum industry, which this young student (above) examines today and 15 years into the future. The 'buzz' at this gathering was what some delegates were calling the last, great energy transformation on earth, namely, the hydrogen-fuel-cell economy. Many believe it will overtake oil in coming decades as the ecological and economic energy system of choice. For a nation whose revenues have been largely dependent upon a unique geological bonanza provided by fossil fuels, this new generation of ecologists is, if anything, a radical departure from the status quo. However, adults in the audience seemed more proud of their fiery youngsters than worried about how they would fuel their cars in the future.

▶ Habiba Al Marashi, chairperson of EEG (partly obscured, top right), listens intently to her young colleagues. Later in the week, Al Marashi would present a compelling talk on the promise and perils of conservation biology in the Gulf states. *Photos by Dariush Zandi.*

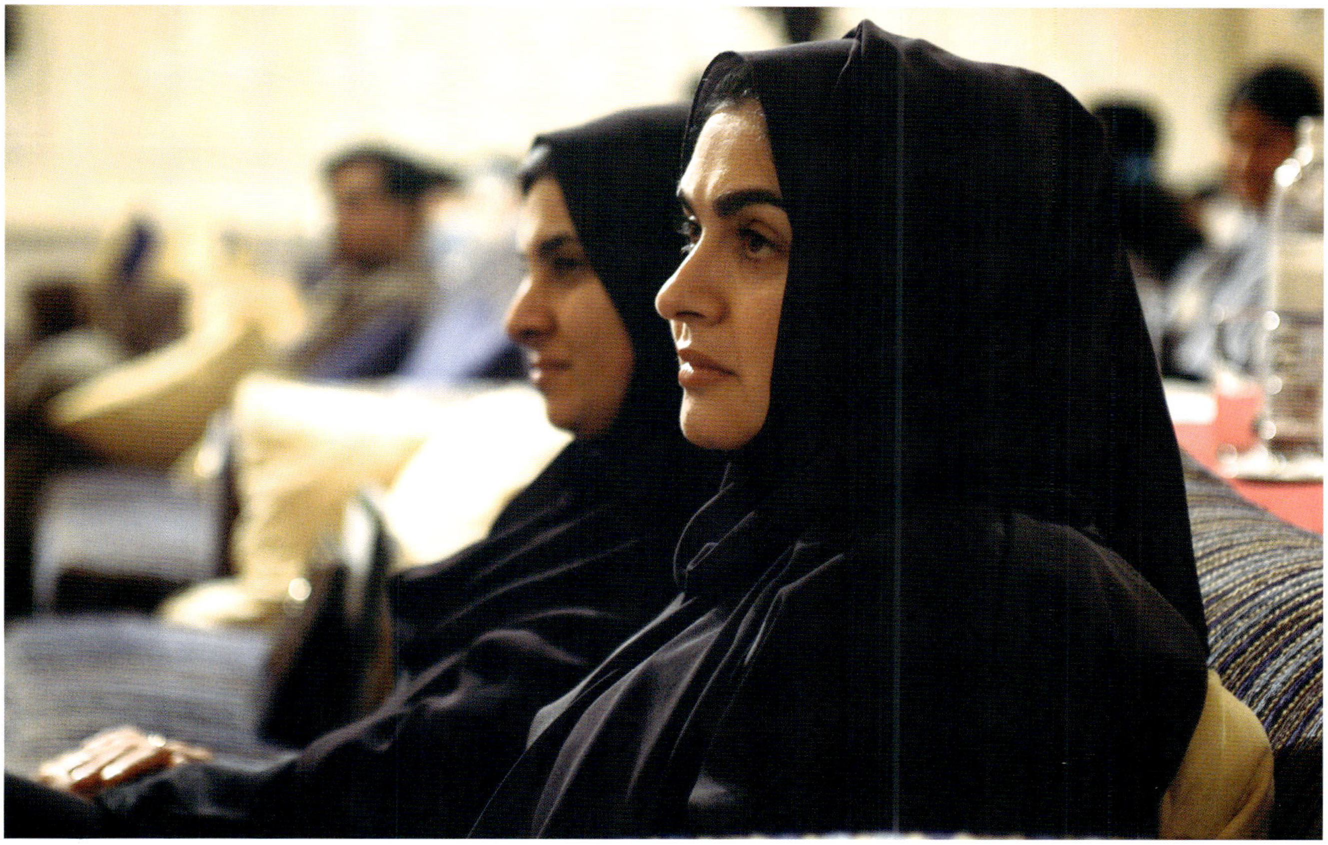

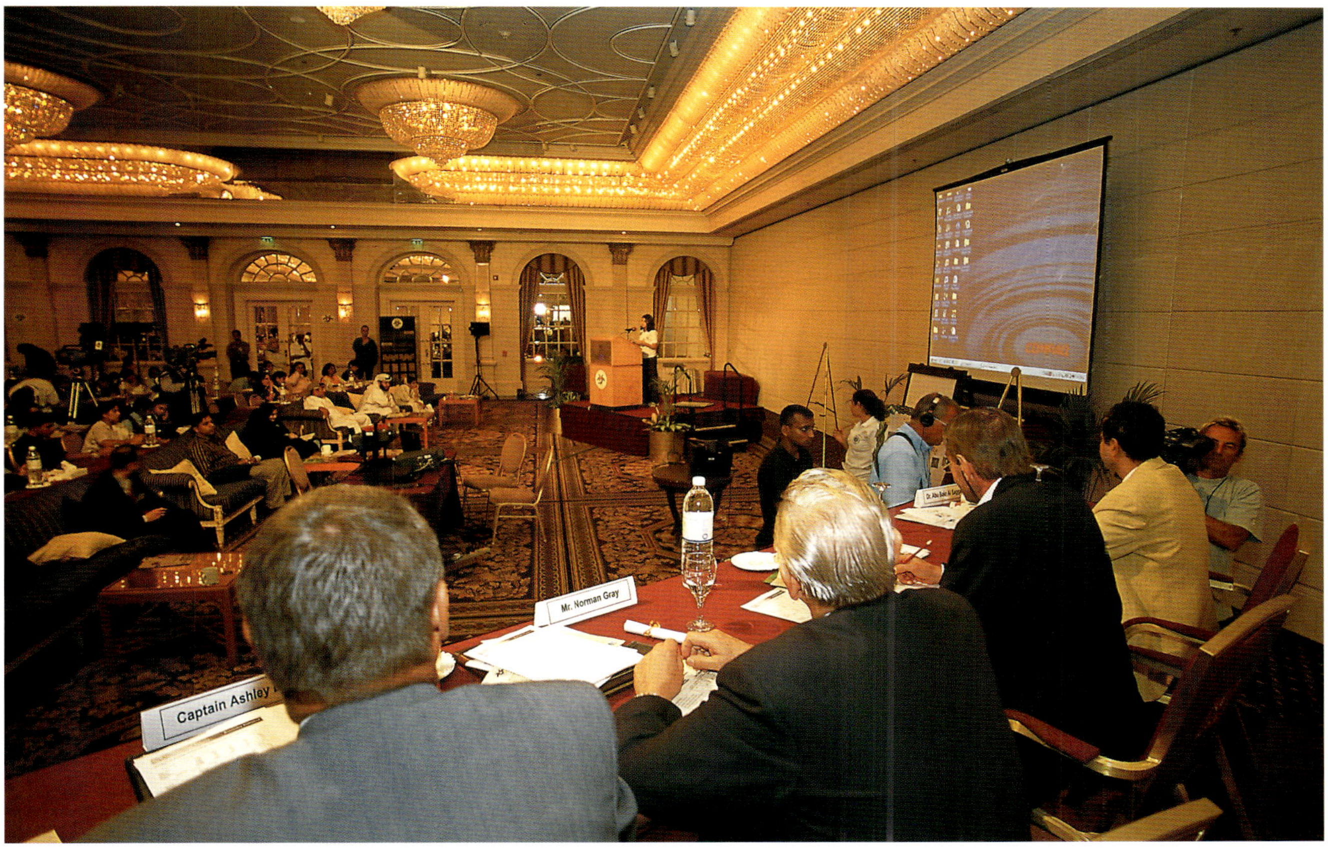
Mr. Norman Gray
Captain Ashley

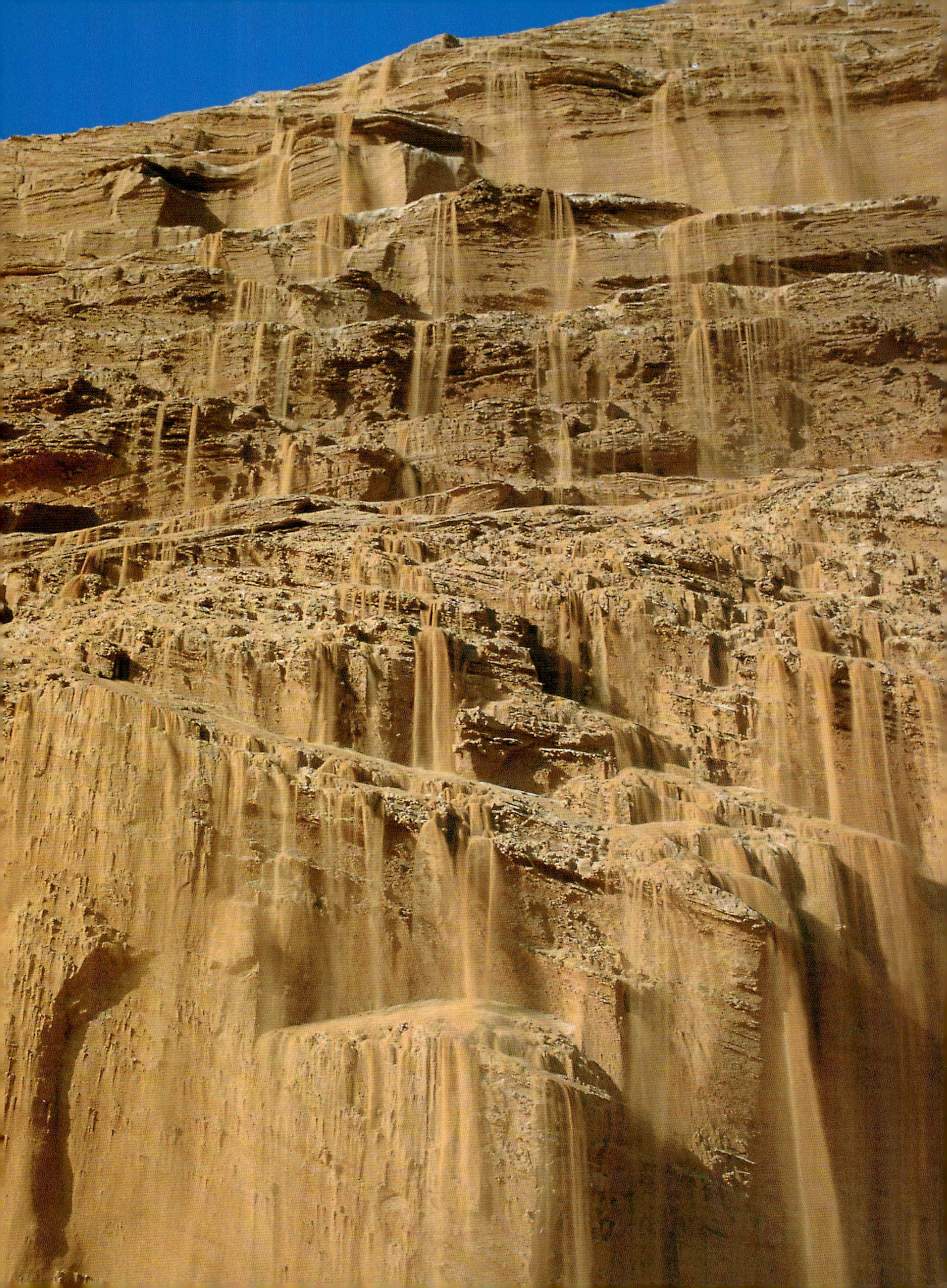

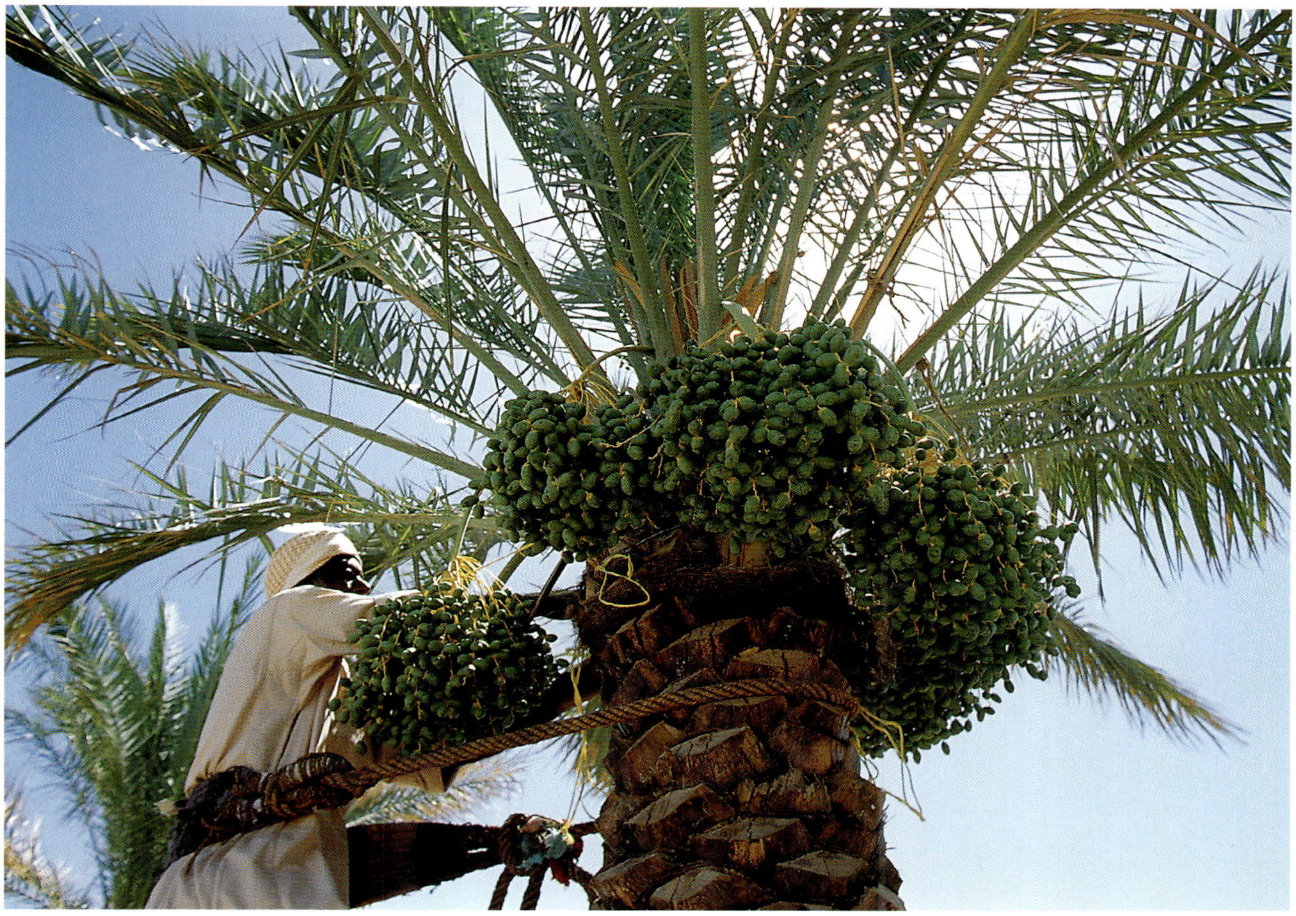

◄ NEAR THE GREAT RED DUNE WEST OF DUBAI, photographer, architect, city planner and author, Dariush Zandi, captured these 'waterfalls' of sand just after sunrise in the vicinity of Nazwa, *en route* to Hatta. The height of the sand wall is approximately 30 metres. At one point during filming, a portion of the wall collapsed upon a videographer and sound technician. No one was hurt, fortunately, but a Dat recording device is still recovering from the fine sands of Arabia.

▲ LATER THE SAME DAY, OUTSIDE THE WALLS OF THE historic Hatta Heritage Village, near the northern tip of Oman, Zandi came upon this local clipping clusters of moist, ripe dates. *Photos by Dariush Zandi.*

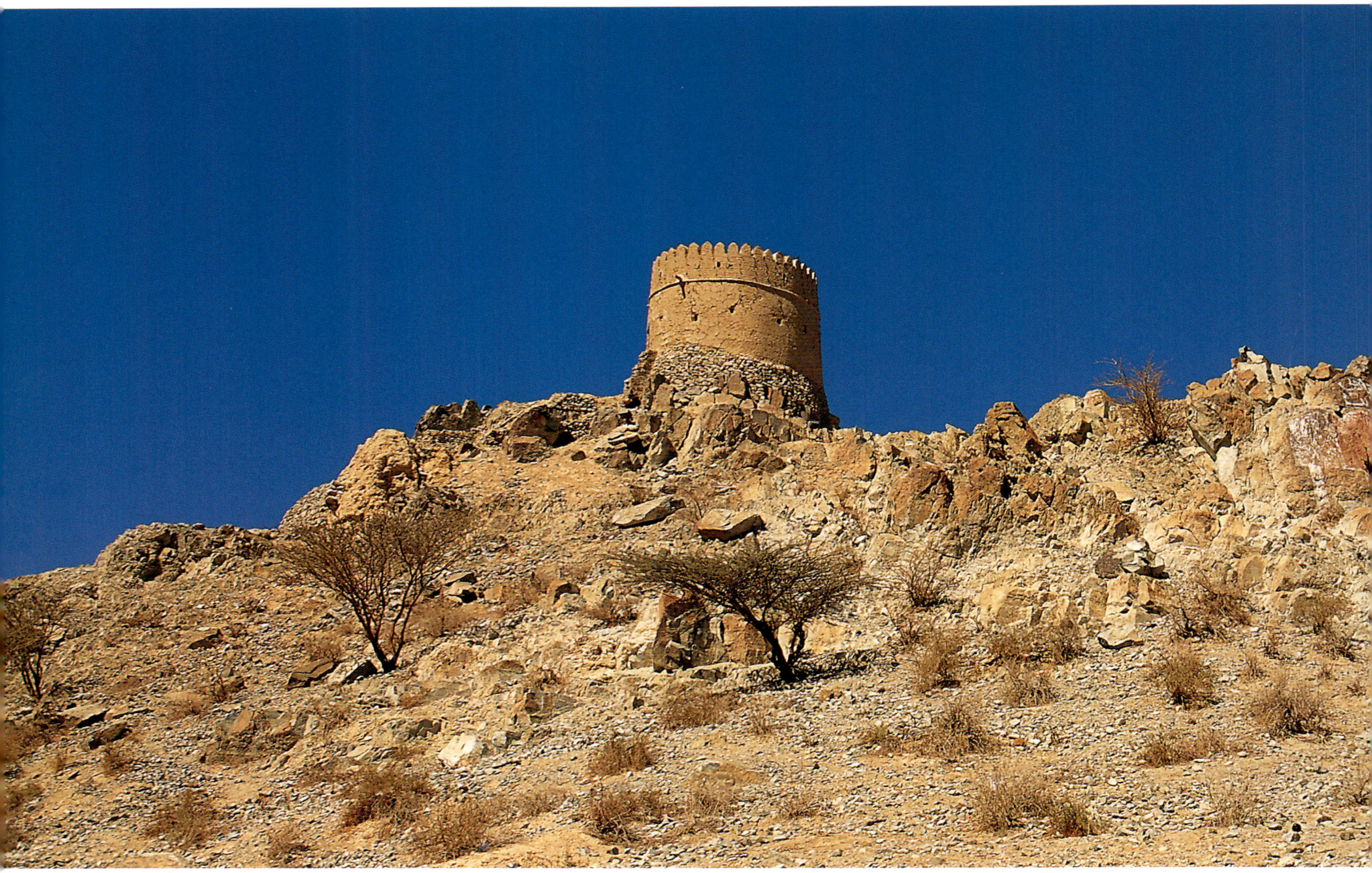

▲ HATTA, JUST TWO HOURS FROM THE CITY OF DUBAI BY freeway, and inhabited for nearly 3,000 years, combines the tranquillity of a traditional mountain village with nearby amenities of high standard. An oasis of palms, a central fort and two watch-towers, surround the original village of 30 old-world houses. Across the way is the Al Hosn Majlis where the traditional governors of the region met, and today's sheikhs still take leisurely meetings with local heads. *Photo by David Steele.*

▶ BEYOND HATTA LIES THE RUGGED HAJAR MOUNTAINS and Wadi Hatta, where four-wheel-drive vehicles take modern-day explorers past hidden wadis, crystals pools and other oases leading into Oman. *Photo by Dariush Zandi.*

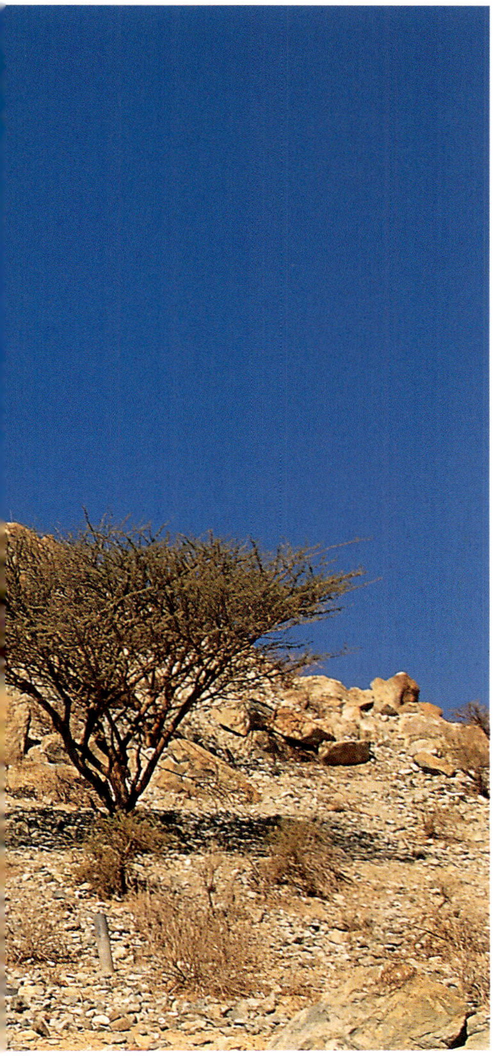

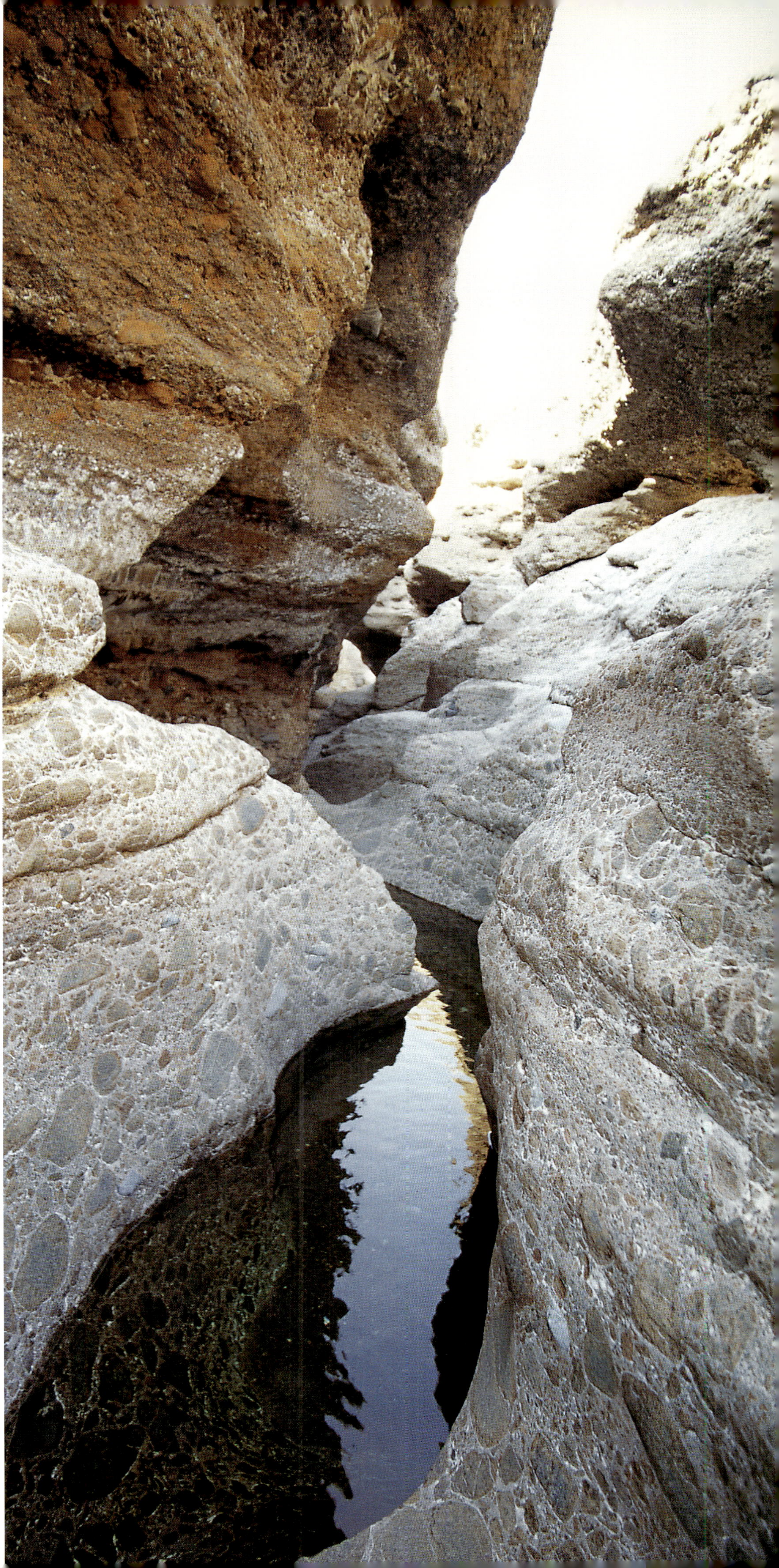

▼ THE SEA OF ROLLING DUNES BETWEEN DUBAI AND Hatta are easily observed from the tarred highway that cuts straight through them. *Photo by Dariush Zandi.*

▶ FRIENDSHIP WITH A PEREGRINE FALCON (*FALCO peregrinus*) or Saker (*Falco cherrug*) – as well as with the captive-bred Gyrfalcon hybrids – has become an expensive obsession for many Emiratis. The biophilial bonds are complex, the veterinary care exclusive, the computer records extraordinarily detailed. And the point of it all? Although no longer used for hunting, there's a fascination with one of the most exquisite of all avians; a ferociously fast and optically spell-binding raptor that confers enormous status on its human companion and displays a range of hunting and flight patterns as elegant and aerodynamically perfect as the bird itself. *Photo by Shankar Adiseshan, Motivate Publishing.*

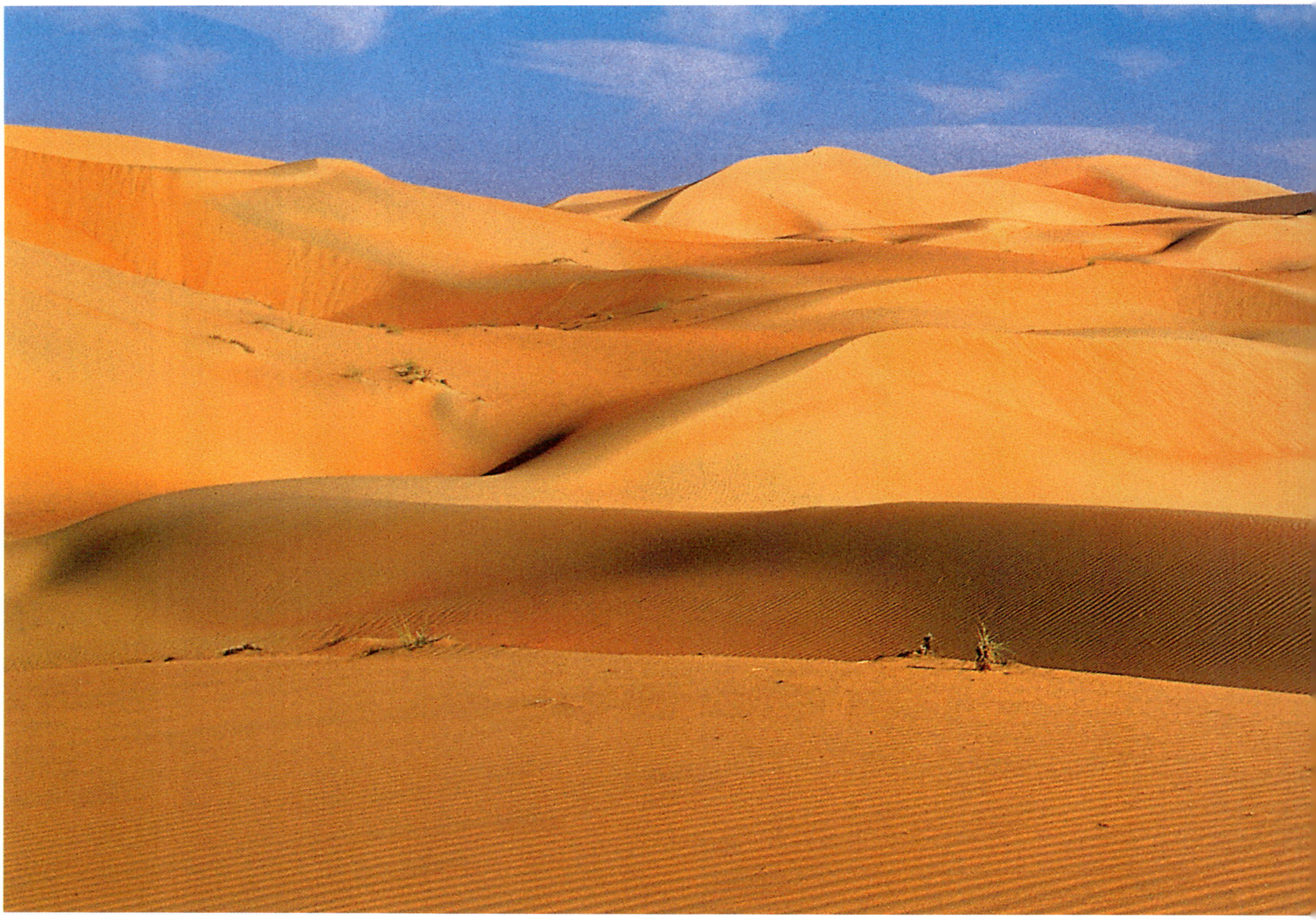

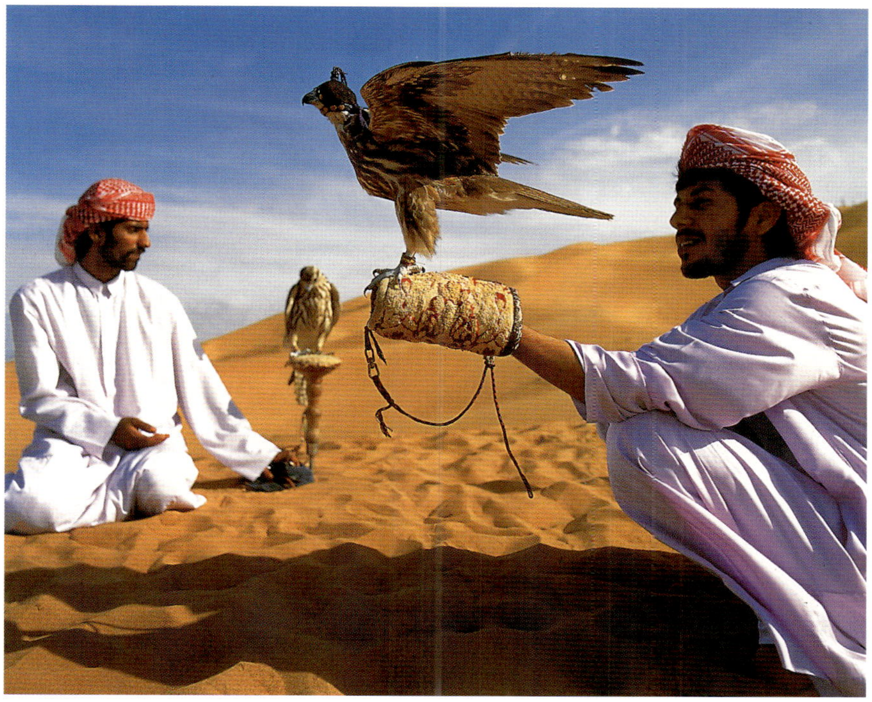

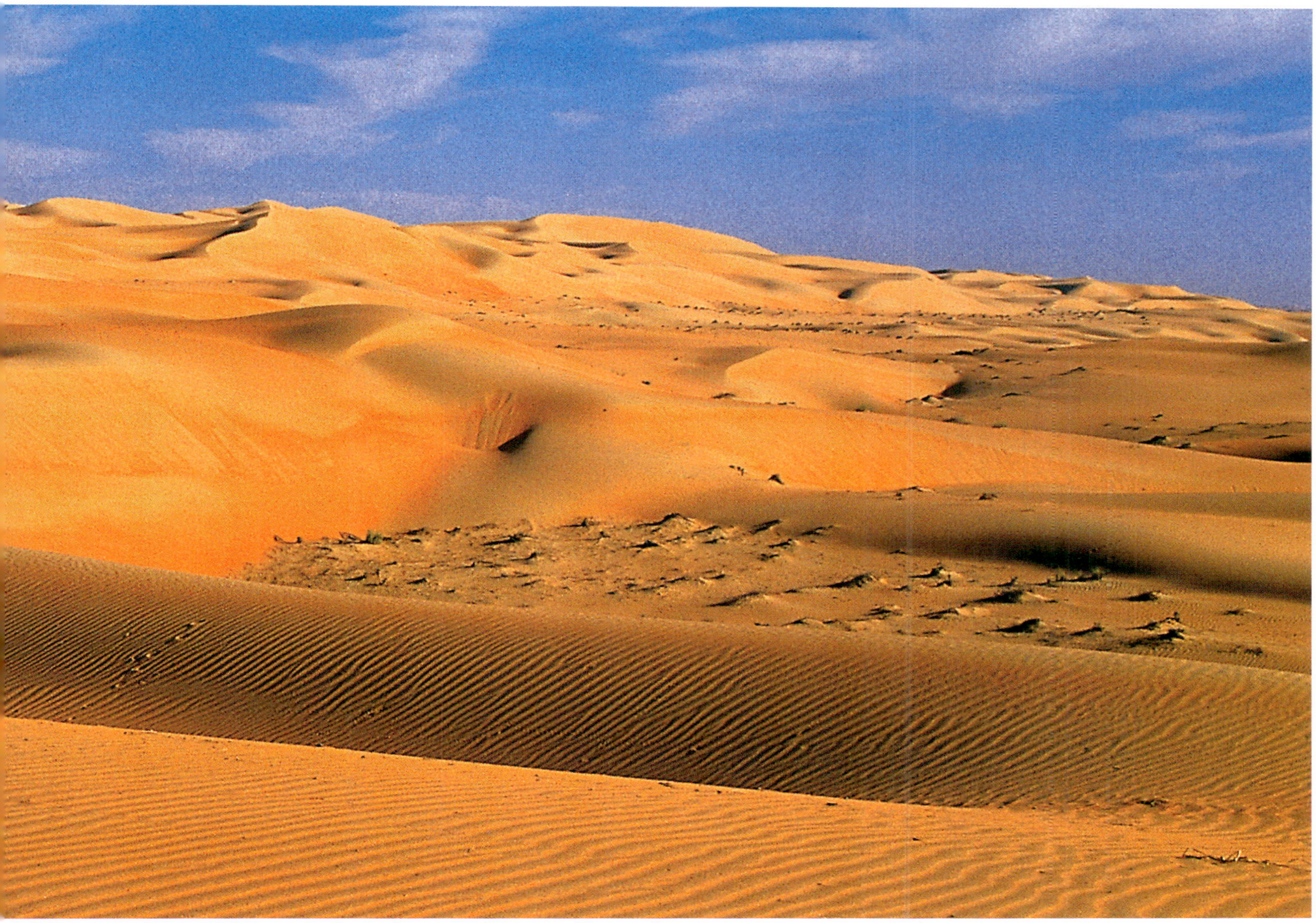

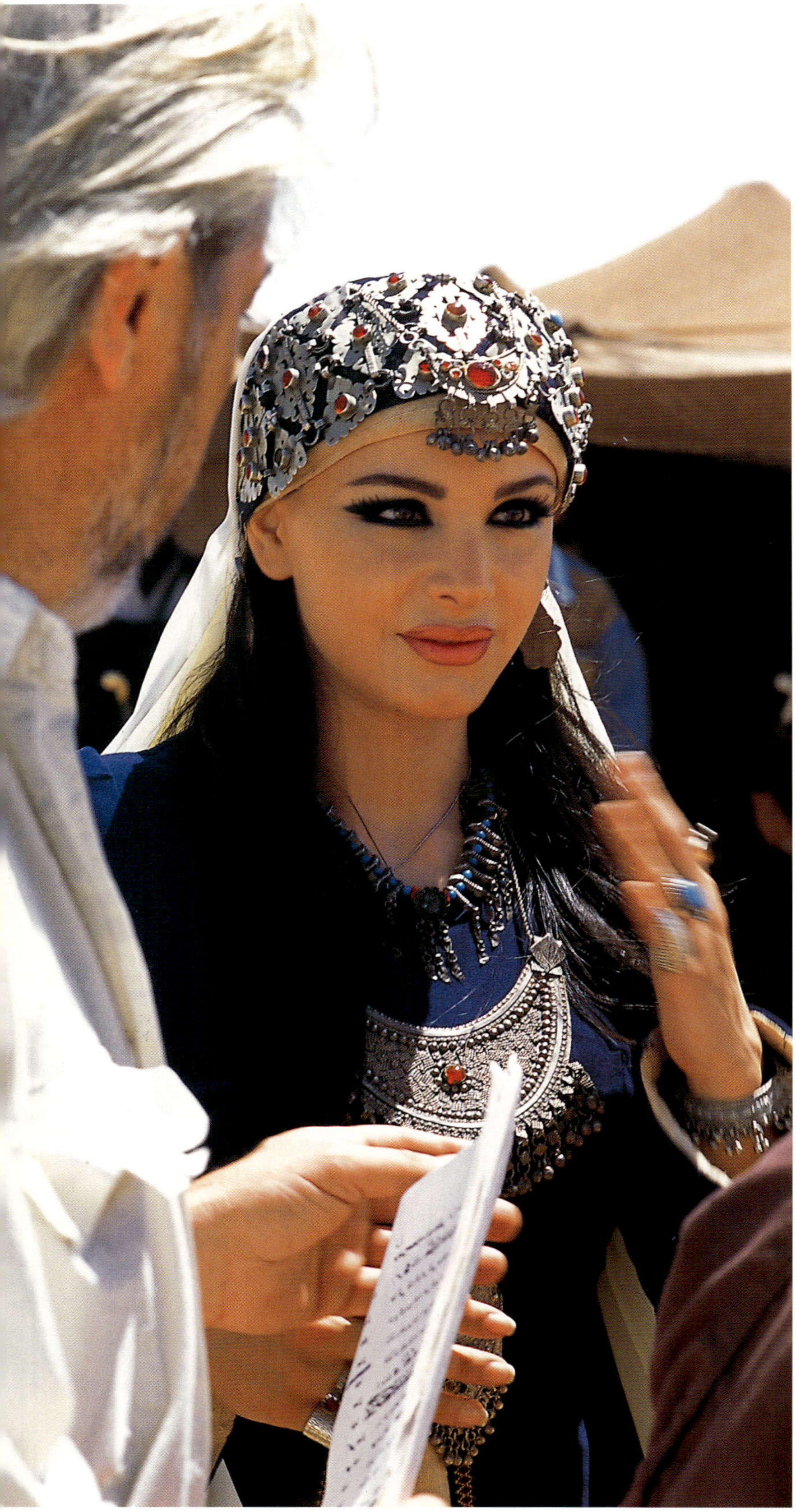

◄ On location with Al Alarabiya's TV drama, *The Last Cavalier*, starring former Miss Lebanon – actress Joelle Behlock, in the role of Shaima, the poetess princess. Here, on set, she is seen rehearsing with celebrated Syrian director Najdat Anzour. The massive, international production is a romantic adventure set in 19th century Arabia (though parts were filmed in China, the Maldives, South Africa, Sudan, Morocco and Jordan) and is based on the poetry of Sheikh Mohammed bin Rashid Al Maktoum.

► Jordanian actor, Hisham Hamadeh, awaiting his cue on an Arabian horse during filming.

►► On location with *The Last Cavalier*, just 25 minutes drive from Dubai. *Photos by Katarina Premfors.*

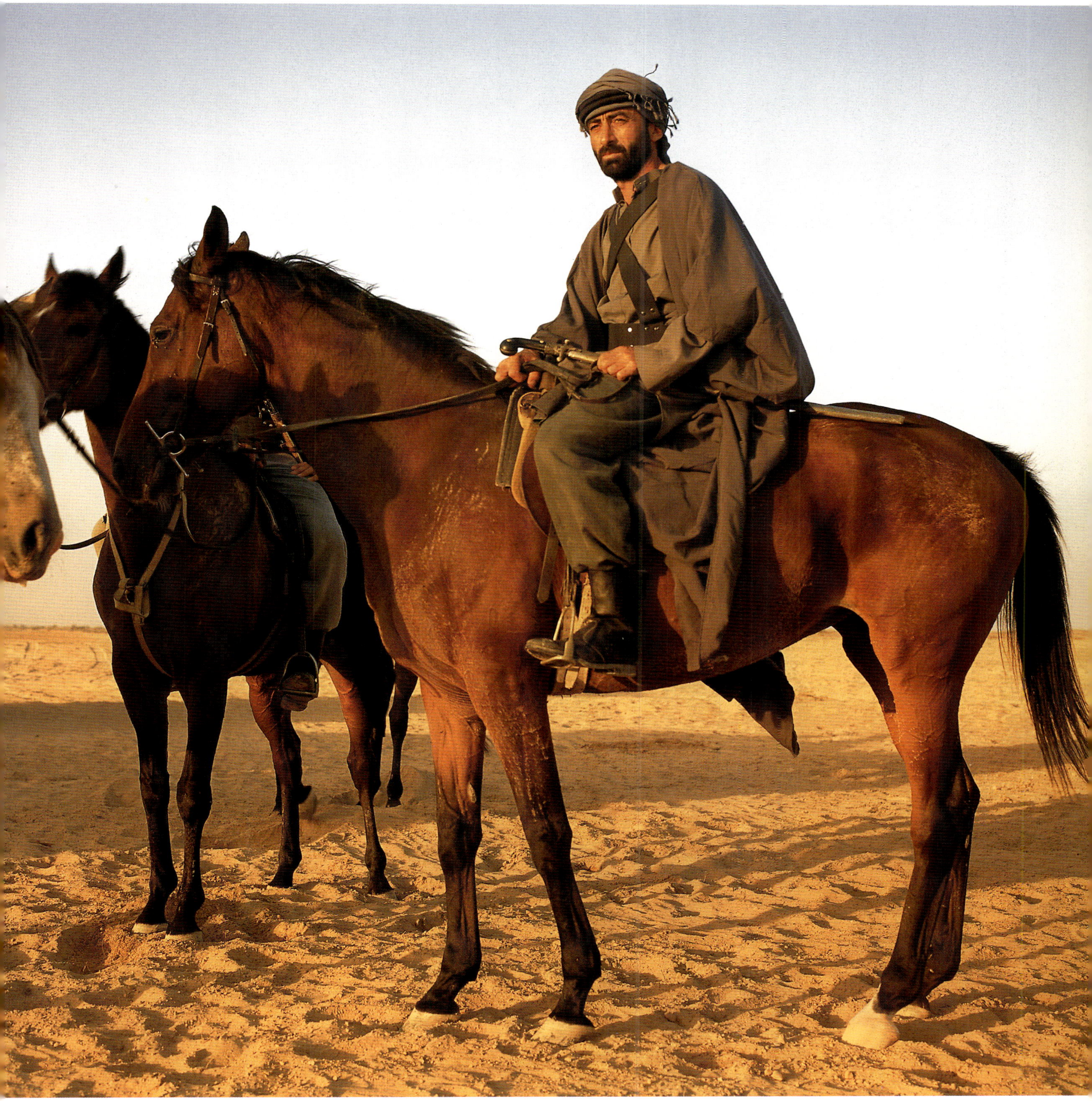

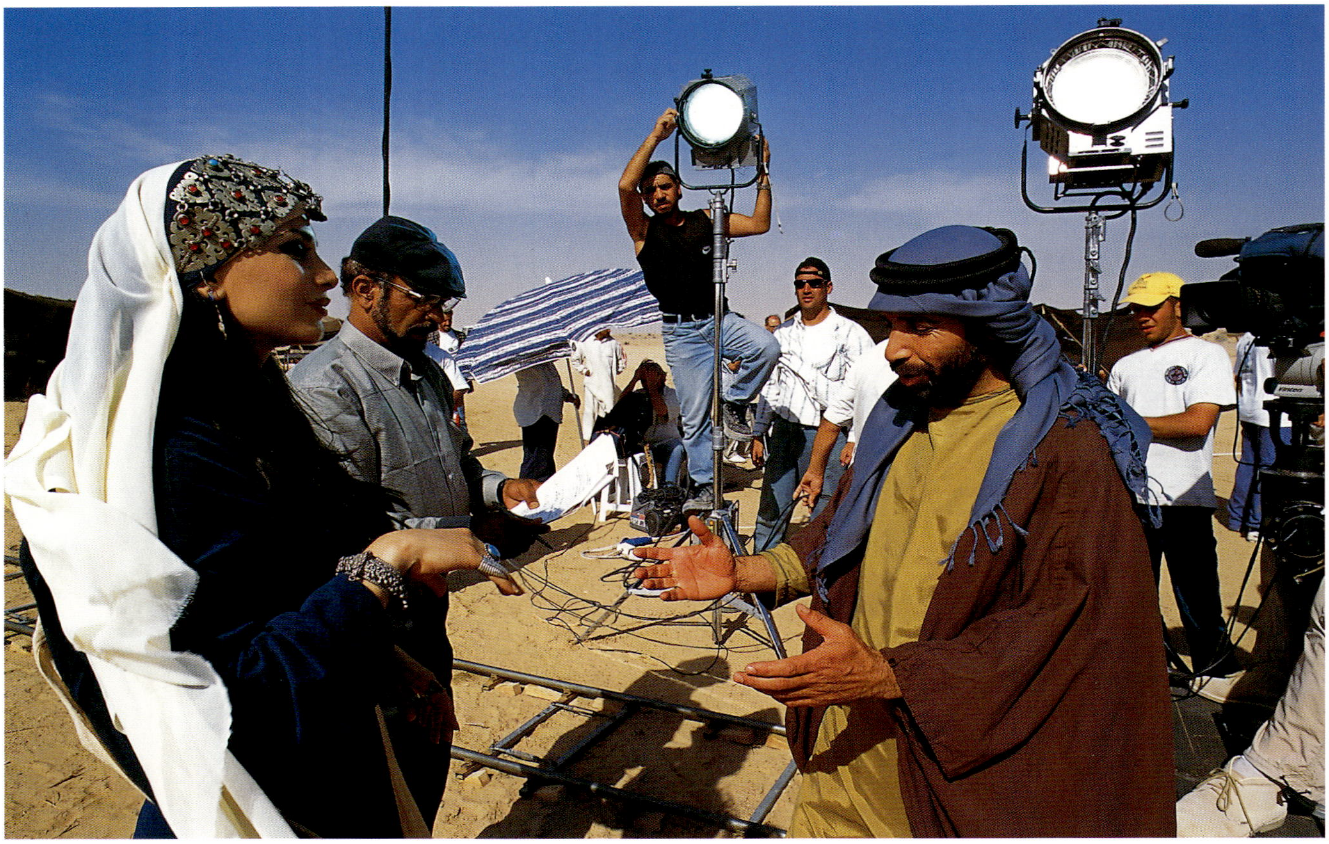

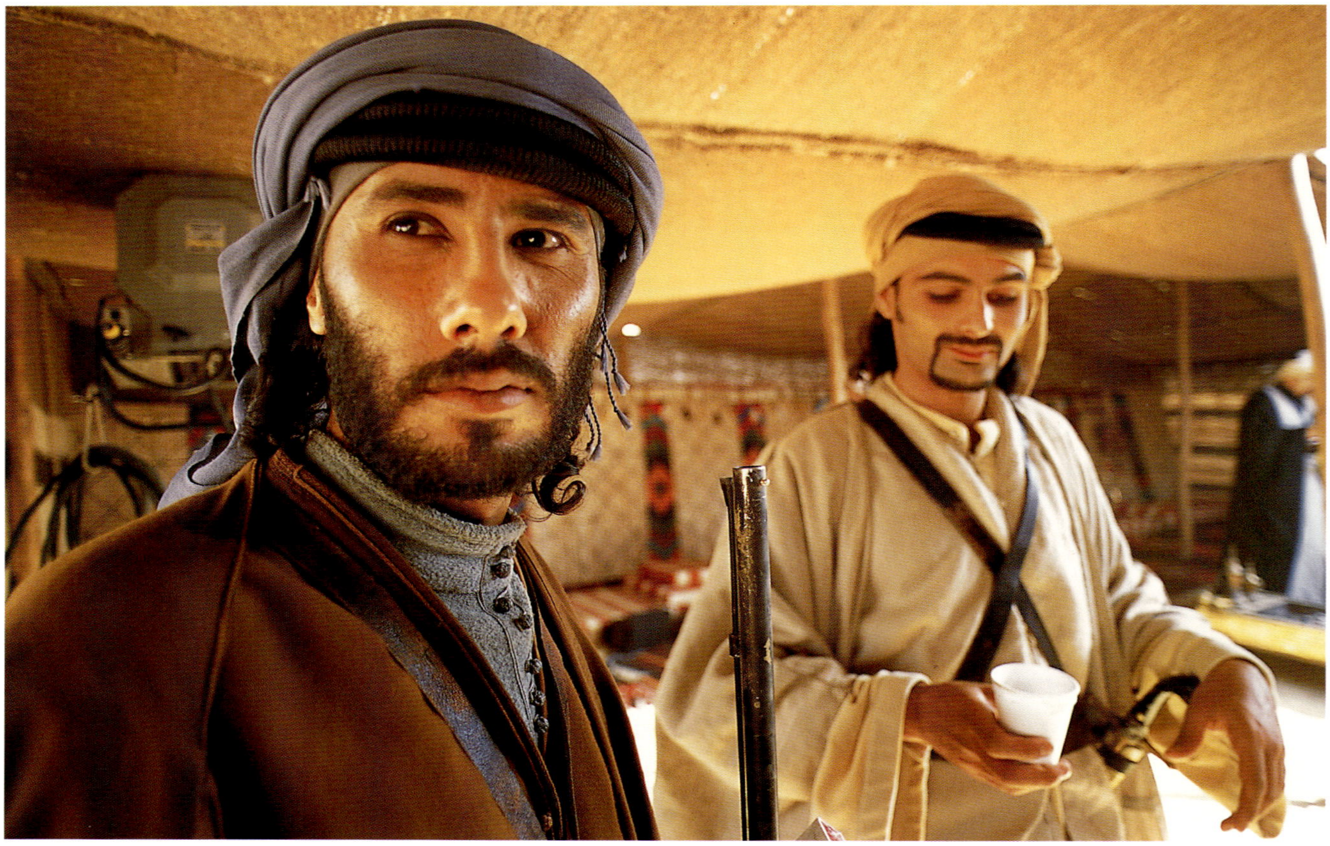

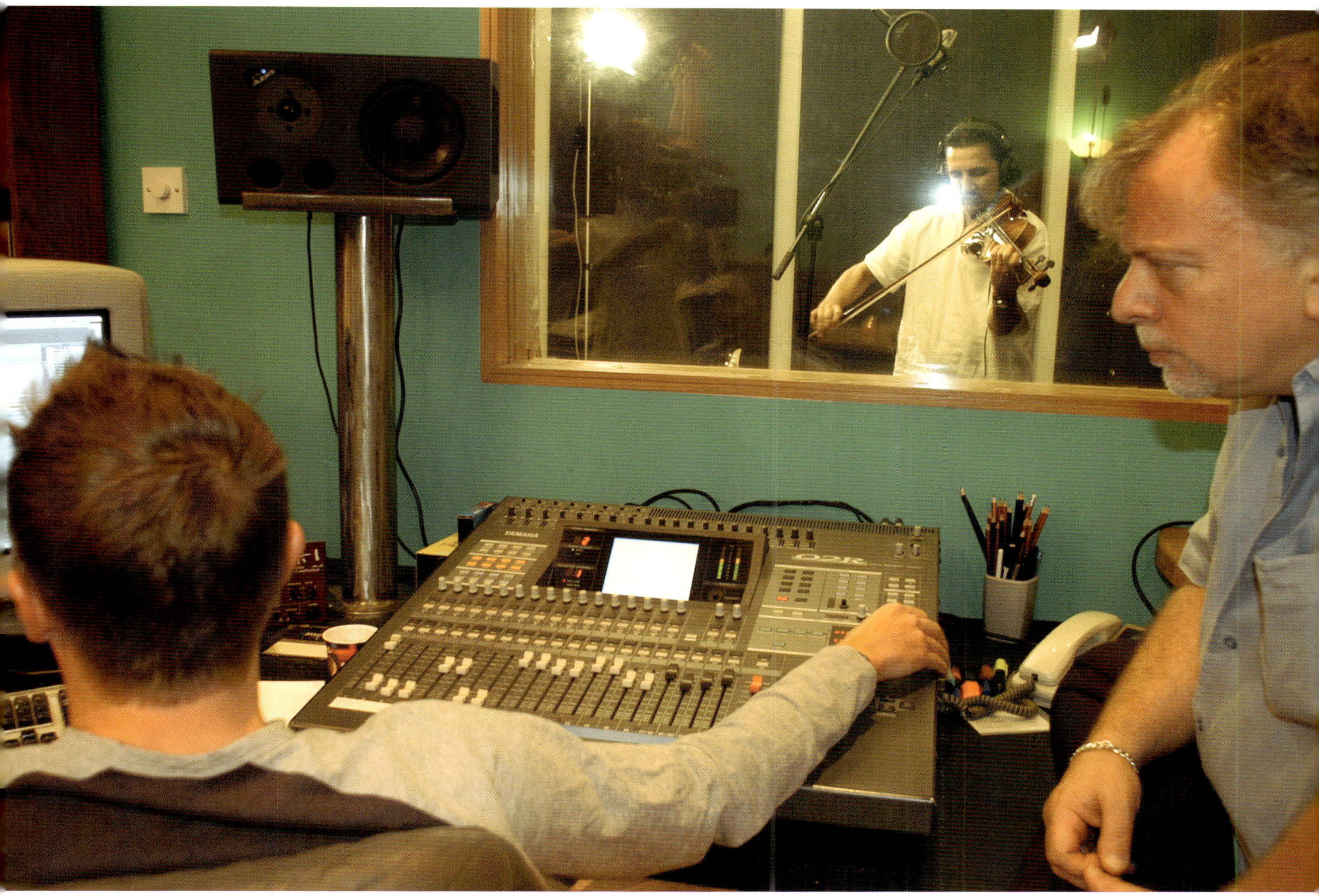

▲ During post-production, talented composer and orchestrator Barry Kirsch (right) works with his sound engineer Matthew Faddy and violinist Khalil in his studio, to produce a sound that has increasingly become his own brand of Western-Arabic fusion. *Photo by Dariush Zandi.*

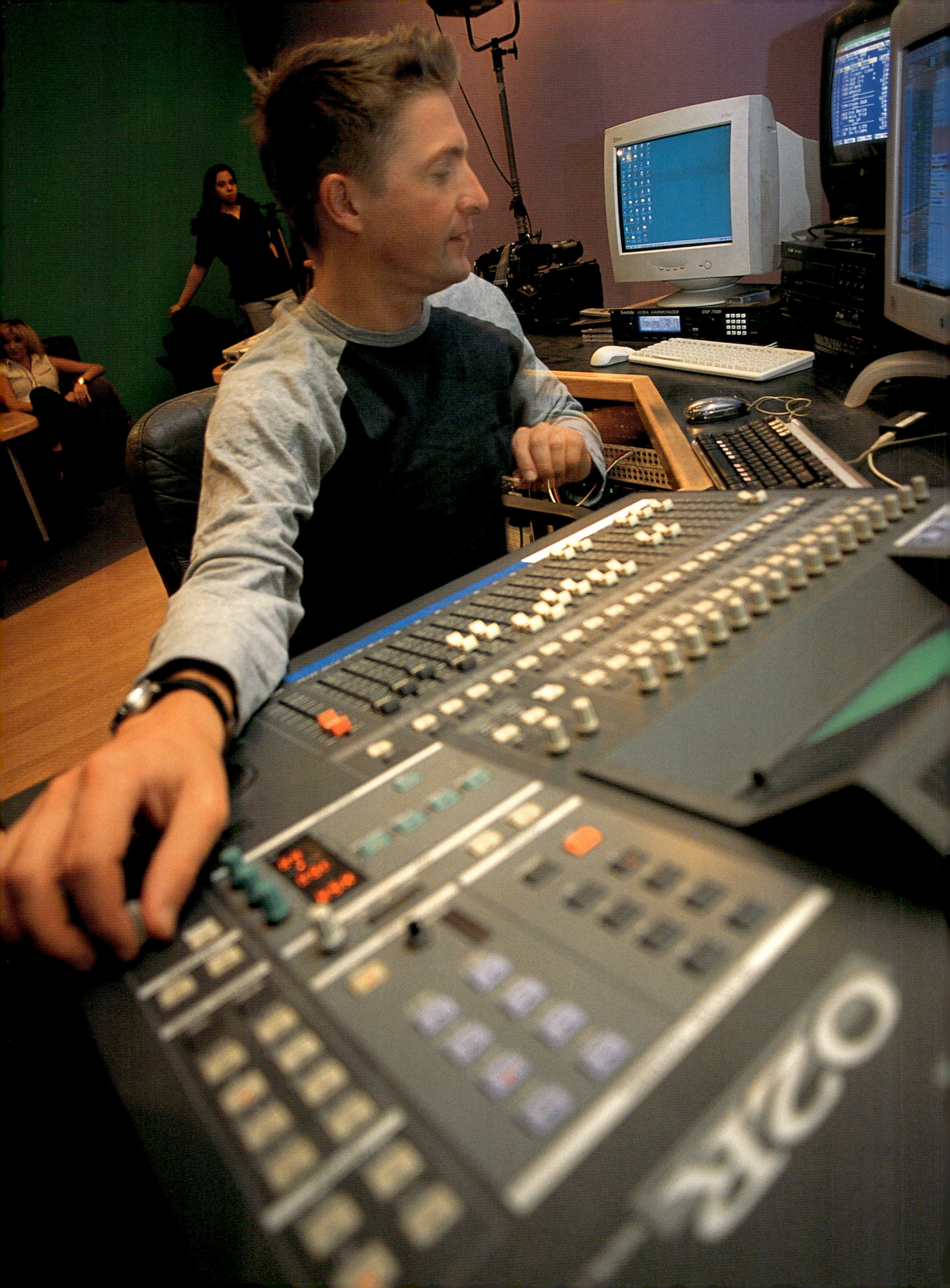

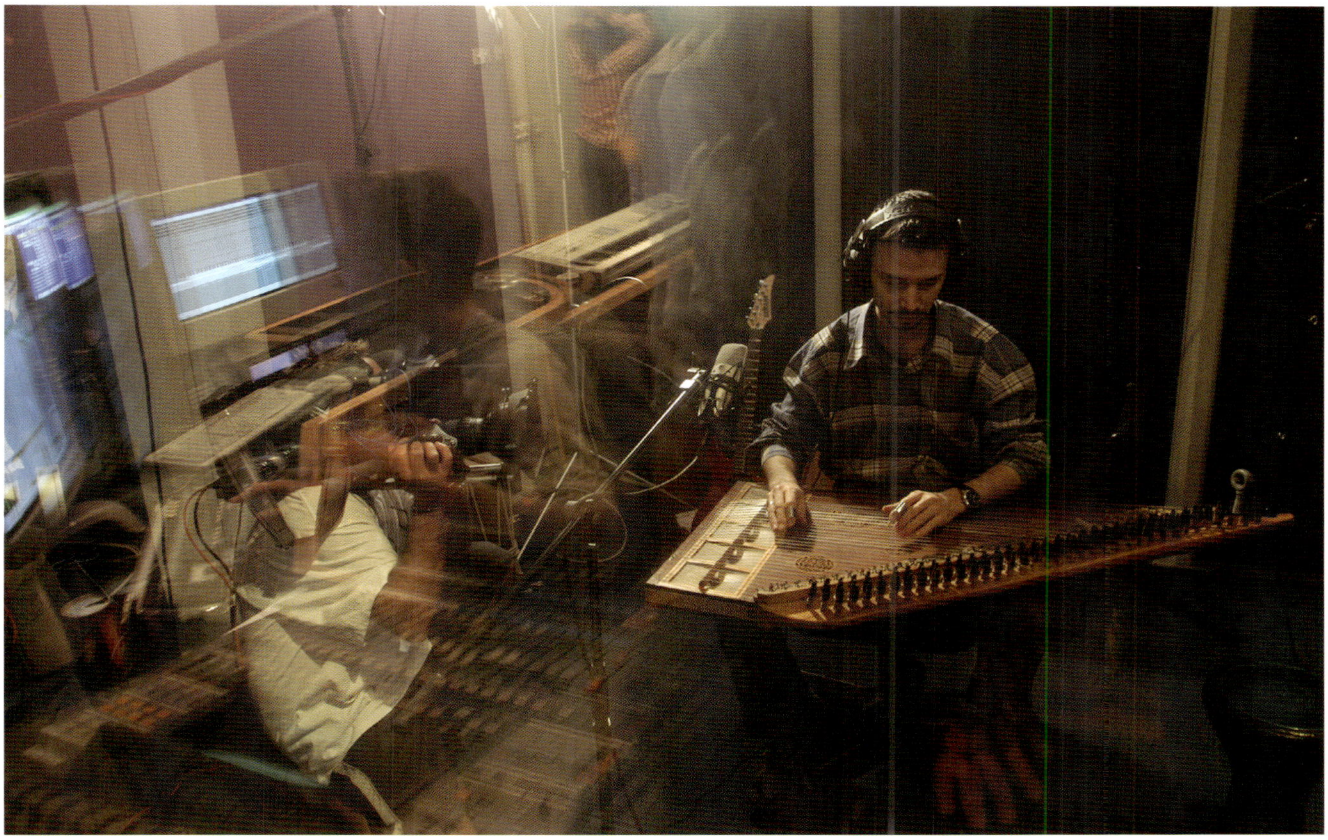

◄ Kirsch has recently worked for the Nobel-winning charity, Medecins Sans Frontieres (Doctors Without Borders), bringing to his bilingual lyrics (penned by Tom Callaghan) such Arabic musical touches as the *chunk* (16-string violins) as well as the traditional *oudh*, *qanoon*, *tabla* and *nai*, all performed by local musicians.

▲ A *Qanoon* performer, Khaled Ghadry, playing at Kirsch's Dubai studio. Traditional Arab music has a distinctive capacity to transcend both the artist and listener into a state of *tarab* (roughly translated as 'ecstatic enjoyment' or 'a nearly mystical trance-like condition'). In his recent study *Making Music in the Arab World*, ethnomusicologist AJ Racy examines the fascinating relationship between performers and listeners, how musicians become inspired, and the use of lyrics of love as tools of ecstasy. *Photos by Dariush Zandi.*

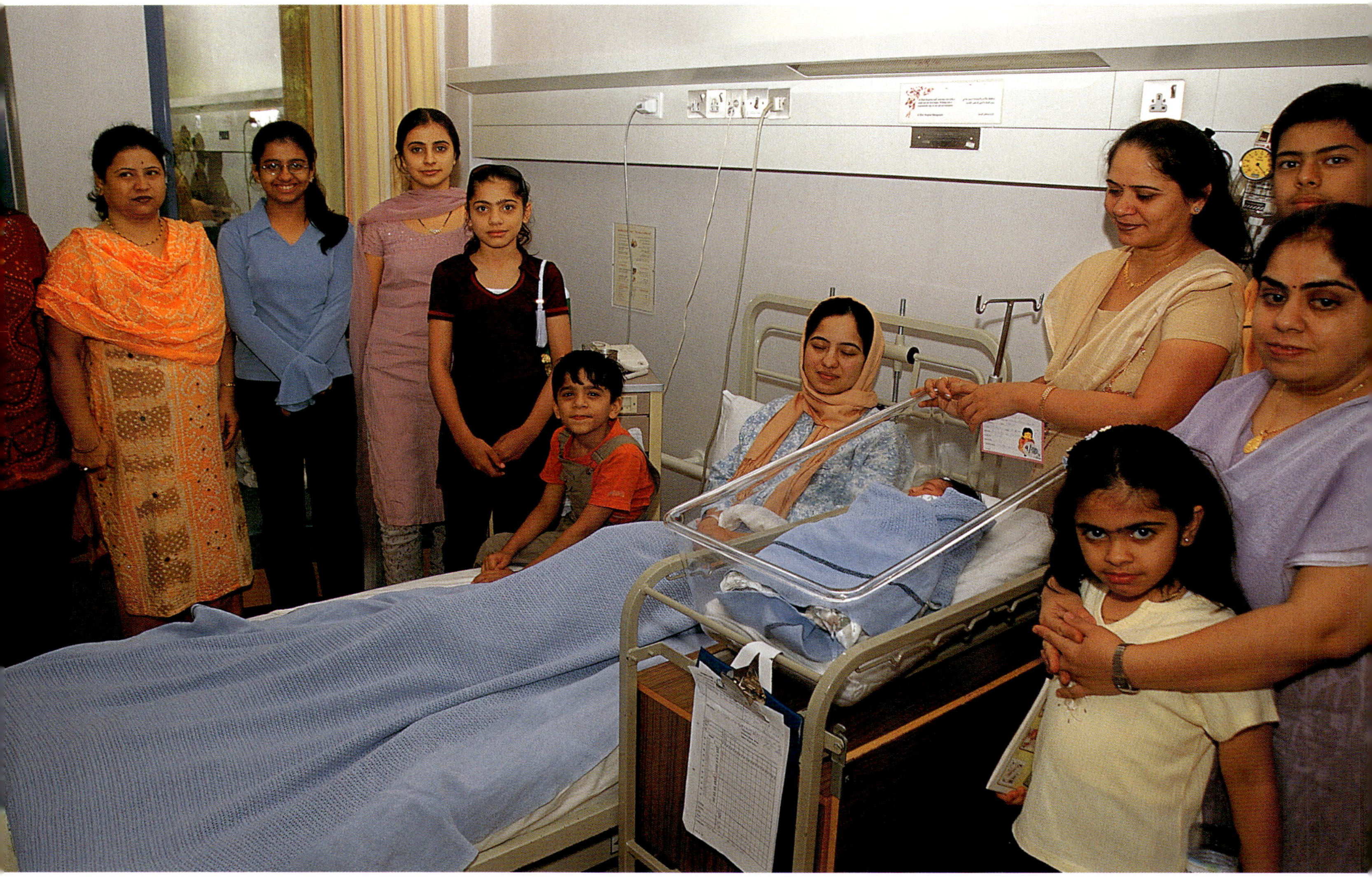

▲ AT AL WASL HOSPITAL MRS NEHA, FROM INDIA, SEEN here surrounded by family and relatives, gave birth to a baby girl. As per Hindu custom, the infant will be named six days later. Al Wasl has a large gynaecological division, a fine maternity ward and offers comprehensive ante-natal care.

▶ AN ARAB WOMAN, MRS GHADEER, HAS GIVEN BIRTH to a child at 4.05 am and wants to name her A'ala, 'Gift of God'. Mrs Ghadeer is a civil engineer and has lived in Dubai for 23 years. Her husband is a pysiotherapist who works for a government hospital in Dubai (right top). A Philippine couple, Rose and Roland, who have named their new son Timothy, beam with joy (right bottom). Emergency medical care in Dubai is free for everyone at government hospitals. In addition to Al Wasl, the Dubai Department of Health and Medical Services runs Dubai Hospital (one of the best medical centres in the Middle East), the Rashid and Maktoum hospitals, and several out-patient clinics. In addition there are a number of well-equipped private hospitals. *Photos by Souheil Semaan.*

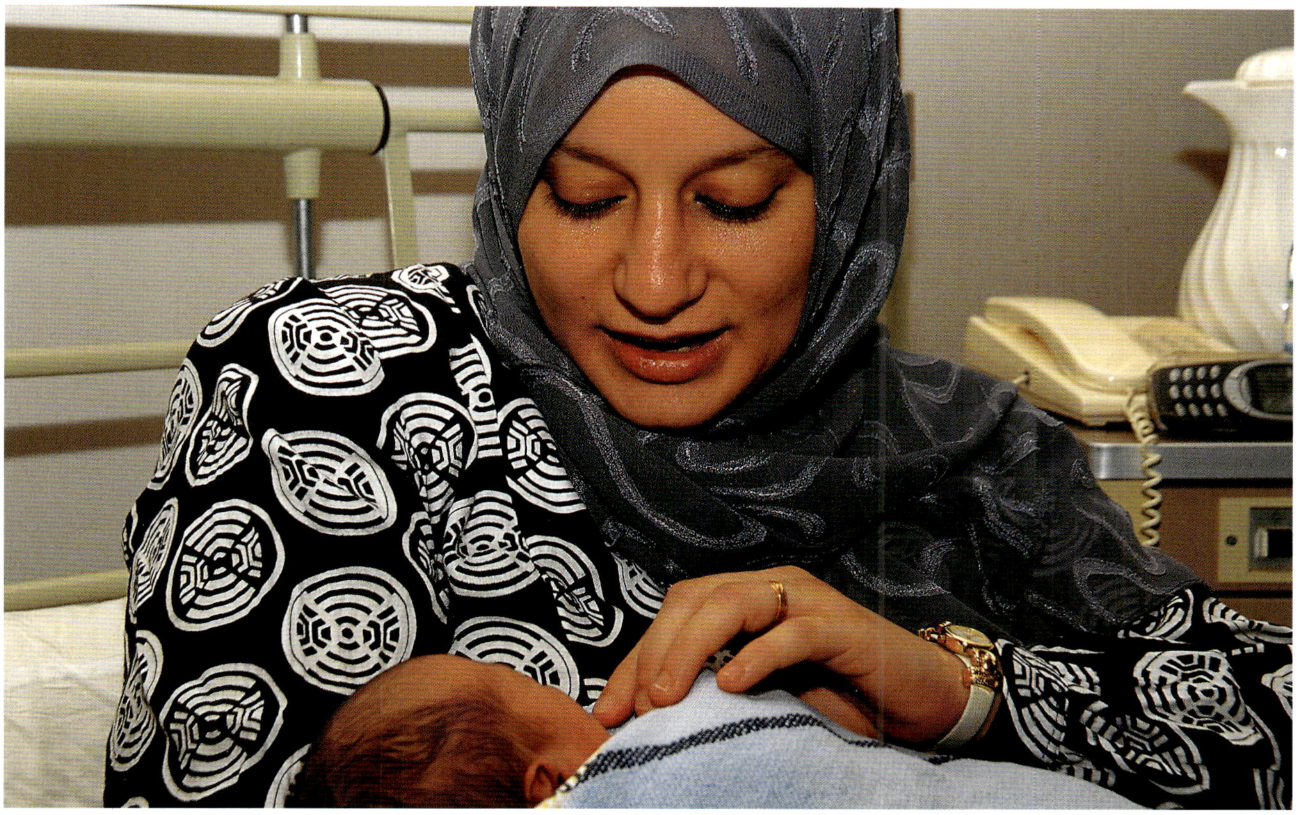

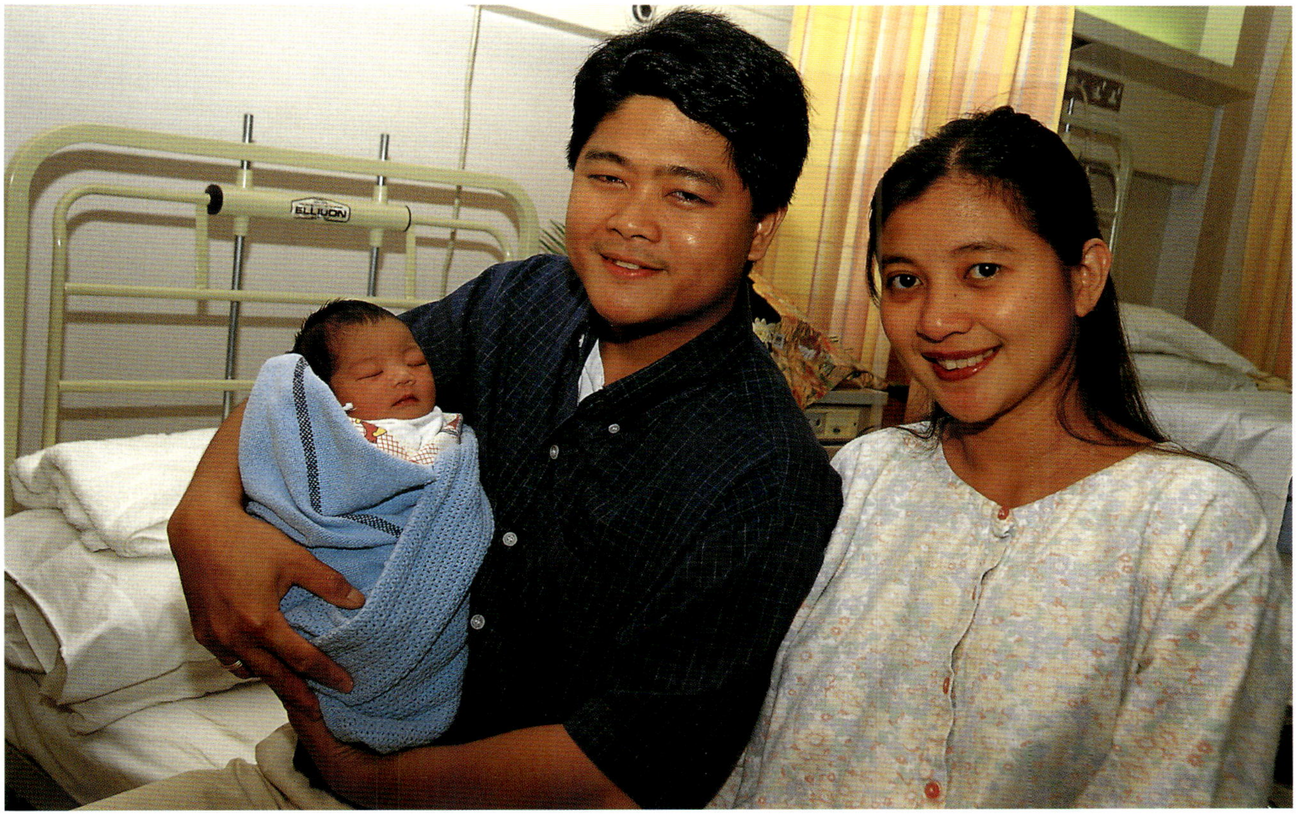

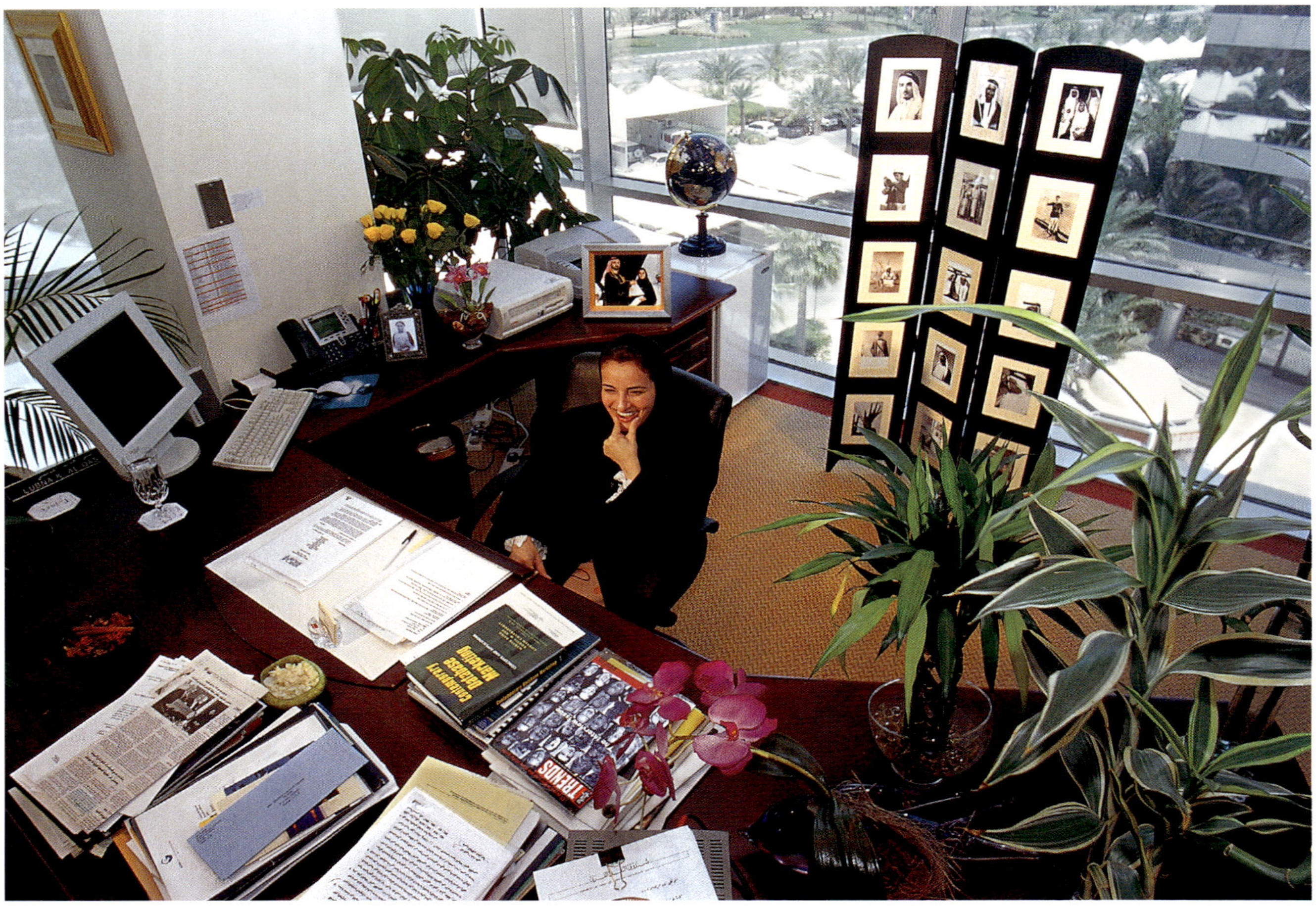

▲ ▶ In her office in Dubai, Sheikha Lubna Al Qasimi discusses her company, Tejari.com, and her long-time involvement in what she terms, "the electronic market place" and Dubai's Jebel Ali Free Zone. This young offspring of the ruling family of Sharjah is a California State University graduate and the success of her business-to-business initiative has positioned her to become a leader not only in industry but also of women's rights. She is accessible, witty, and brilliant; serves in the fight to heal cancer and helps individuals afflicted with autism. *Photos by Dariush Zandi.*

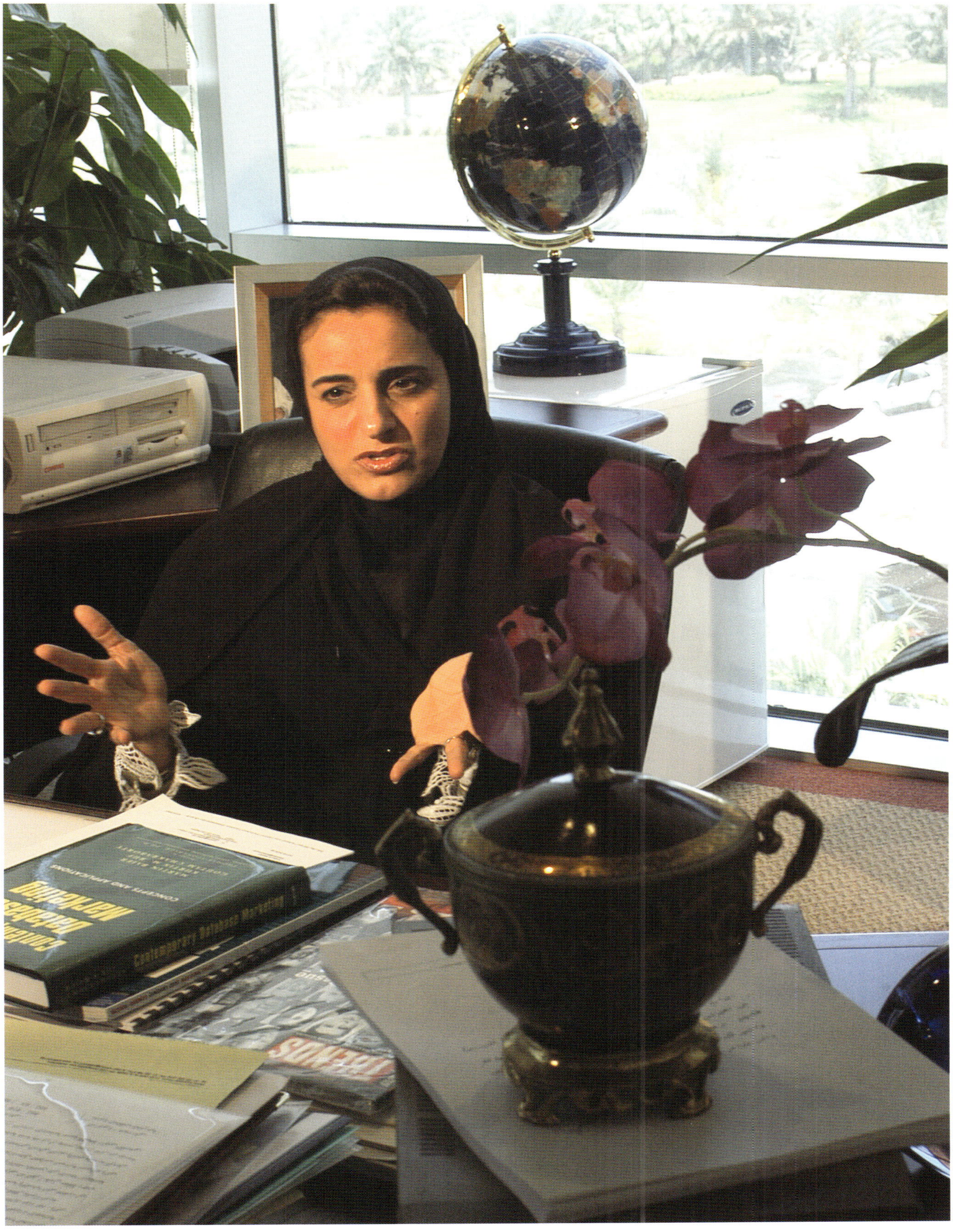

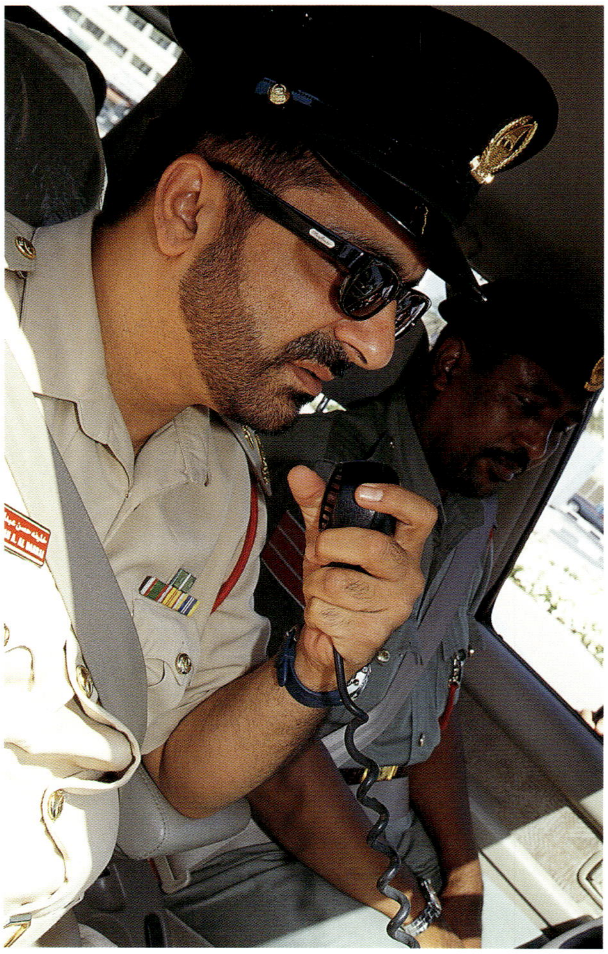

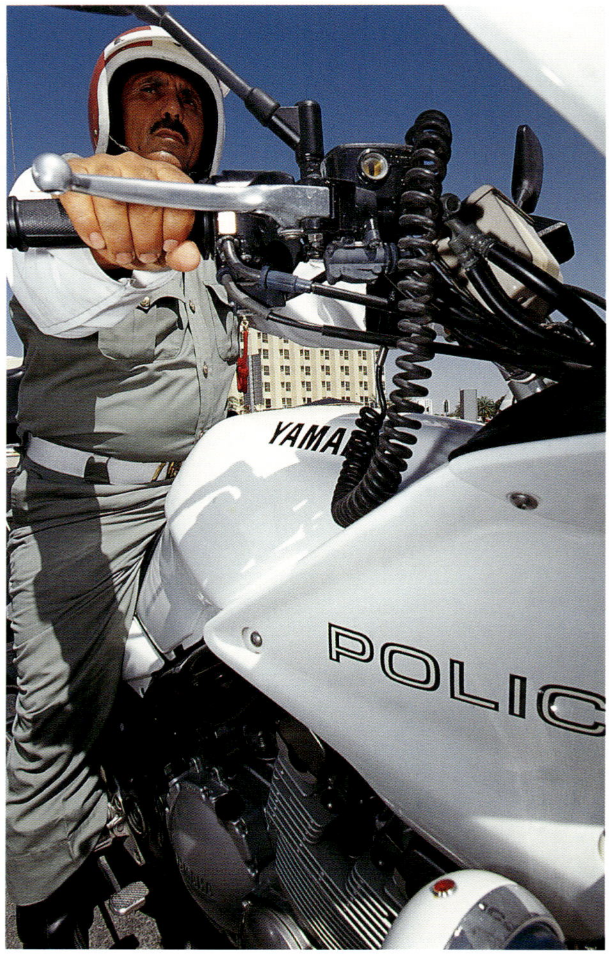

▲ ▶ IN THEIR WHITE-AND-GREEN VEHICLES, THE POLICE patrols of Dubai seem almost obsolete, because crime is extraordinarily low. When the *Dubai 24 hours* film crew double-parked near a Satwa roundabout, in the crowded souk area, they were approached by two serious-looking policemen. Michael Tobias remembered an earlier incident when Italian police surrounded a film crew of his near Venice, their machine guns raised, for simply using a tripod. In Dubai, the crew was treated with courtesy and kindly assistance. *Photos by Paul MacLeod.*

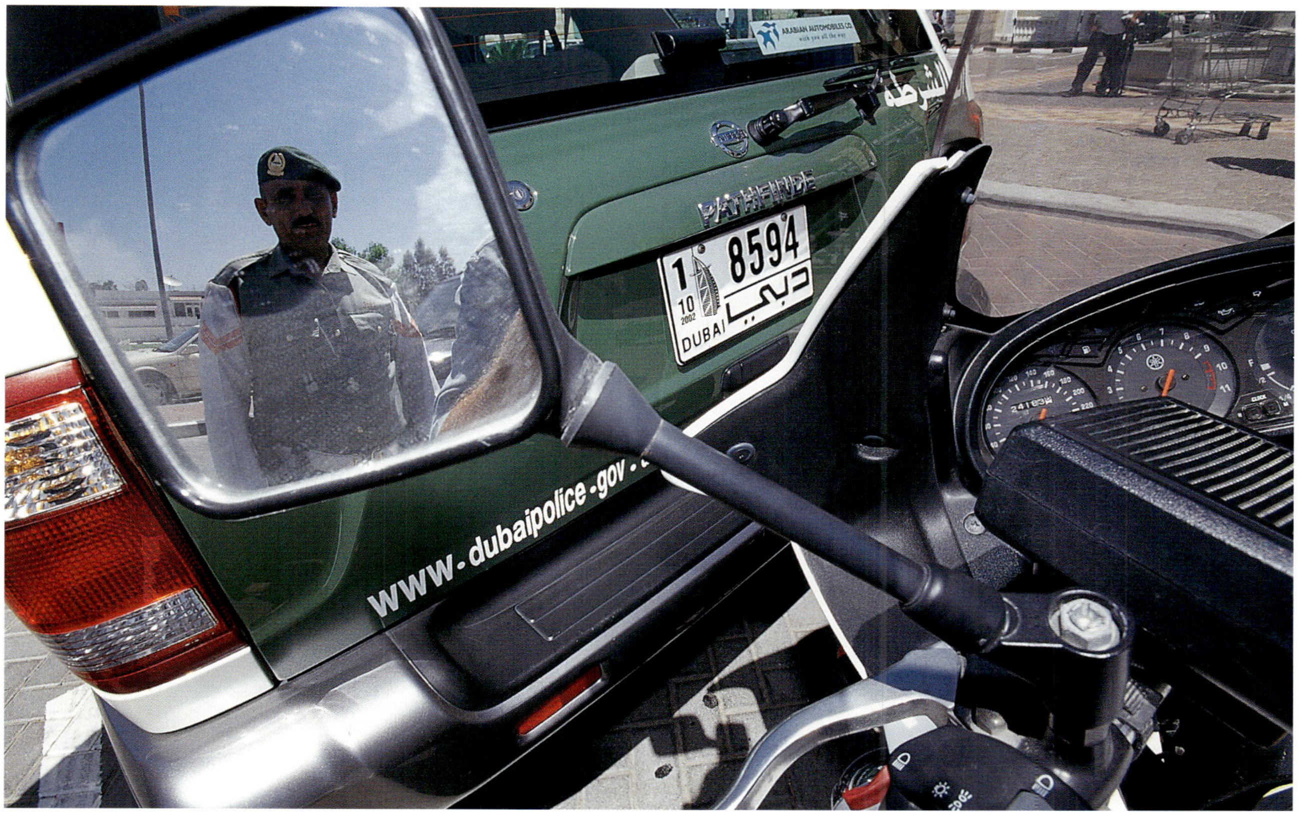
1 8594
10
2002
DUBAI
www.dubaipolice.gov

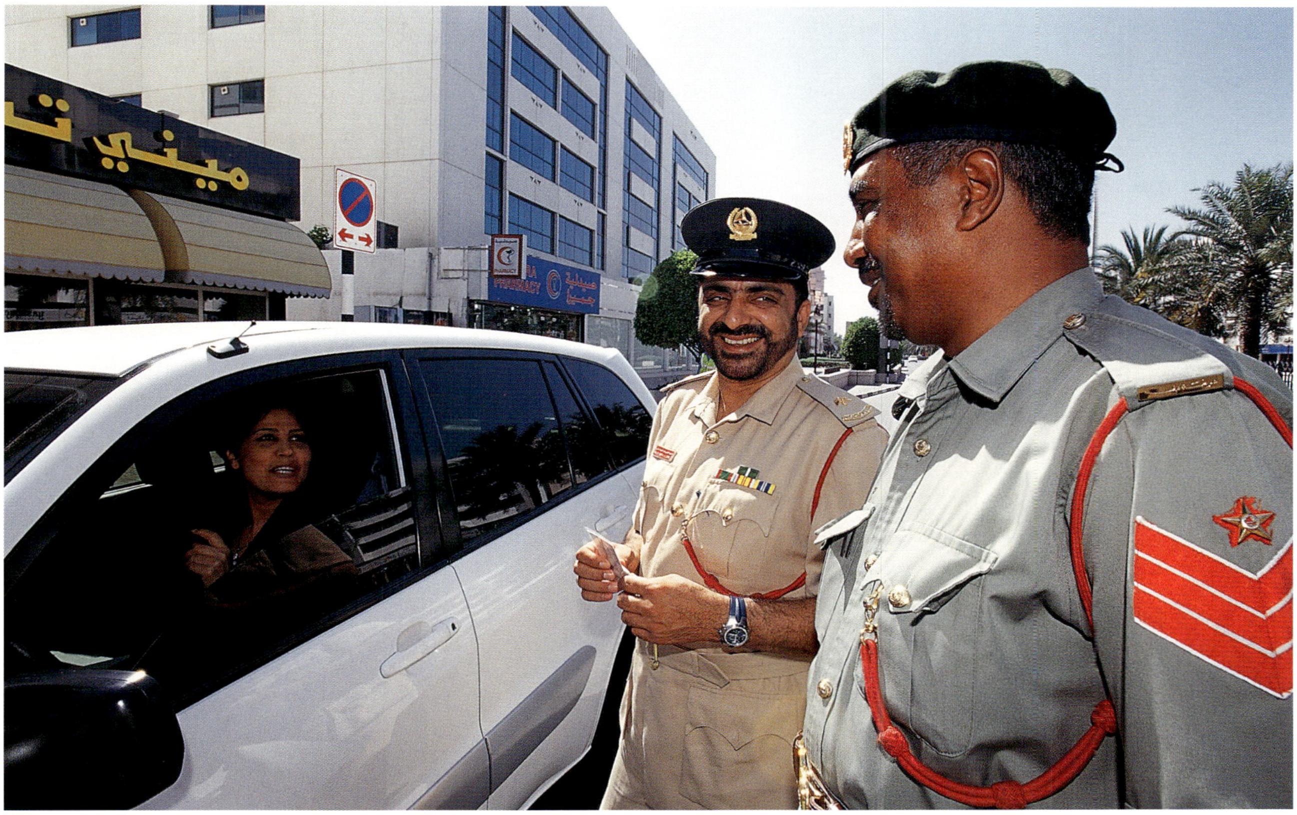

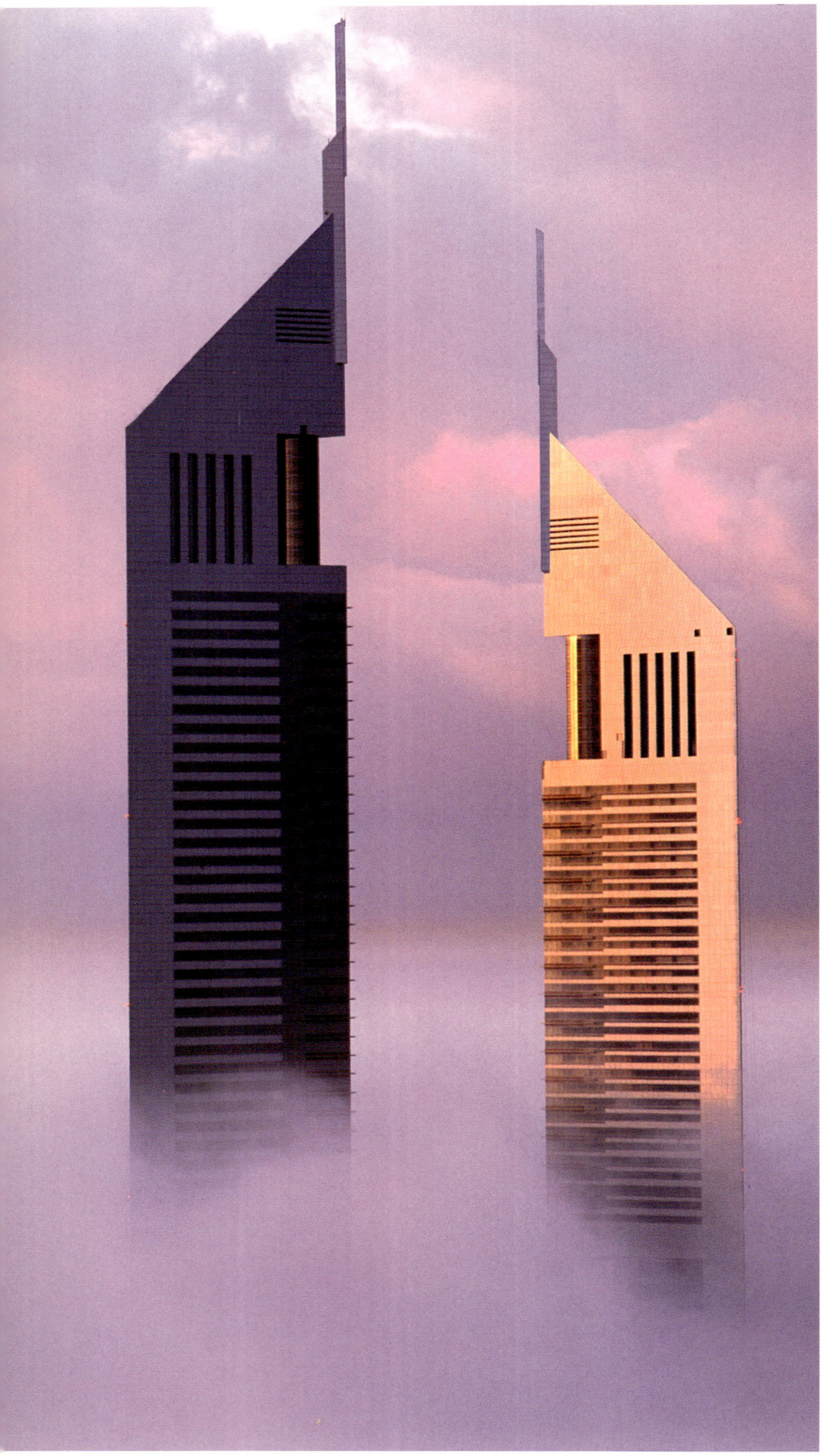

◀ ▼ TO MANY OBSERVERS, EMIRATES TOWERS – AT 350 metres the tallest buildings in the Middle East and Europe – seen here in an unusual early-morning fog – may well be the most beautiful skyscrapers in the world. One tower serves as an office block and the other is a five-star business hotel. Part of the Jumeirah International Group, a Dubai-based hotel company, Emirates Towers was designed by Hazel Wong of NORR Architects (pictured below), who comments: "Dubai is an architect's dream because of its readiness to accept new ideas." In Dubai, the buildings, not the streets, have become the icons of daily life. And there's probably no comparable juxtaposition in the world than clearing the last sand dune when approaching the city and suddenly confronting the distant horizon of elegant high-rises dominated by these two exquisite peaks of bustling human life. *Photo by Jumeirah International.*

▶ INSIDE THE EMIRATES TOWERS, A GLANCE UPWARDS reveals a spectacular atrium flanked by four glass-fronted elevators that provide hotel guests with panoramic views of Dubai's coastline as they glide skywards at four metres per second. *Photo by Dariush Zandi.*

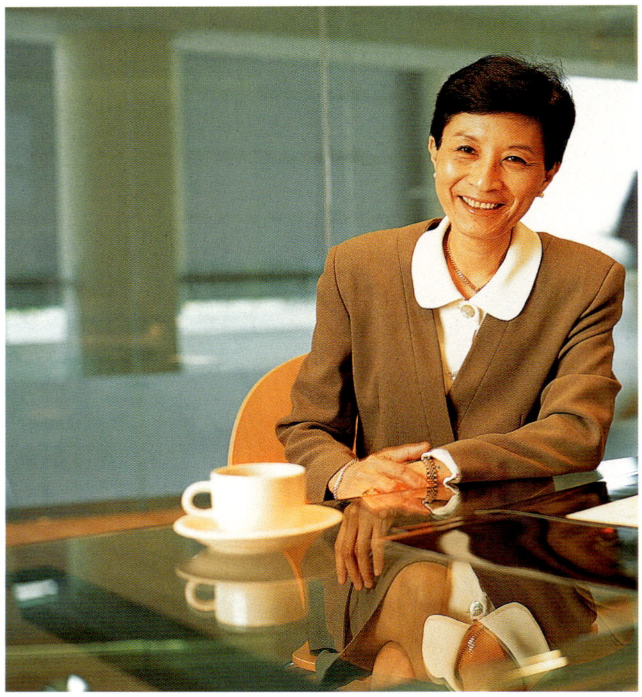

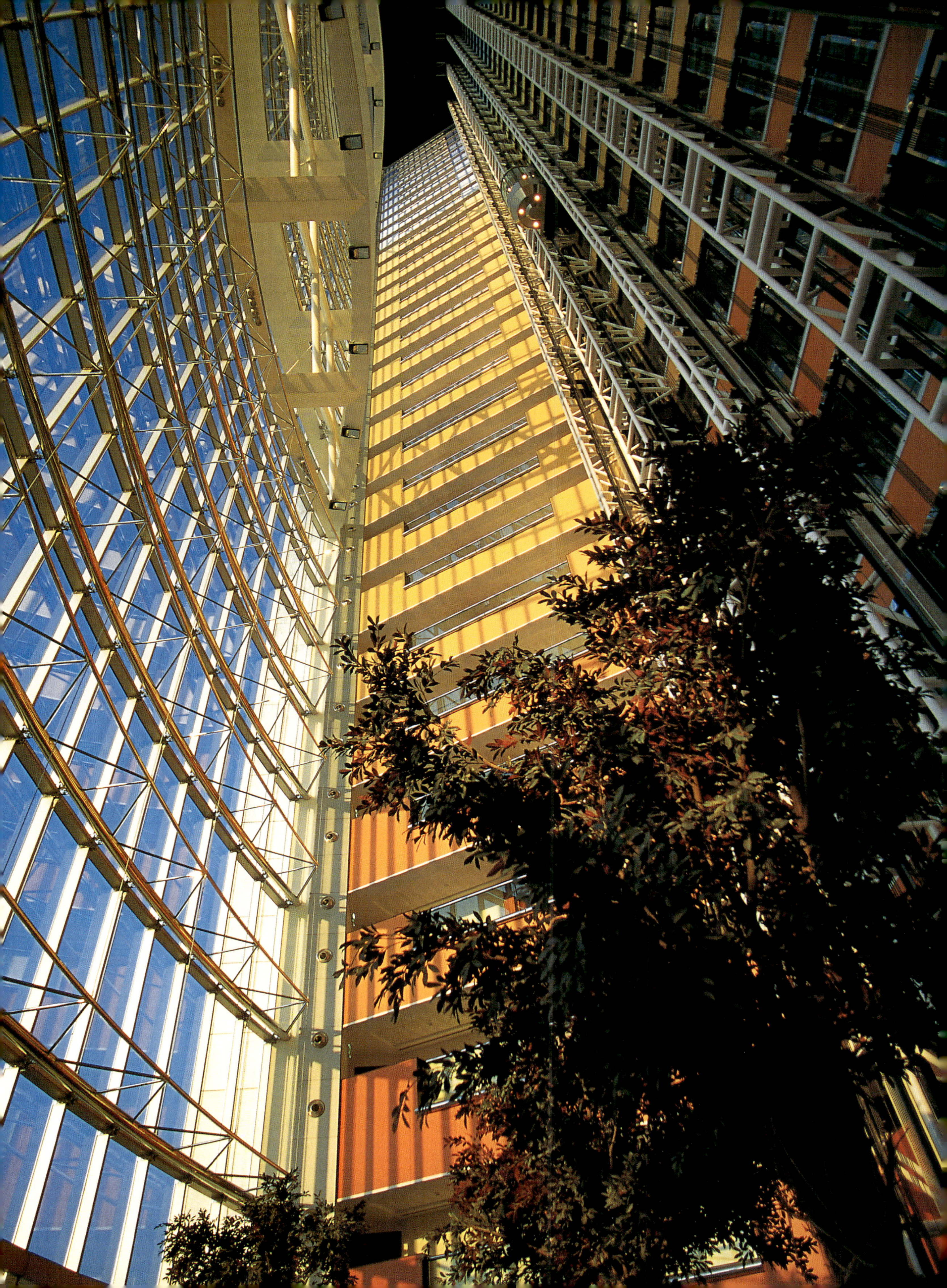

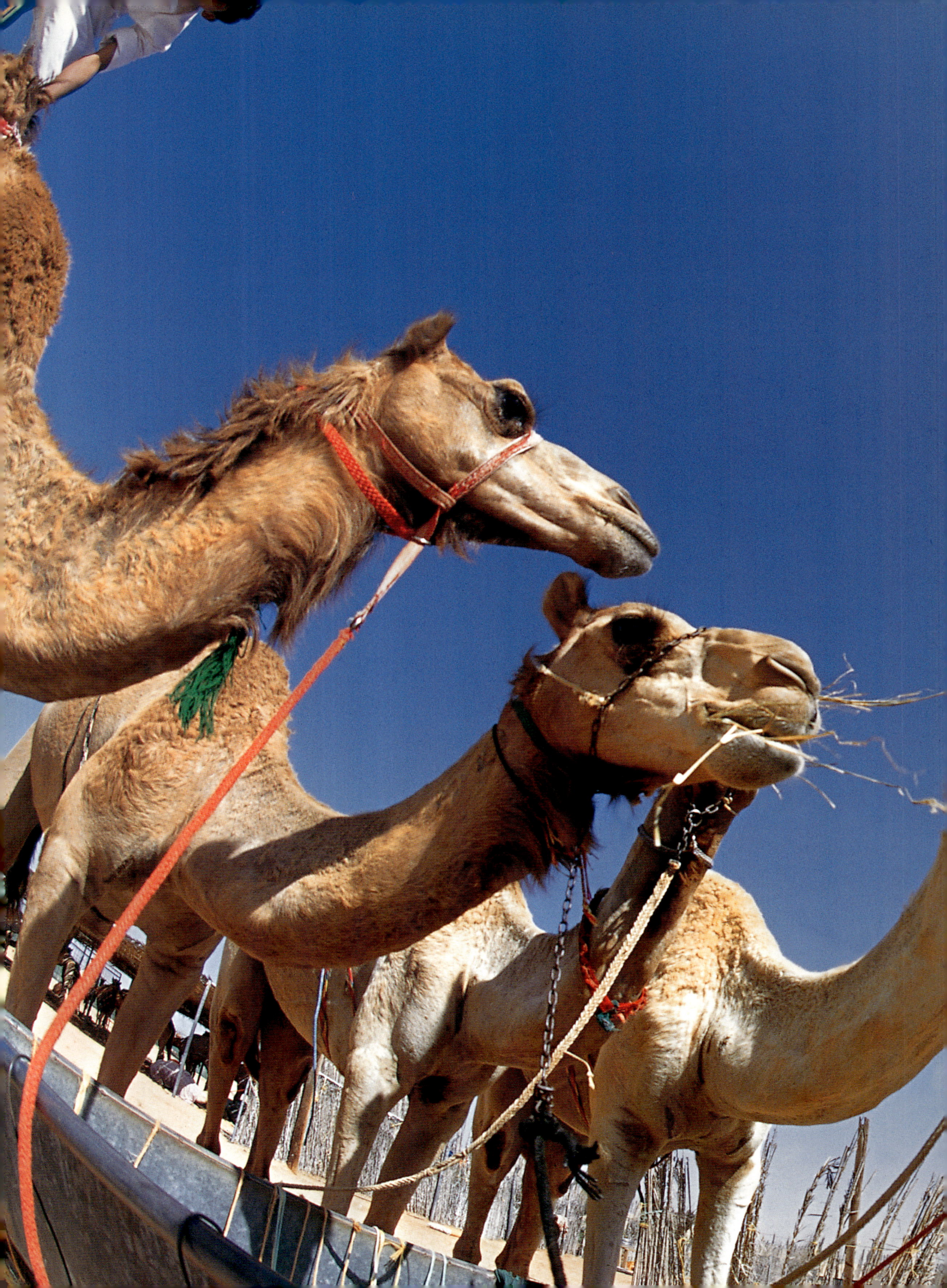

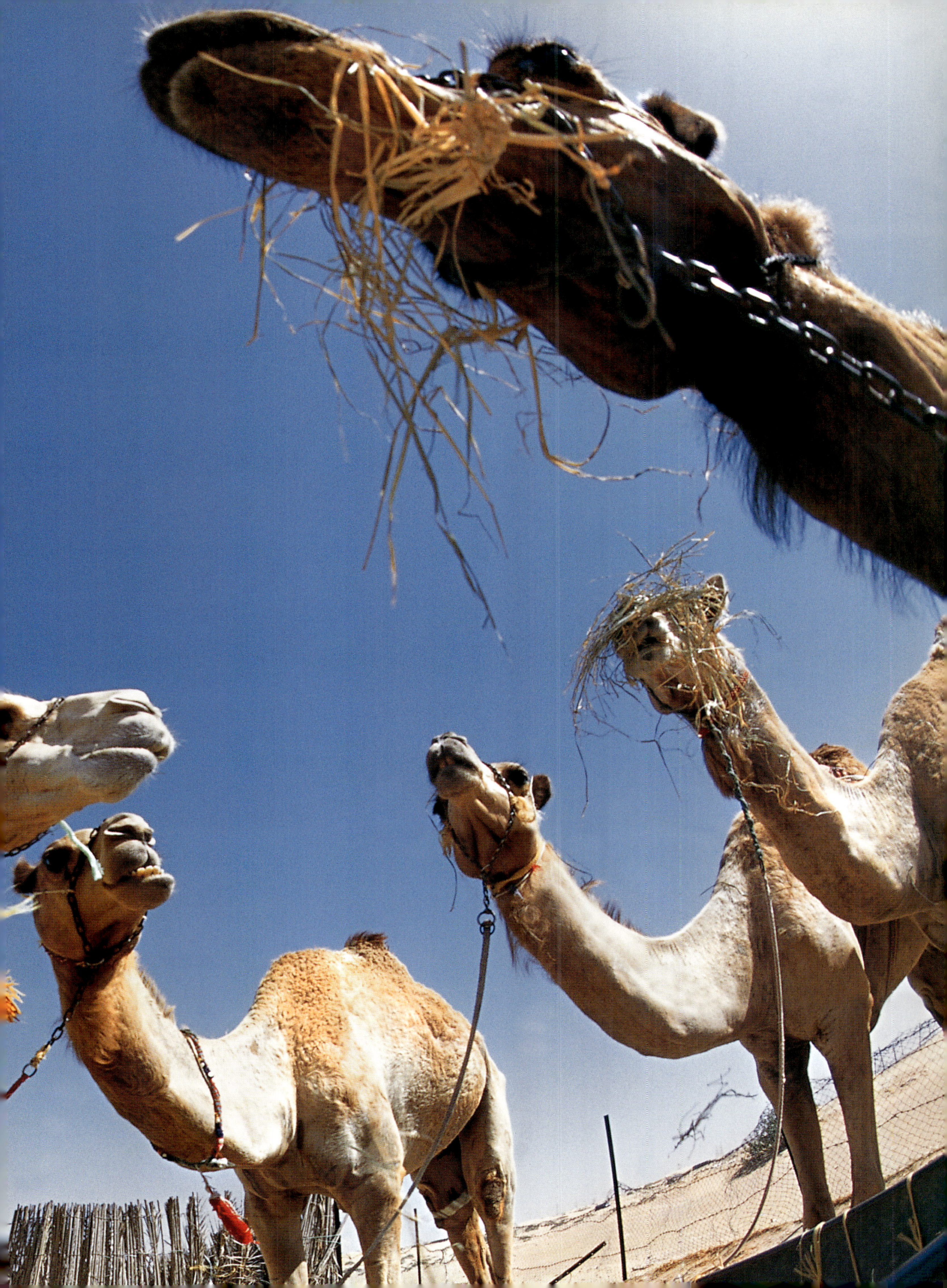

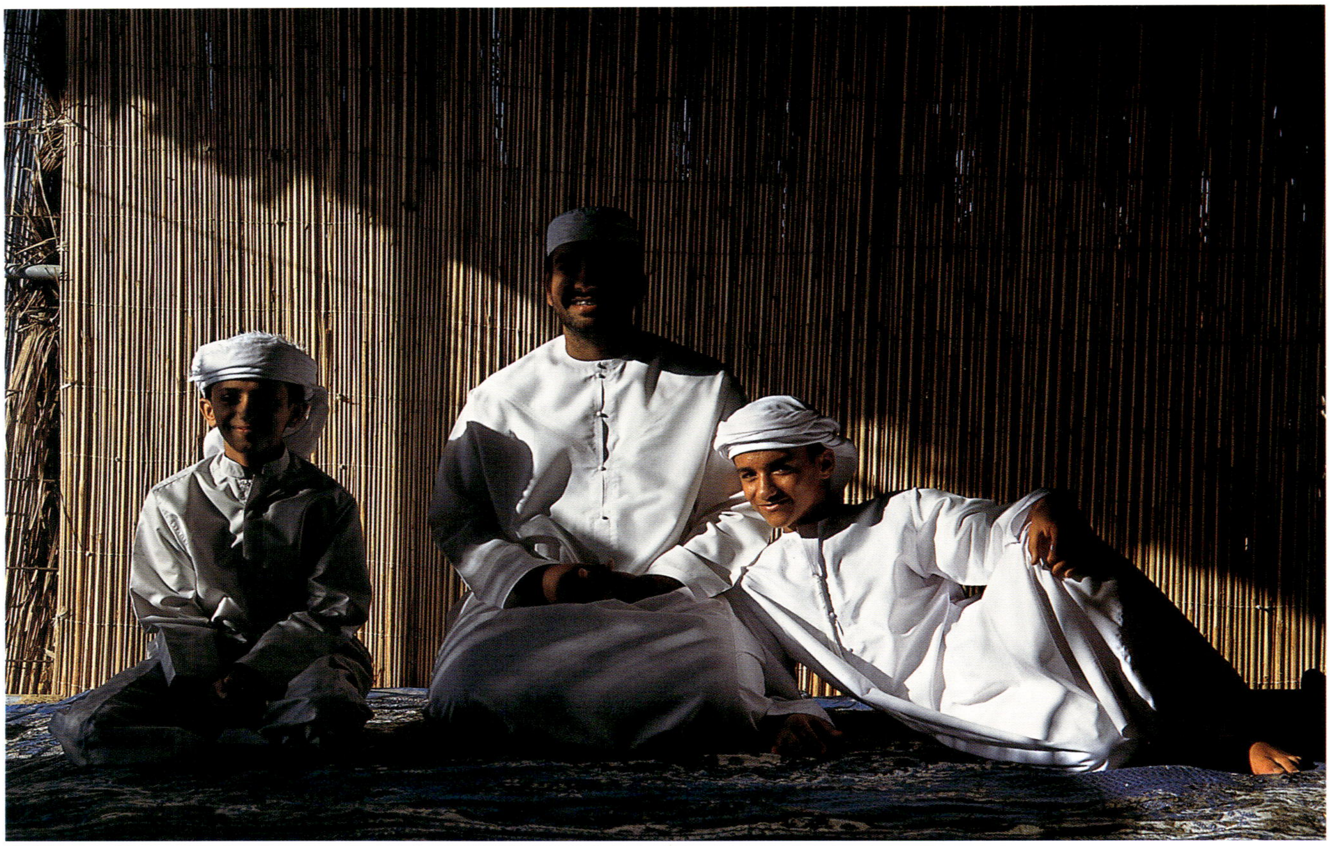

◀◀ Khawaneej, about 20 minutes drive from Dubai, is a good place to observe camels. Bedouin camel trainers also come here to learn an ancient art of dealing with one of the most stubborn, loving and intelligent of all the creatures of the desert. *Photo by Joe Sassine.*

▲ Mohammed Ali Alrezi, Ahmed Al Shaer and Khalifa Ali Alrezi at the Khawaneej Bedouin camp prior to their camel migration to Ajman. *Photo by Joe Sassine.*

▶ Camels and their Emirati owners (Ali Humaid Ali Alrezi and his friend, Tariq Jasim Rashid Alaraidi), walk hand in hand: their history is inextricable, the bonds almost mystical. To the Bedu the animal's vigour is legendary, and until recent times, they were their essential allies. They remain ubiquitous, and camel milk is still available throughout the United Arab Emirates, but many camels are now bred almost exclusively for racing and can command very high prices. *Photo by Paul MacLeod.*

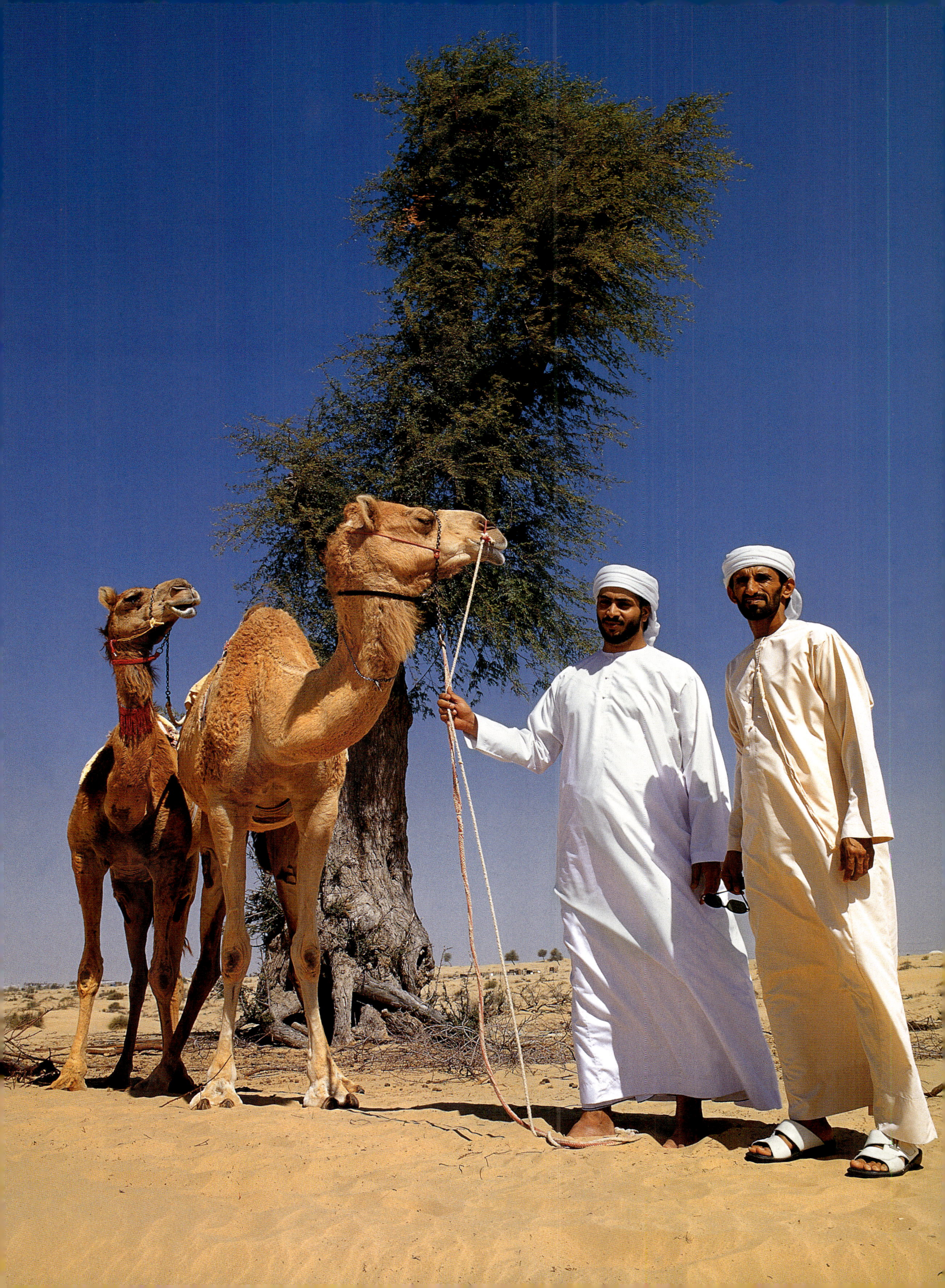

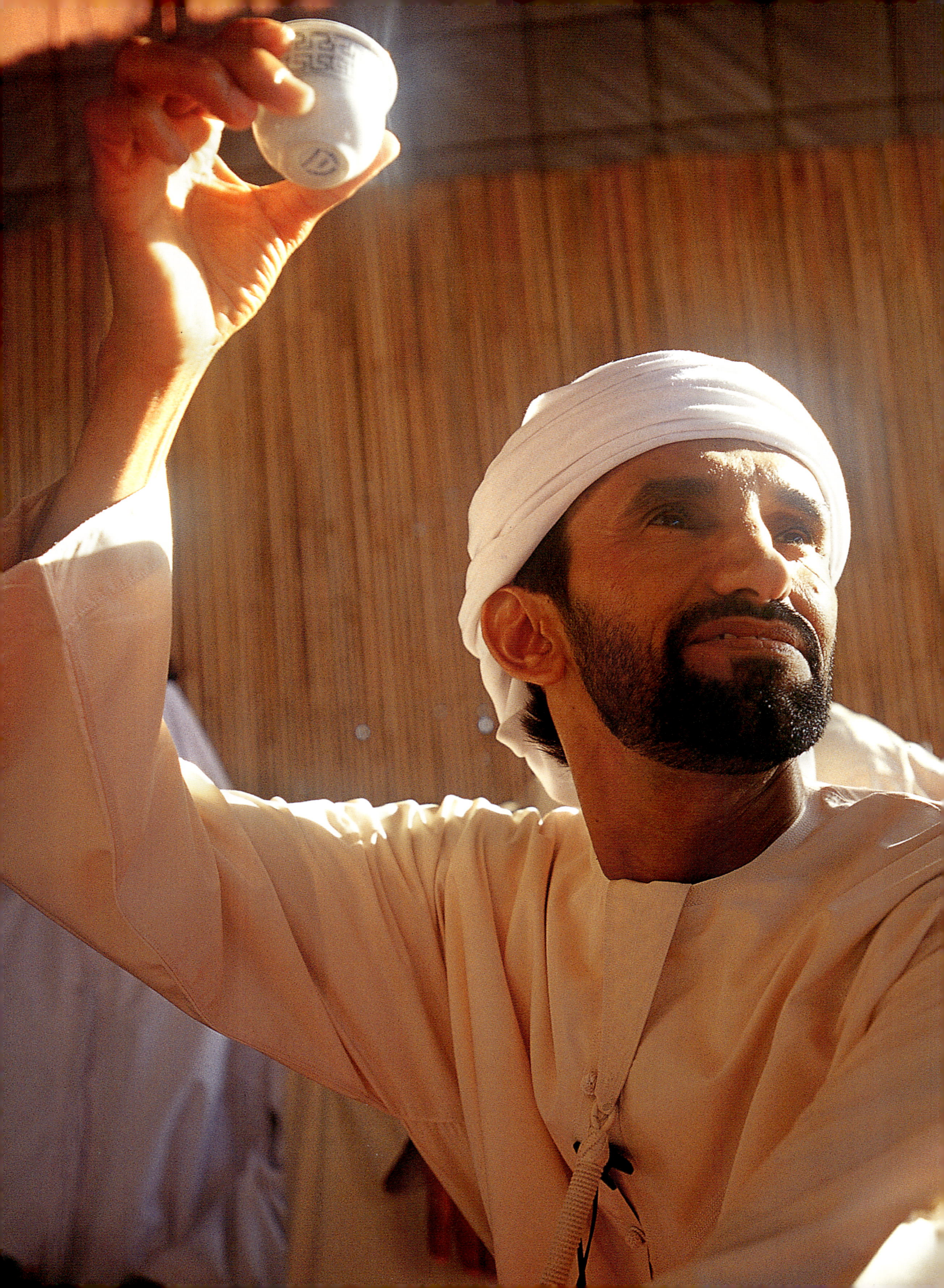

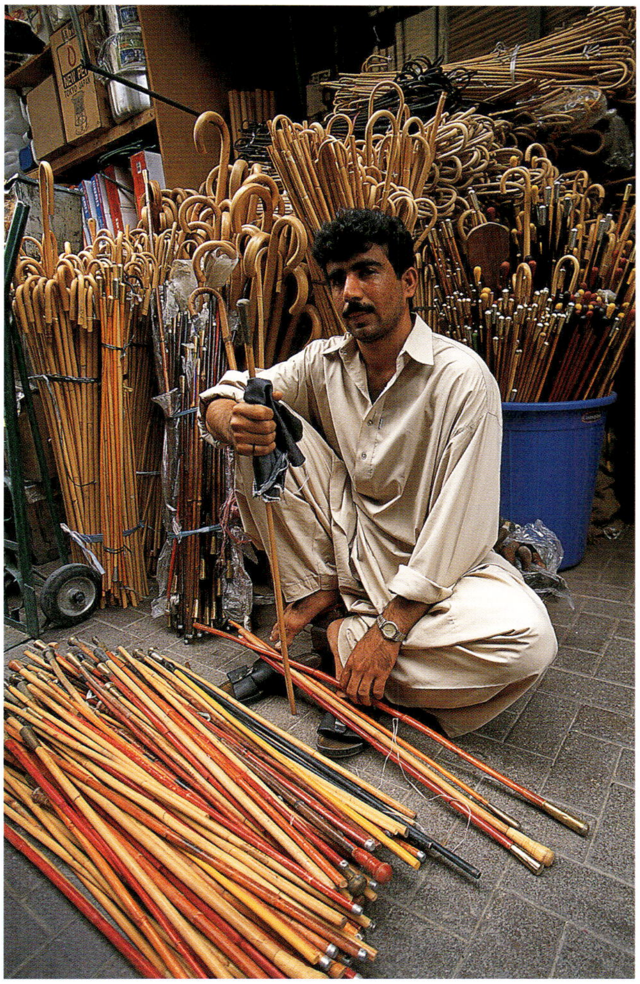

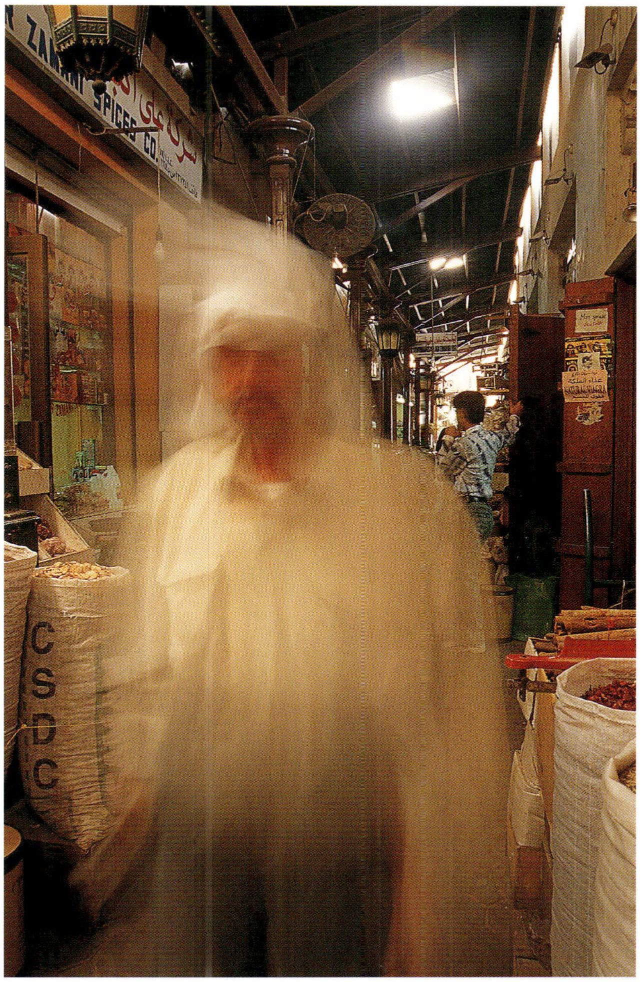

◄ Bedouin Ali Humaid Ali Alrezi with a cup of *kehwa*, strong Arabic coffee spiced with cardamom. Coffee is appreciated in Dubai and is also available at a number of modern, Western-style franchises. *Photo by Paul MacLeod.*

▲ Souk is Arabic for 'market'. In Dubai, numerous such hubs brim with shoppers and the stalls breathe life into even the most mundane walking canes – known as *khayzaraneh* and actually used by the affluent elite as well as those who need them (left). In these tightly packed alleys, every price is negotiable, even gold. Dubai is known as the 'City of Gold' throughout the Gulf. Its prices are competitive and the workmanship is of a high standard. *Photos by Dariush Zandi (left) and Souheil Semaan (right).*

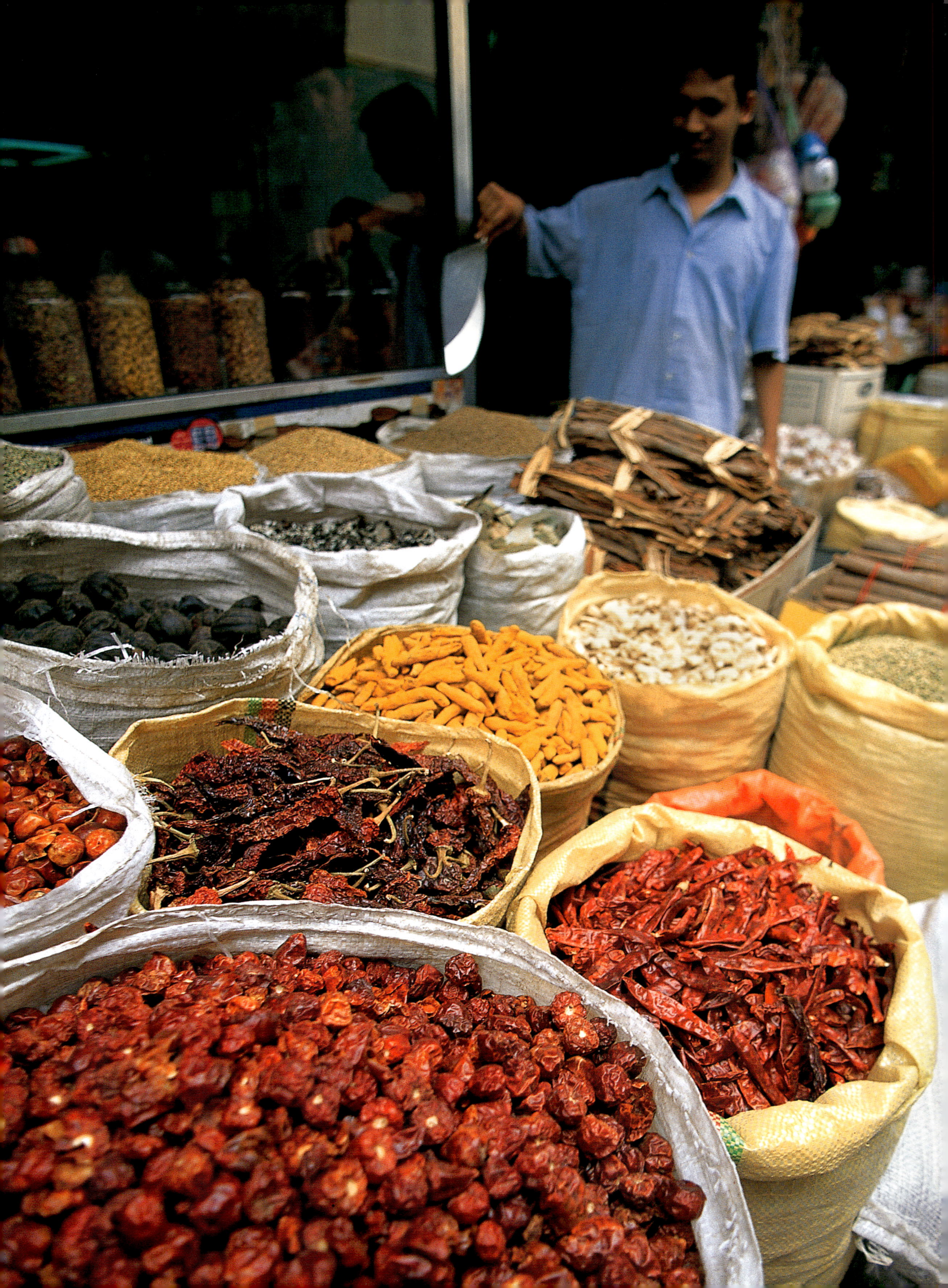

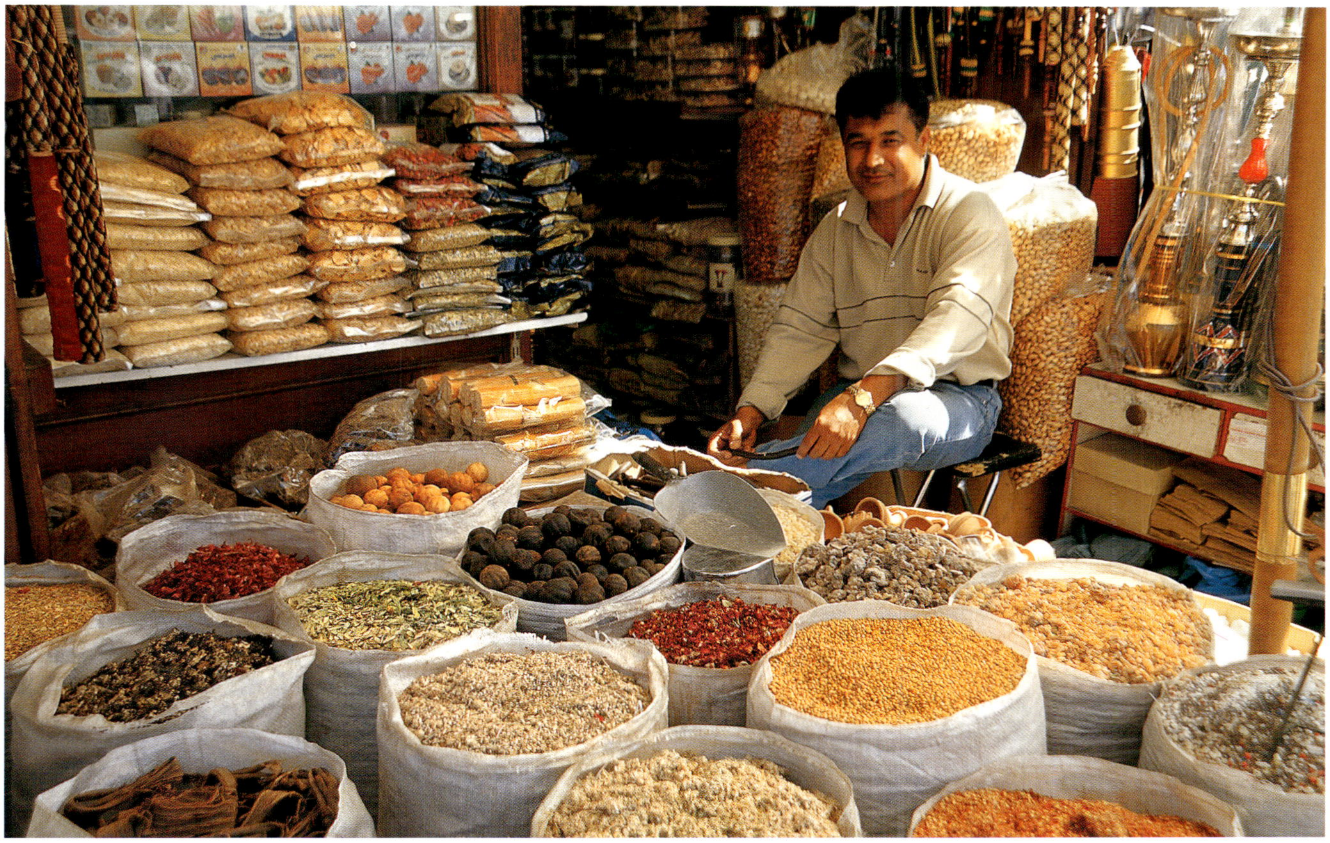

◀ ▲ AT THE SPICE SOUK BETWEEN AL NASR SQUARE AND the Creek, these gentlemen display their sacks of spices, perfumed oils and dried herbs, some of which are sold for medicinal purposes. The spices, including chillies, samak, mustard, dried lime, cardamom, cinnamon, pepper, saffron and clove, have been imported from throughout the Gulf, as well as from Africa and the Indian sub-continent. *Photos by Dariush Zandi (left) and Souheil Semaan (above).*

▶▶ SHOPPING IS NOT RESTRICTED TO SOUKS AND DUBAI has a wonderful choice of shopping malls where the prices of goods are often cheaper than in their home countries. Promoting this shopping paradise, the annual Dubai Shopping Festival attracts visitors from all over the world. *Photo by Shankar Adiseshan, Motivate Publishing.*

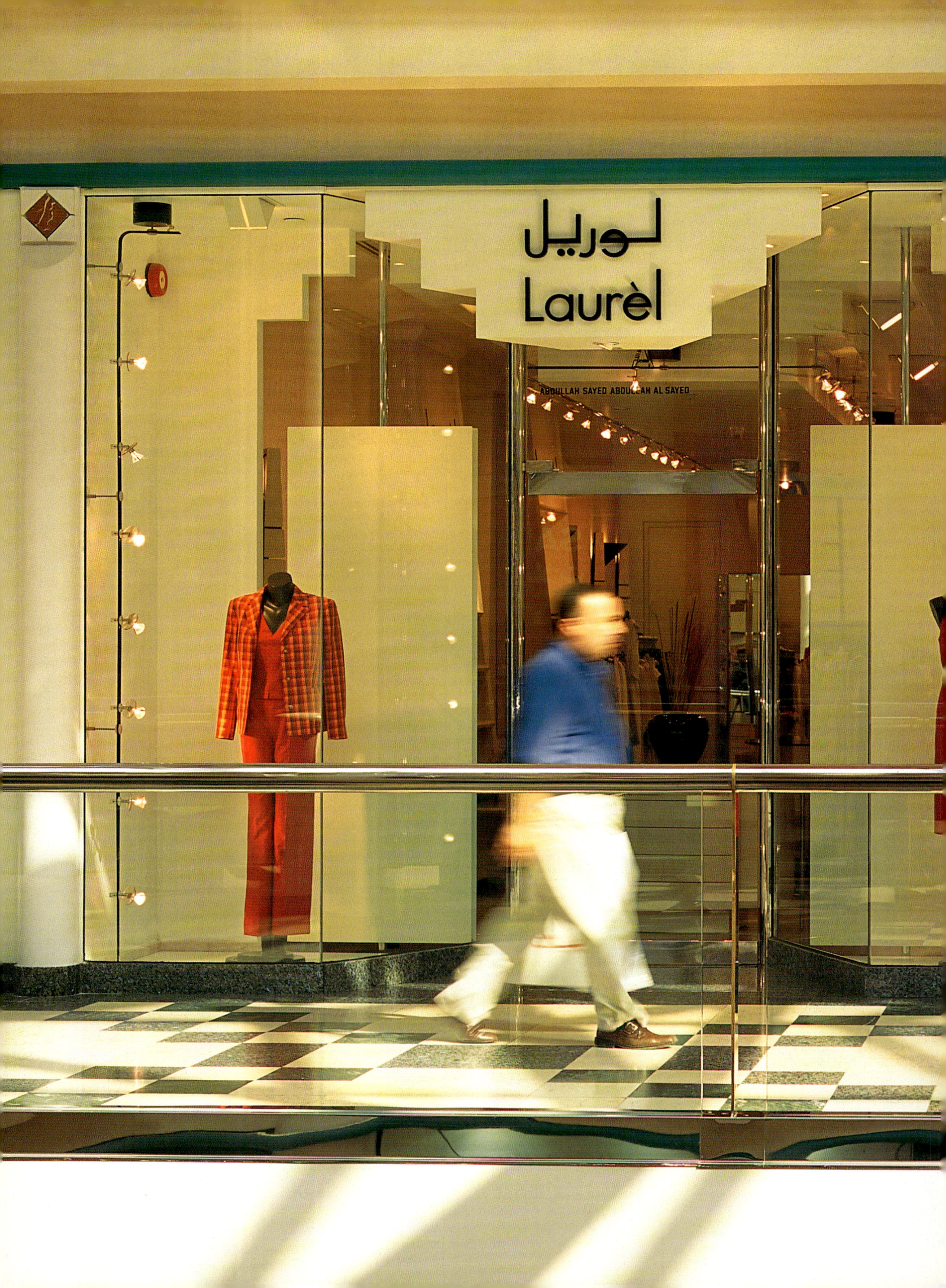

لوريل
Laurèl

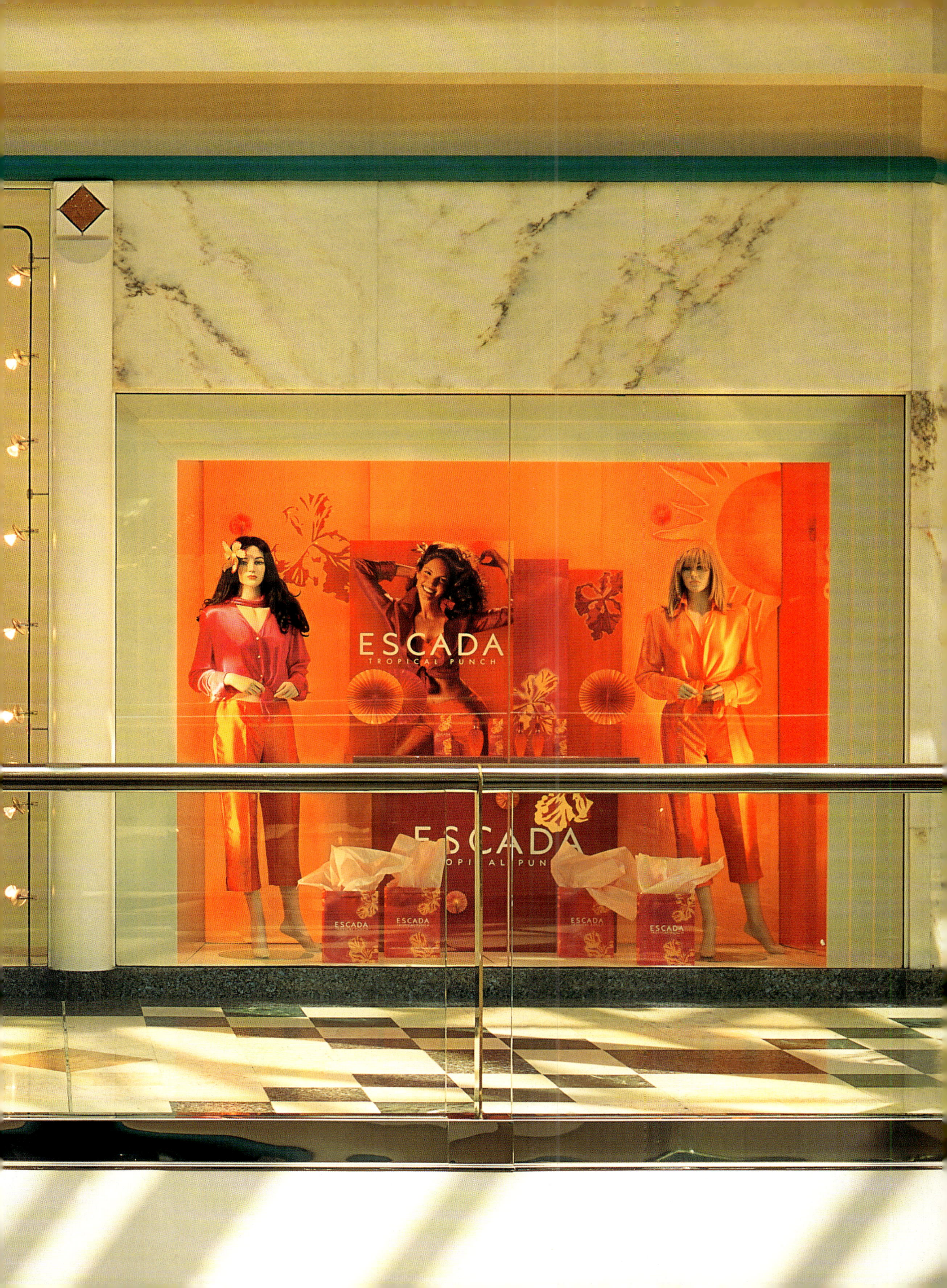
ESCADA
TROPICAL PUNCH
ESCADA

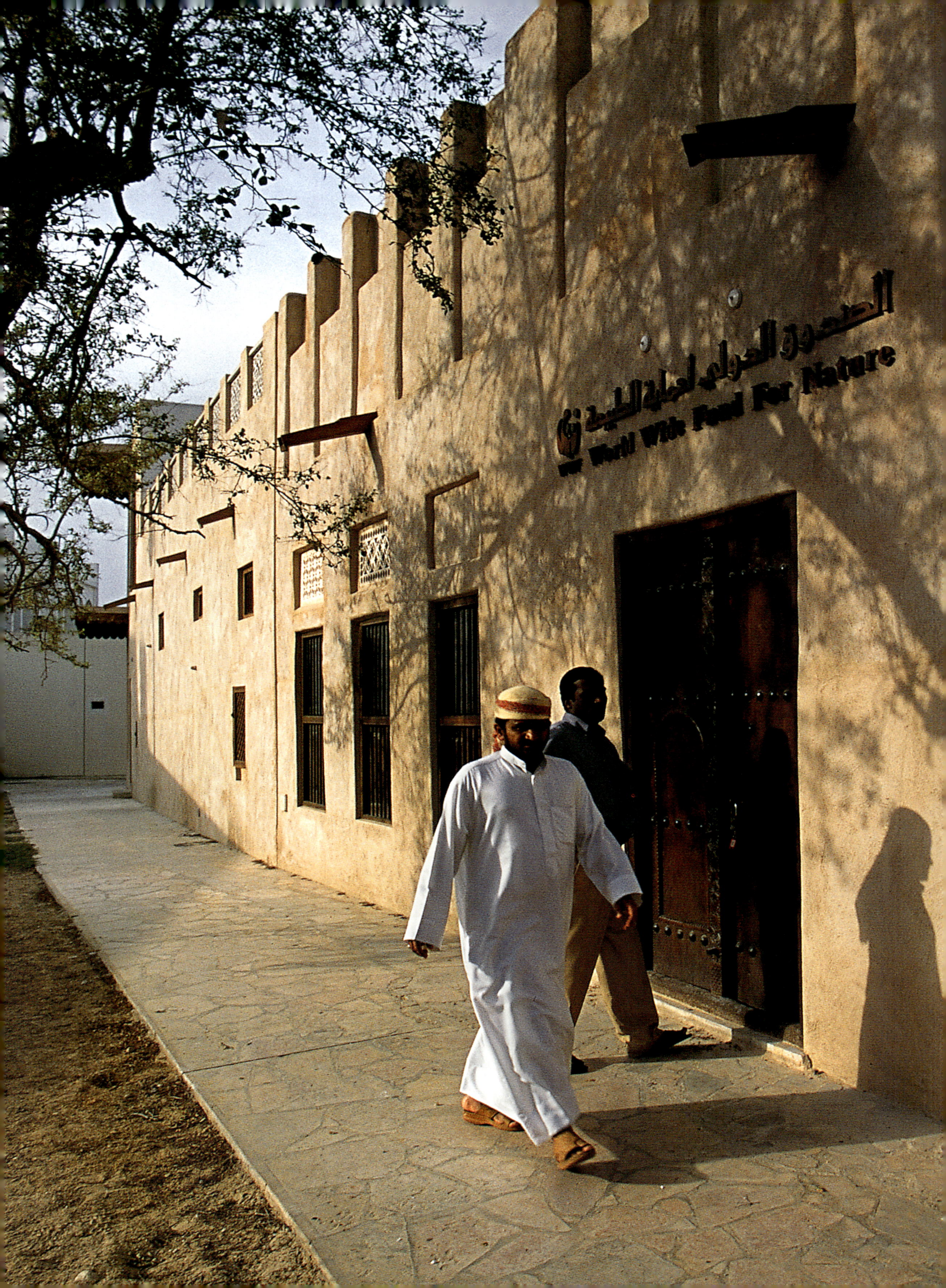
الصندوق الدولي لحماية الطبيعة
WWF World Wide Fund For Nature

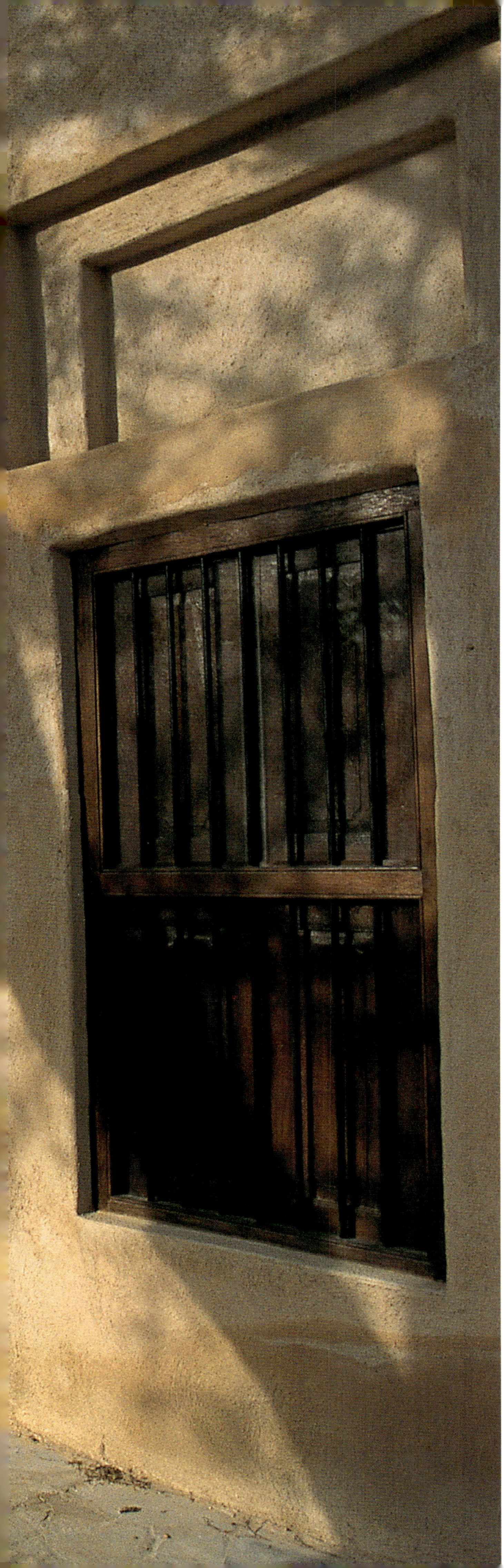

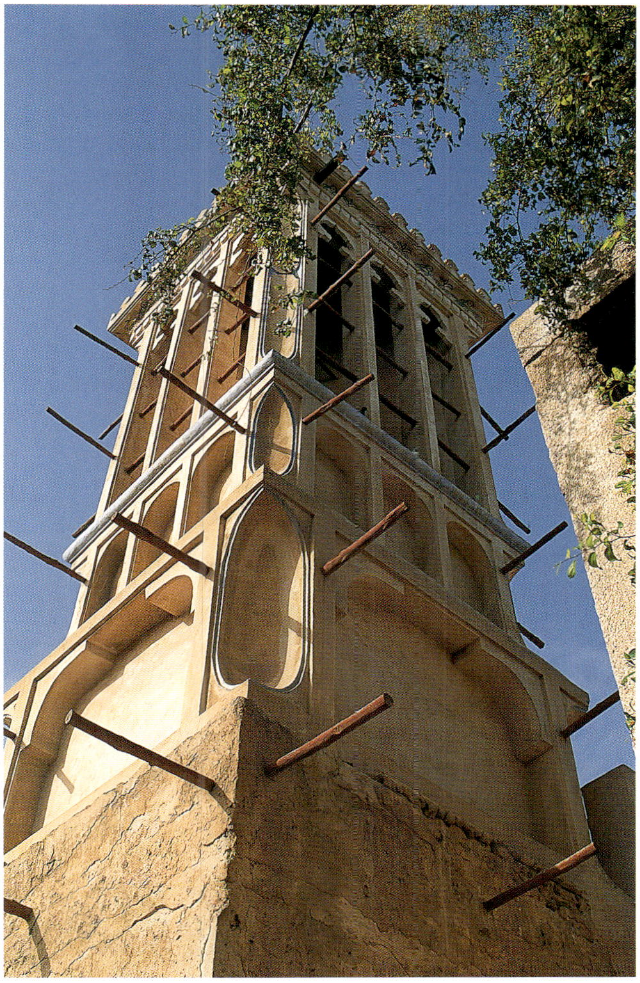

◄▲ Bastakiya, the former merchant area of Bur Dubai, to the east of Al Fahidi Fort, has distinctive traditional architecture featuring imposing houses with central courtyards and wind-towers. At one time, masses of towers lined the Creek. Today, many of the houses in Bastakiya have been carefully restored. *Photos by Dariush Zandi.*

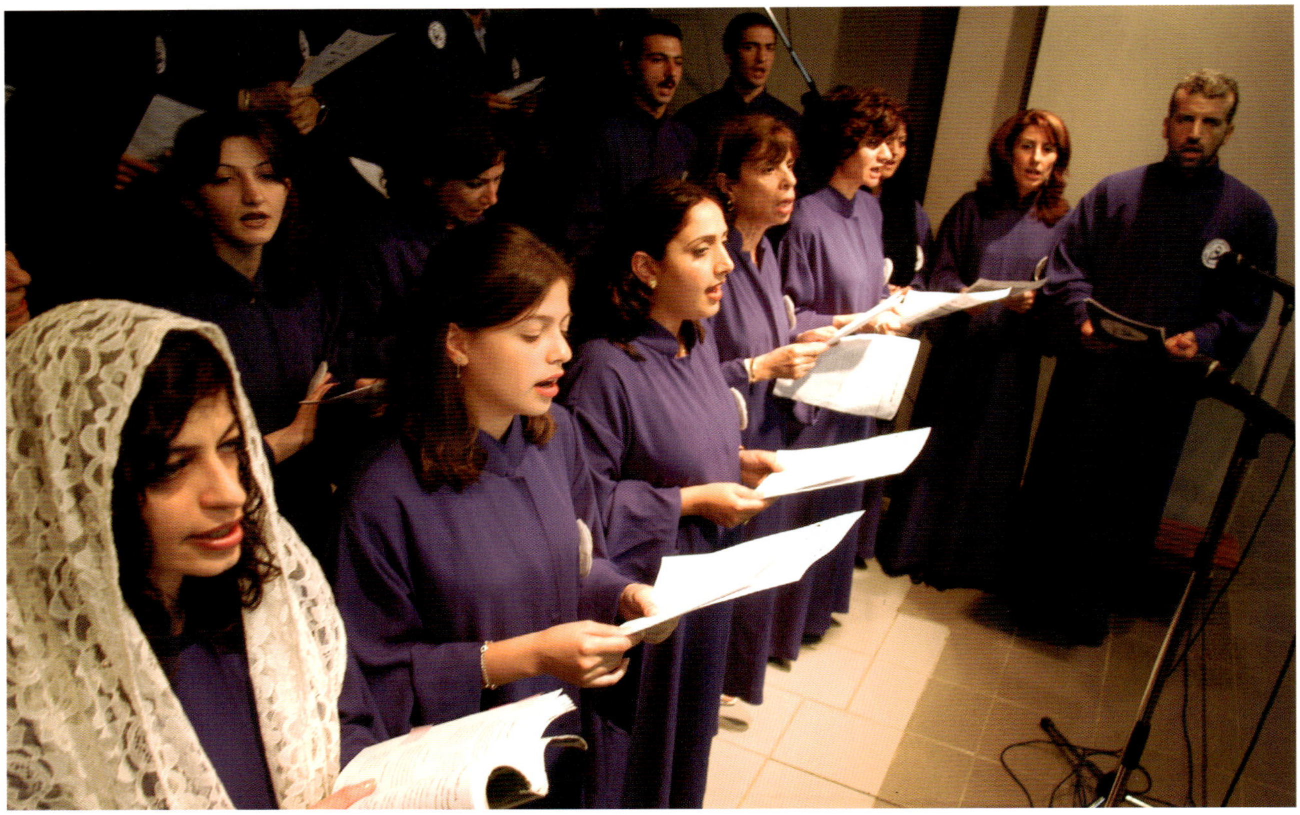

▲ ▶ ALTHOUGH ISLAM IS THE OFFICIAL RELIGION OF THE UAE (right), other religions are respected and Dubai has several Christian churches, including St Mary's (Roman Catholic) – where the above photo was taken – and Holy Trinity (interdenominational); both of which have services in Arabic and other languages. There are also two Hindu temples in Dubai. *Photos by Dariush Zandi.*

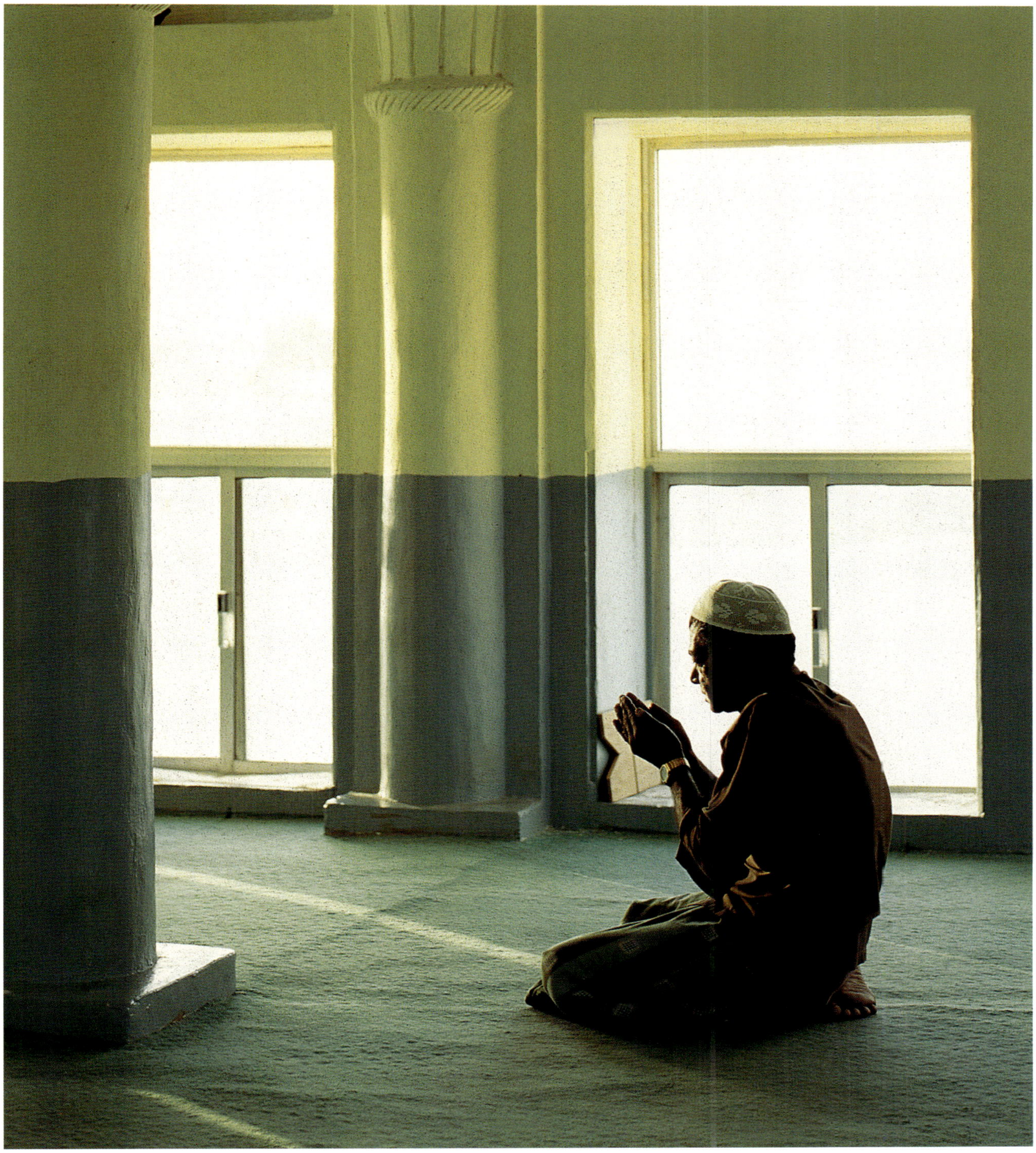

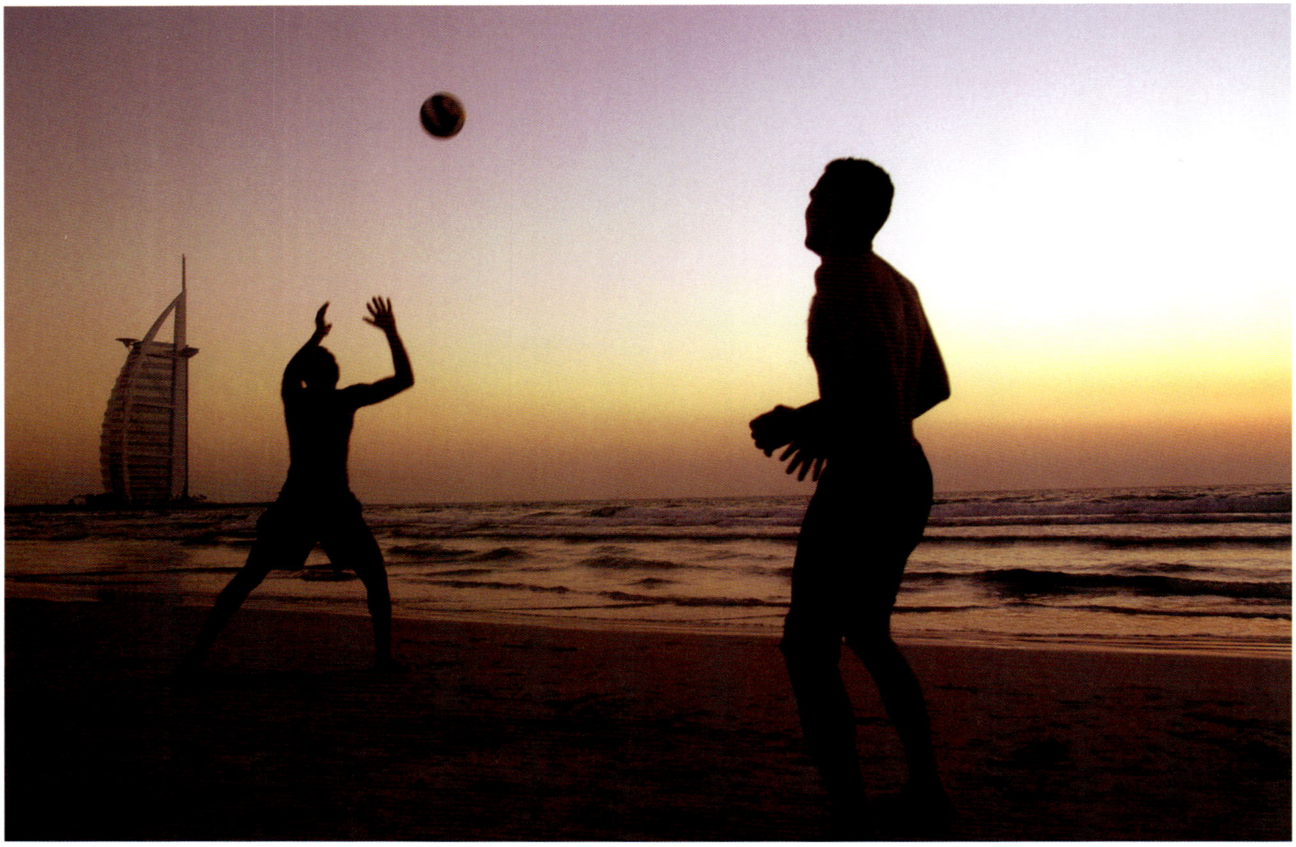

▲ ▶ One of Dubai's most compelling architectural icons, Jumeirah International's Burj Al Arab – or Arabian Tower – was completed in late 1999. It's shaped like a sail and rises 321 metres into the sky from a man-made island just off the city's popular Jumeirah Beach. The last word in luxury, Burj Al Arab is a hotel that aspires to be the best anywhere and is thought of locally as the only seven-star hotel in the world. *Photos by Jumeirah International.*

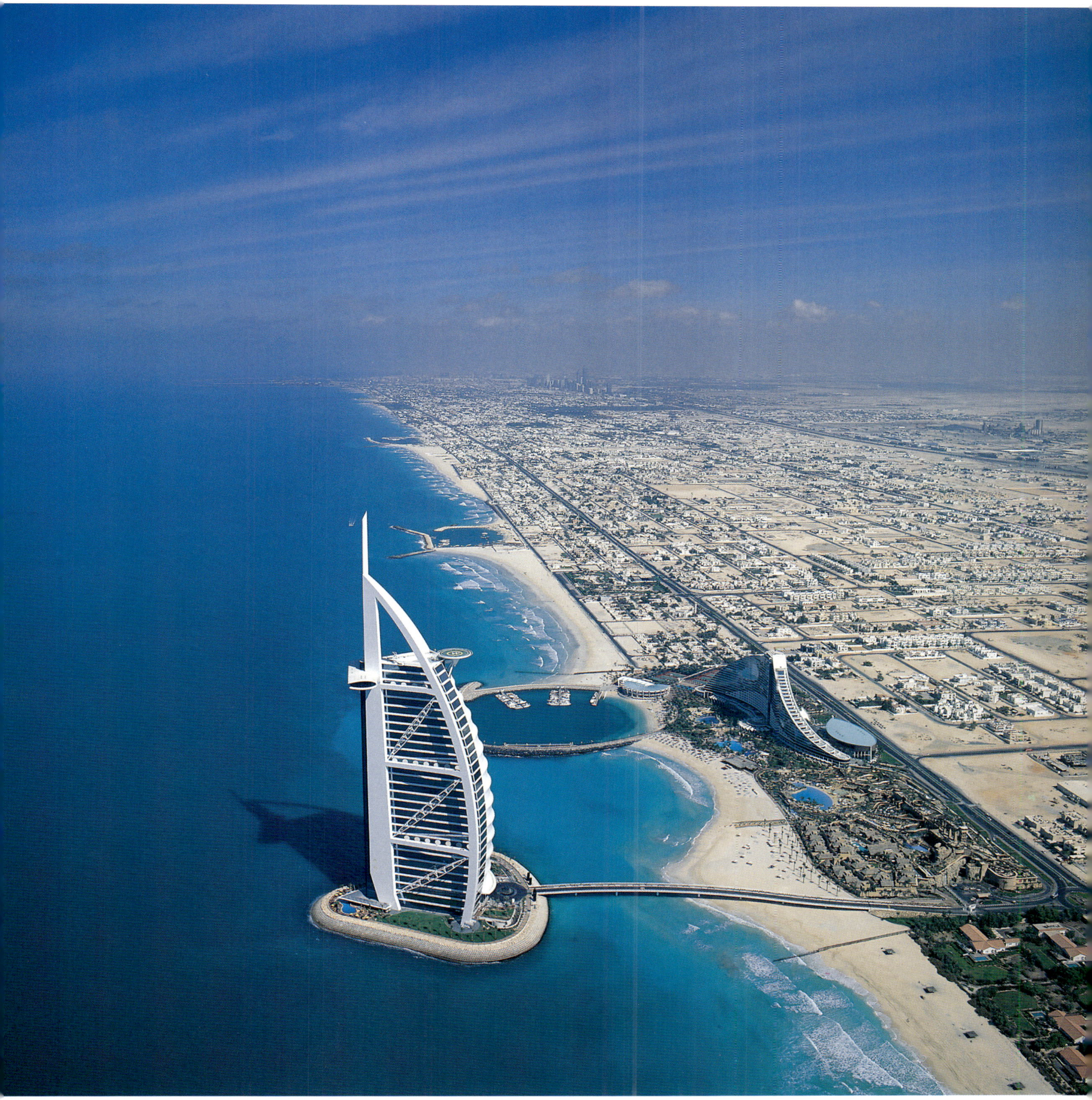

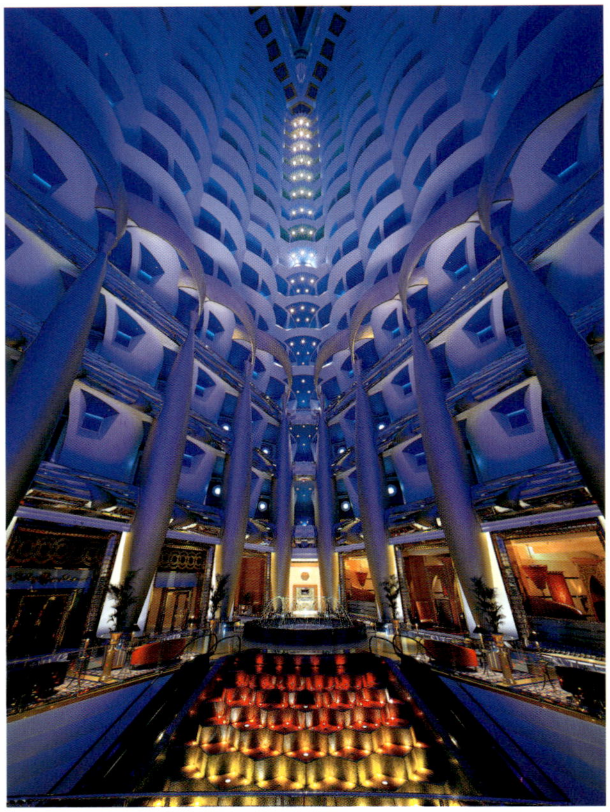

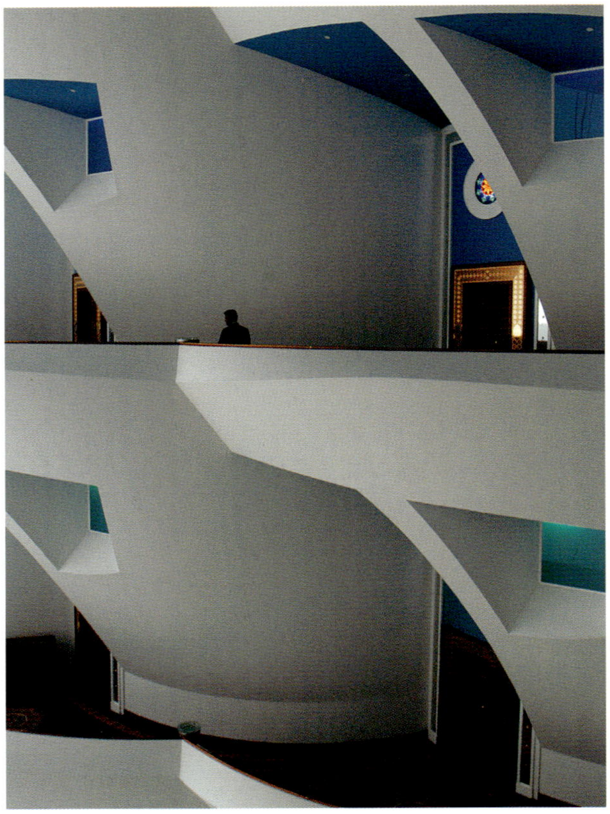

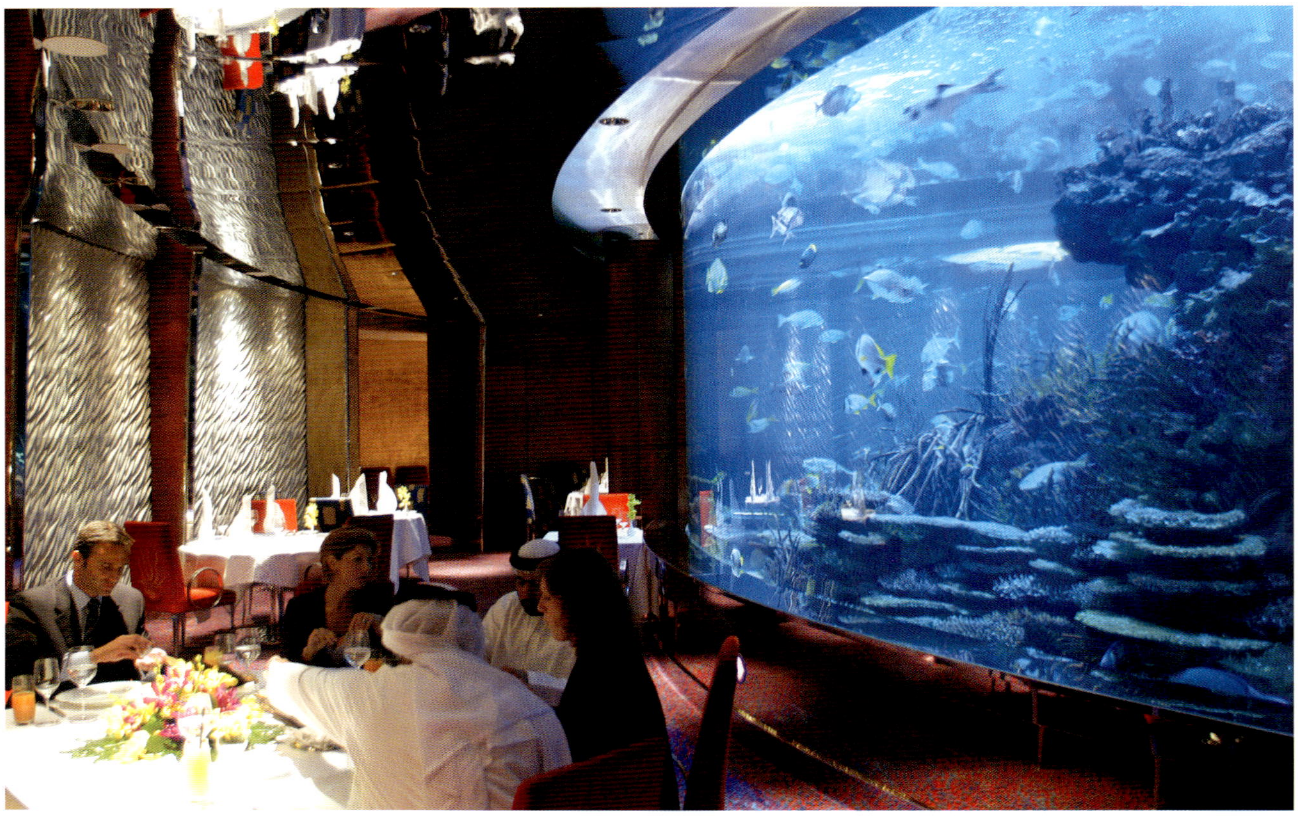

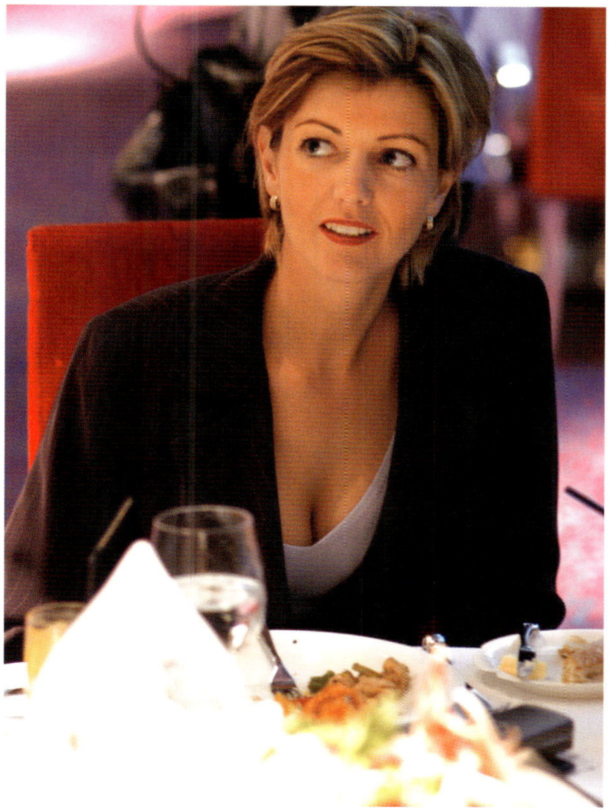

▲ BURJ AL ARAB'S CELEBRATED HOSPITALITY IS MATCHED by its passionate, multi-cultural team. Here, Sue Wheatley, during a lunch meeting with the Dubai Duty Free management, discusses a forthcoming international tennis tournament in the city. *Photo by Samar S Jodha.*

◀ BURJ AL ARAB'S INTERIOR, REMINISCENT OF *THE Thousand and One Nights,* offers a truly magical Arabian experience for guests and diners alike. Transporting you to another world, Al Mahara (The Shell) restaurant is where you can 'truly dine with the fish" (bottom left). *Photos by Jumeirah International (top left) and Samar S Jodha.*

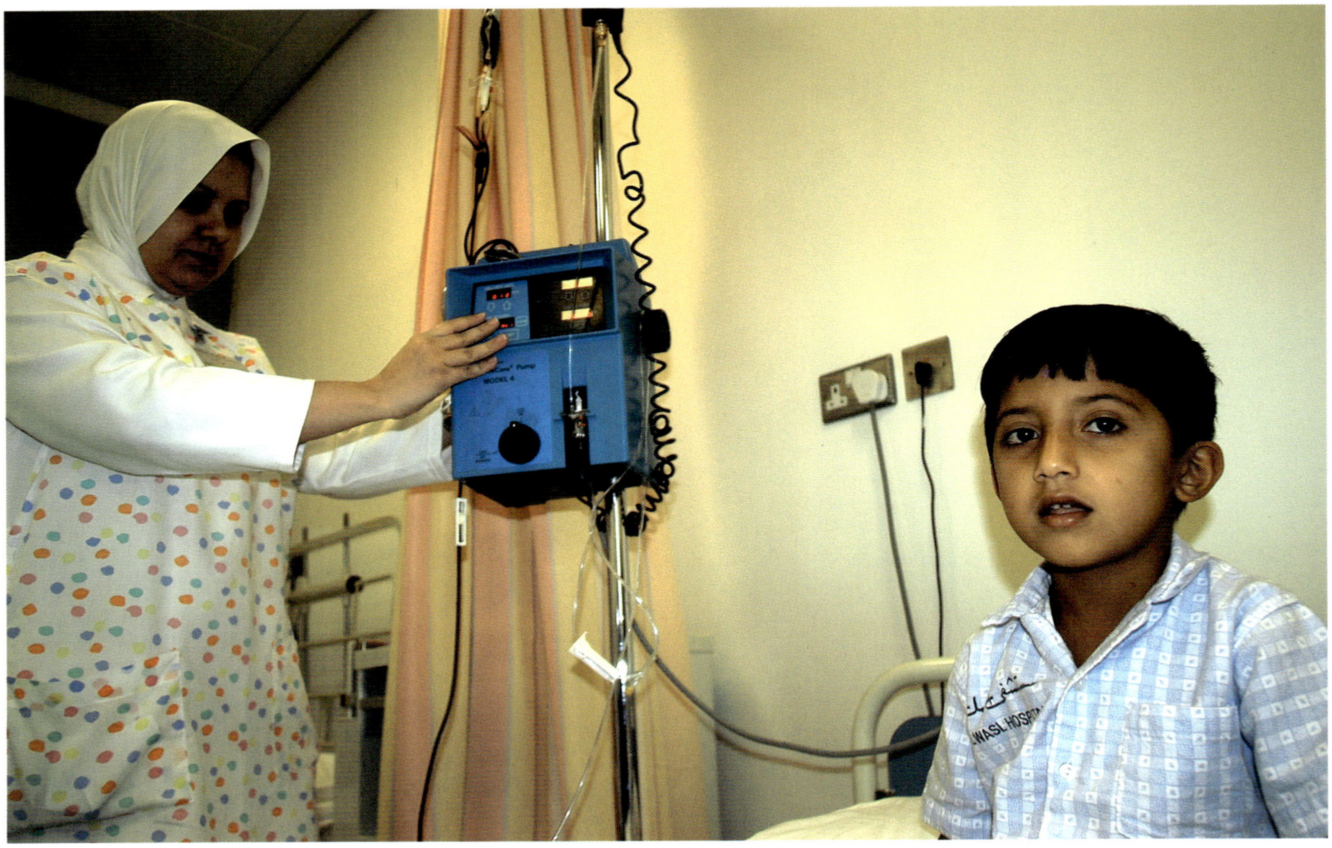

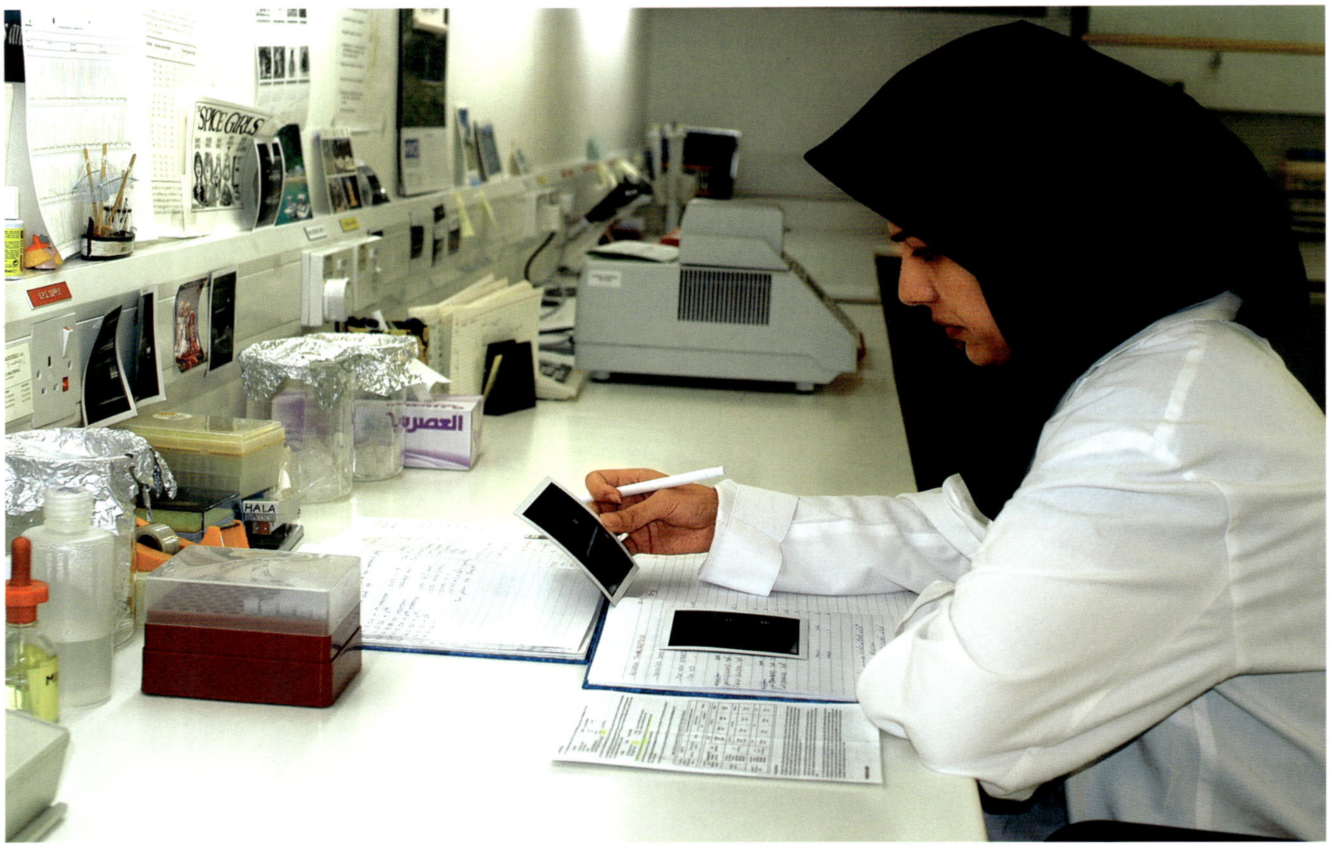
SPICE GIRLS
HALA

◀▶ Five-year old Mohammed Abdul Hameed receives a blood transfusion at the Al Wasl Hospital Thalessemia unit (left top) while his sisters 12-year old Khadija Abdul Hameed (right top) and seven-year old Fatima Abdul Hameed (right bottom) undergo the same procedure. The children come to receive blood for several hours every three weeks; there's obviously some discomfort, but little pain, and they seem remarkably stoic, almost like angels all things considered. The UAE suffers from one of the highest rates of this incurable genetic disease and it can be fatal if left untreated. Patients come to the hospital from the other emirates and Gulf states because Al Wasl – with its Centre for Arab Genomic Studies – is considered to have the best facilities in the region. Mahnaz Zeinali is one of the dedicated research workers at the Genetic Unit of the hospital (left bottom). *Photos by Dariush Zandi.*

▶▶ Nuha Al Safar at her desk, where she sports a collection of delicate glass spheres filled with snowflakes. Nuha is the Deputy Chief Co-ordinator of the 'Dubai – the City that Cares' campaign and has headed 'Events and Promotional Campaigns' for the Dubai Chamber of Commerce and Industry. *Photo Souheil Semaan.*

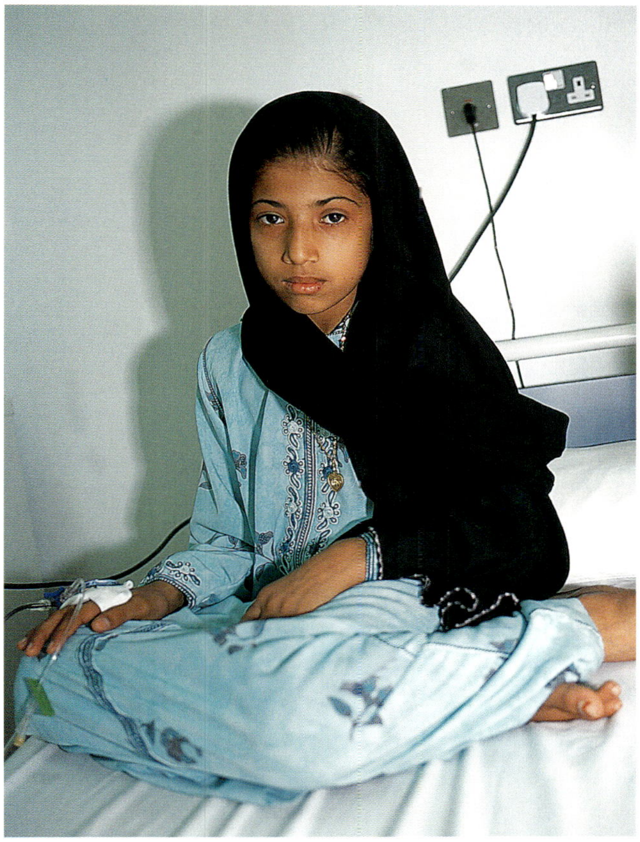

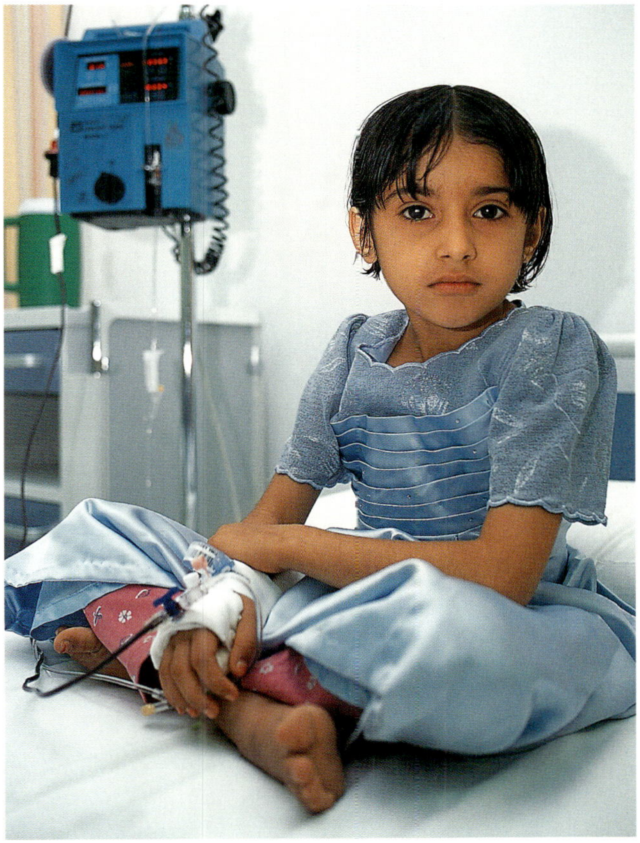

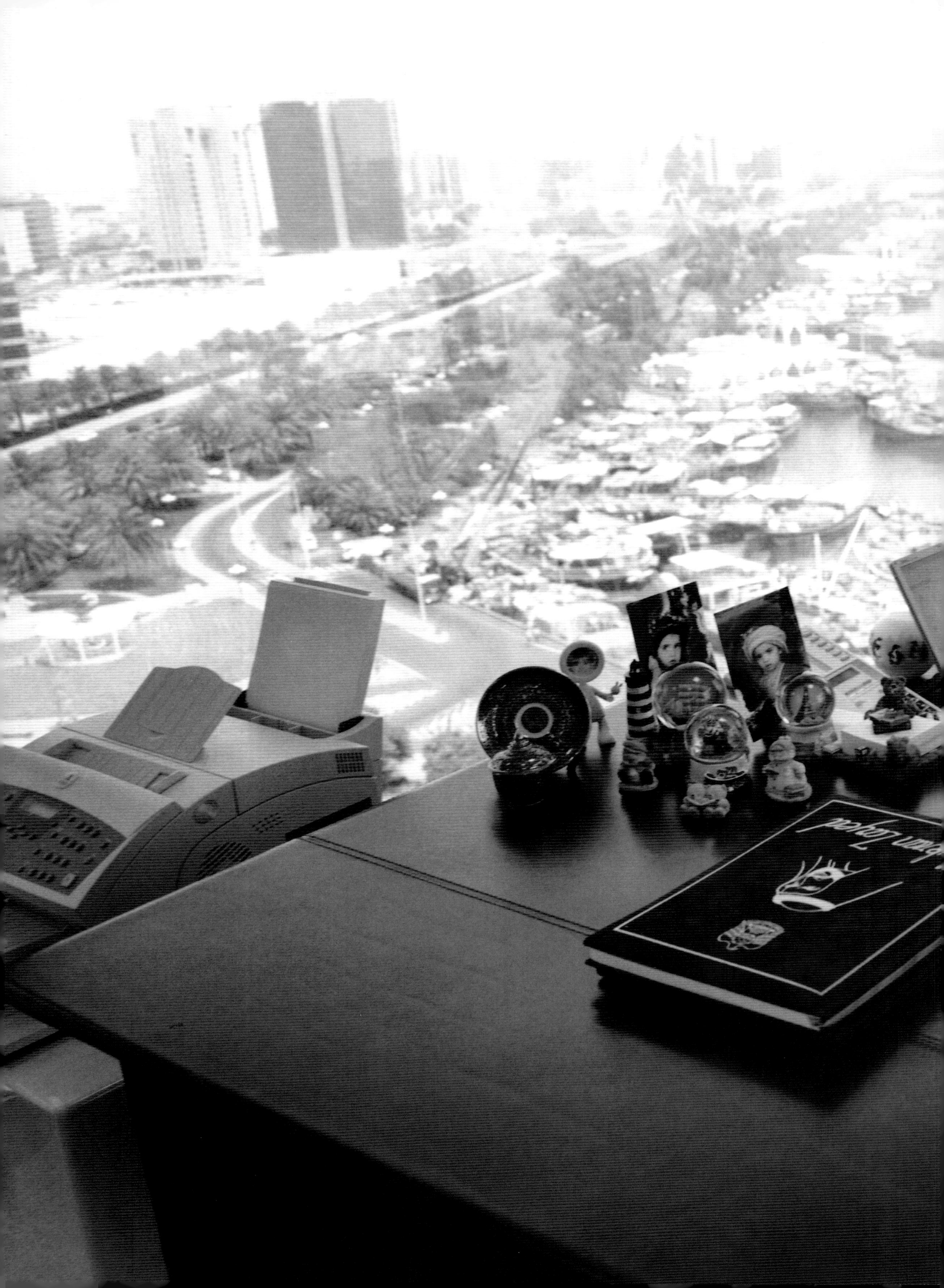

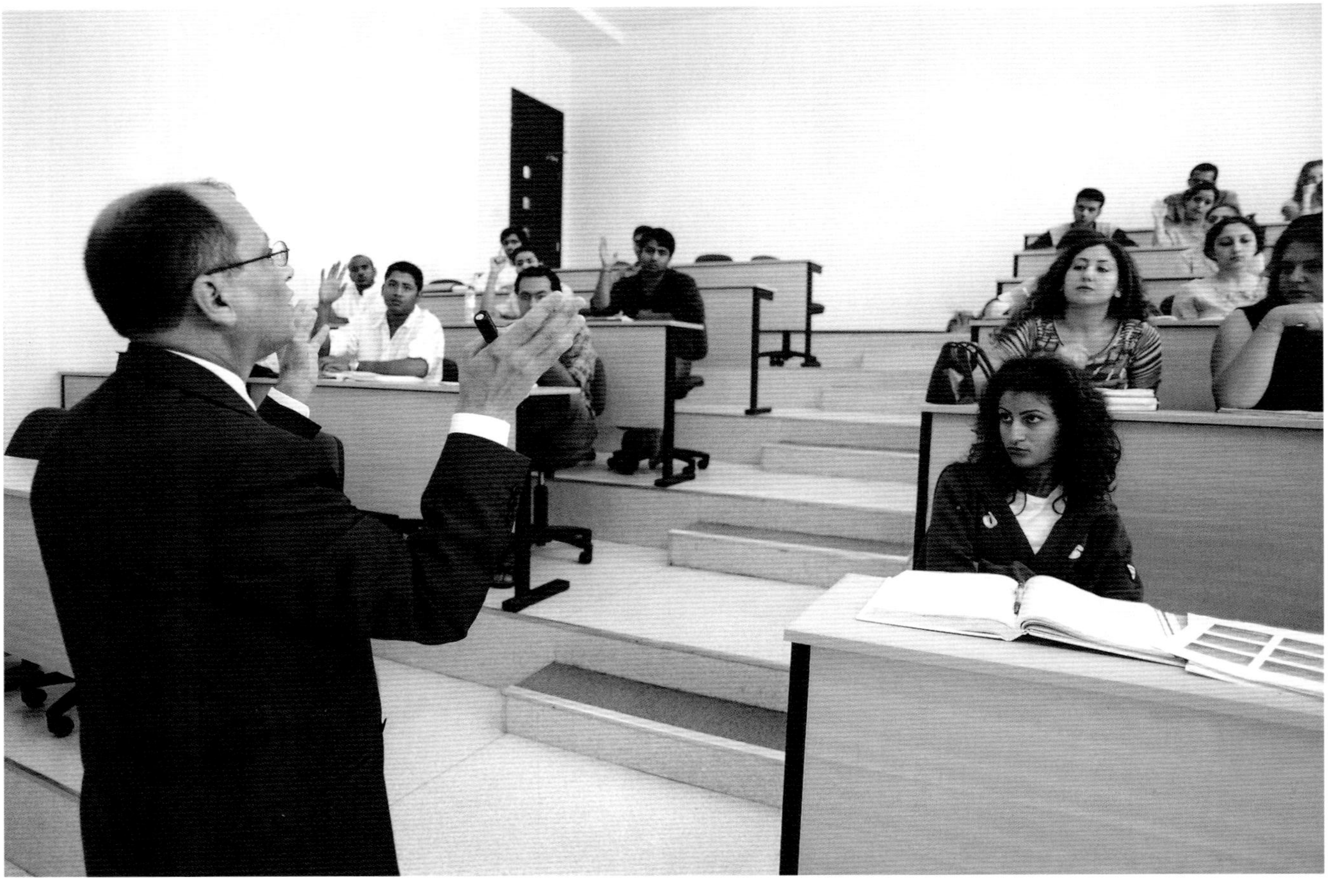

▲ LANCE DE MASSI, PRESIDENT AND CHIEF ACADEMIC Officer at the American University of Dubai, lectures on advertising and global marketing, a subject that has become key to Dubai's commercial success. In fact, Dubai is considered as the advertising capital of the Middle East.

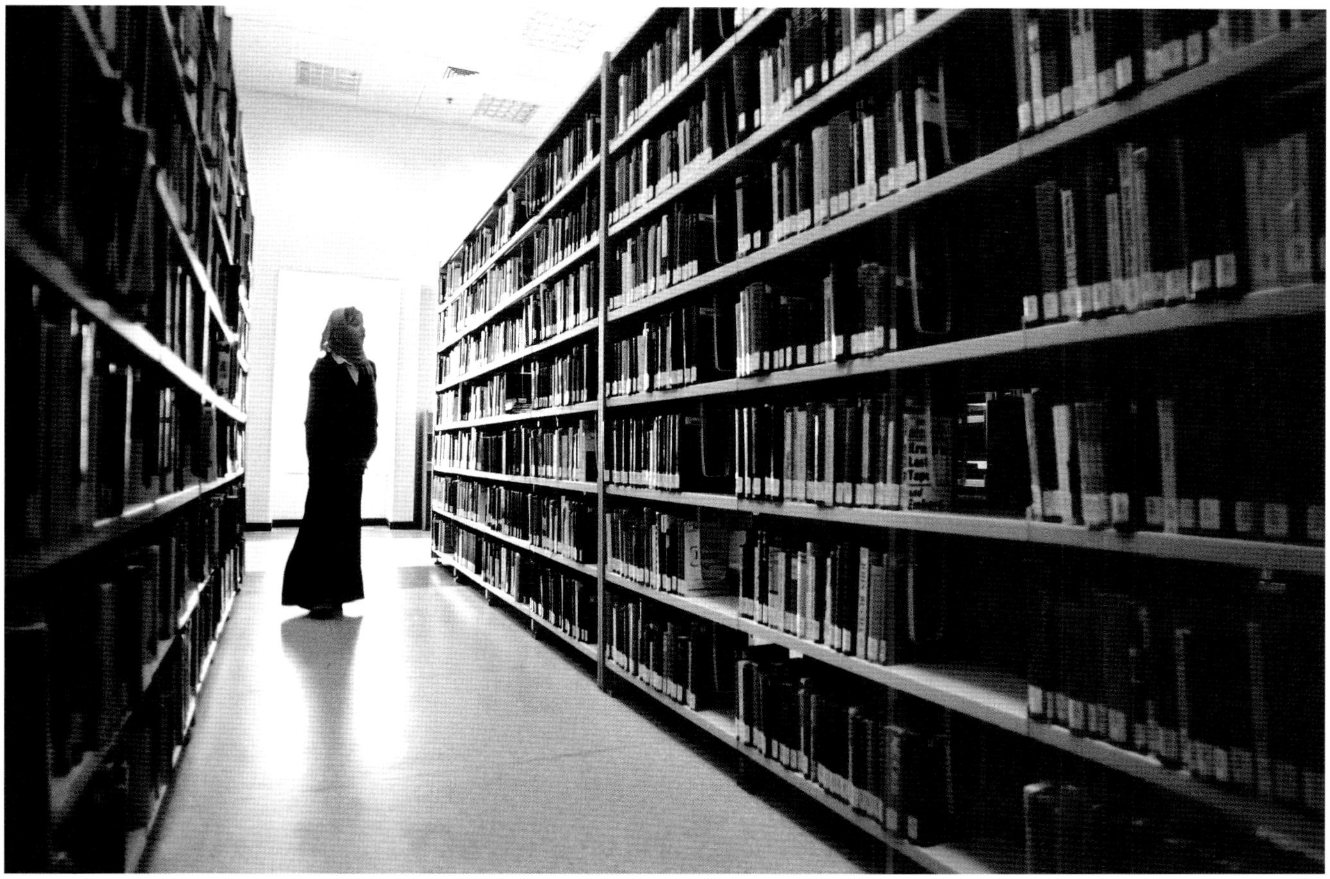

▲ A STUDENT WANDERS THROUGH THE LIBRARY AT THE American University of Dubai. The university is the first and only American-accredited university in the Gulf and serves UAE nationals and international students seeking career-oriented education. *Photos by Katarina Premfors.*

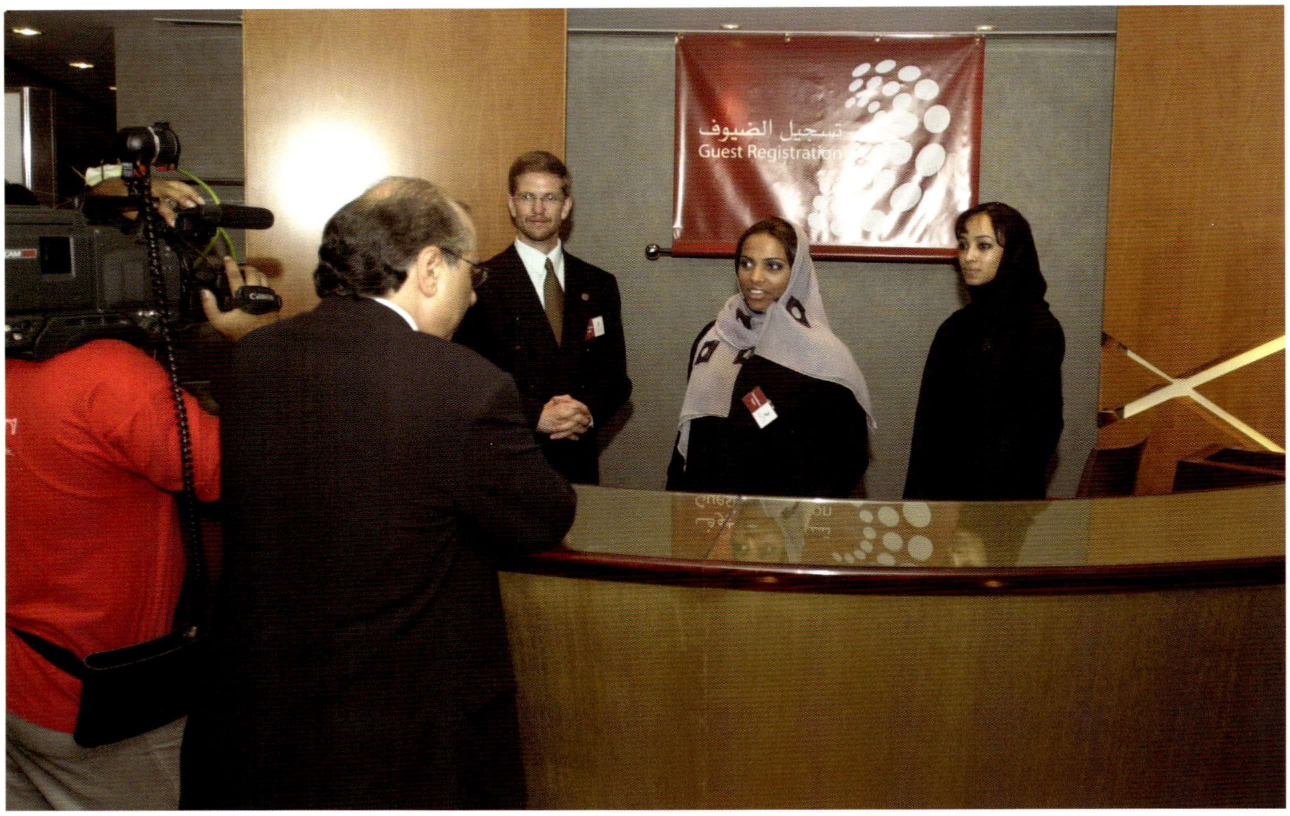
تسجيل الضيوف
Guest Registration

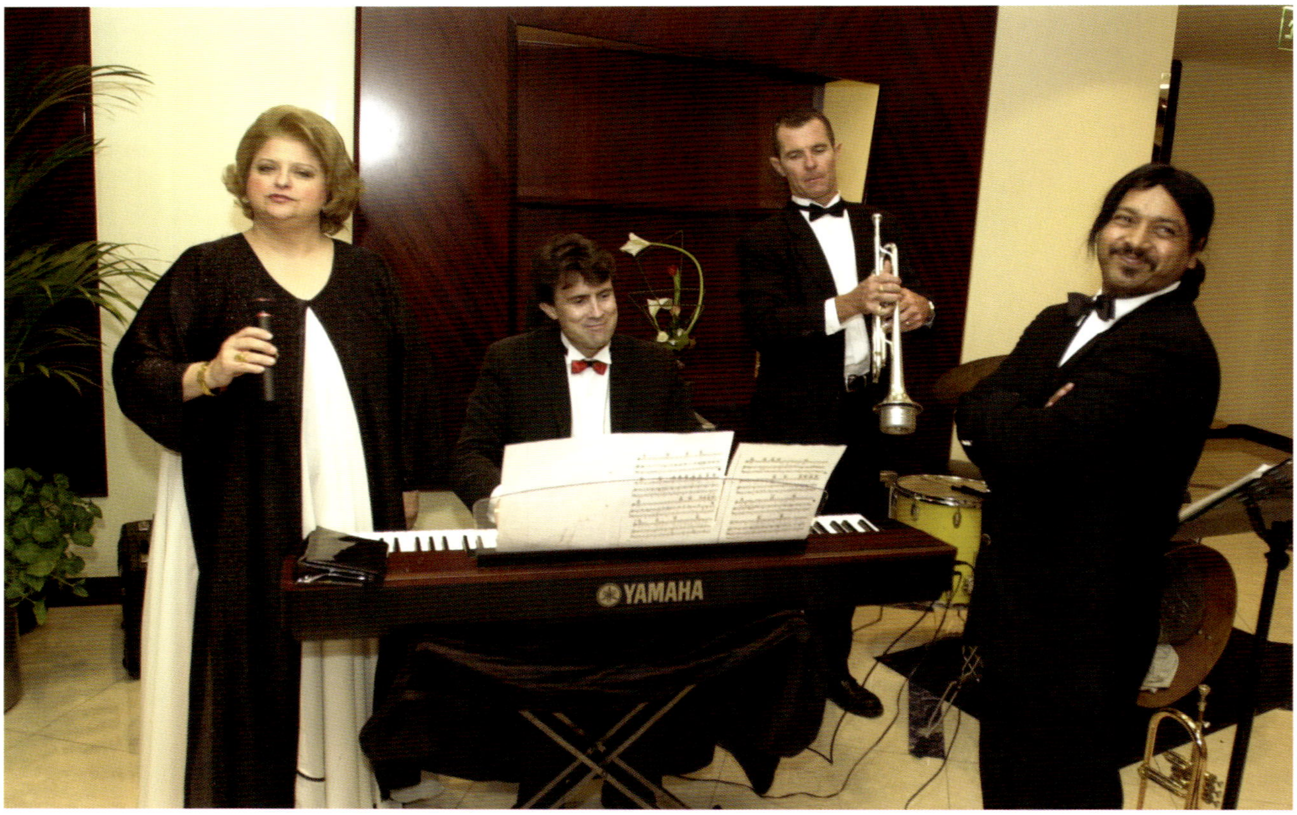
YAMAHA

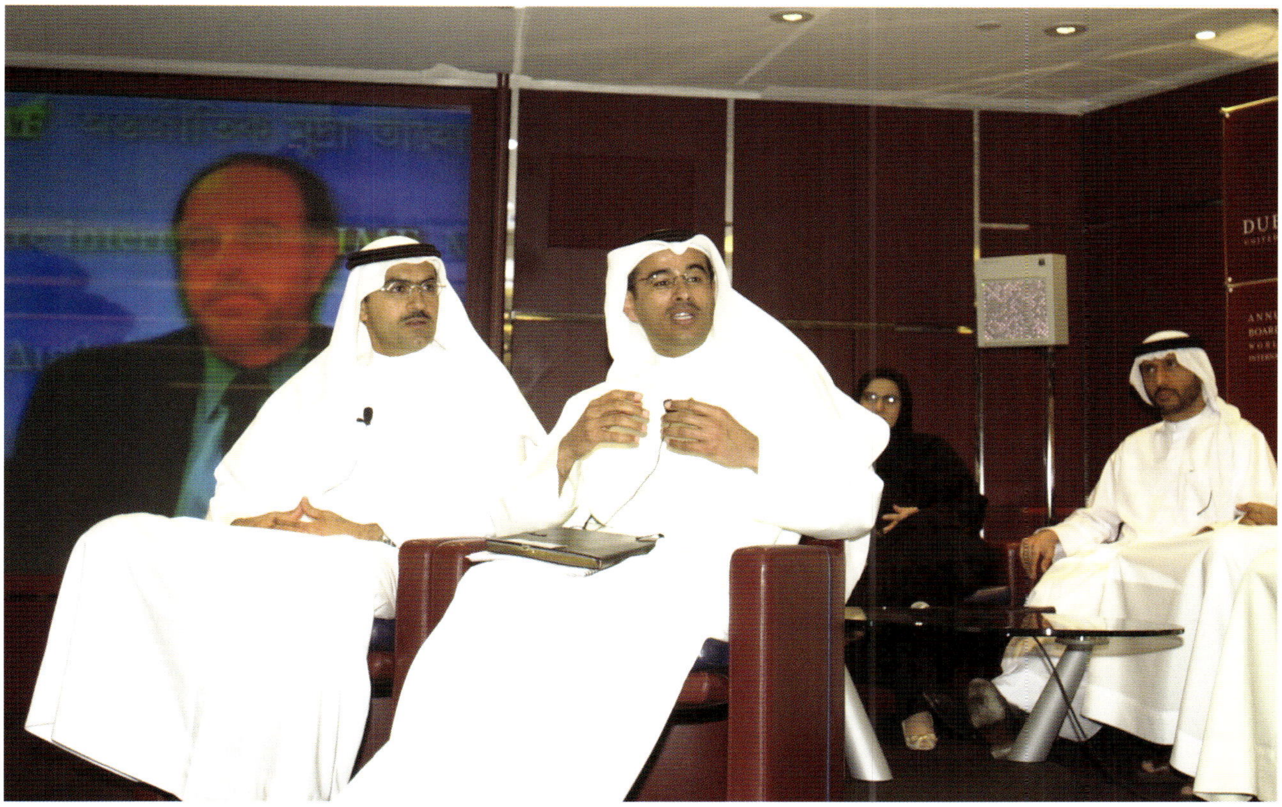

▲ Dubai, 15 June 2003: Dubai 2003 holds a press conference to mark the 100-day countdown to the Annual Meetings of the Boards of Governors of the World Bank Group and the International Monetary Fund (IMF) in September. Ibrahim Belselah, General Coordinator of Dubai 2003, and Mohamed Ali Alabbar, Director General of the Dubai Department of Economic Development and Chairman of Emaar properties, during their brief to the international media. Dubai 2003 committee members briefed attendees on the progress made in organising the world's most influential financial meetings. The UAE and Dubai were selected because of their highly developed transportation and logistics infrastructure, their growing importance as a financial hub and their established position as an oasis of opportunity. The United Arab Emirates' hosting of the Annual Meetings mark the first time they were held in an Arab country.

◄ At least 200 journalists and television crews from all round the world, including a *Dubai 24 hours* film crew, attended the media event, which included live entertainment. *Photos by Mohammed Hisham,* Al Bayan.

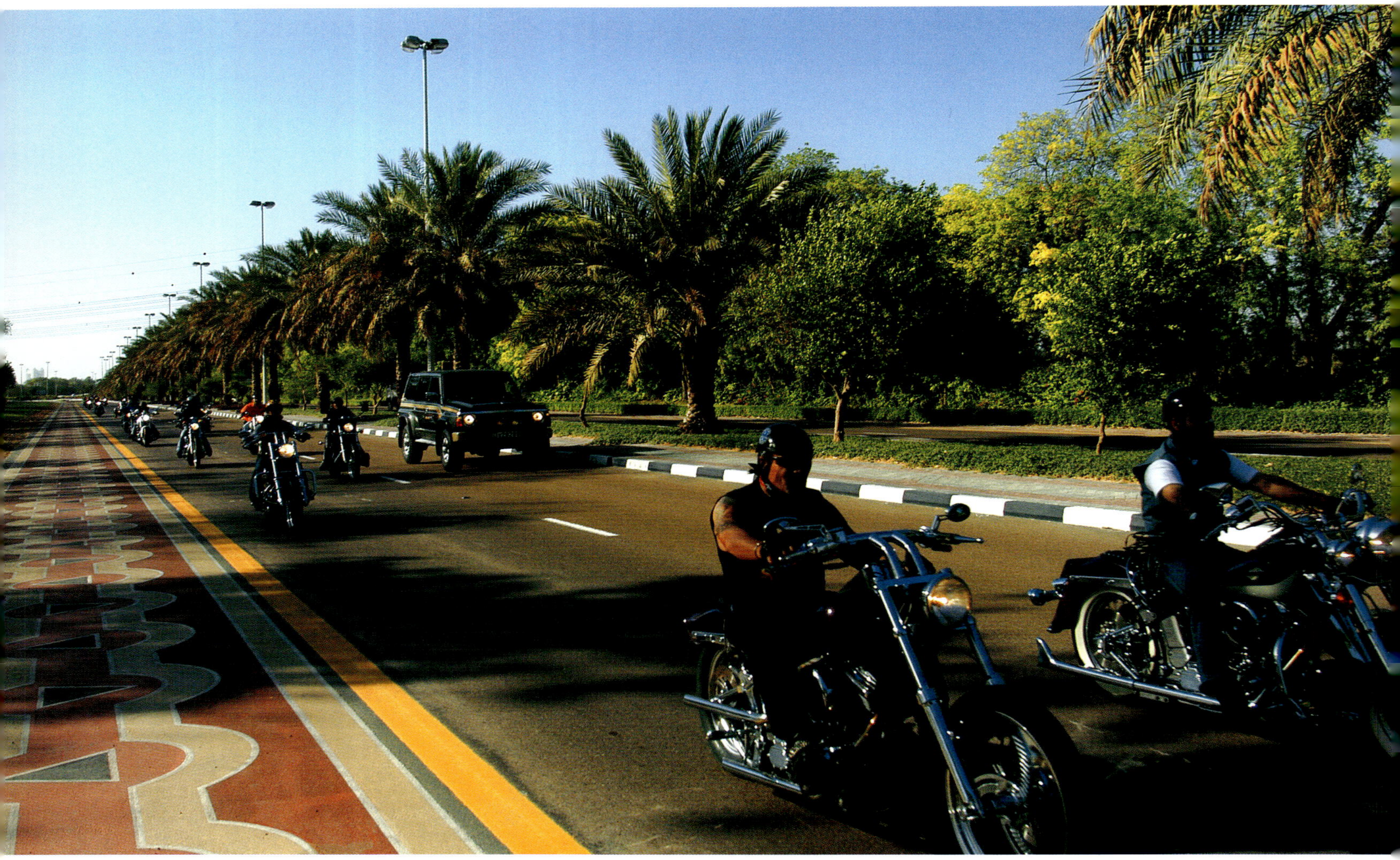

▲ ▶ Men will be men and from New York to New Zealand, and Dublin to Dubai, the Harley-Davidson heavy metal exerts its mystique. The Harley boys of Dubai – seen here on their way into Oman – include some unexpected professionals. A typical group may encompass as many as 20–45 bikers. *Photos by Samar S Jodha.*

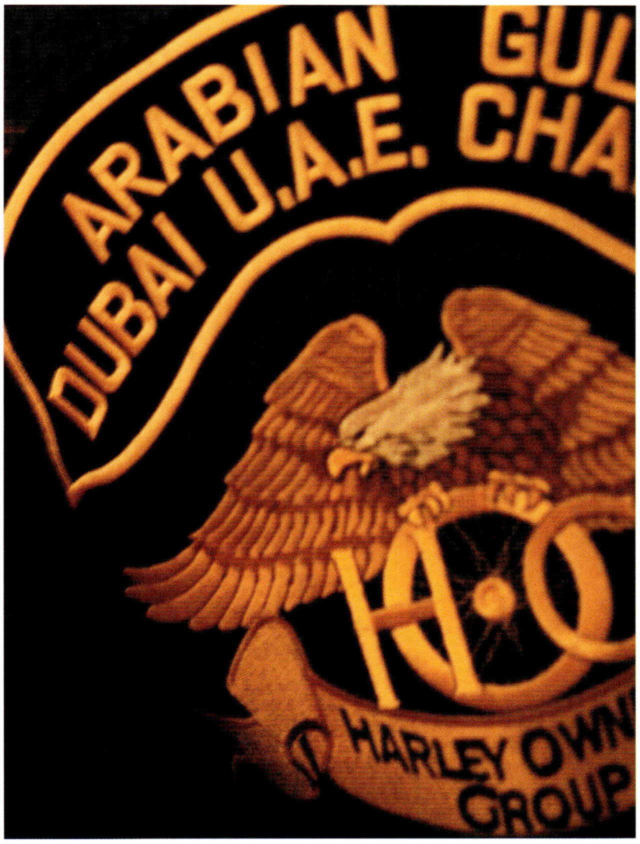
ARABIAN
DUBAI U.A.E.
HARLEY
GROUP

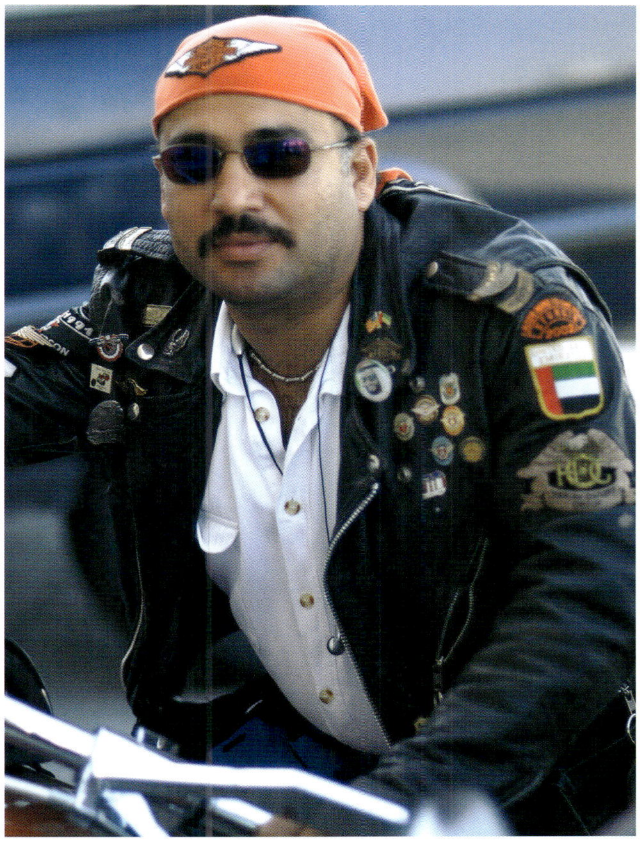

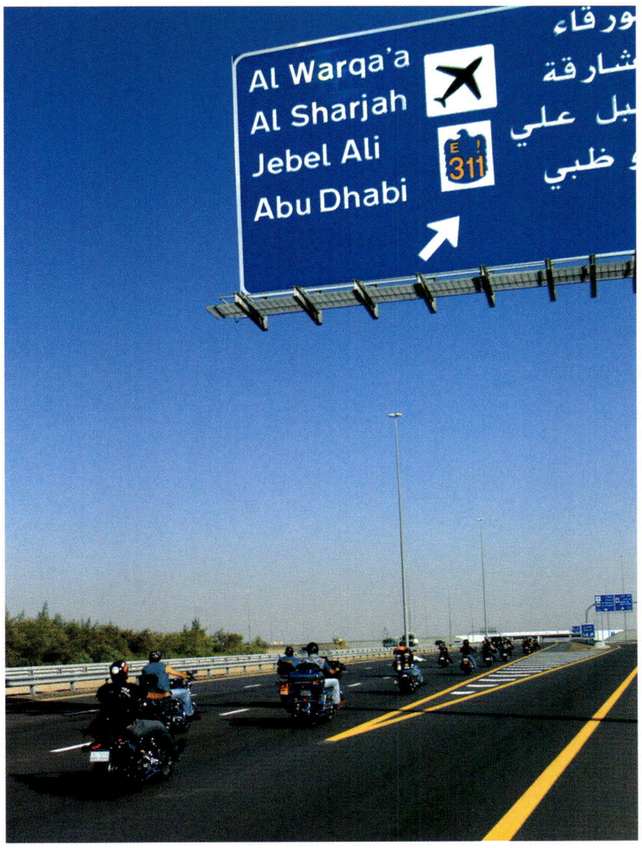
Al Warqa'a
Al Sharjah
Jebel Ali
Abu Dhabi
311

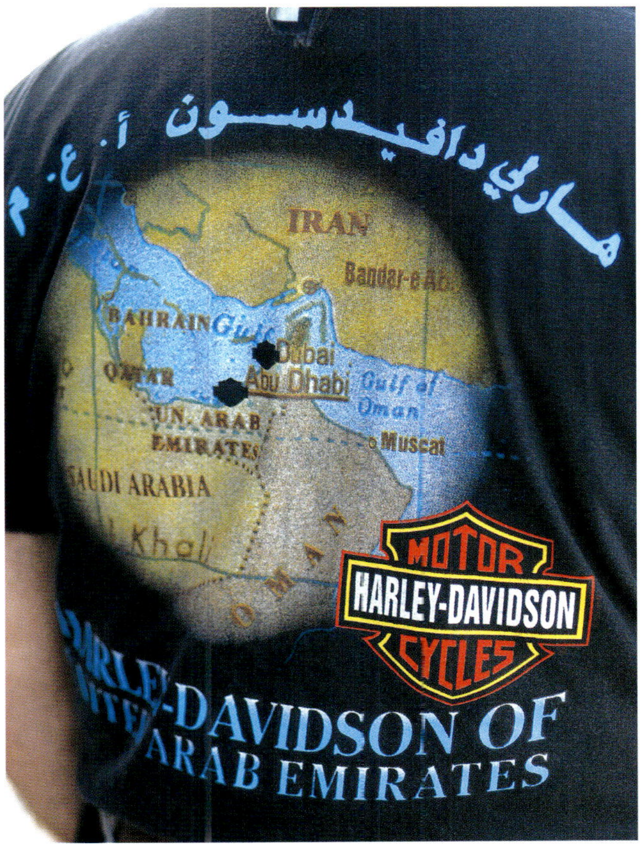
IRAN
BAHRAIN
QATAR
Dubai
Abu Dhabi
Gulf of Oman
U.N. ARAB EMIRATES
Muscat
MOTOR
HARLEY-DAVIDSON
CYCLES
DAVIDSON OF
ARAB EMIRATES

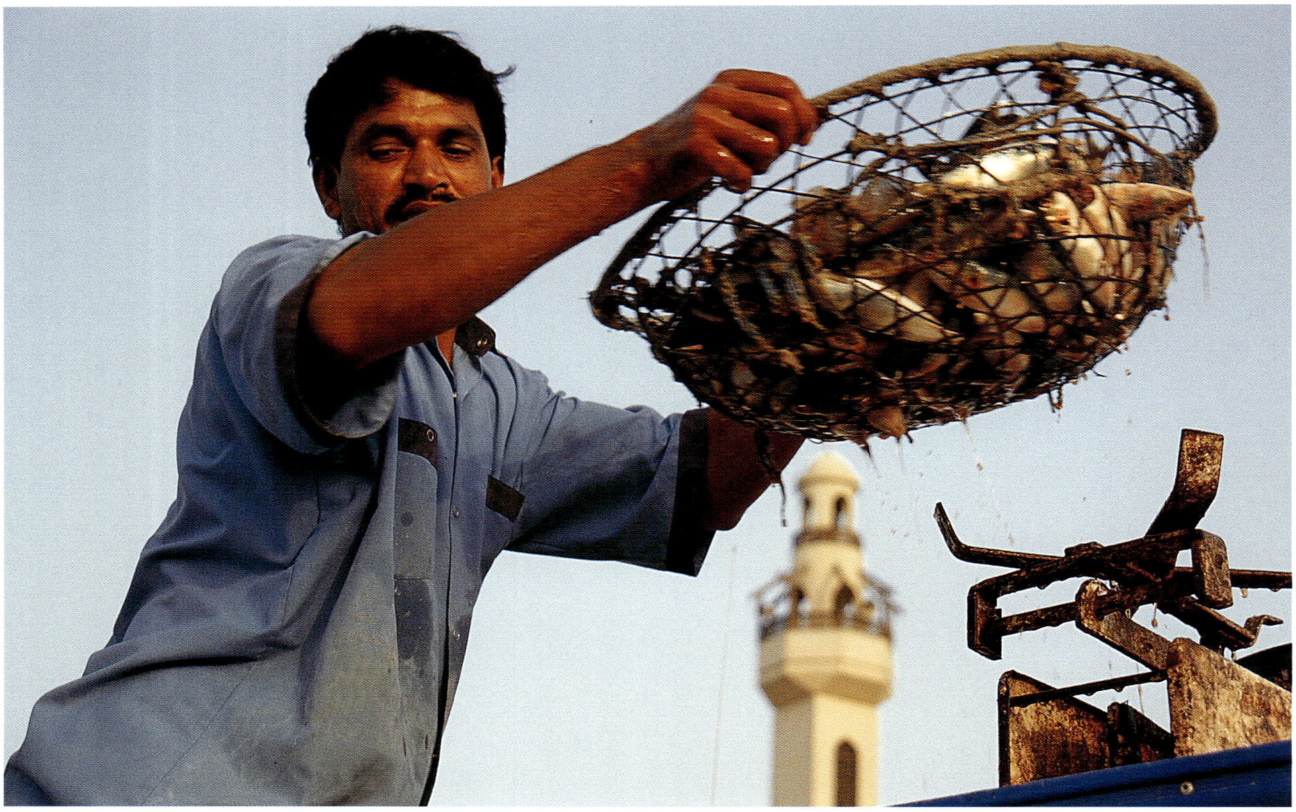

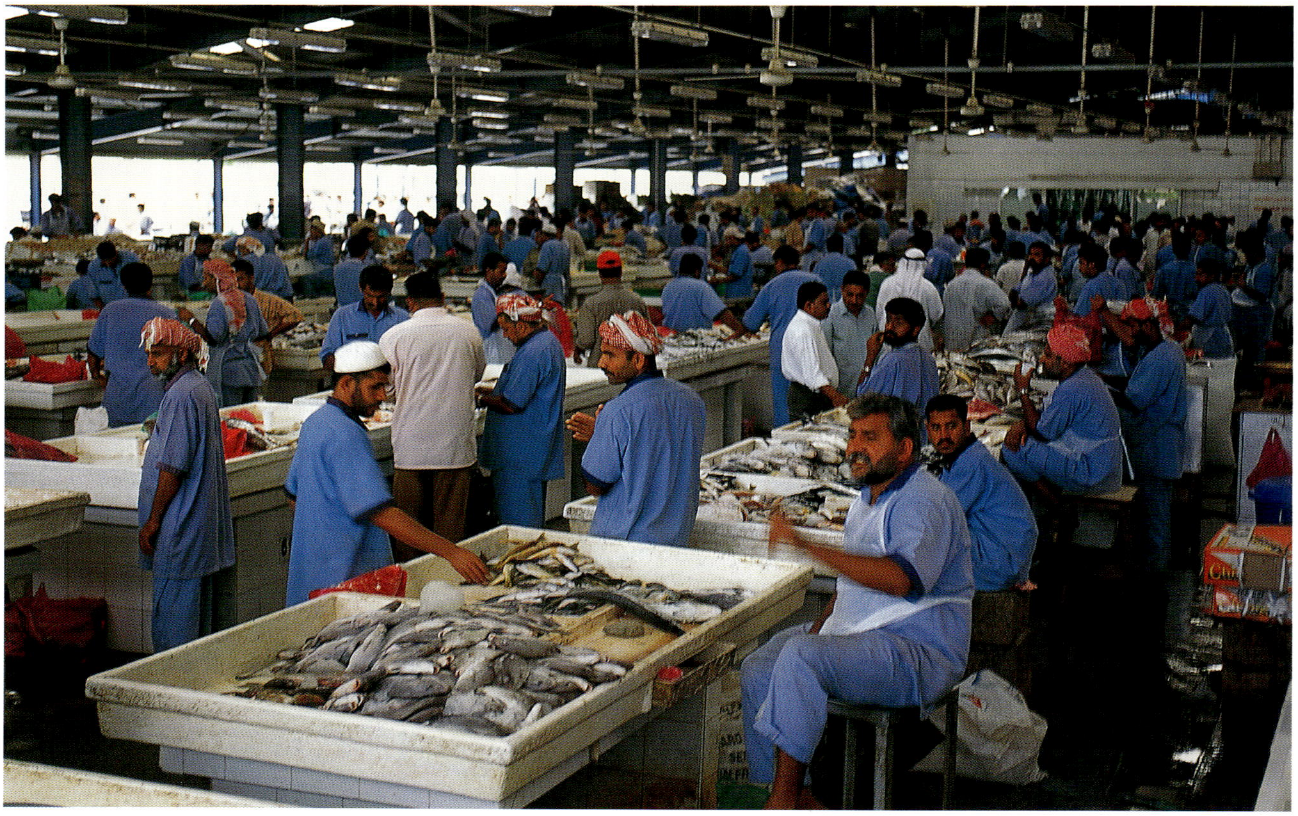

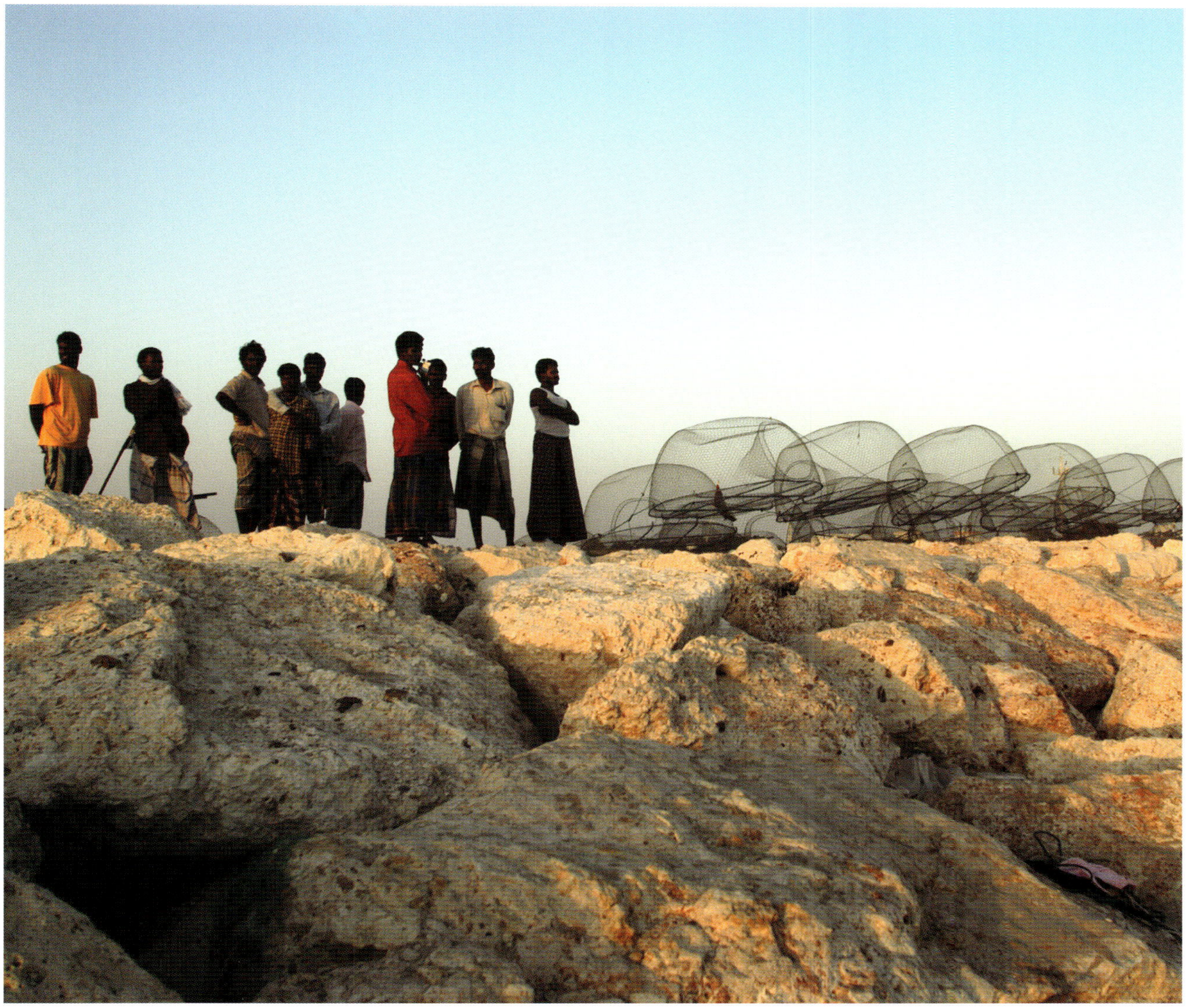

▲ EARLY ONE MORNING, FISHERMEN GATHER ON THE breakwater of one of Dubai's small fishing harbours. Stacked next to them are their traditional *gargours* or fish traps. The variety of species in the Arabian Gulf and Gulf of Oman includes lobster, prawns, shrimps, crab, kingfish, tuna, pomfret and the delicious local favourite *hammour* (rock cod). *Photo by Samar S Jodha.*

◄ AT THE COLOURFUL FISH MARKET AT SHINDAGHA, workers sort out the day's catch. Quotas on many species have been imposed, as local fisheries have begun to witness serious declines, not unlike those throughout the world. *Photos by Paul MacLeod (top) and Dariush Zandi (bottom).*

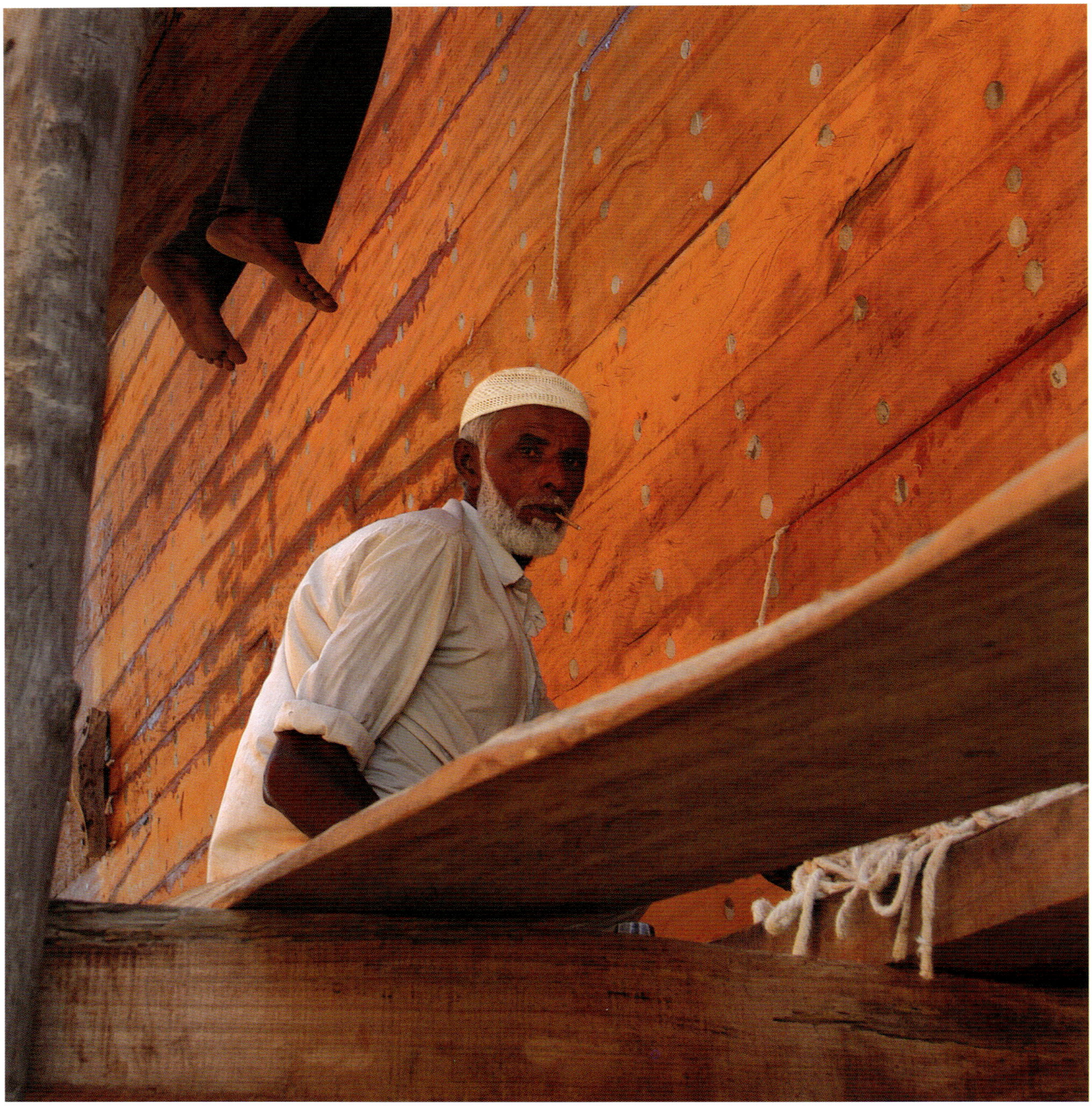

▲ ▶ BABA SAEED, A VETERAN OF *AL QALAFA*, OR DHOW-building, poses beside an enormous hull of a dhow being built in the Jaddaf district, near Al Garhoud Bridge. Dubai-born Saeed used to use the sun (and, he says, "coffee beans") to help him position his boats, which he's skippered from Mombasa to Mumbai. Today, teak is still the choice material but engines have replaced sails. Prior to the introduction of nails, these hulls were sewn together with hardened fibre from palm fronds. These days, the large dhows may be 20 metres in length and weigh as much as 1,400 tonnes. During weekends in winter, large fleets of elegant racing dhows sail against each other, while there are also special races for long, narrow rowing dhows with up to 100 oarsmen in each. *Photos Samar S Jodha.*

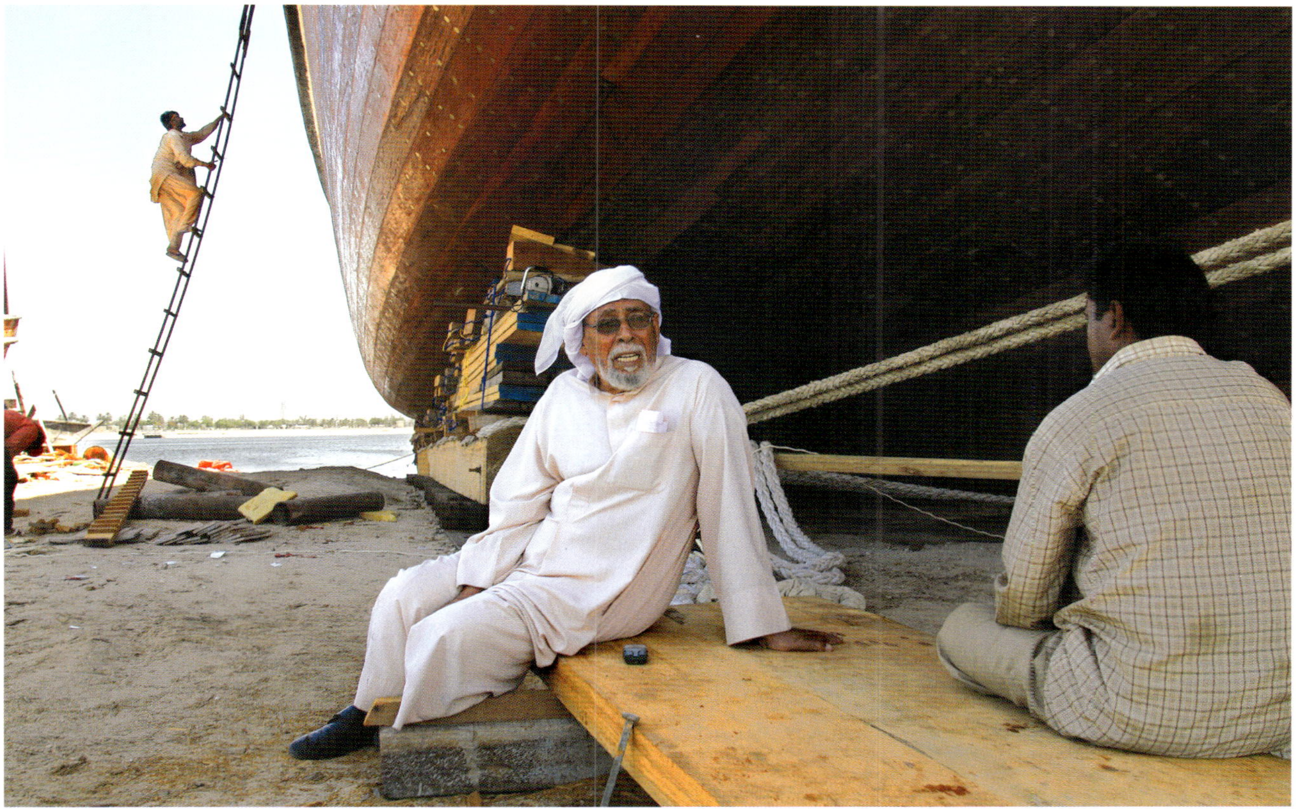

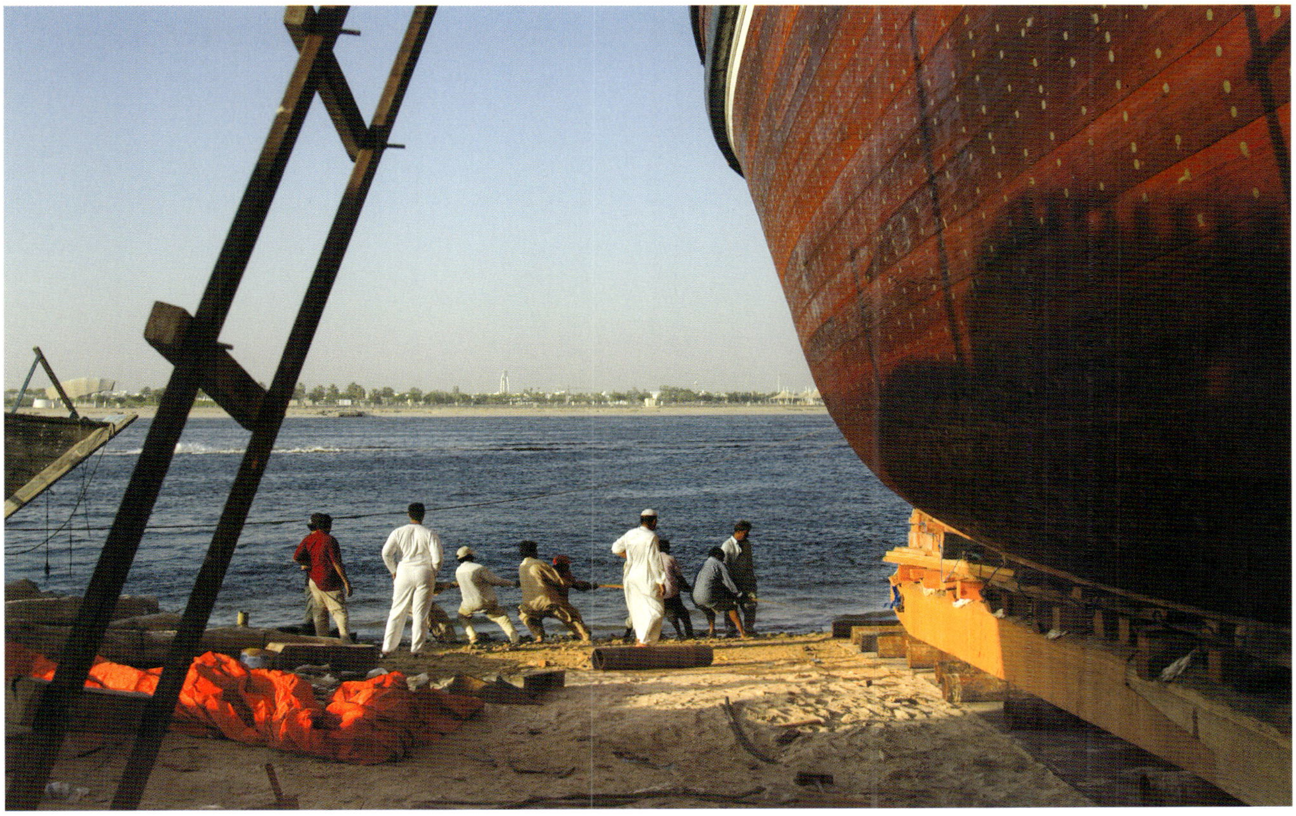

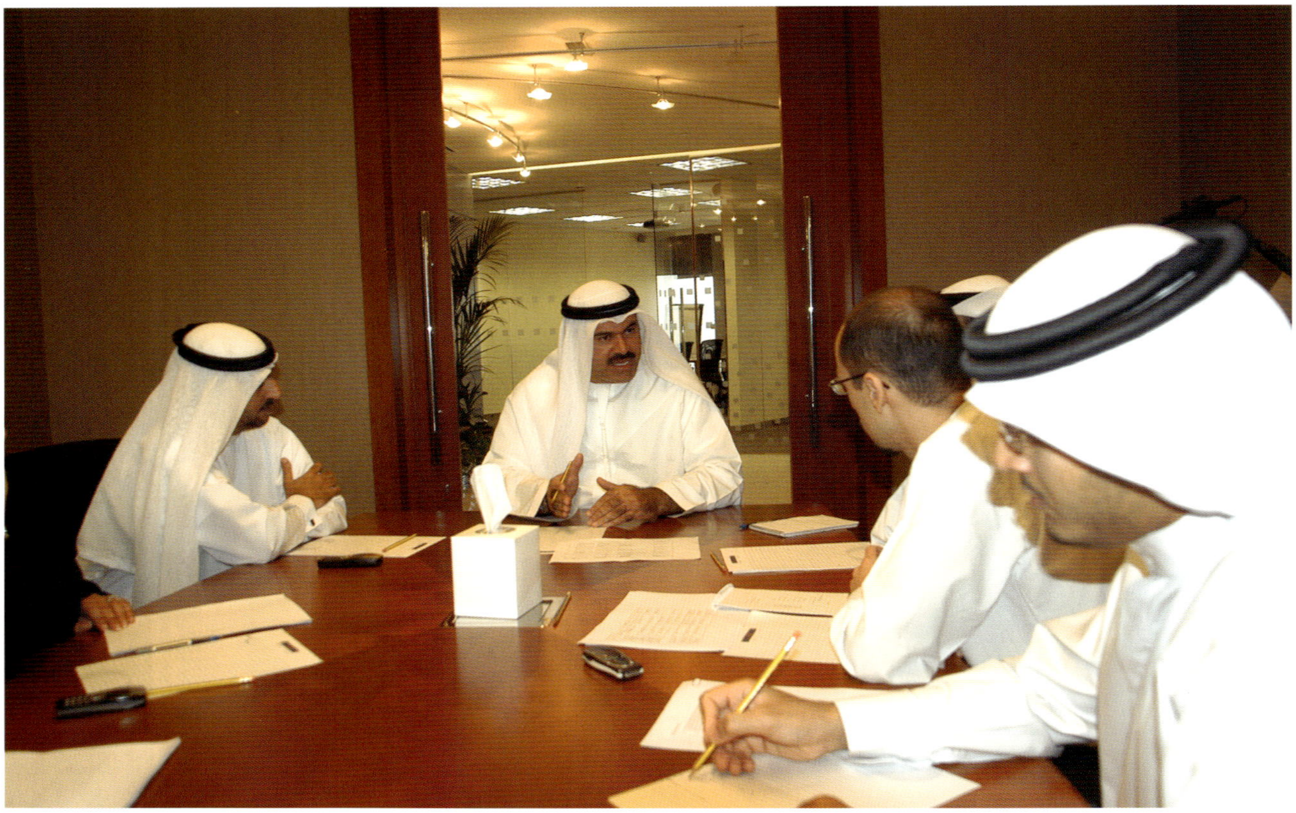

▲ ▶ Mohammed Gergawi, chairman of Dubai Development and Investment Authority, conducts a creative think-tank session with some of his team. This engaging captain of industry is noted for his warmth and ability to bring out the best in people. He's worked in the government's Ministry of Finance, as Vice Chairman of the Dubai Handicapped Club, as Secretary General of the UAE Federation of Disabled Athletes, and in dozens of other high-level capacities. This is certainly one 'athlete' whose energy levels and productivity are anything but compromised. *Photos by Dariush Zandi.*

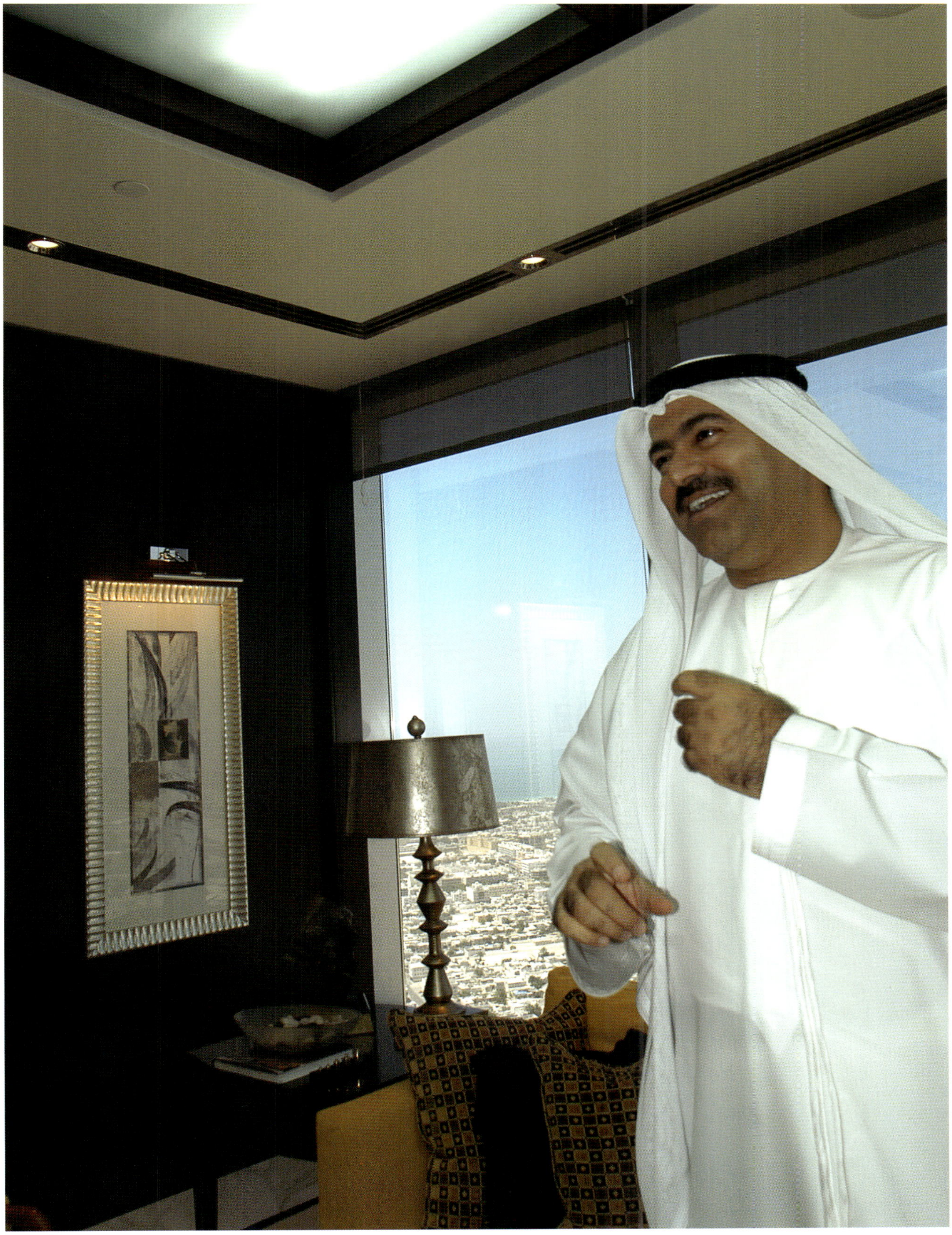

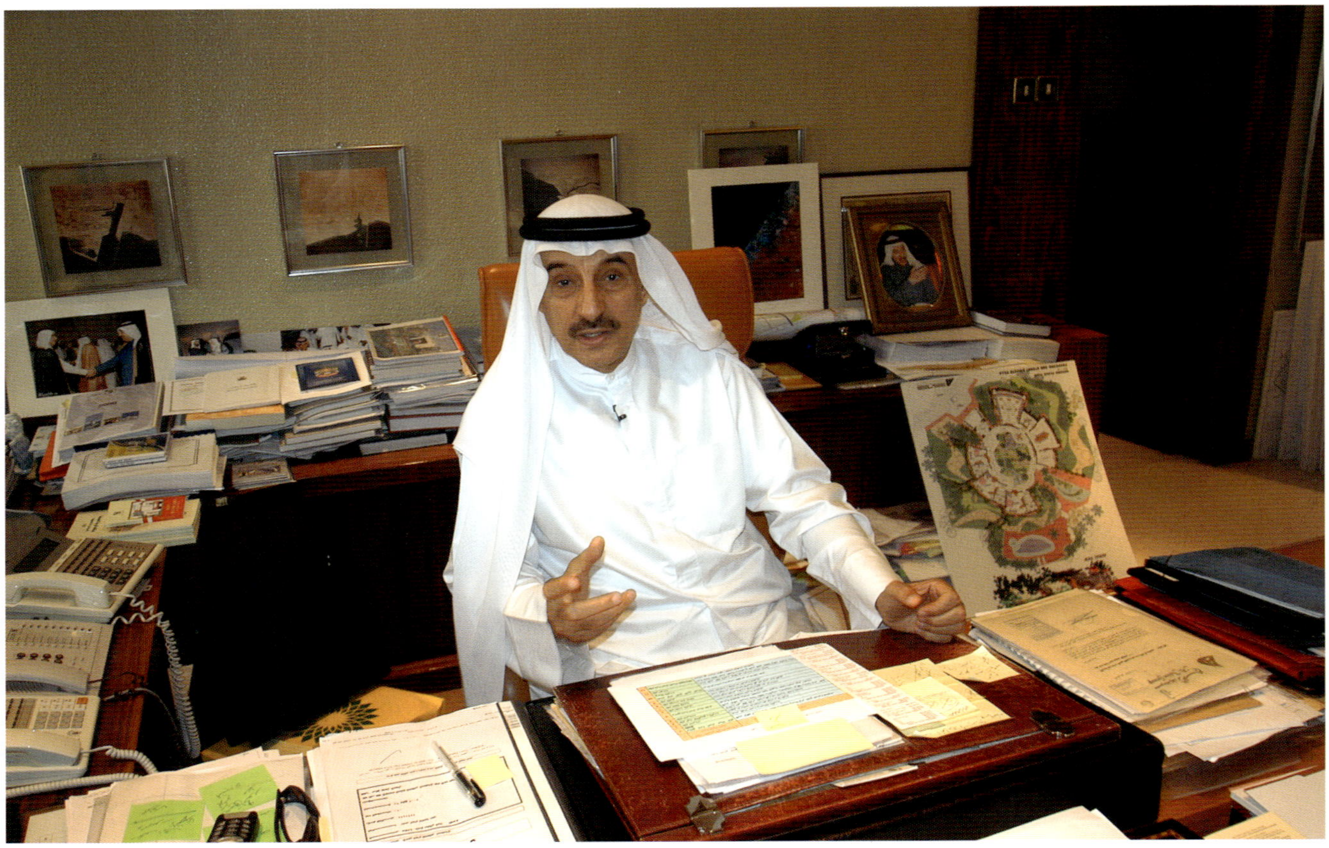

▲ Qasim Sultan is Director General of the Dubai Municipality and has helped transform Dubai into a city with an effective infrastructure. One of his most cherished and successful goals is the facilitating of an investment-friendly region. *Photo by Dariush Zandi.*

► A salesman spreads out his carpets in one of the city's souks. Hand-knotted, piled carpets (looped, as opposed to woven) evolved within the Middle East and Dubai has now become a major import/export centre for such carpets. *Photos by Samar S Jodha.*

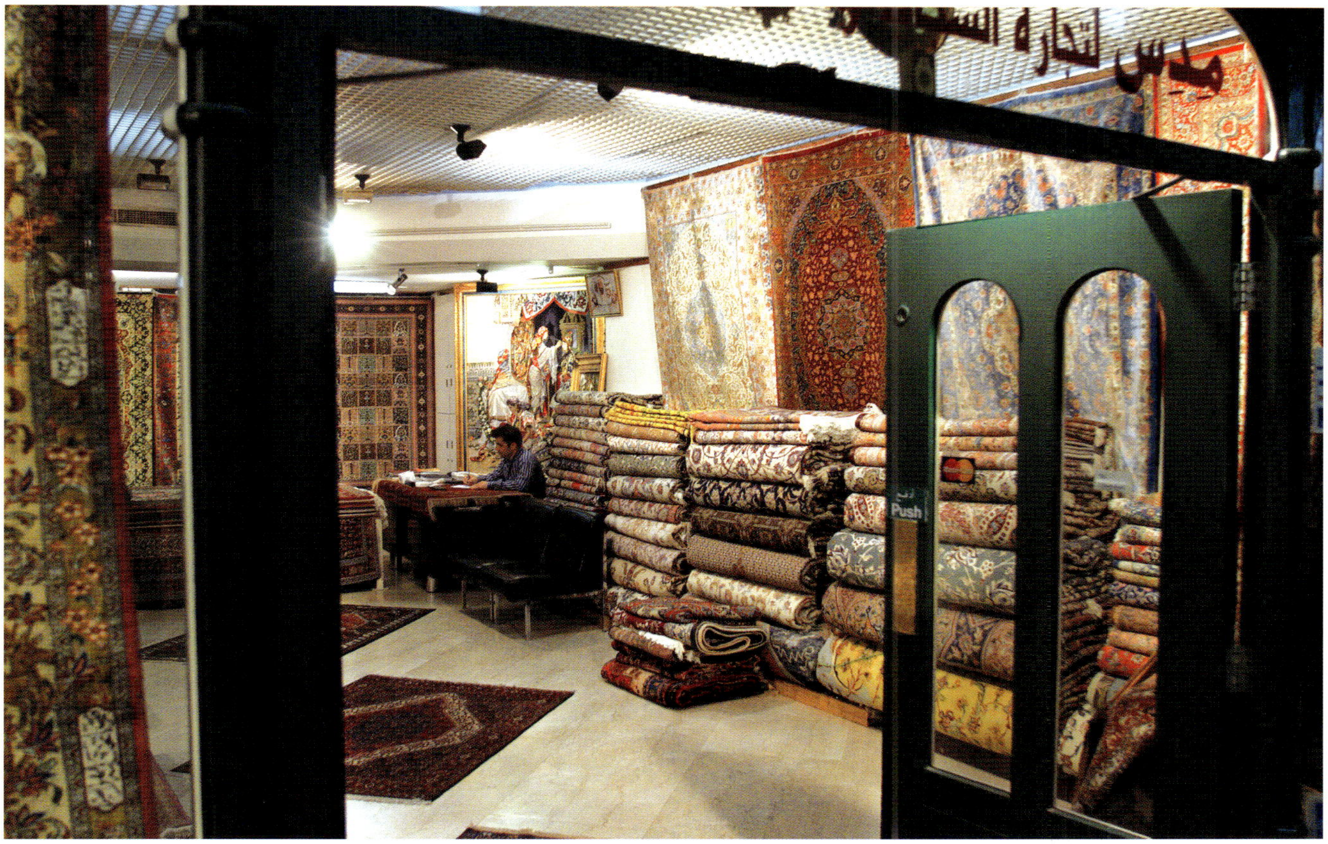
Push

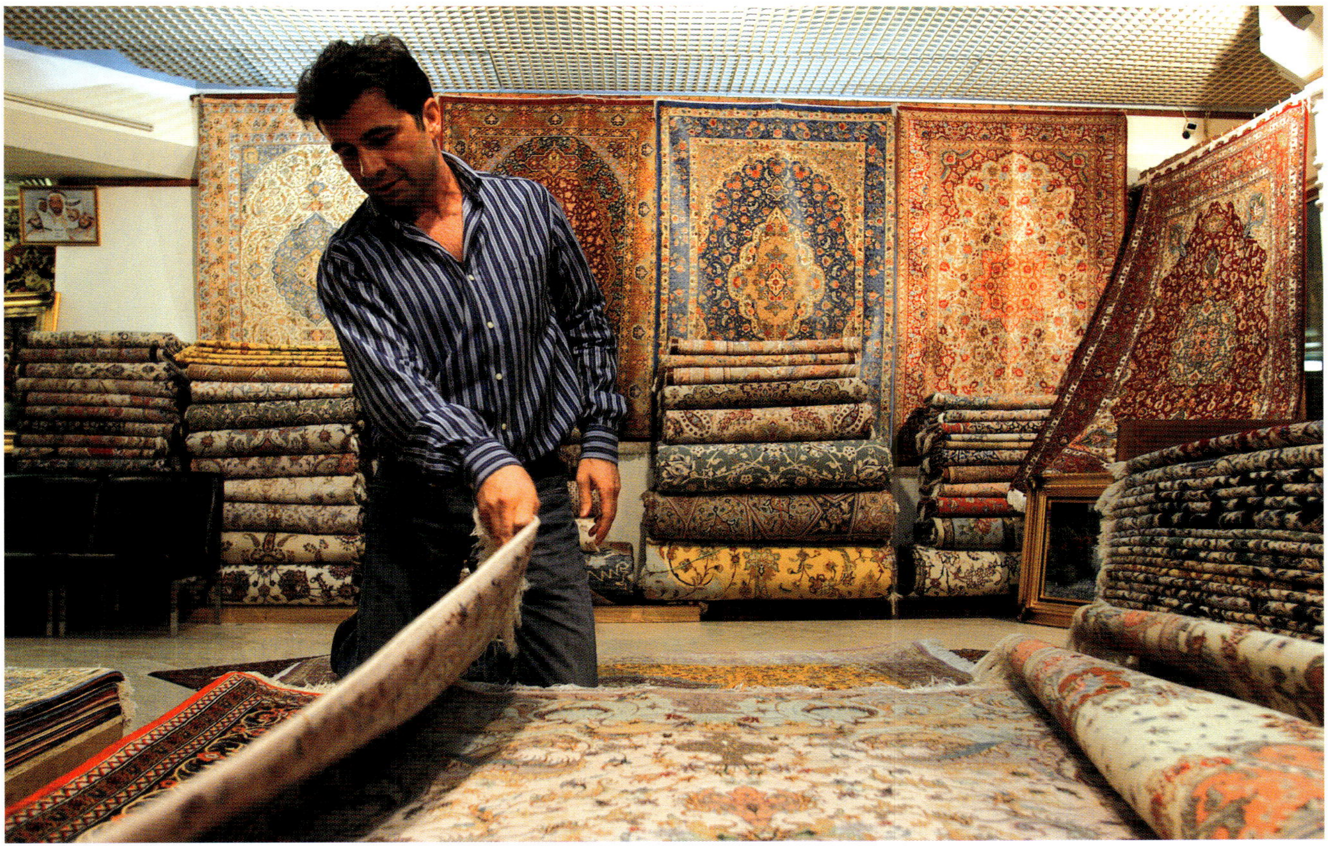

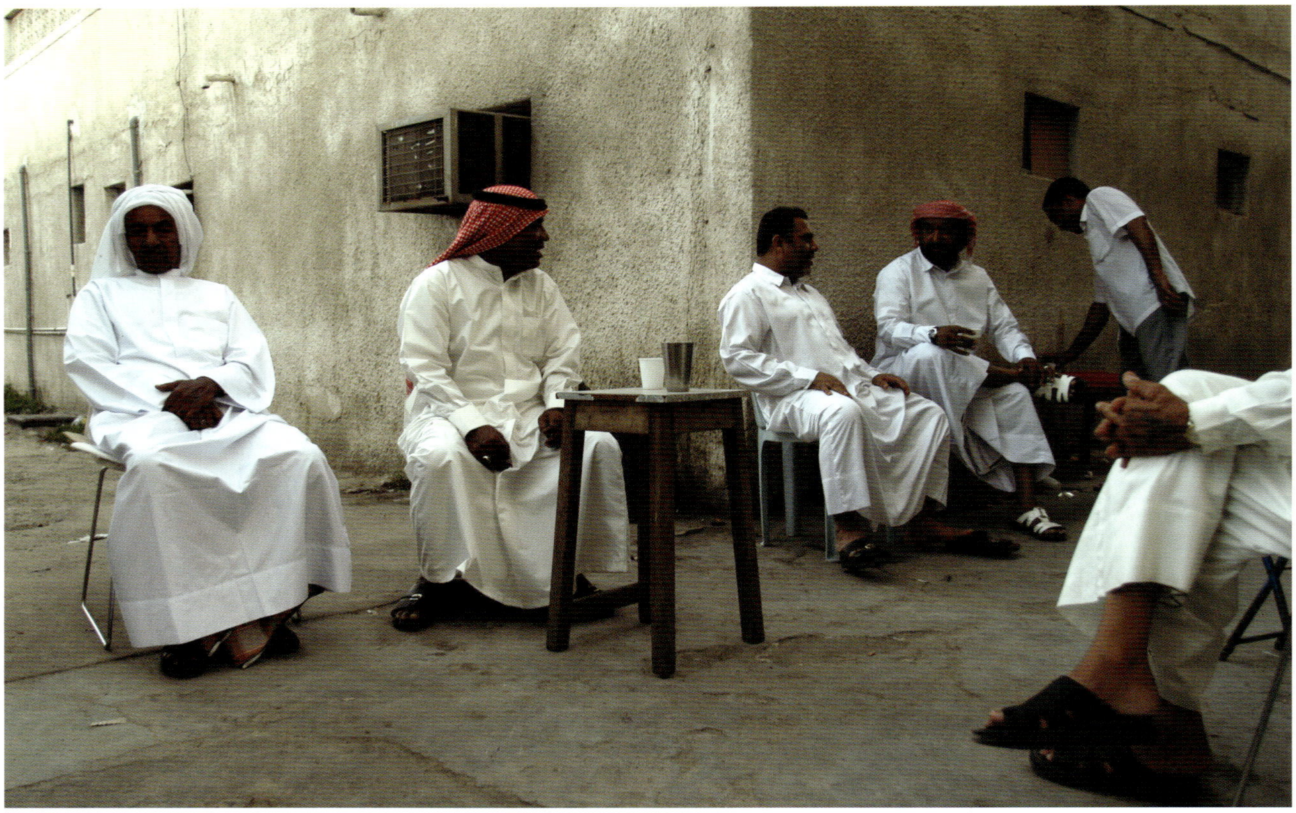

▲ ▶ WITH HUNDREDS OF THOUSANDS OF INDIAN AND Pakistani workers, consuming customary *chai*, it's little wonder that a tradition of Indian tea stalls has grown up in Dubai, contributing to a culture of pause, reflection, and community *rapprochement*. The Satwa area is at the heart of this local custom. *Photos by Samar S Jodha.*

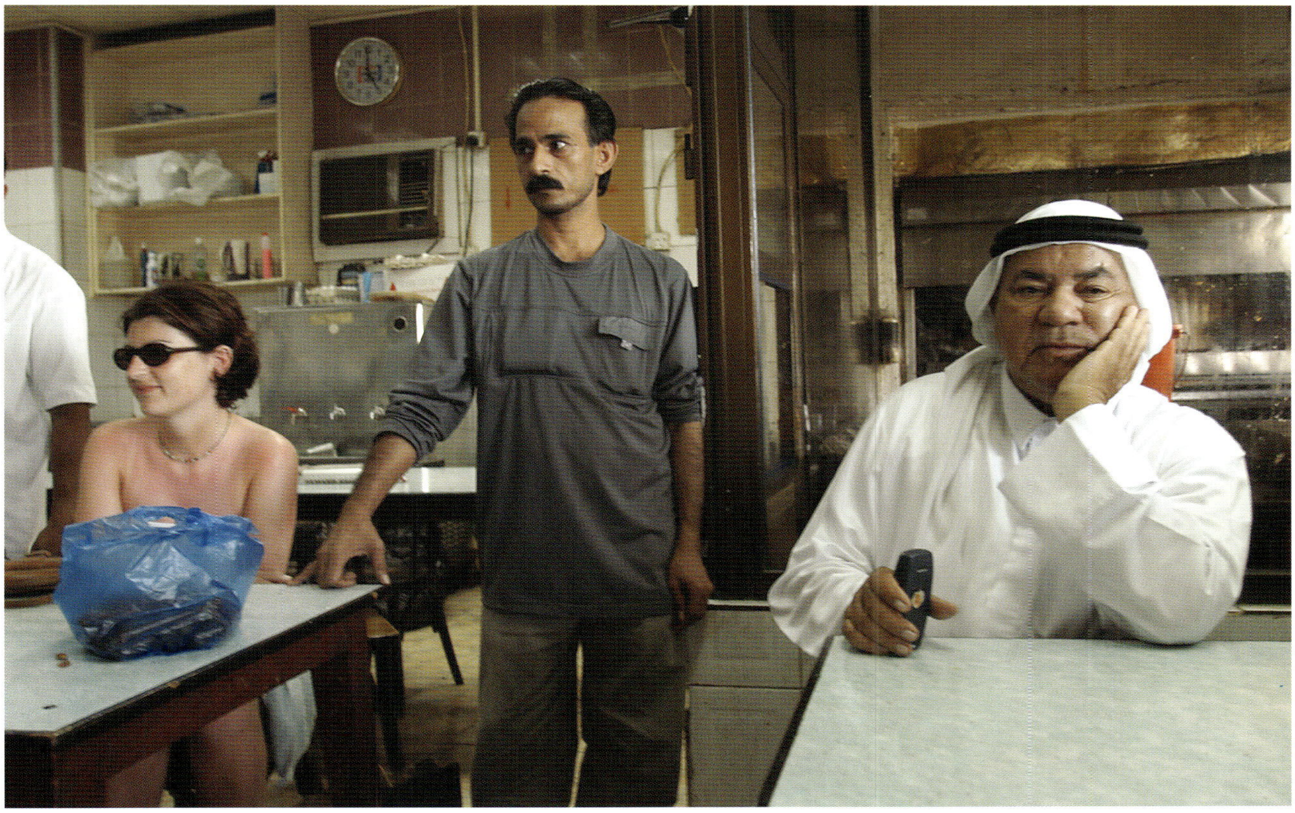

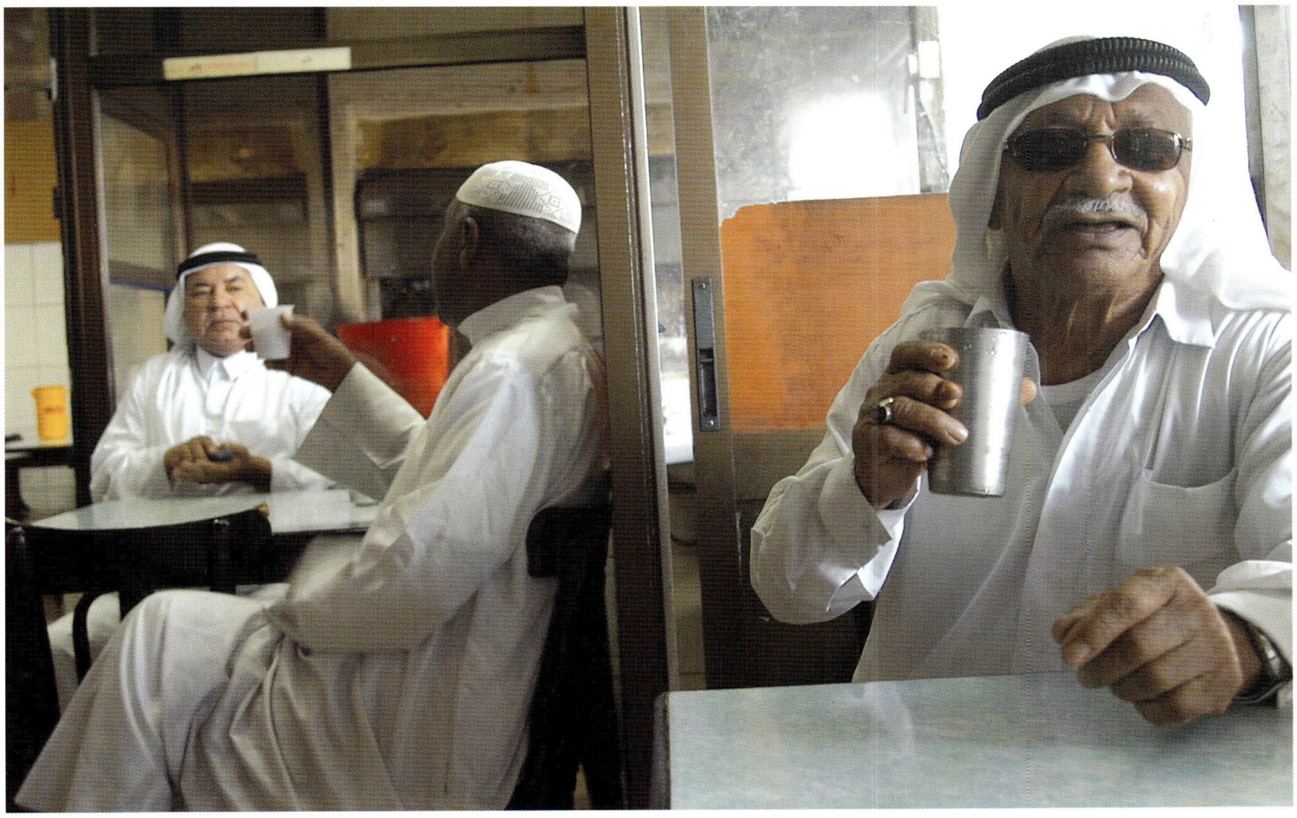

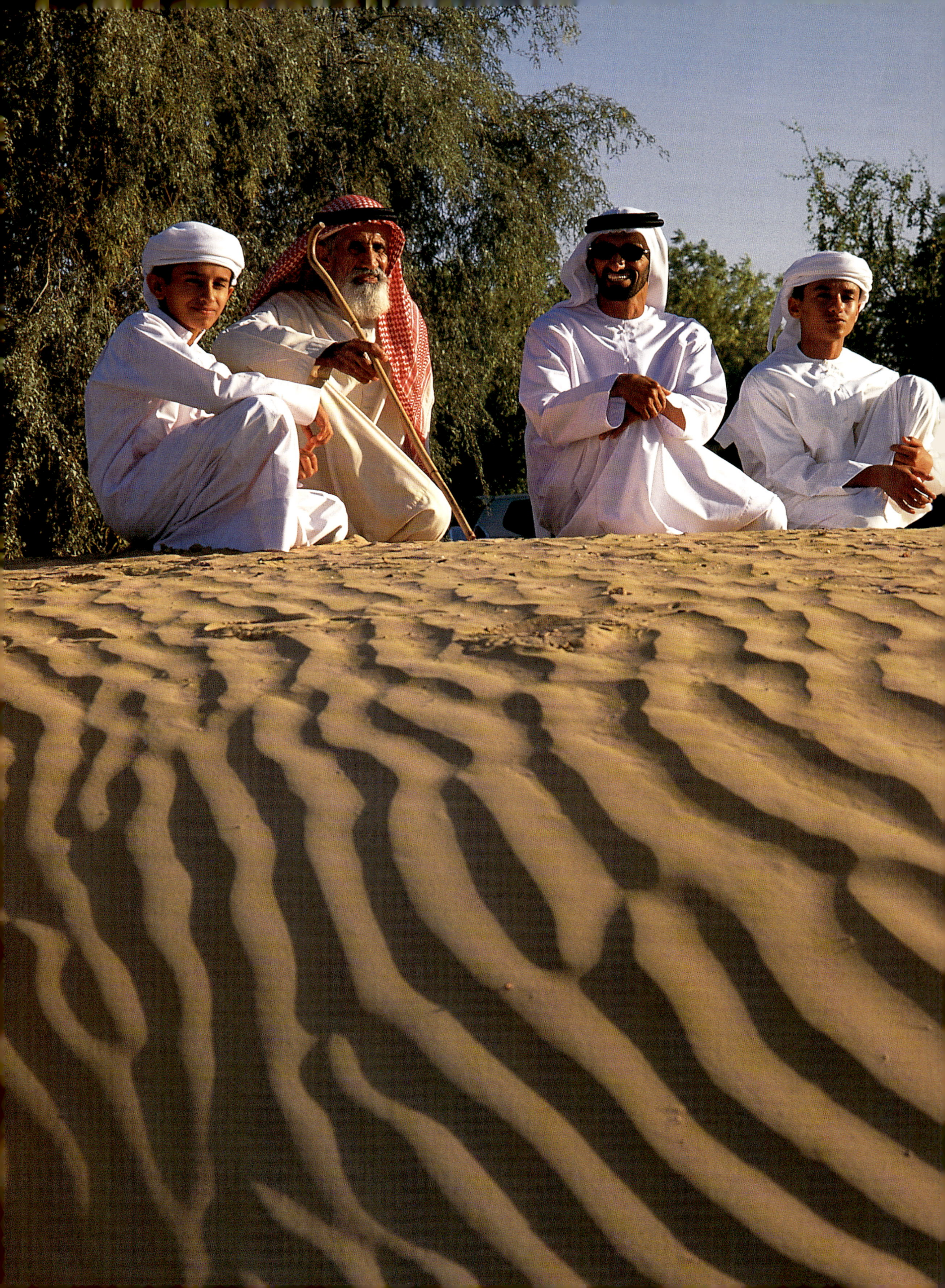

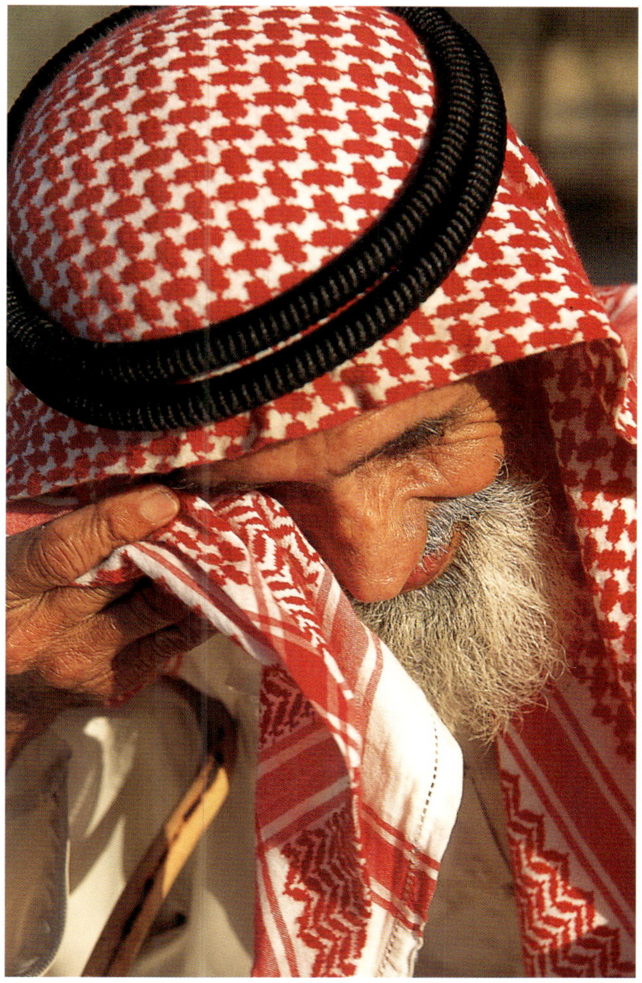

◄ ▲ CONTEMPORARY ARABIC POETRY IS A FAVOURITE pastime of the Emirati, particularly the Bedu, with three generations of the Ali Alrezi family seen here in a poetry-reading session in the soft evening light of the desert – not an uncommon sight. Where else but in Dubai would a political leader establish a precedent for spreading poetry on the radio, TV and Internet? The Crown Prince may be a soldier, a diplomat, a horseman, a falconer, and the current visionary of his emirate, but he is, first and foremost, a great poet. *Photos by Joe Sassine.*

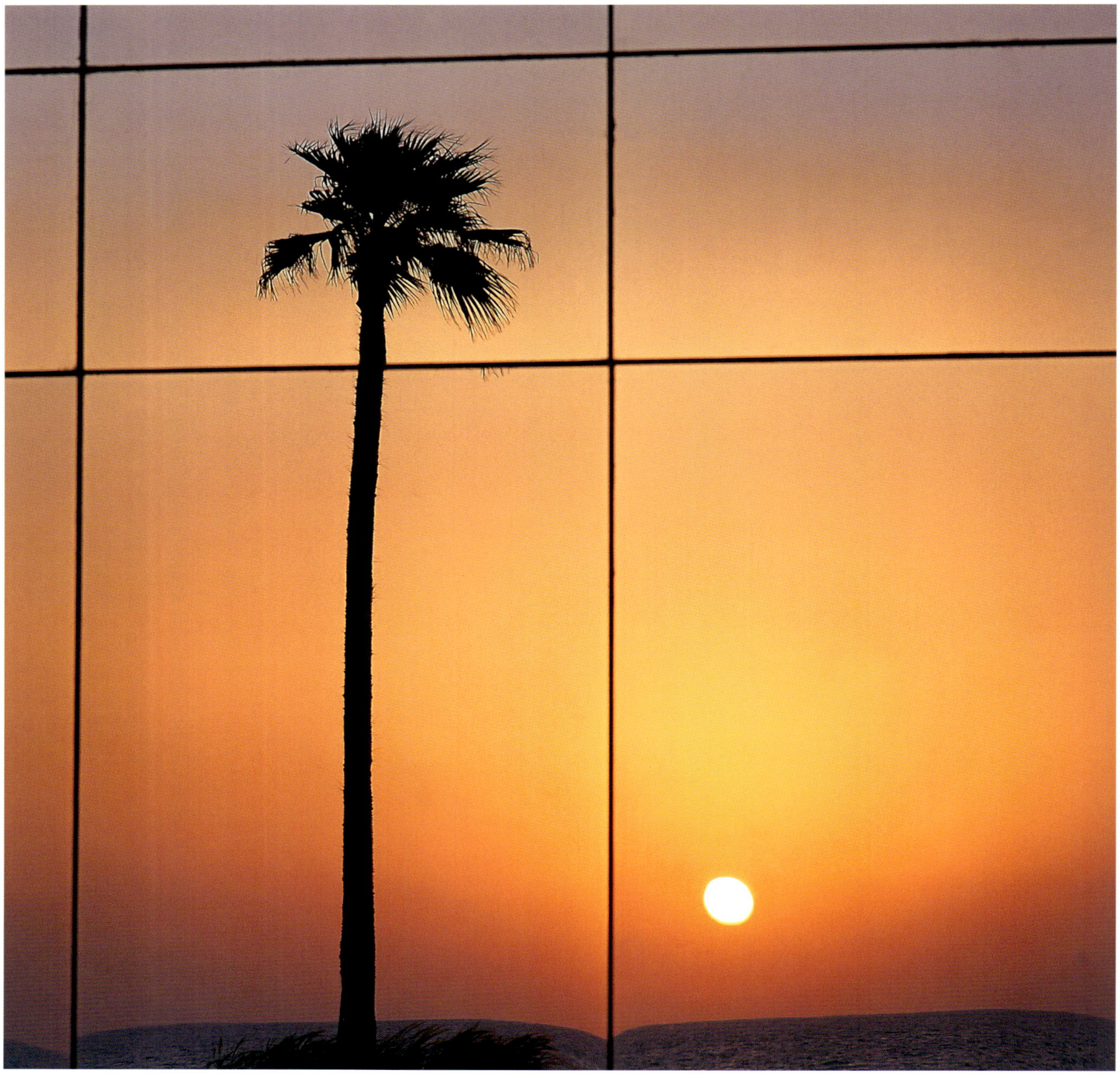

▲ Hardly a day goes by in Dubai when you'll not be able to bask in the warmth of the sun or relish a splendid Arabian sunset. Here, without the use of trick photography, the photographer has cleverly combined the great outdoors with a large plate-glass window in the city. *Photo by Shankar Adiseshan, Motivate Publishing.*

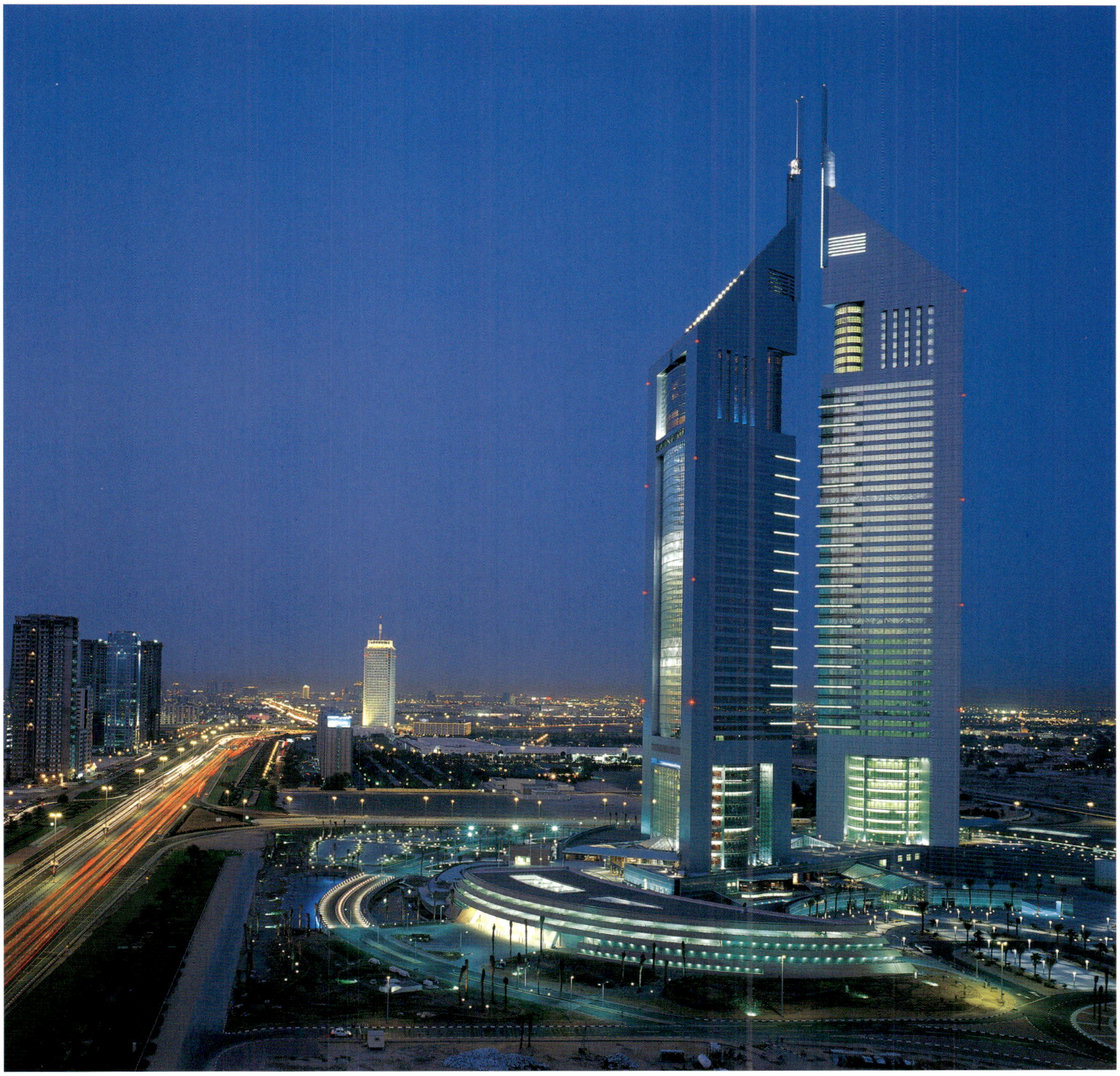

▲ Night falls on Sheikh Zayed Road, the main highway to Abu Dhabi. The four-lane highway starts in a busy commercial, residential and hotel district and continues past Jebel Ali and through the desert to Abu Dhabi. The photo also provides another striking view of Emirates Towers. *Photo by Jumeirah International.*

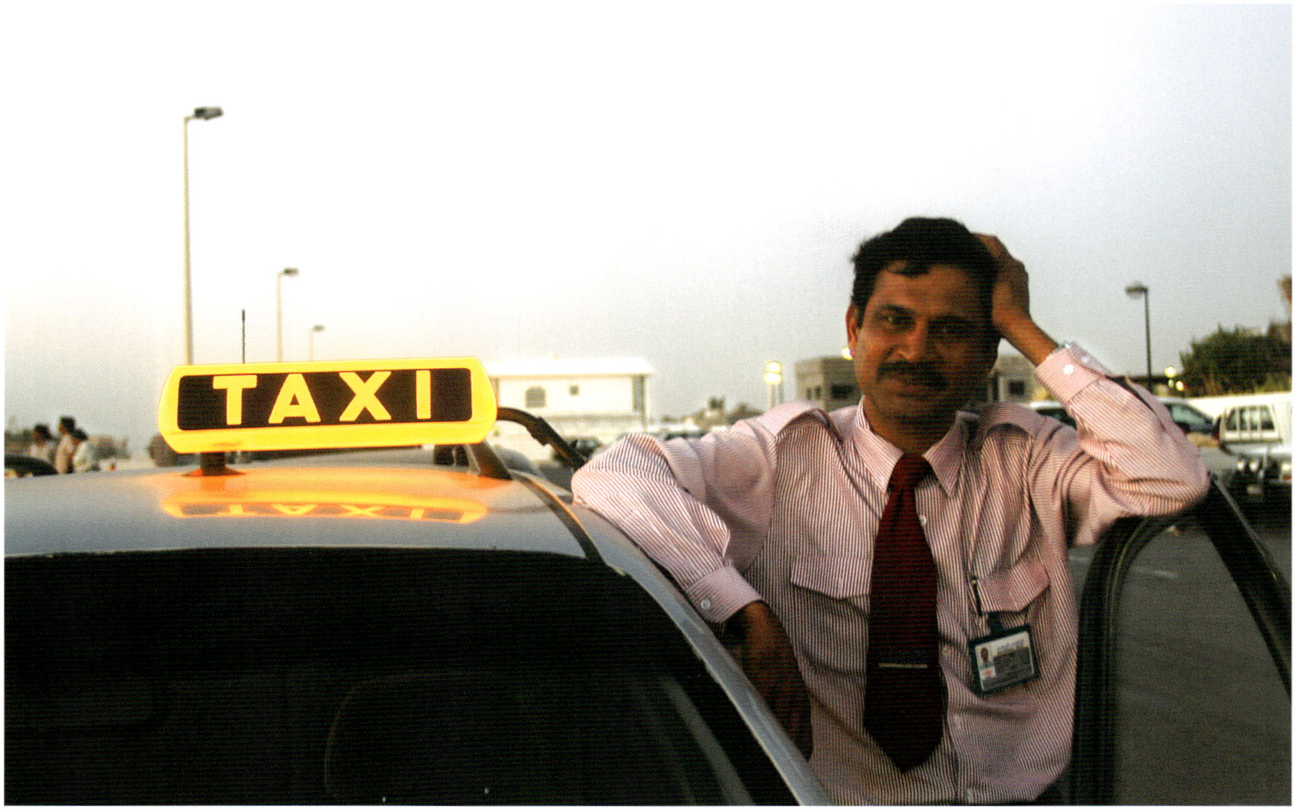

▲ A taxi driver poses just before dark in Satwa. In plying the often choked streets of Dubai, these men will characteristically earn double what they would receive in their home country. What's more, compared to the flow of traffic in Karachi or Mumbai, negotiating the spanking-clean motorways of Dubai is a breeze.

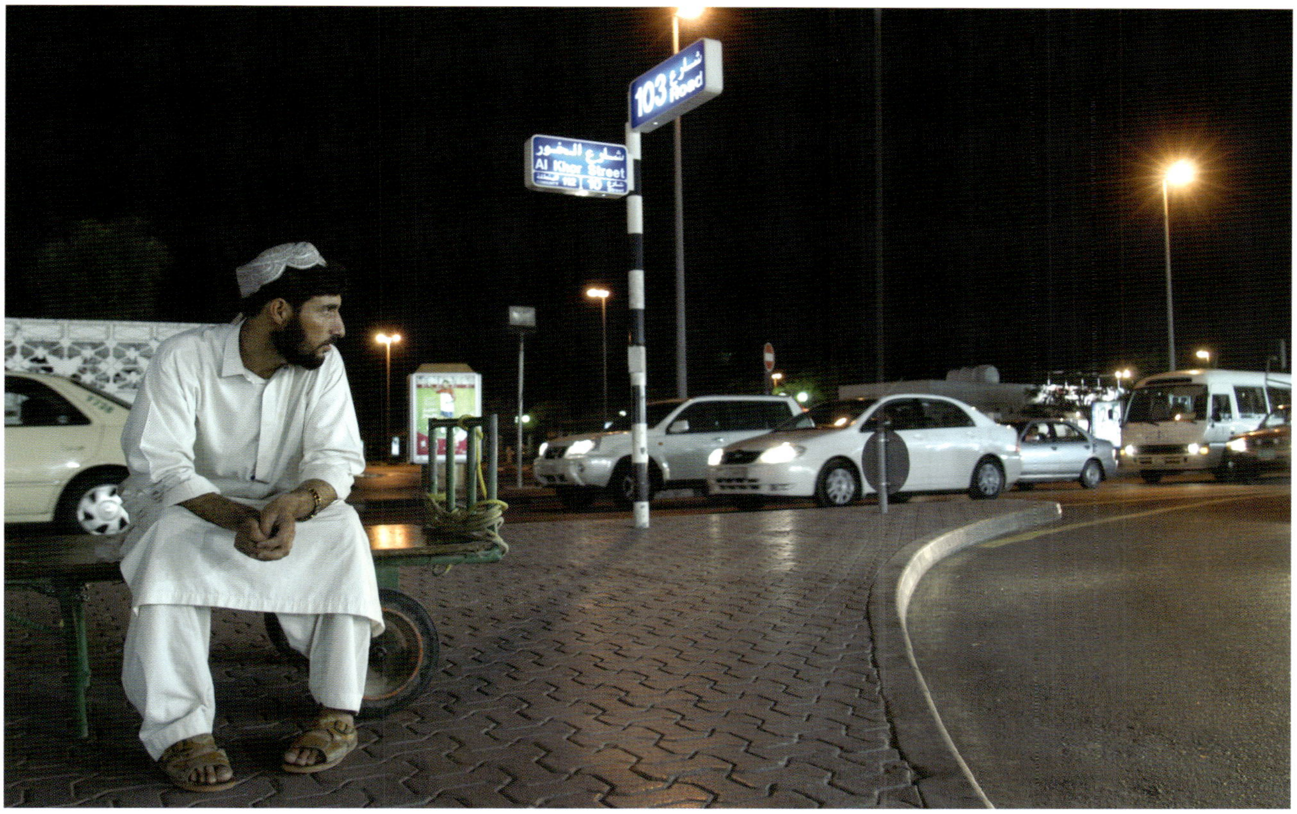

▲ The lively suburb of Satwa combines dirt roads and carriageways, souks and modern shops, traditional restaurants and fast-food joints, and a good variety of dwellings. It is also home to people of many nationalities. Here, while waiting for a friend, a Pakistani expat quietly contemplates his future in Dubai. *Photos by Samar S Jodha.*

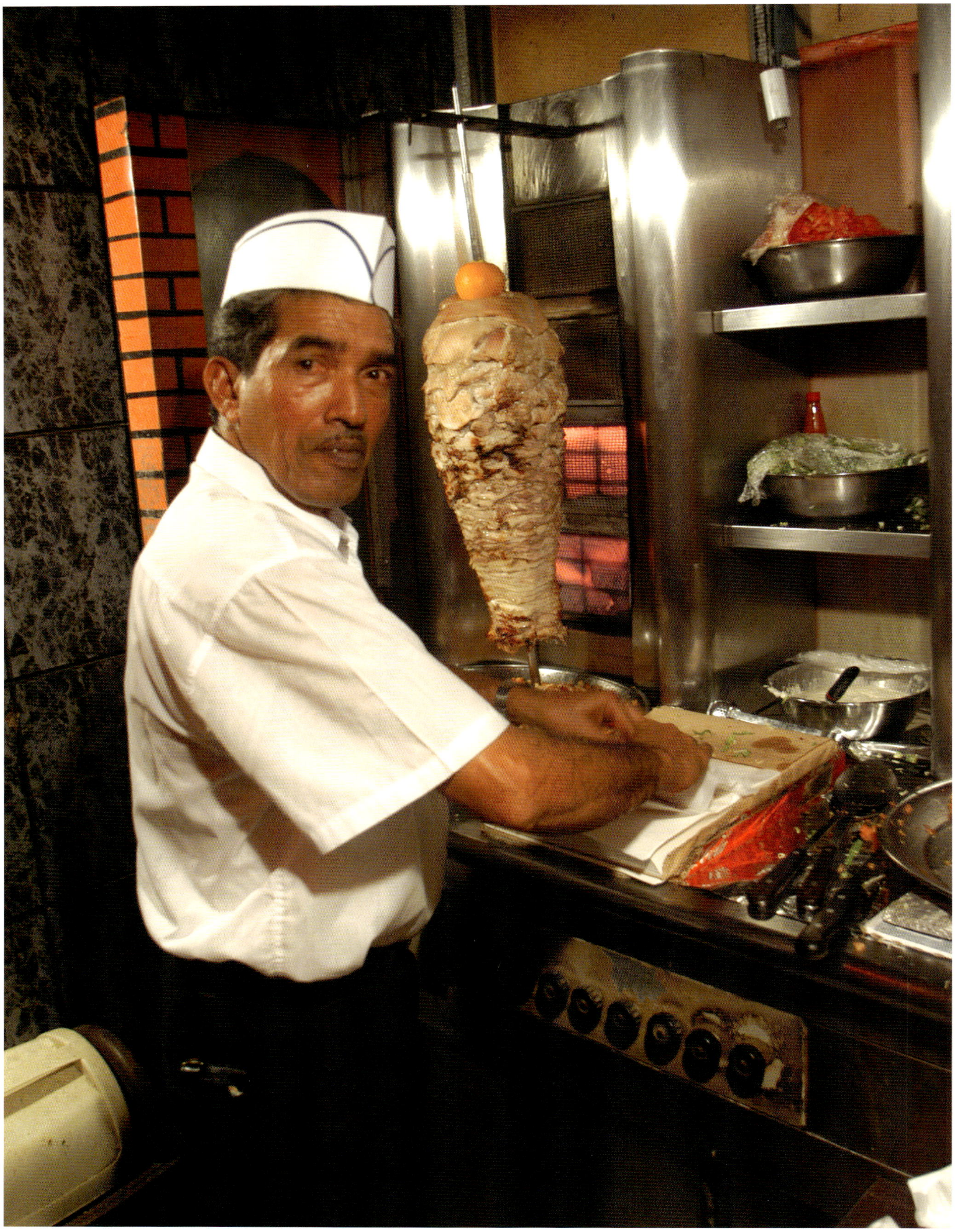

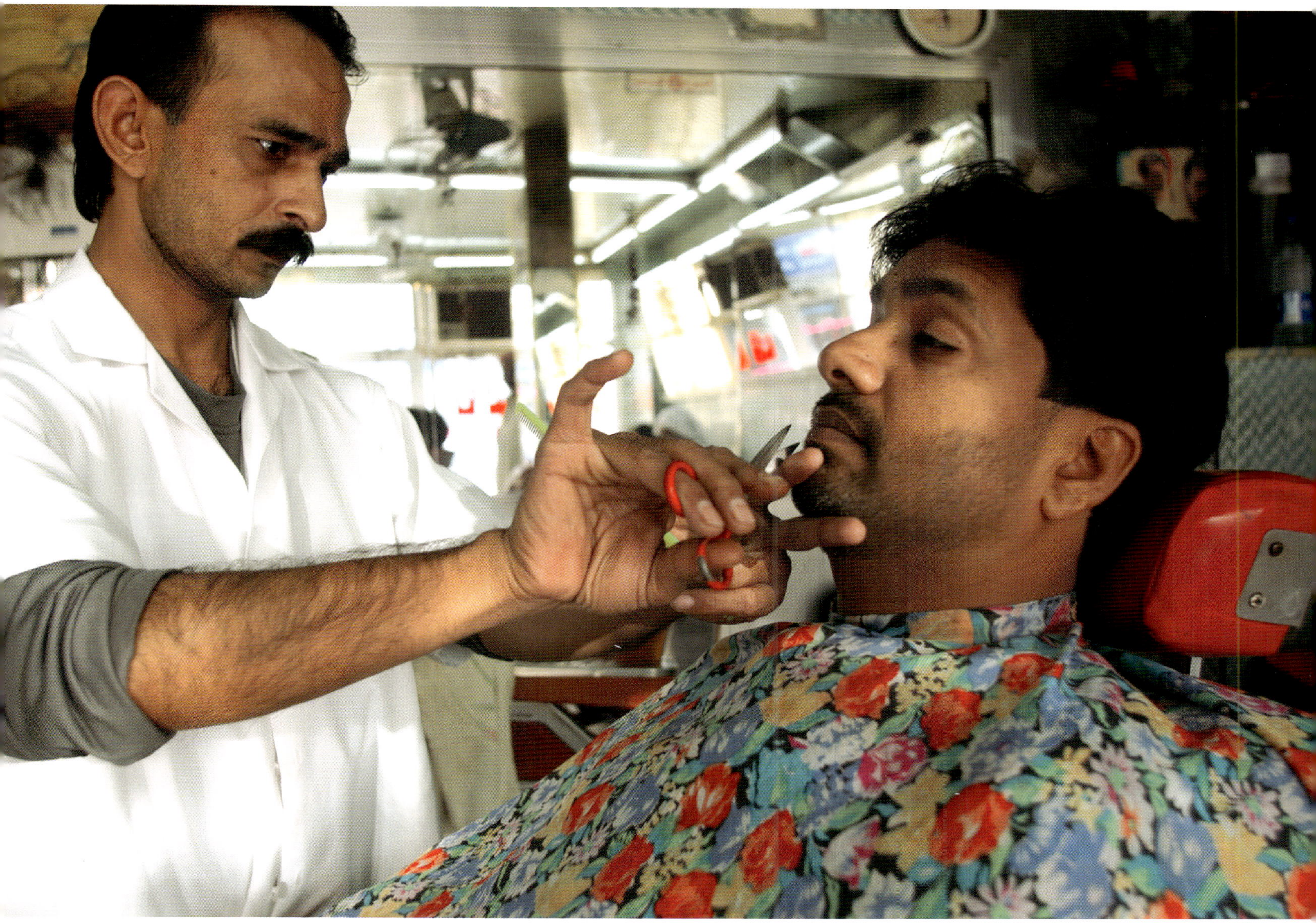

◀ A Syrian prepares *shawarma*, a typical Middle-Eastern fast food, served with lamb or chicken and extremely popular in the region. In Dubai, you'll pay less than one US dollar for one. In London, probably 10 times more. *Photo by Souheil Semaan.*

▲ A Pakistani barber at work in Satwa. Here, at Haji Sharief Hair Dressers, near the post office, a stylish man's haircut costs about 10 dirhams (less than three US dollars). Barber shops abound in Dubai and they're great places for cross-cultural discussions. *Photo by Samar S Jodha.*

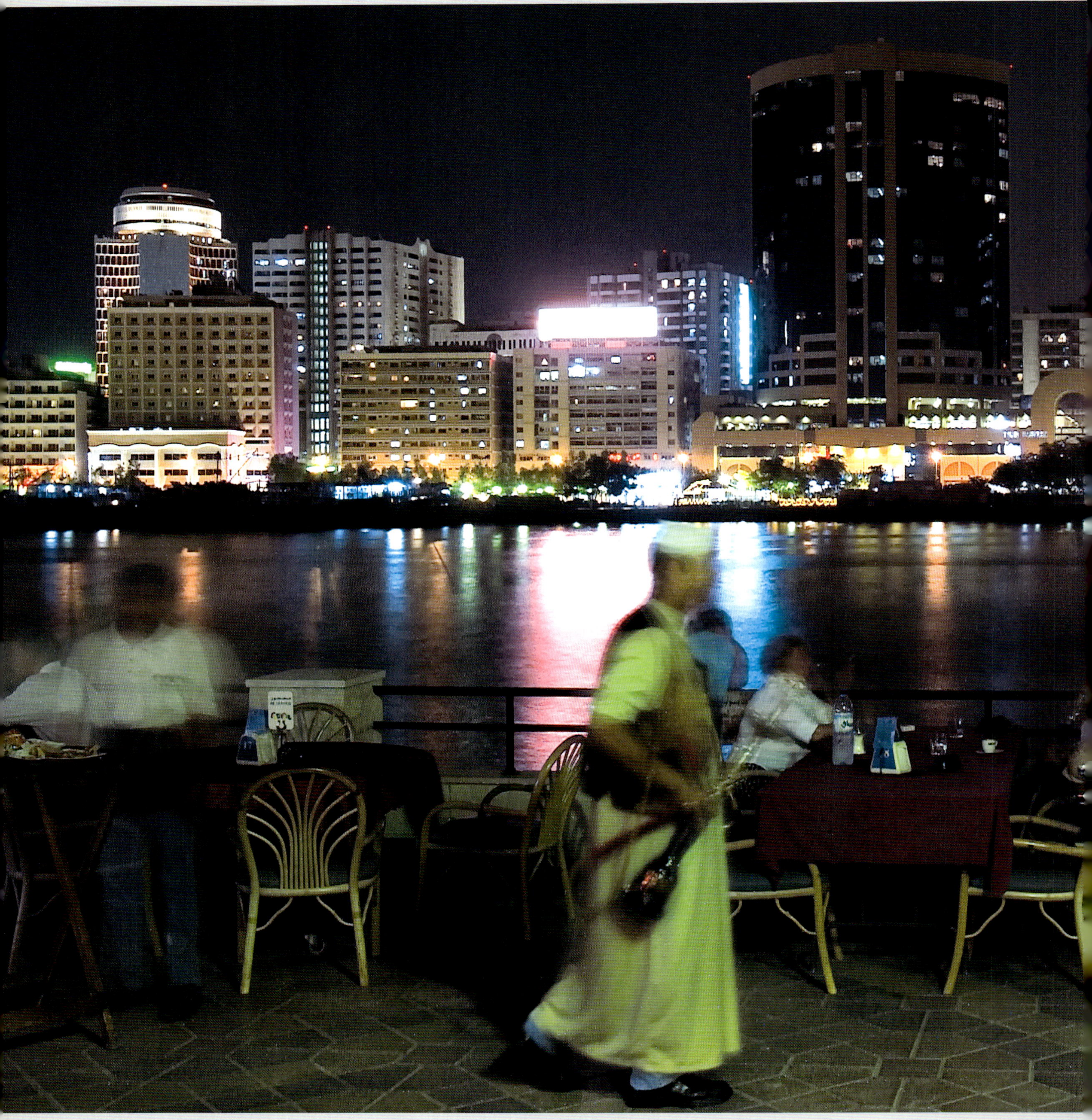

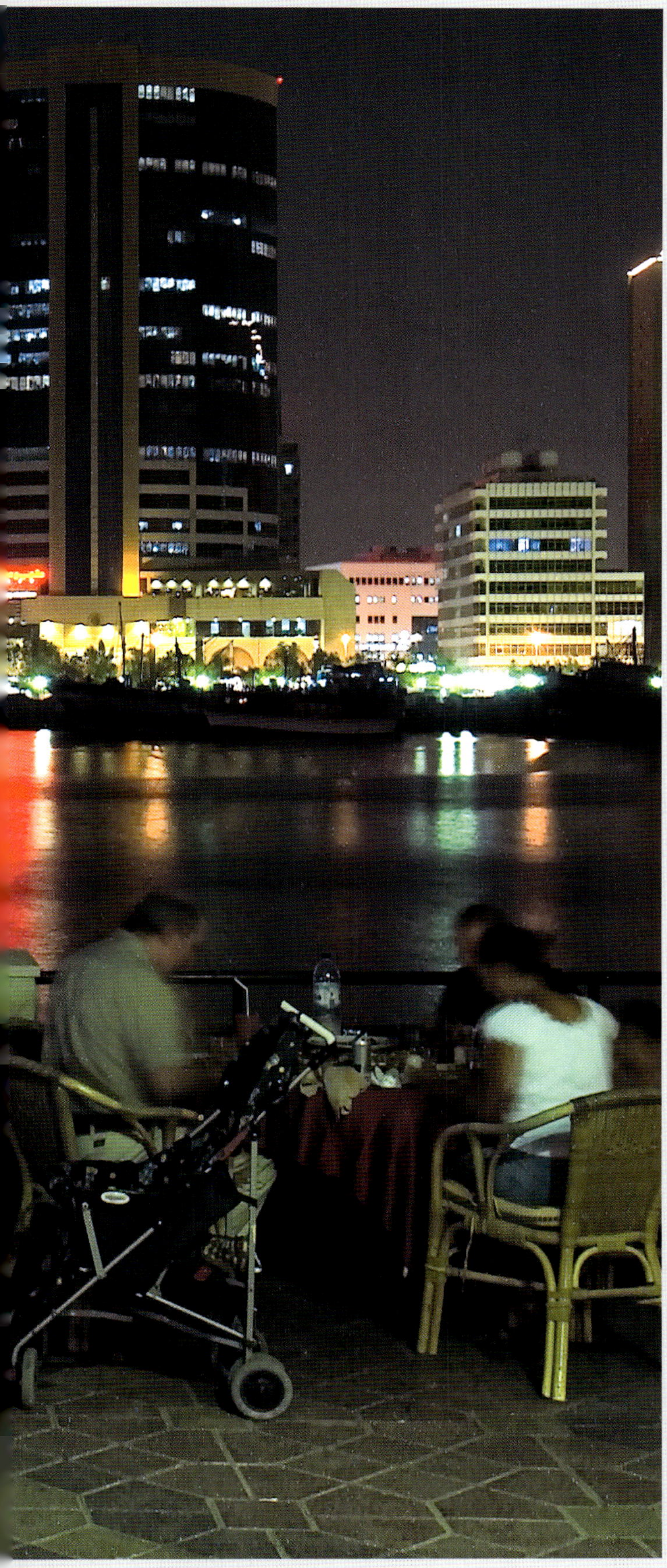

◄ SAMPLING *SHEESHA* OR *SHISHA* (AROMATIC TOBACCO) at the Fatafeet Restaurant facing Dubai Creek. Traditional Arabic culture flourishes in the thick of such philosophical aroma, where casual coffees and teas are also imbibed, and all the problems of the world discussed with quiet conversation. *Photo by Karel Kita, Motivate Publishing.*

►► THE CREEK AT NIGHT, WITH BUR DUBAI ON THE right bank and Deira on the left. The buildings of this particular part of Bur Dubai (centred round the Textile Souk) contrast with the modern buildings of Deira, while the lights of *abras* linking the two sides can be seen on the water. *Photo by Shankar Adiseshan, Motivate Publishing.*

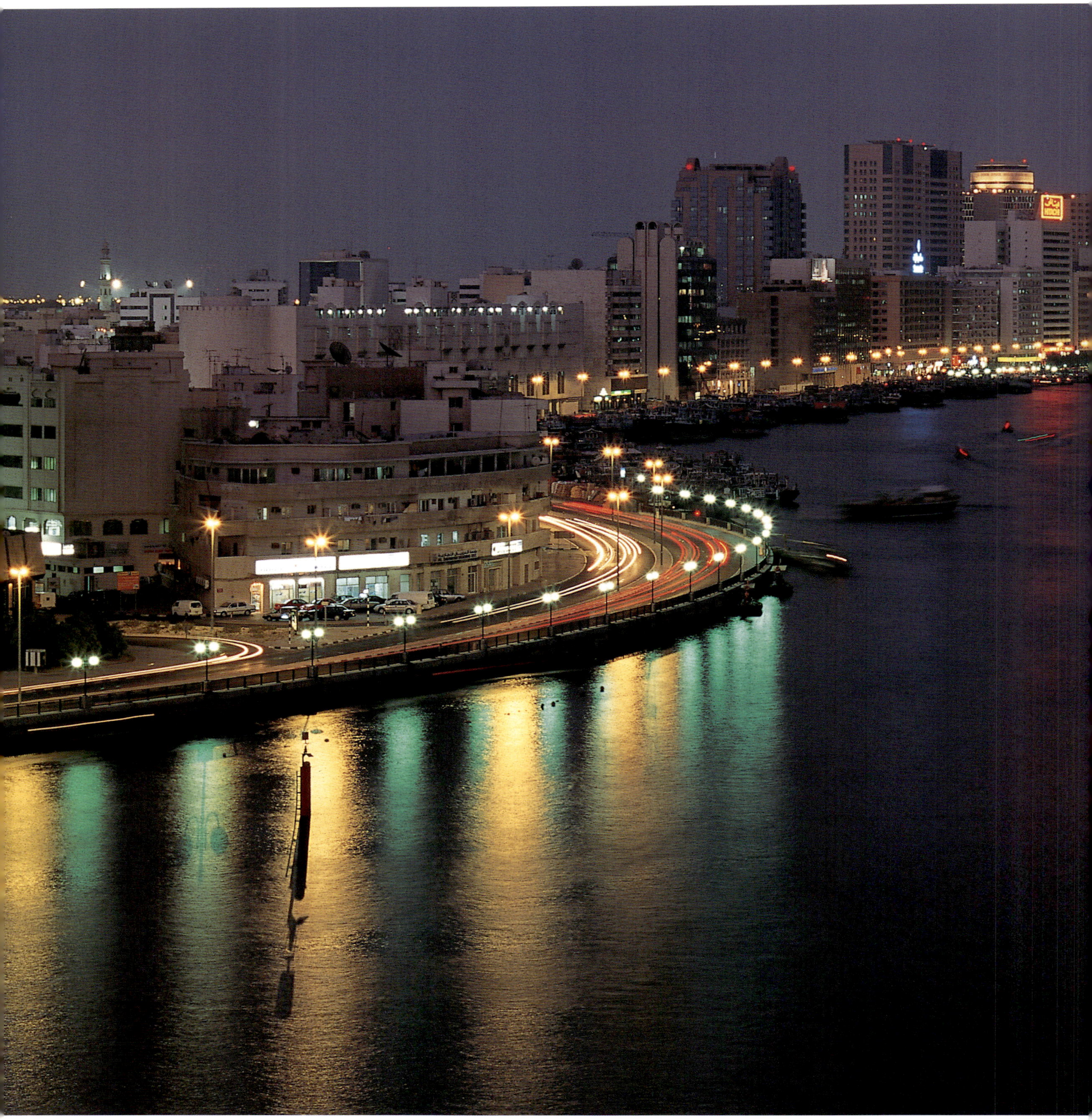

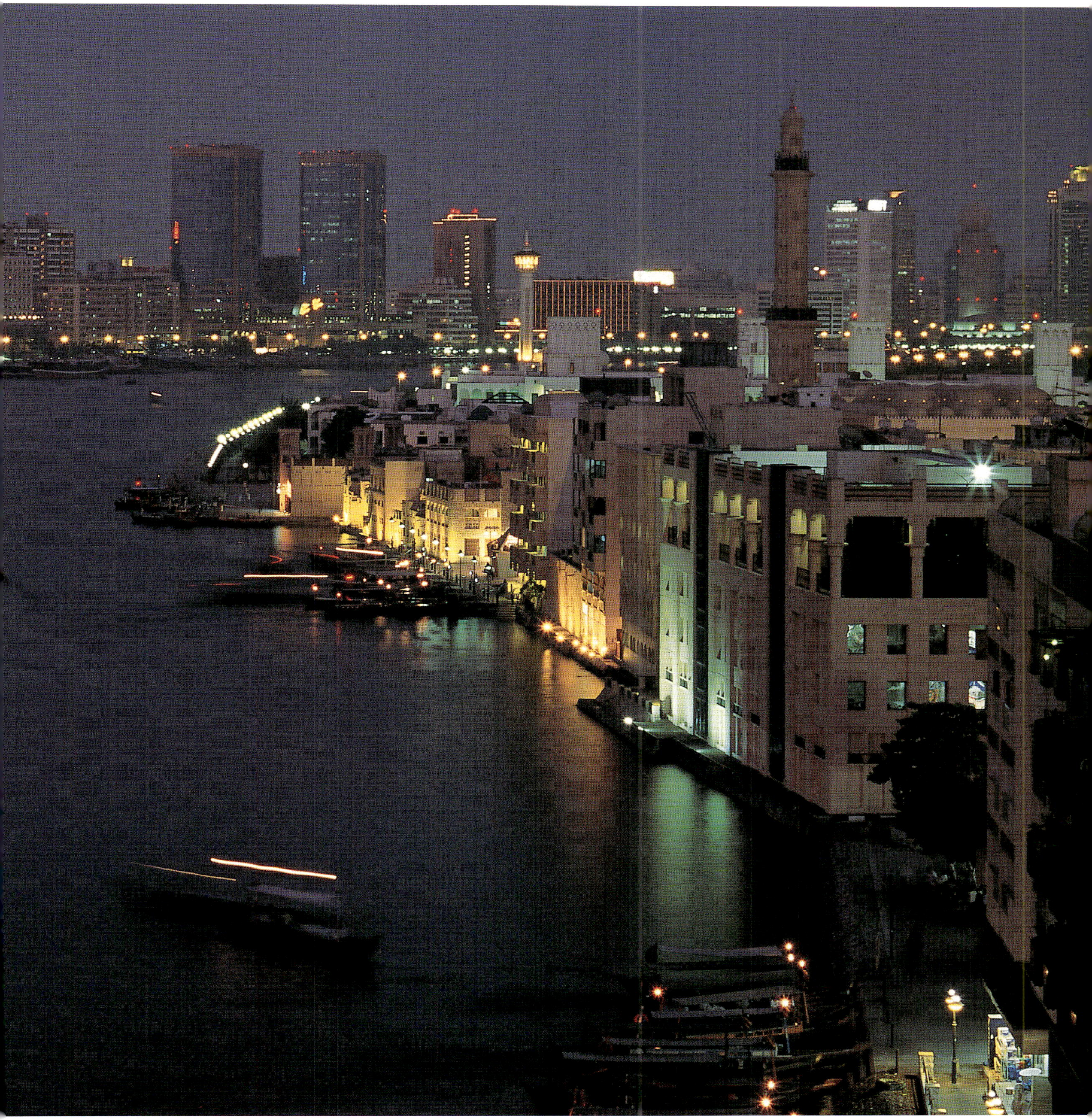

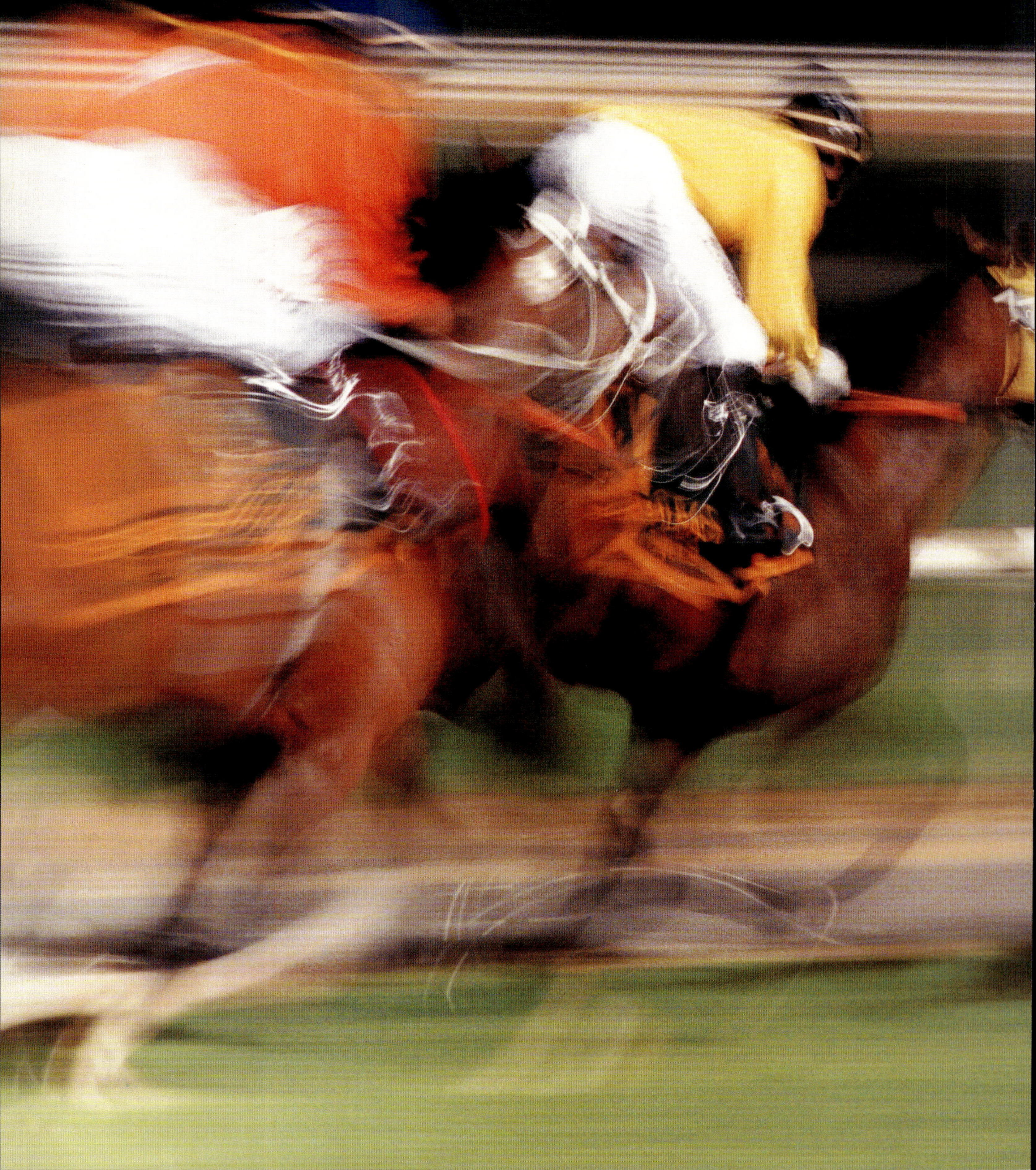

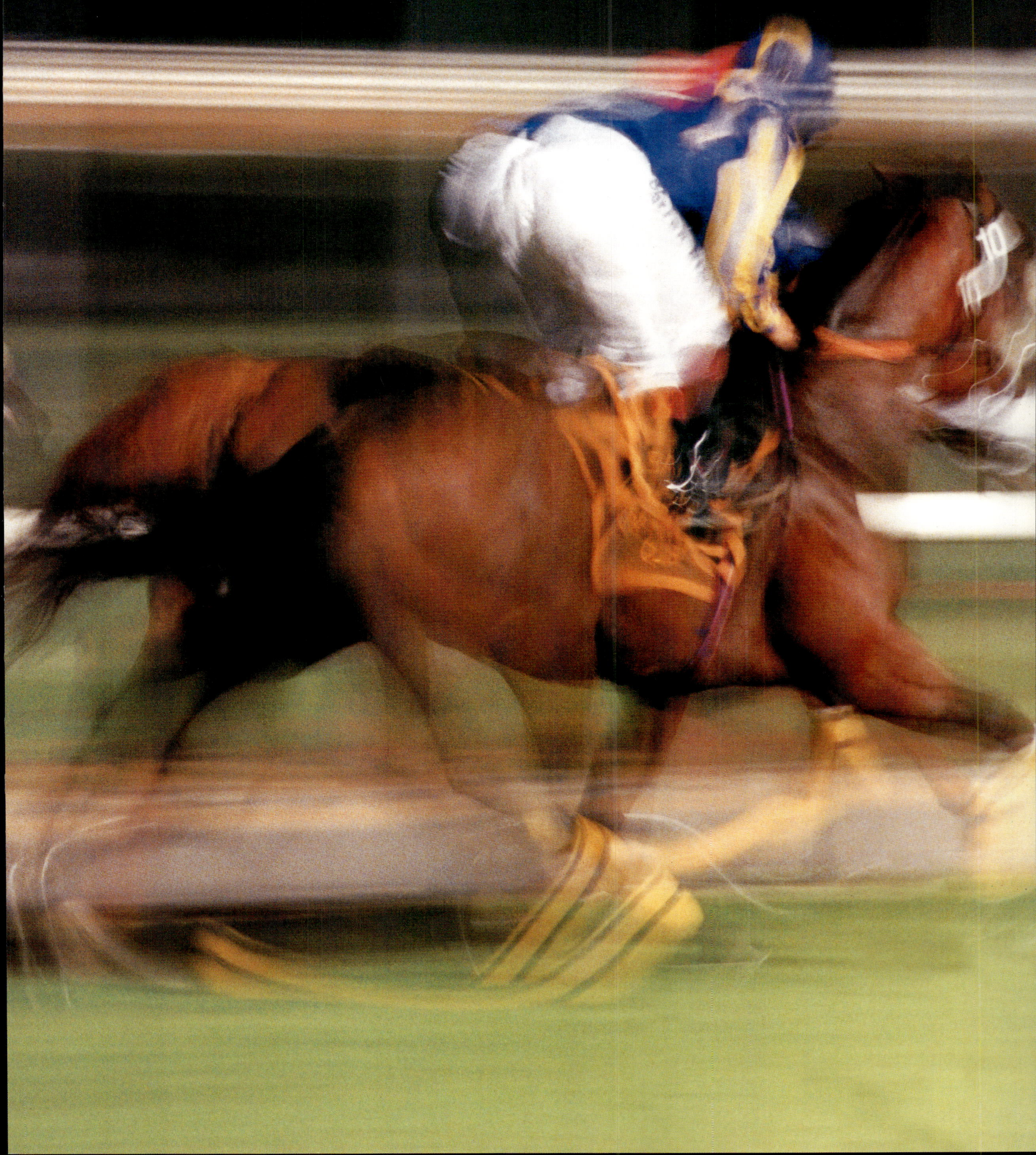
10

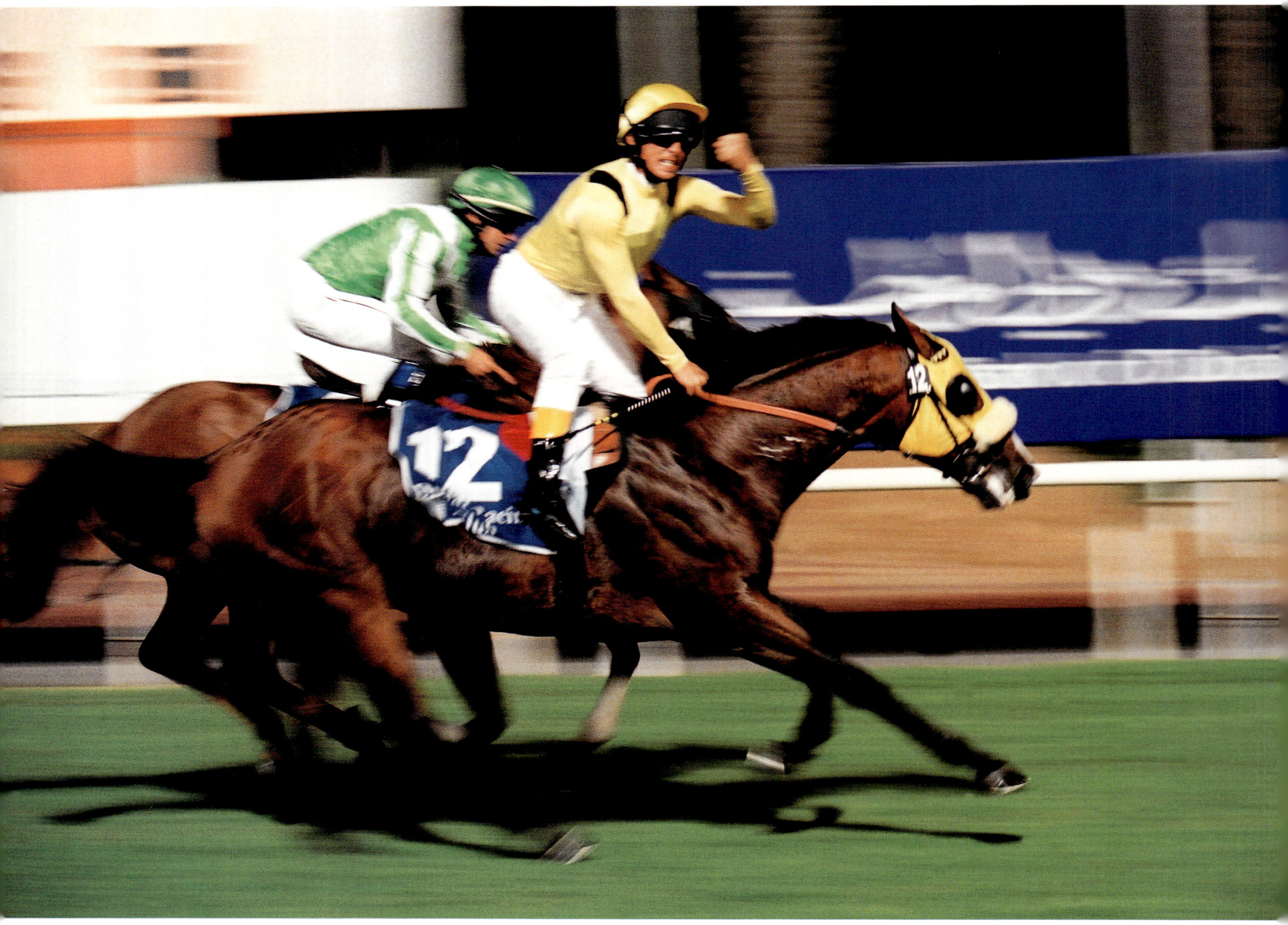

◄◄ ▲ ► Horse racing is popular in Dubai. These images from the Arabian Derby at Nad Al Sheba, won by HH Sheikh Rashid bin Mohammed bin Rashid Al Maktoum (pictured right top after his win), capture the sheer burst of energy which infects the event. Although betting is not allowed, considerable prizes can be won through raffle predictions of winning horses. Thousands of expats throng to Nad Al Sheba in the hope of winning a prize and spending some leisurely time after work (right bottom). In Dubai, horse racing is predicated upon the ebb and flow of the Gulf weather. After late April, when the derby takes place, the horses will be returned to their air-conditioned stalls and will not race again until the following November. *Photos by Lucy Monro.*

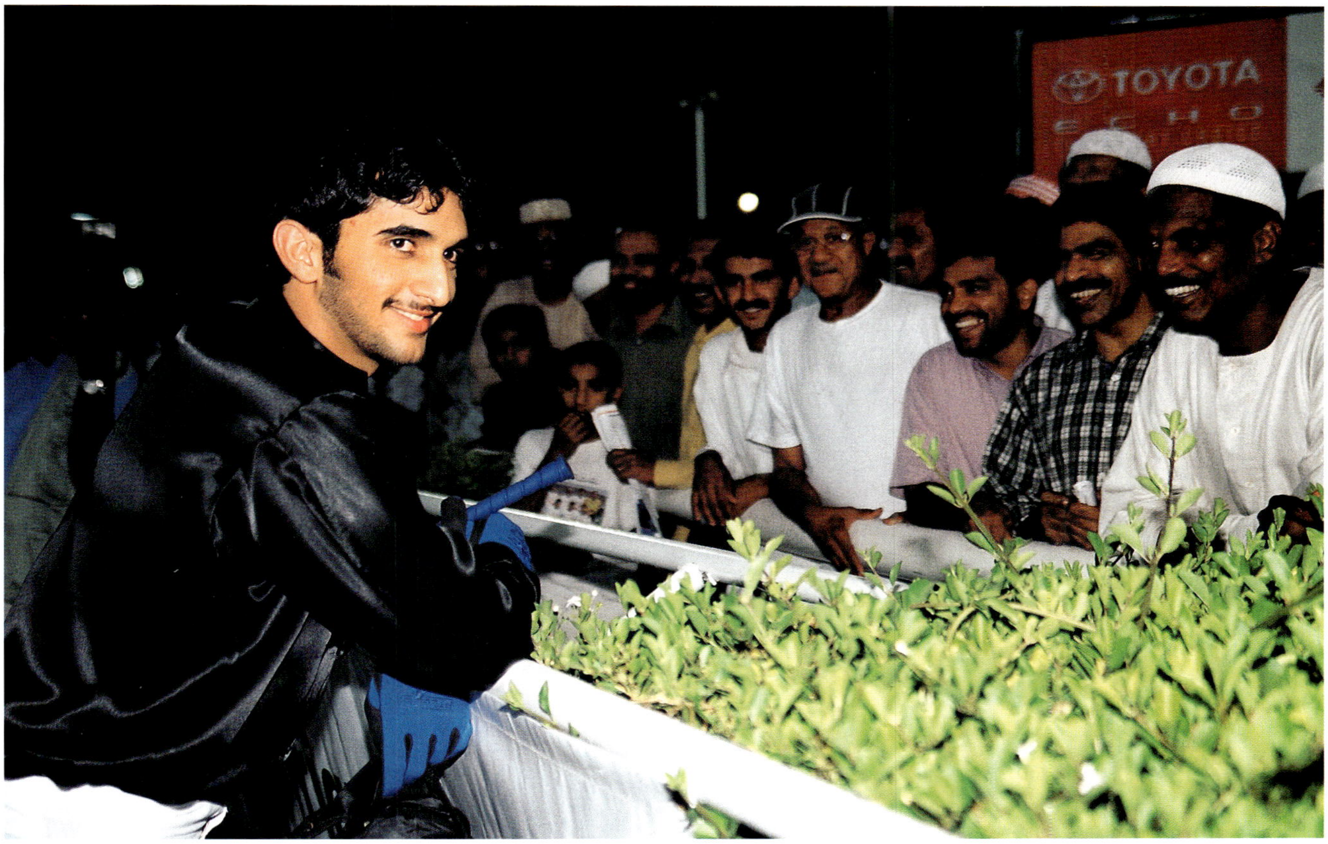
TOYOTA
ECHO

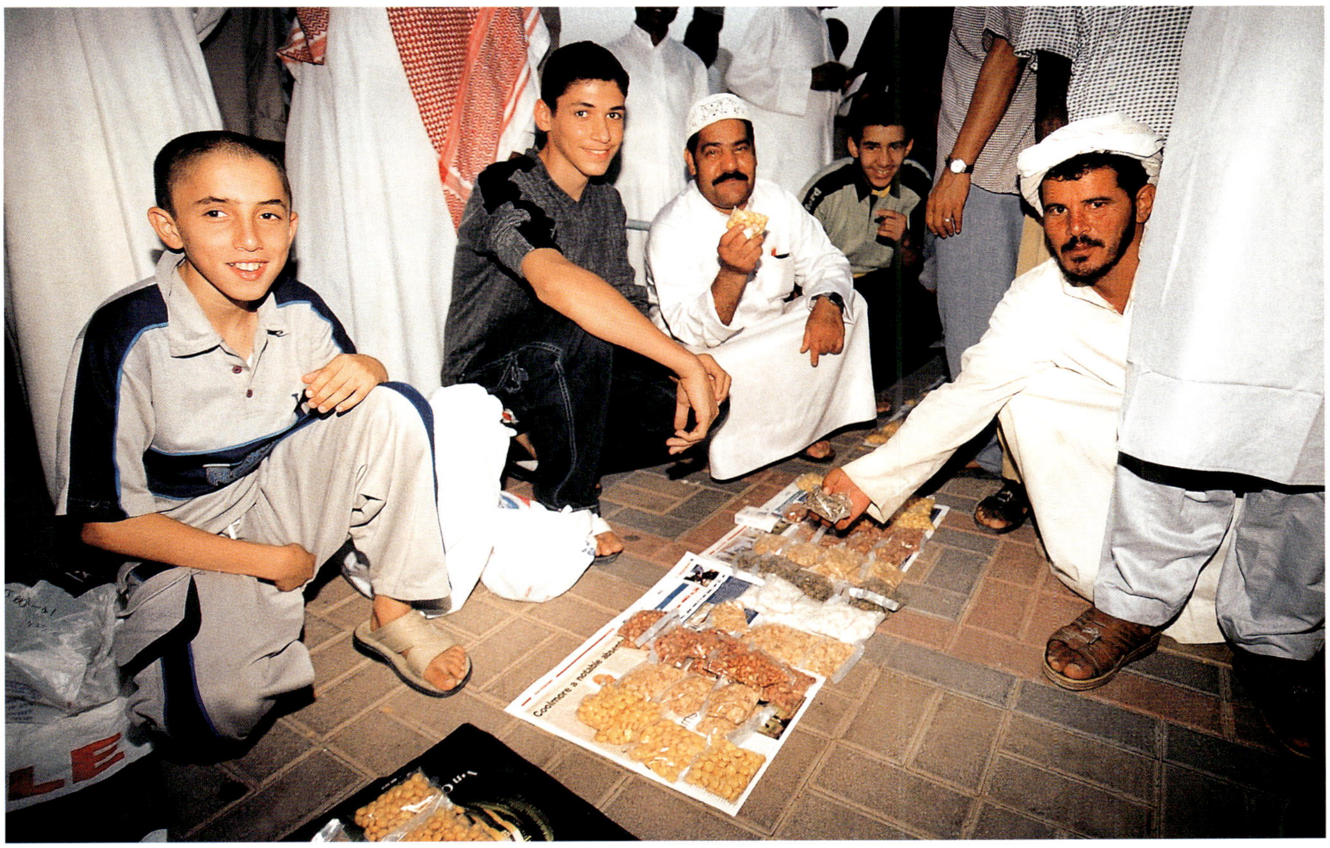

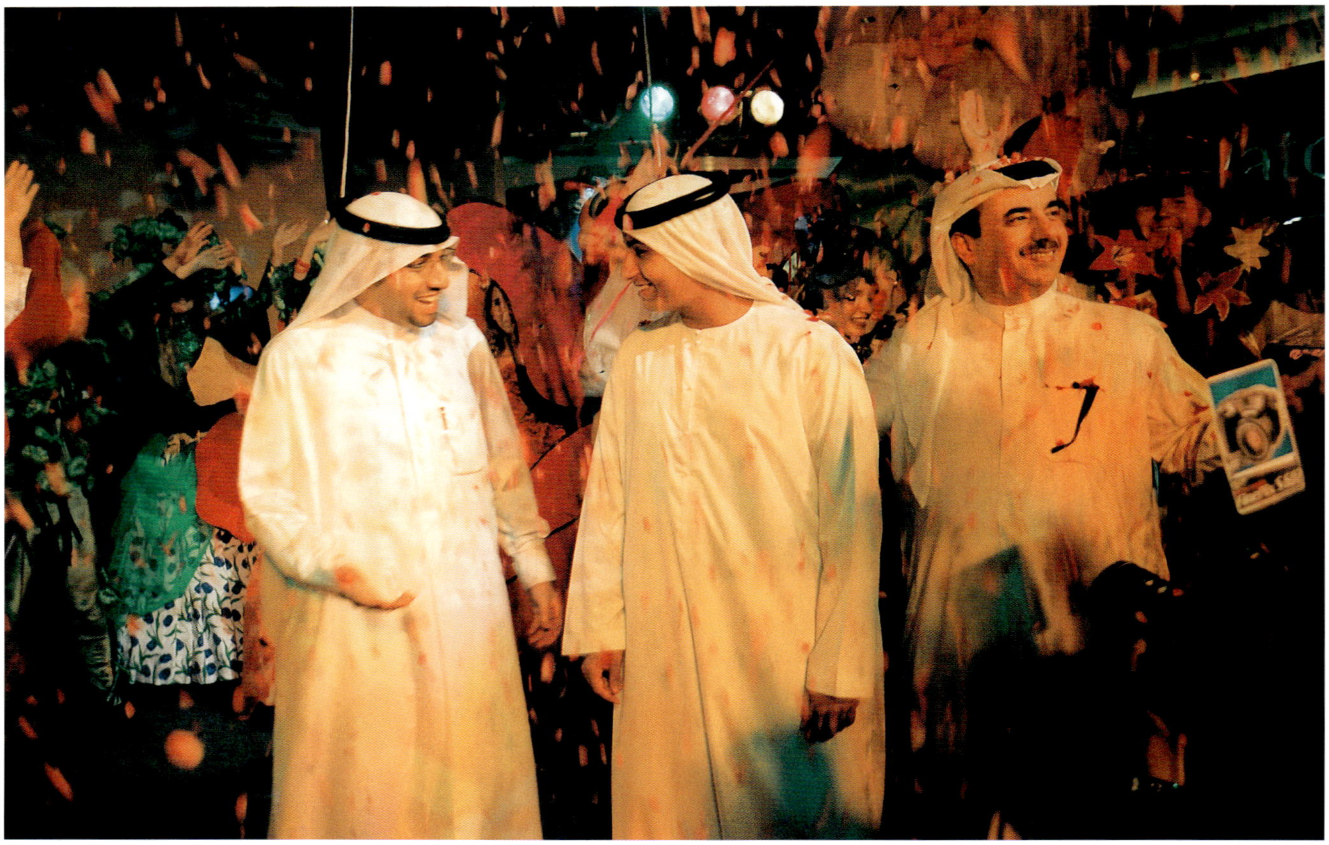

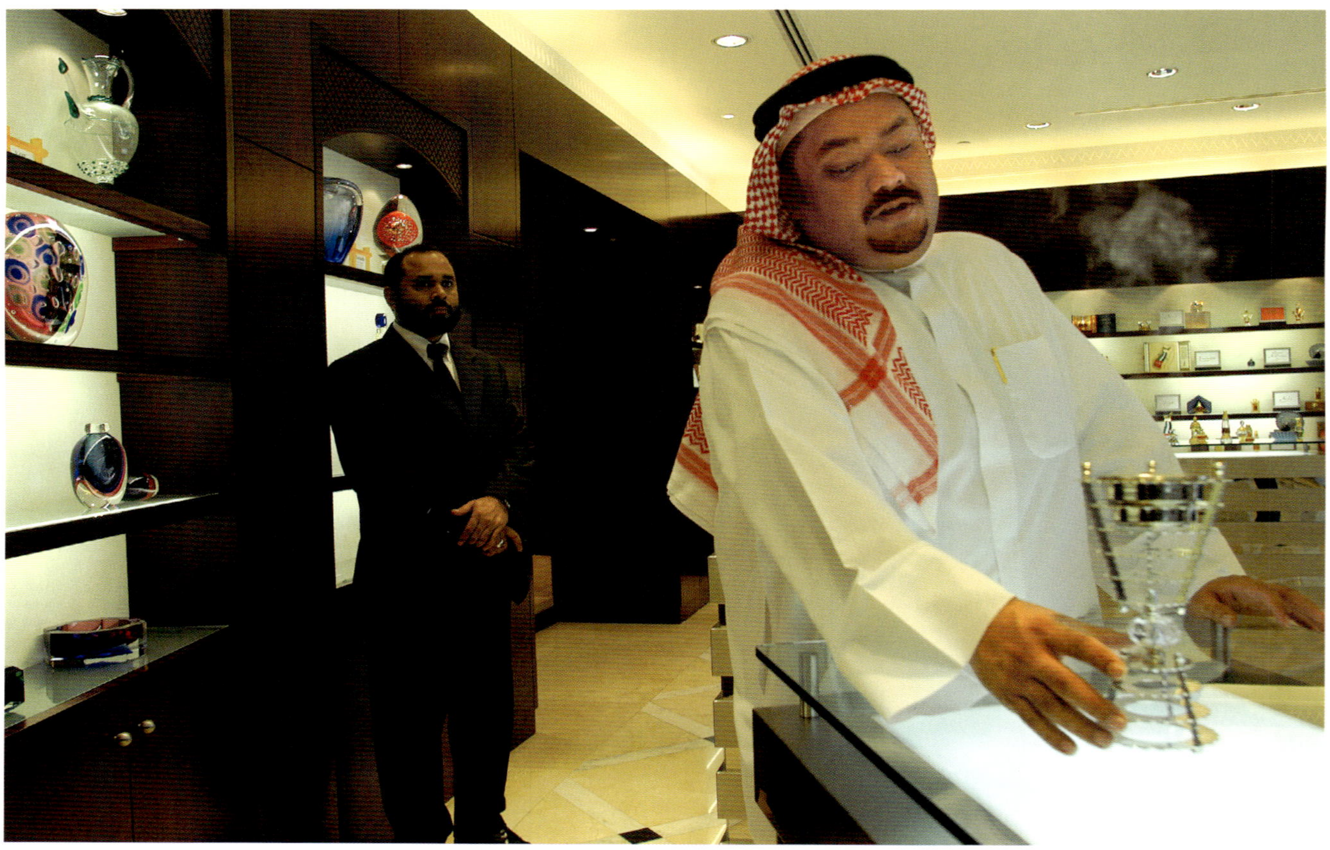

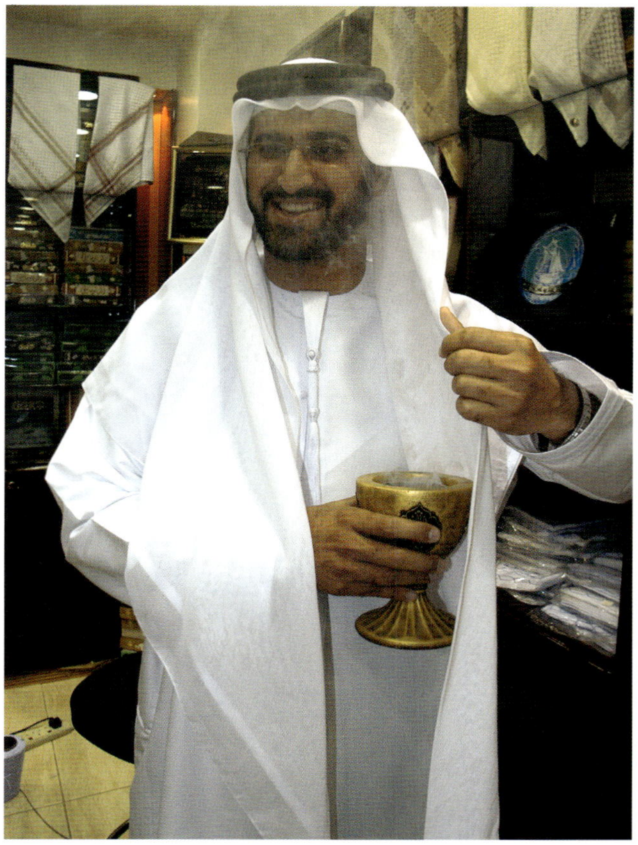

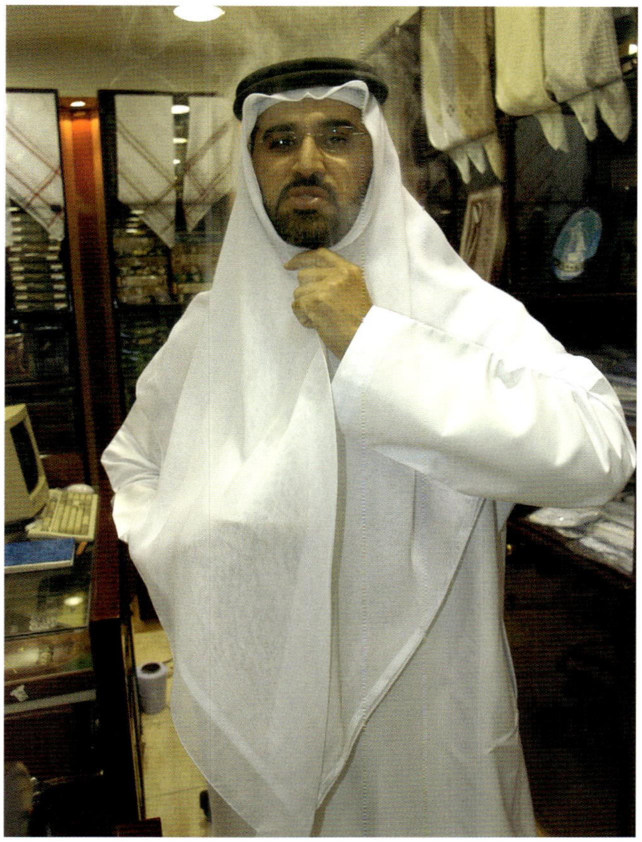

◄ It rained flowers in Dubai during one of the major festivities of the summer. HH Sheikh Rashid Bin Hamdan Bin Rashid Al Maktoum (centre) smiles as he inaugurates the festivities marking the beginning of Flower Surprises, one of the many themed weeks held during the annual Dubai Summer Surprises festival. On the left is the CEO of Dubai Summer Surprises and the Dubai Shopping Festival, Saeed Mohammed Al Nabouda; on the right is Ahmed Abdul Karim, Head of the Flower Surprises Organising Committee. *Photo by Ramesh Shukla.*

◄ The Ajmal Corporation has been concocting glorious perfumes for a quarter of a century and has 24 retail outlets in the United Arab Emirates alone. Whether Cold White Musk, Amber Spirit, Tayef Rose or the glorious Oud (one of the highest priced of all), the tradition of scents and perfumes in Arabia is believed to go back 4,000 years (left bottom). *Photo by Samar S Jodha.*

▲ ► The owner of a traditional Dubai tailor shop, Jabal Arafat, playfully displays an alternative method of perfuming himself – by placing a container of *bakhoor* incense inside his *kandoura*. *Photos by Dariush Zandi.*

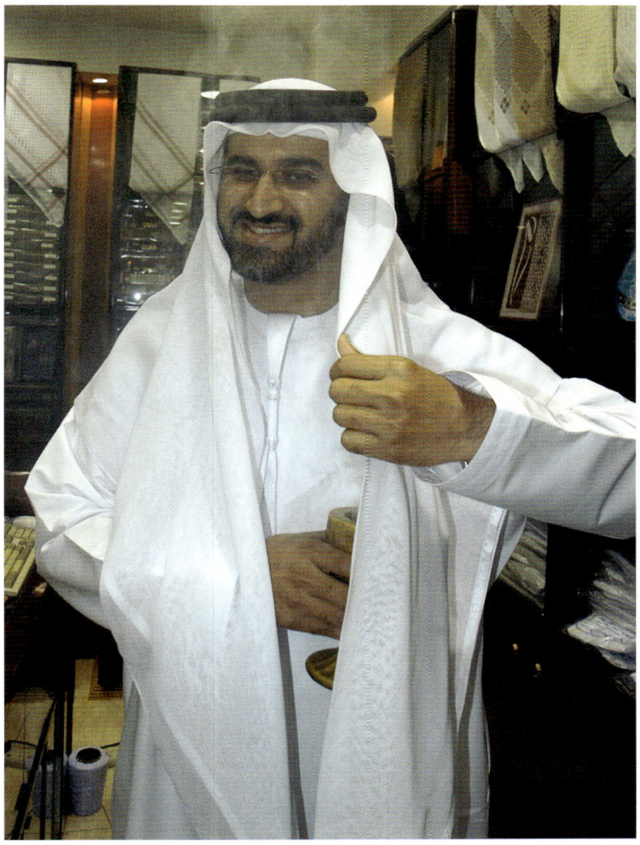

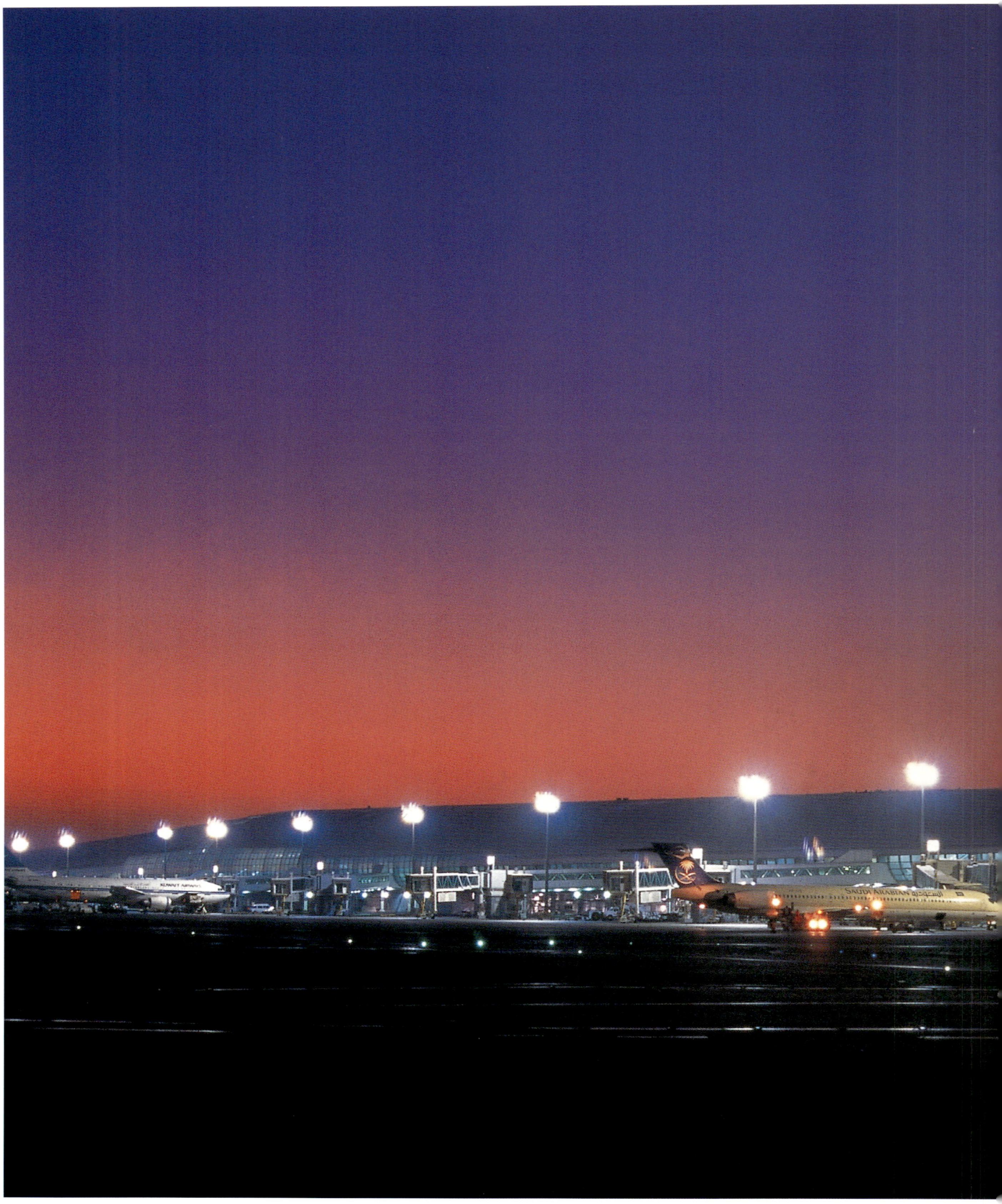

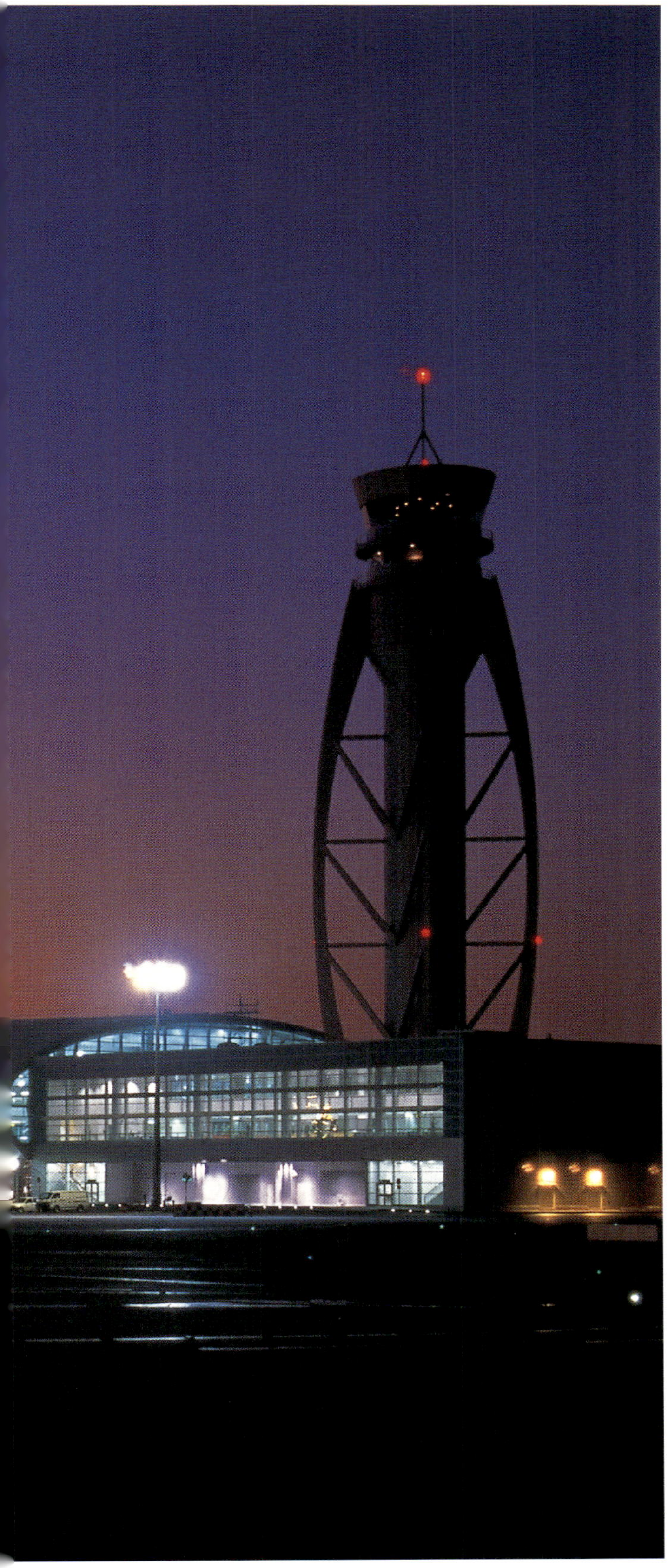

▶ ▶▶ DUBAI INTERNATIONAL AIRPORT MAY BE THE MOST user-friendly airport in the world. Enormous, glossy, utterly spotless and efficient, it caters to human beings, whether in its elegant expanse of duty-free shopping, or Parisian-like coffee houses. Attractive hostesses from all round the world welcome and escort arriving passengers and customs officials make it unbelievably easy to come and go. In 2002, Dubai's Department of Civil Aviation invested US$4.1 billion into the airport's new expansion, to accommodate nearly 20 per cent annual growth in passenger use. By 2010, 30-million travellers a year are expected to land or take off at Dubai International Airport. As for Dubai's own airline, Emirates, it's the fastest-growing airline in the world and regularly wins top international awards. *Photos by Dubai International Airport (left) and Shankar Adiseshan, Motivate Publishing (overleaf).*

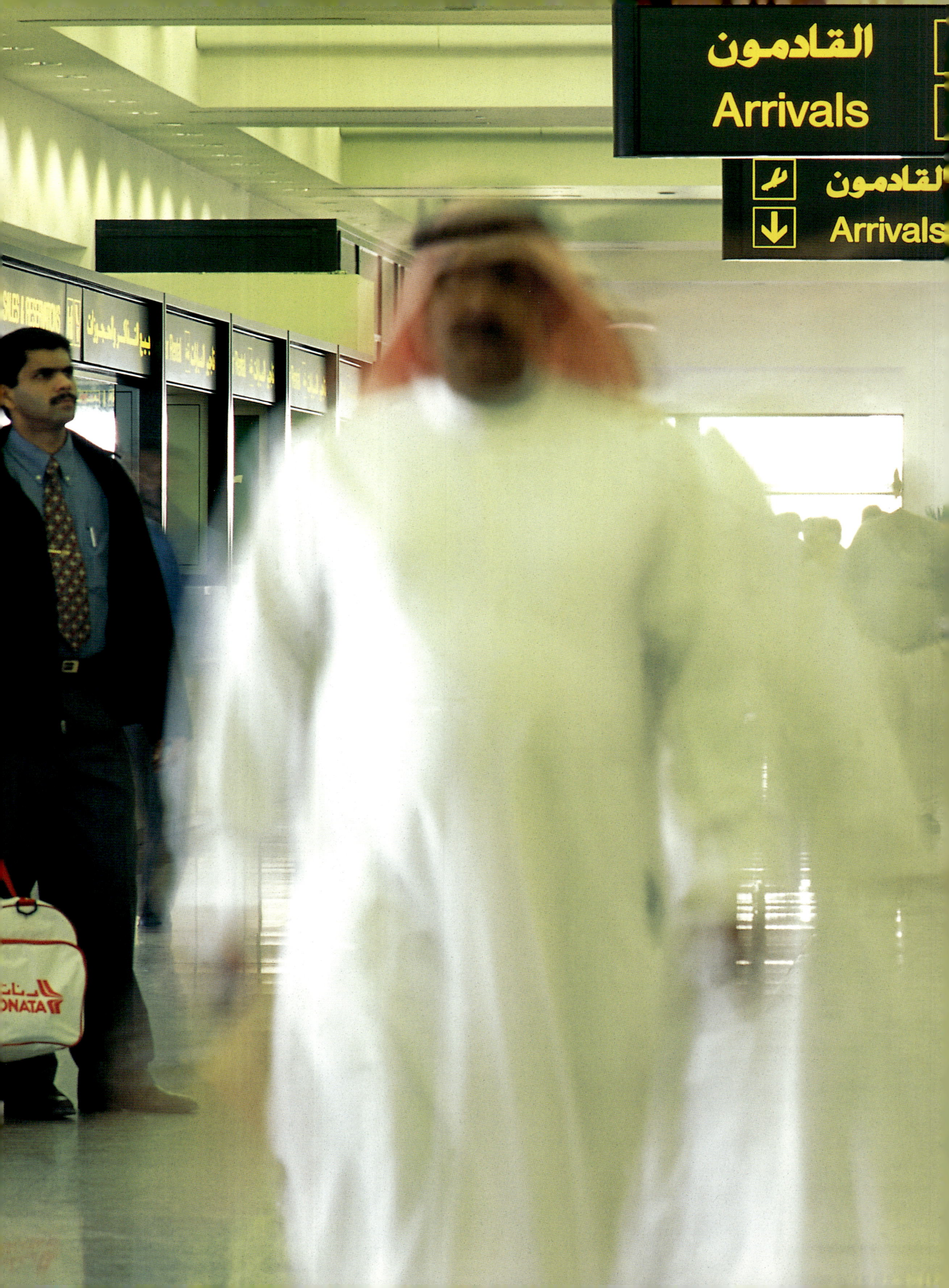
القادمون
Arrivals
القادمون
Arrivals

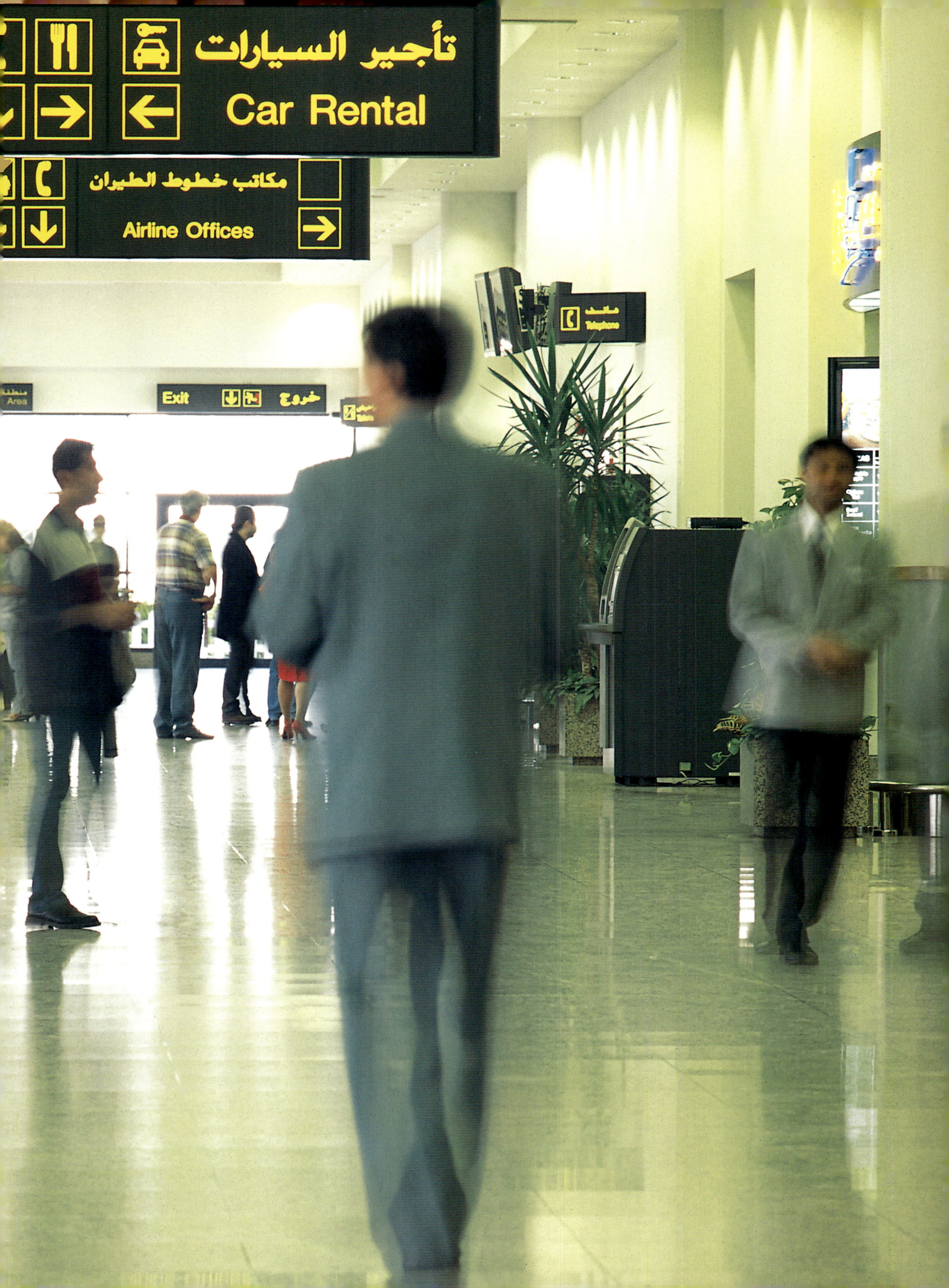
تأجير السيارات
Car Rental
مكاتب خطوط الطيران
Airline Offices
Exit
خروج

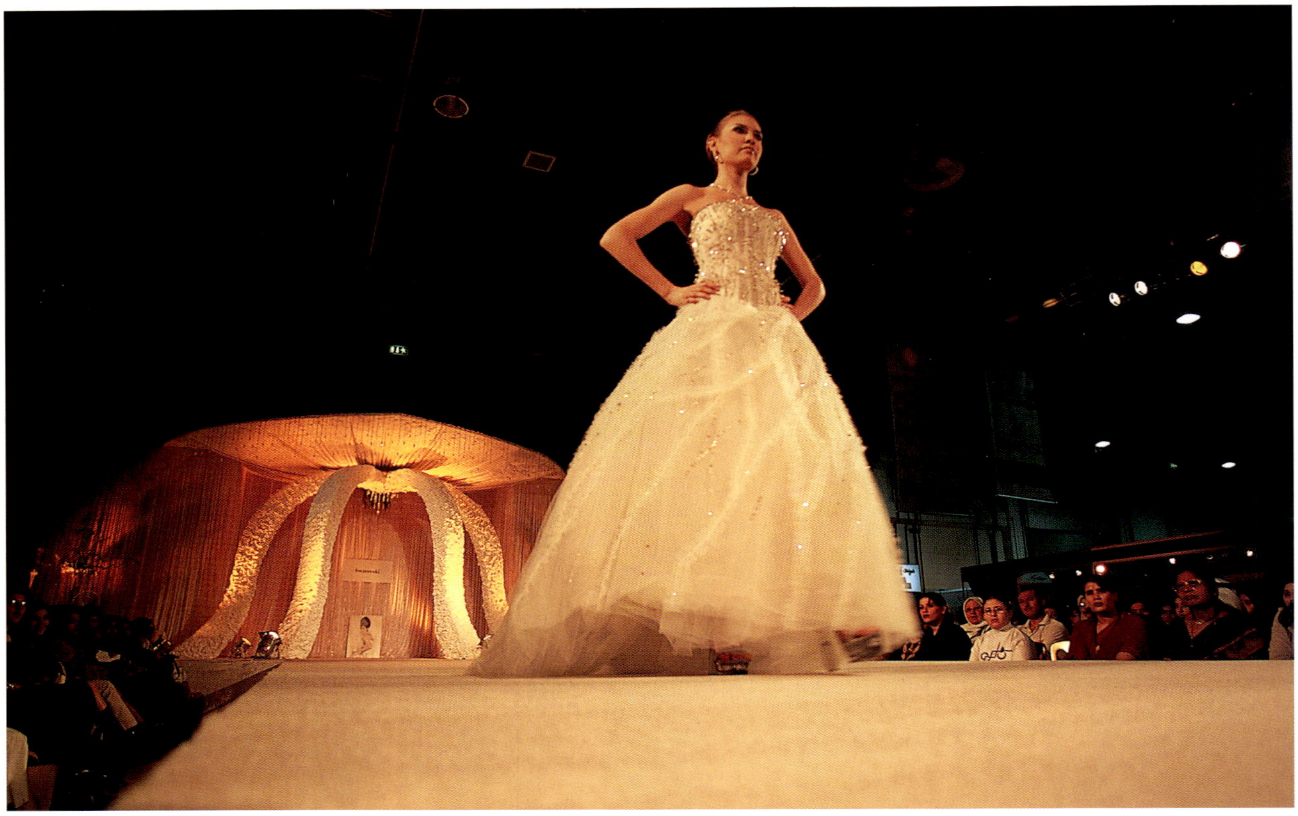

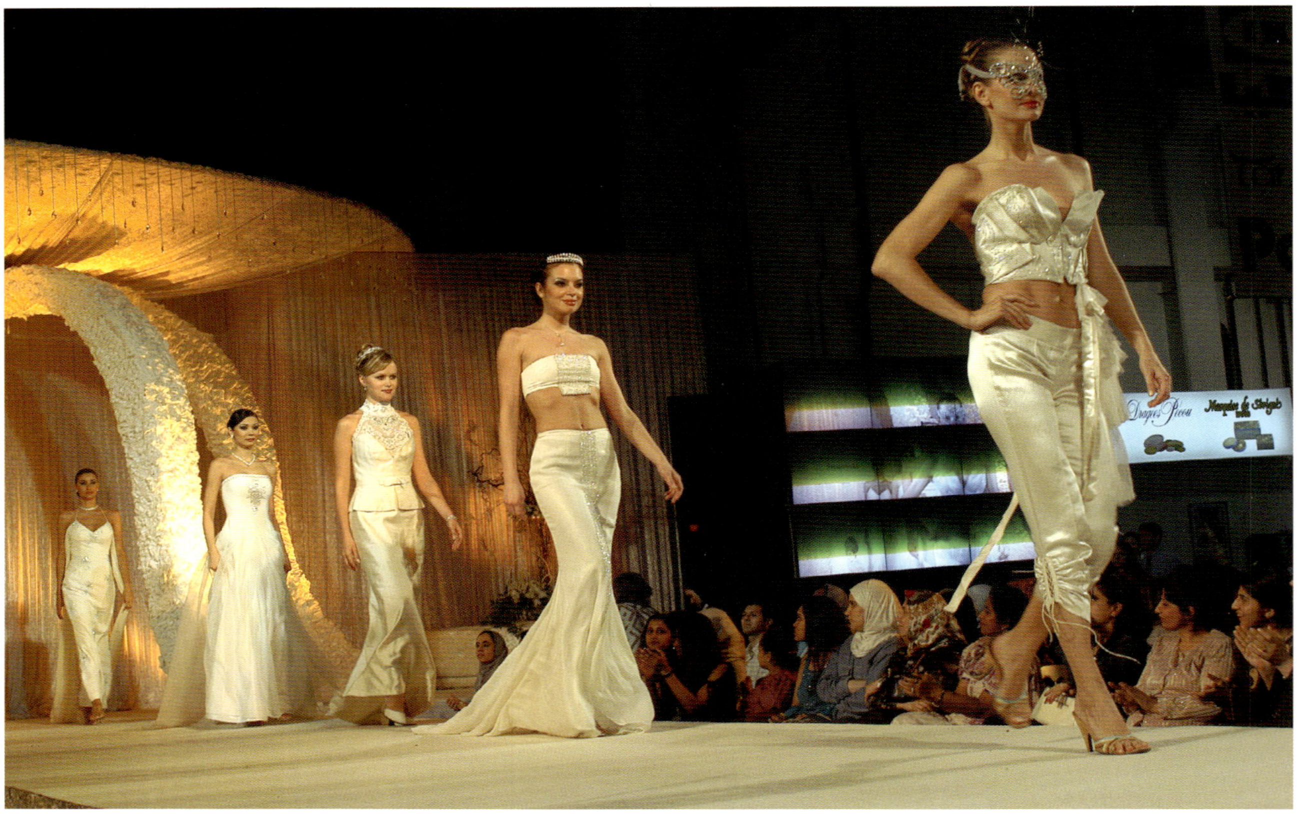

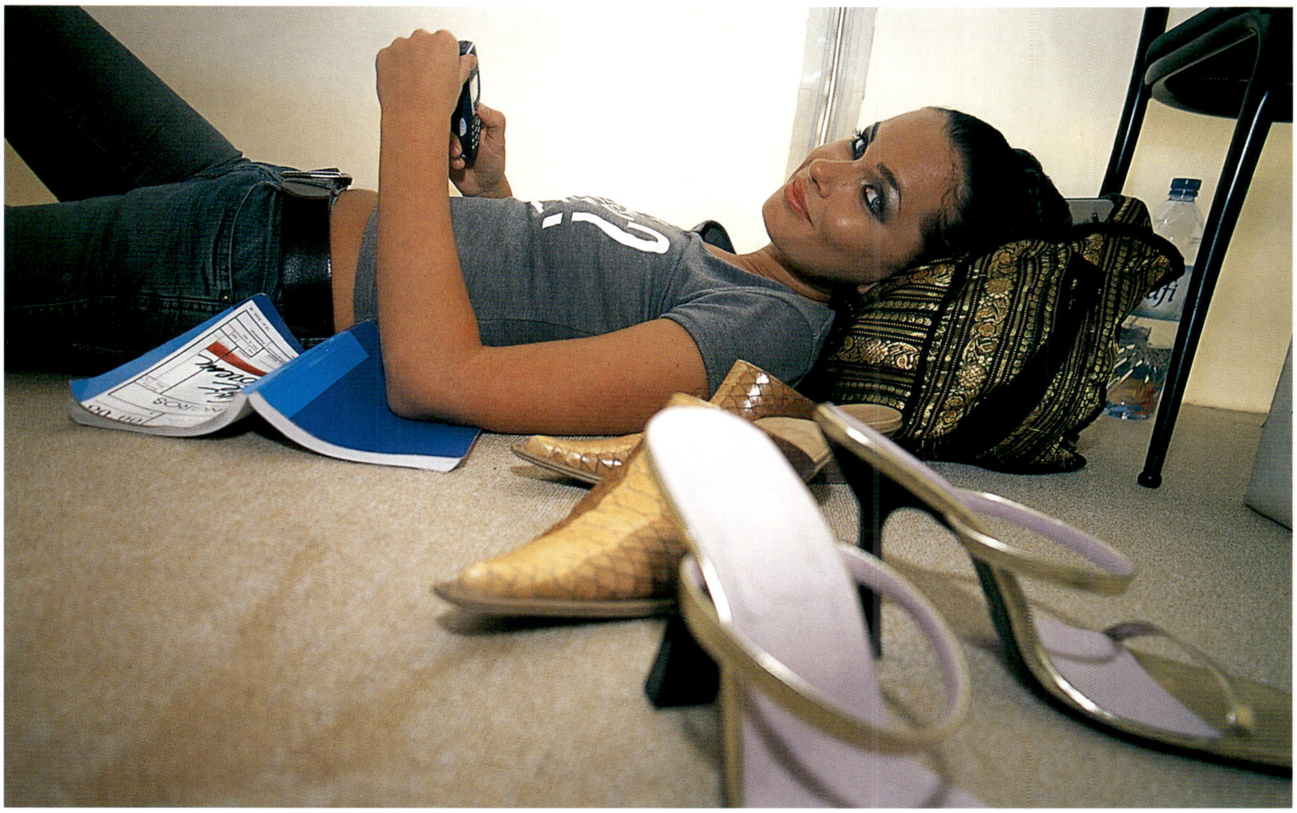

◀ ▲ ▶▶ DURING A MAJOR BRIDAL FASHION SHOW, glamorous models at the Dubai World Trade Centre contradict yet again the dogged stereotype that would have Islamic communities sheltered from female glamour and the pizazz of the global fashion industry. Yet, if anything, Dubai's beauty as an emirate, a city, a people, is reflected in its vibrant fashion scene. *Photos by Dariush Zandi.*

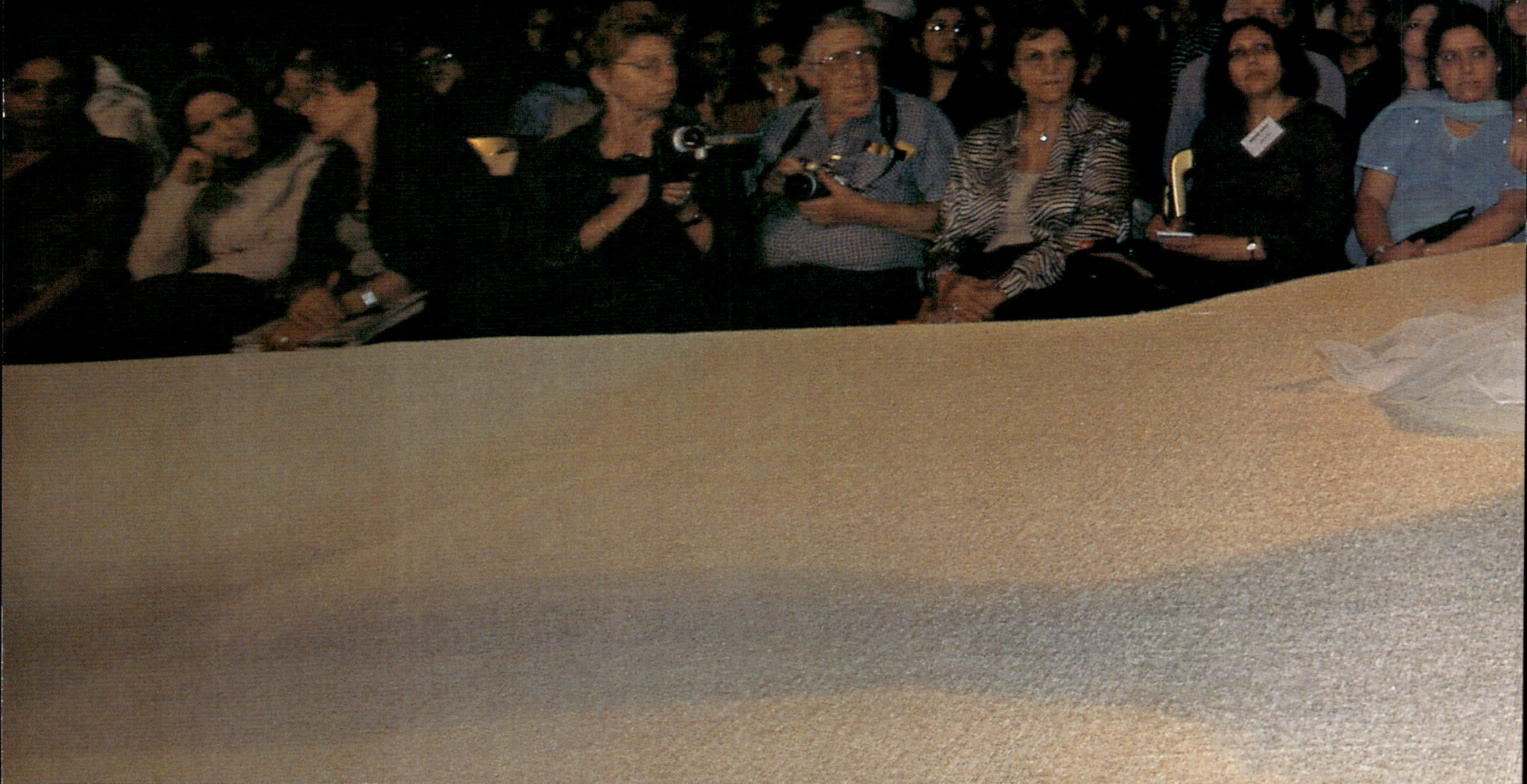

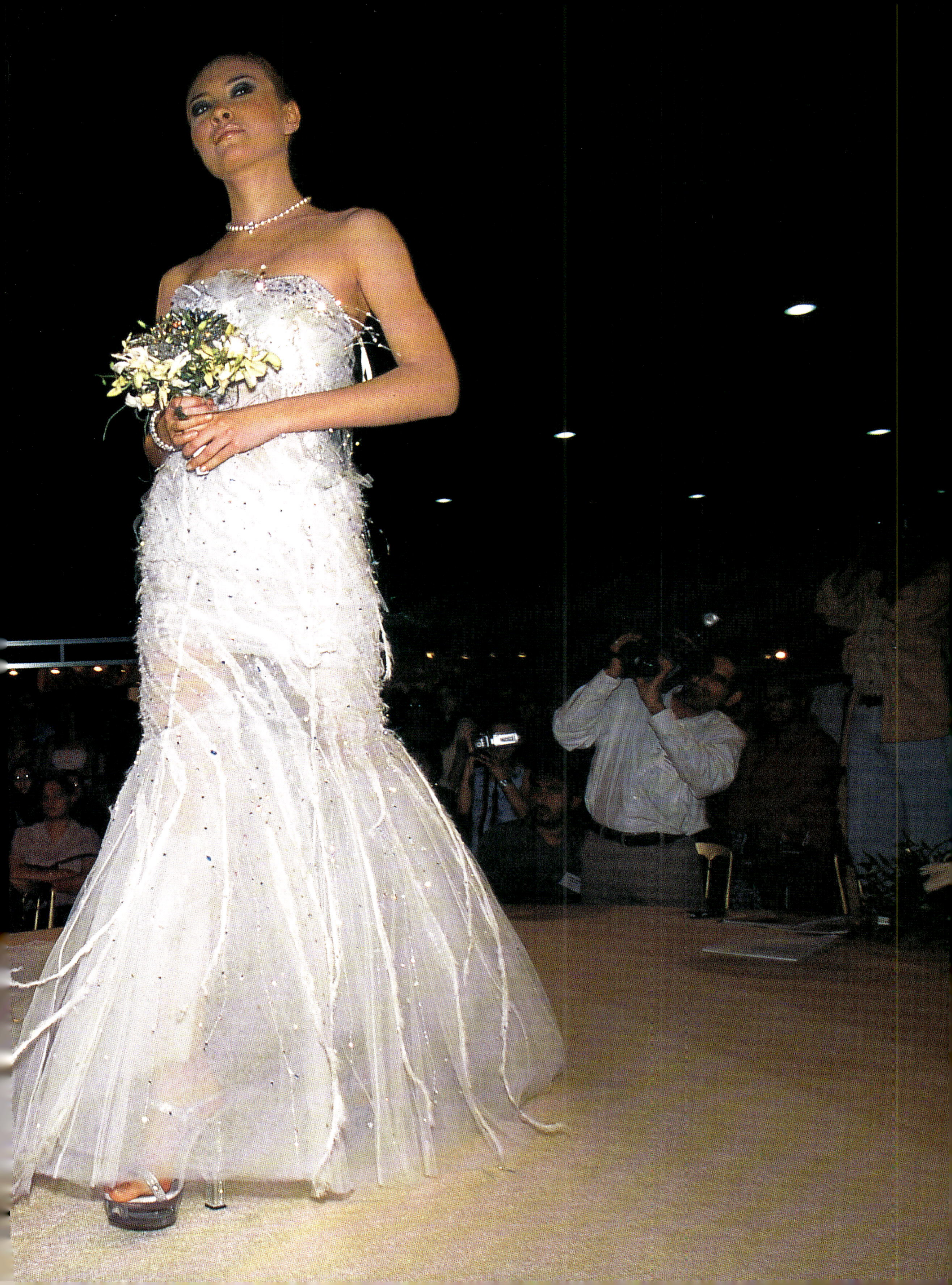

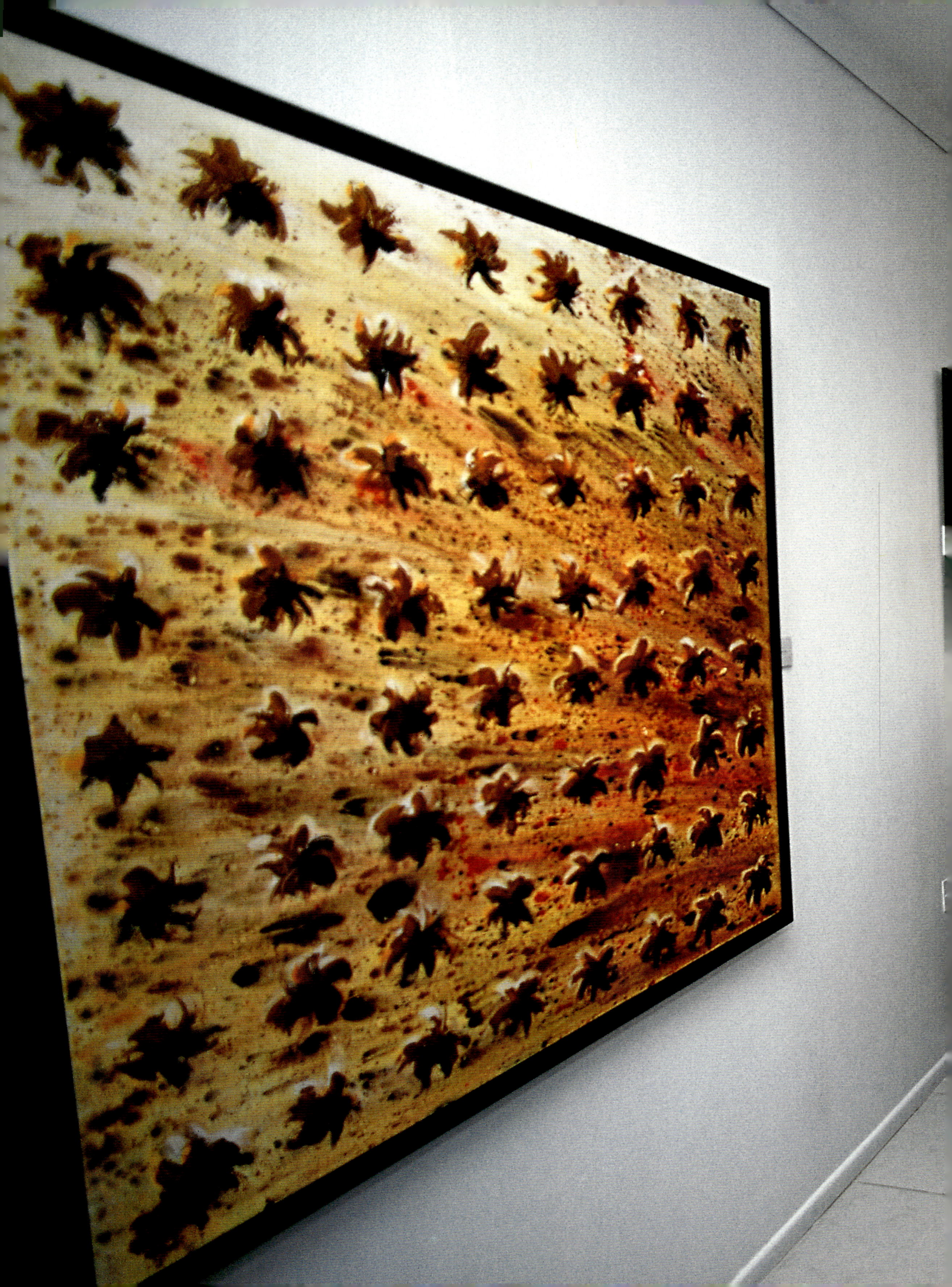

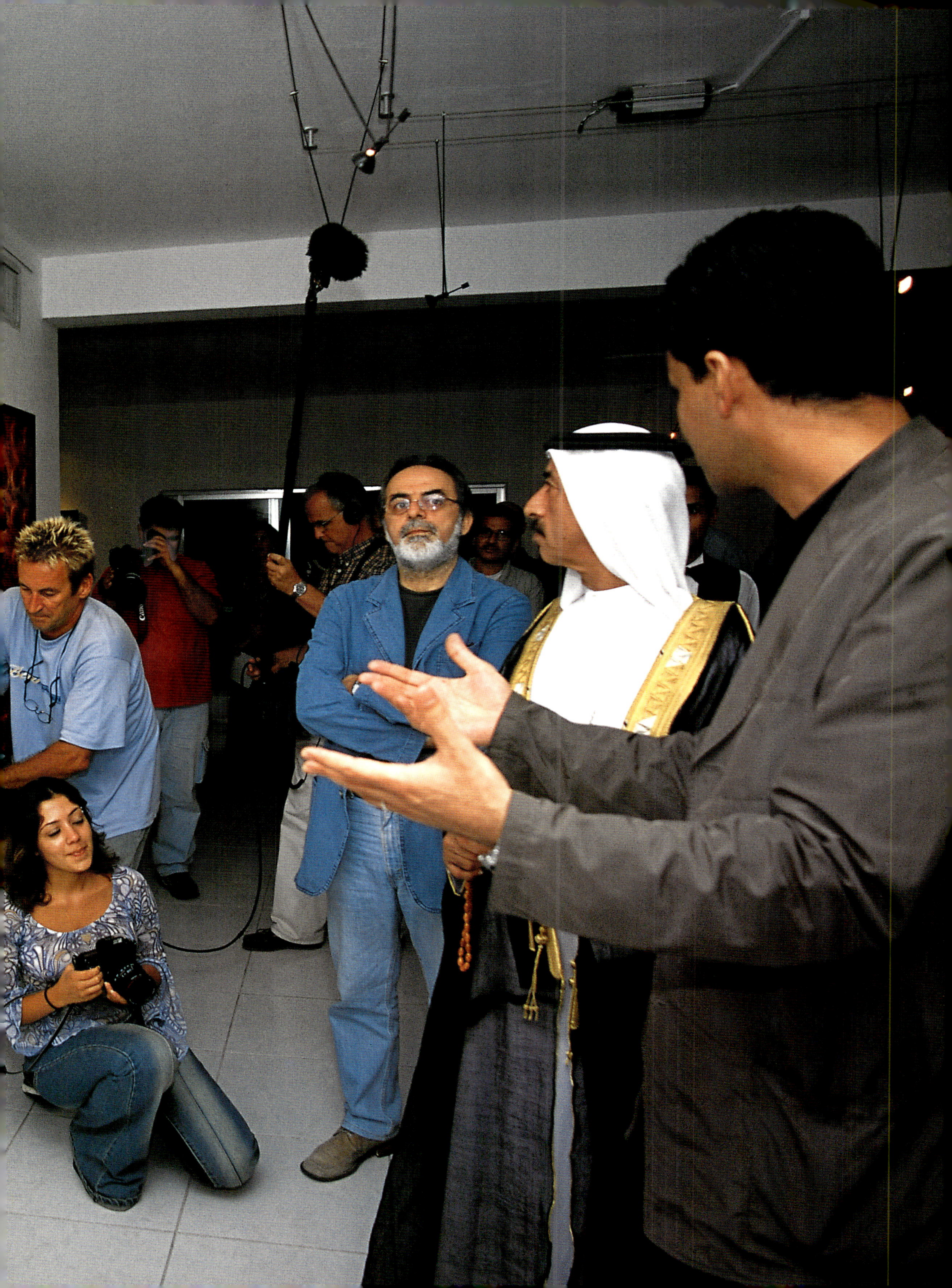

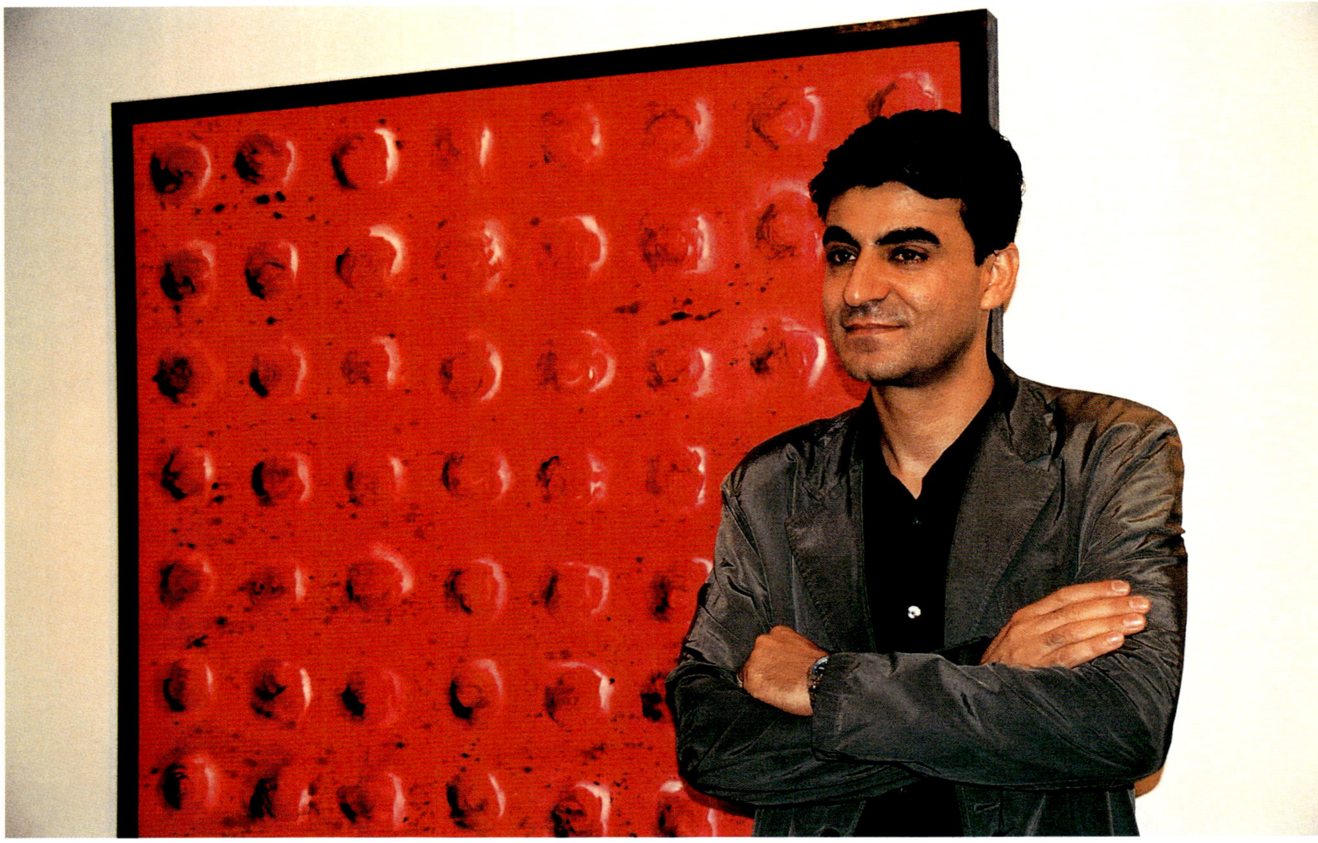

◀◀ ▲ GREEN ART GALLERY IN JUMEIRAH HAS SPONSORED emerging talent and been in the vanguard of Arab culture, as heralded by a new generation of local artists. Limited-edition prints, original paintings and photographs, as well as certain handicrafts unique to Dubai, have set the pace and sensibility for a wide-ranging array of native acumen as figured in pictorial arts. While being filmed by the *Dubai 24 hours* crew and photographer Sara Masinaei at the opening of a new exhibition, HH Sheikh Hasher bin Maktoum Al Maktoum listens while artist Thaier Helal introduces his work (previous spread) before posing in front of another of his paintings (above). *Photos by Dariush Zandi (previous spread) and Sara Masinaei (above).*

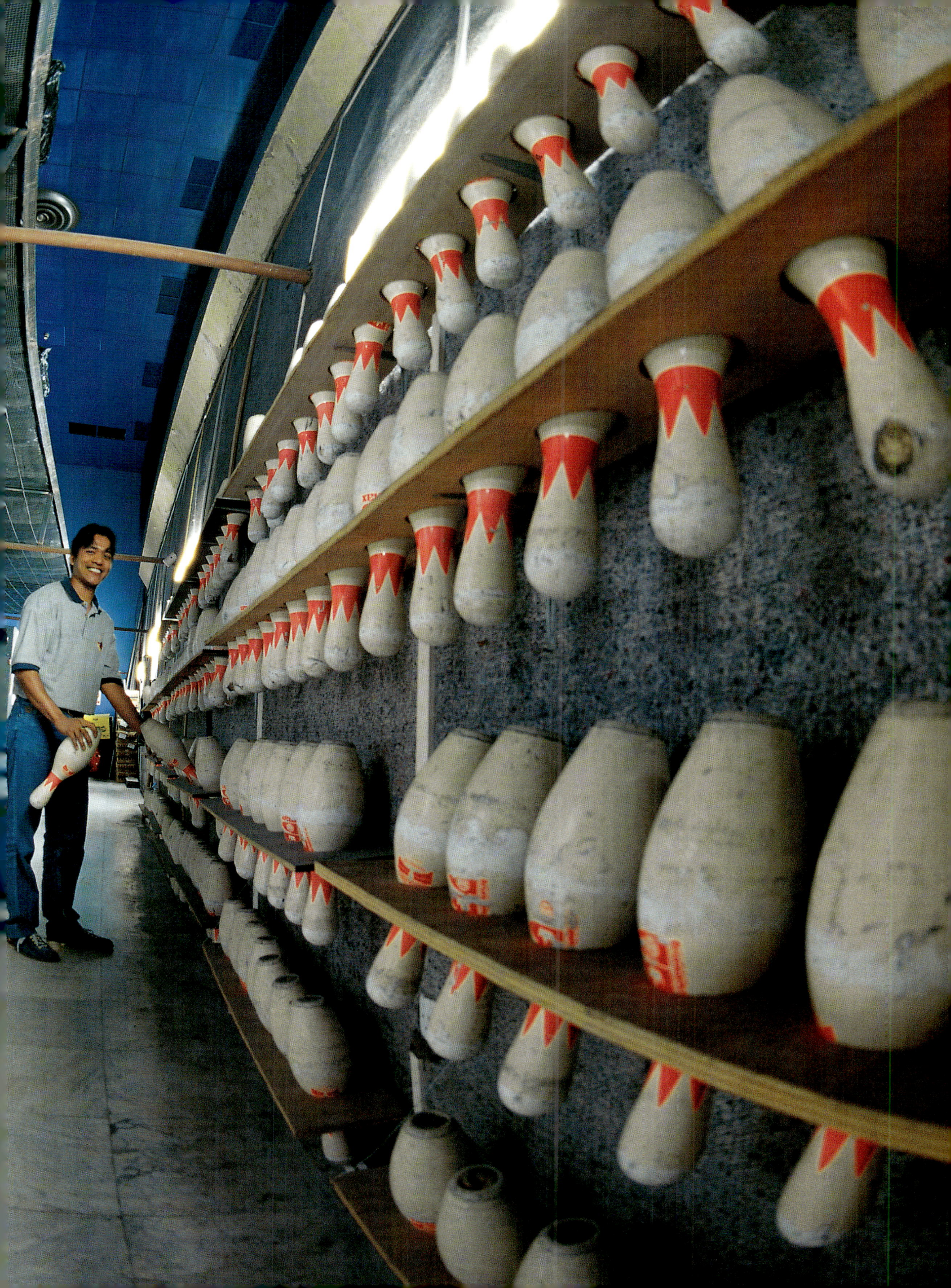

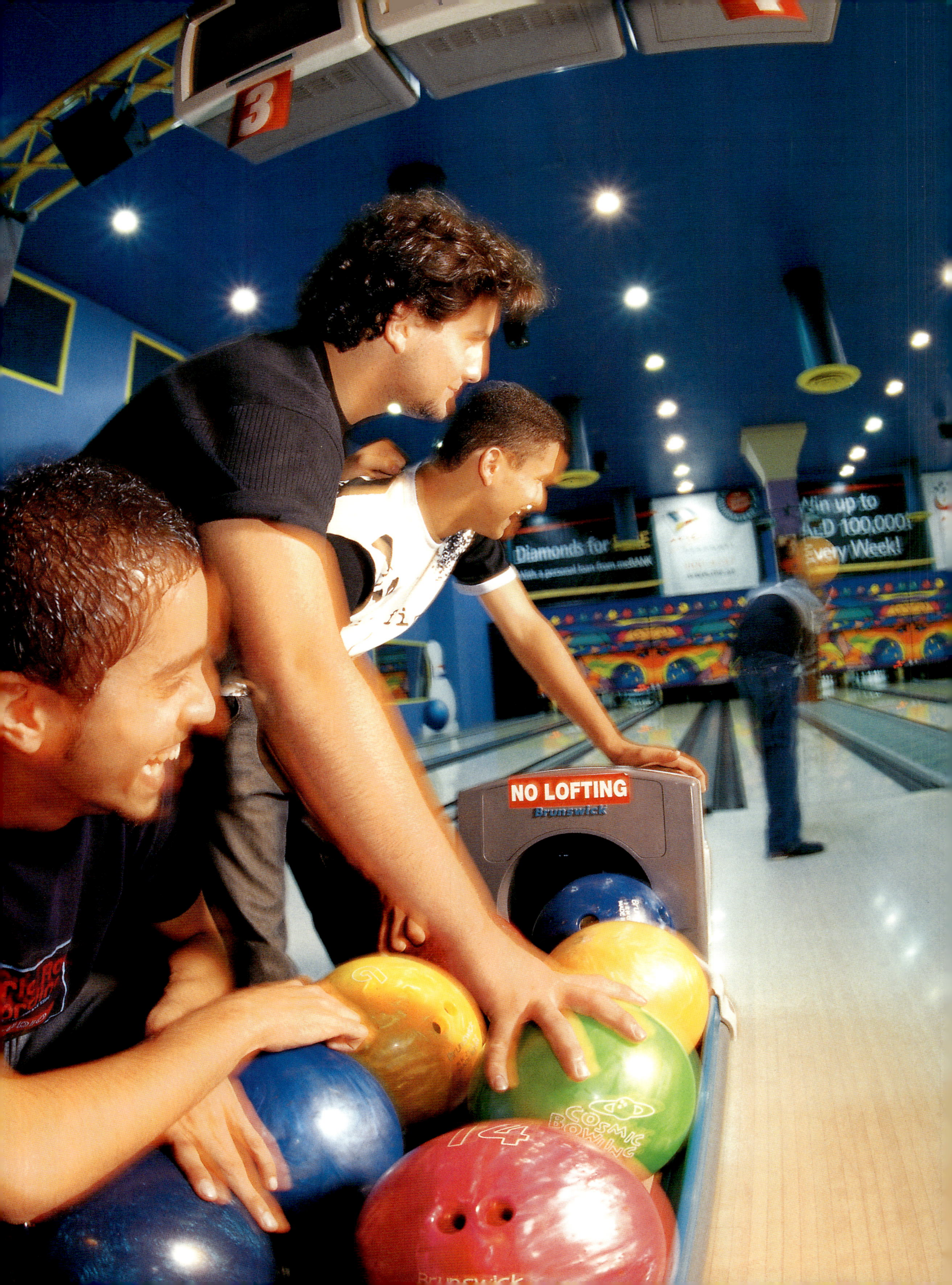
3
Diamonds for
Every Week!
NO LOFTING
Brunswick
COSMIC BOWLING
14

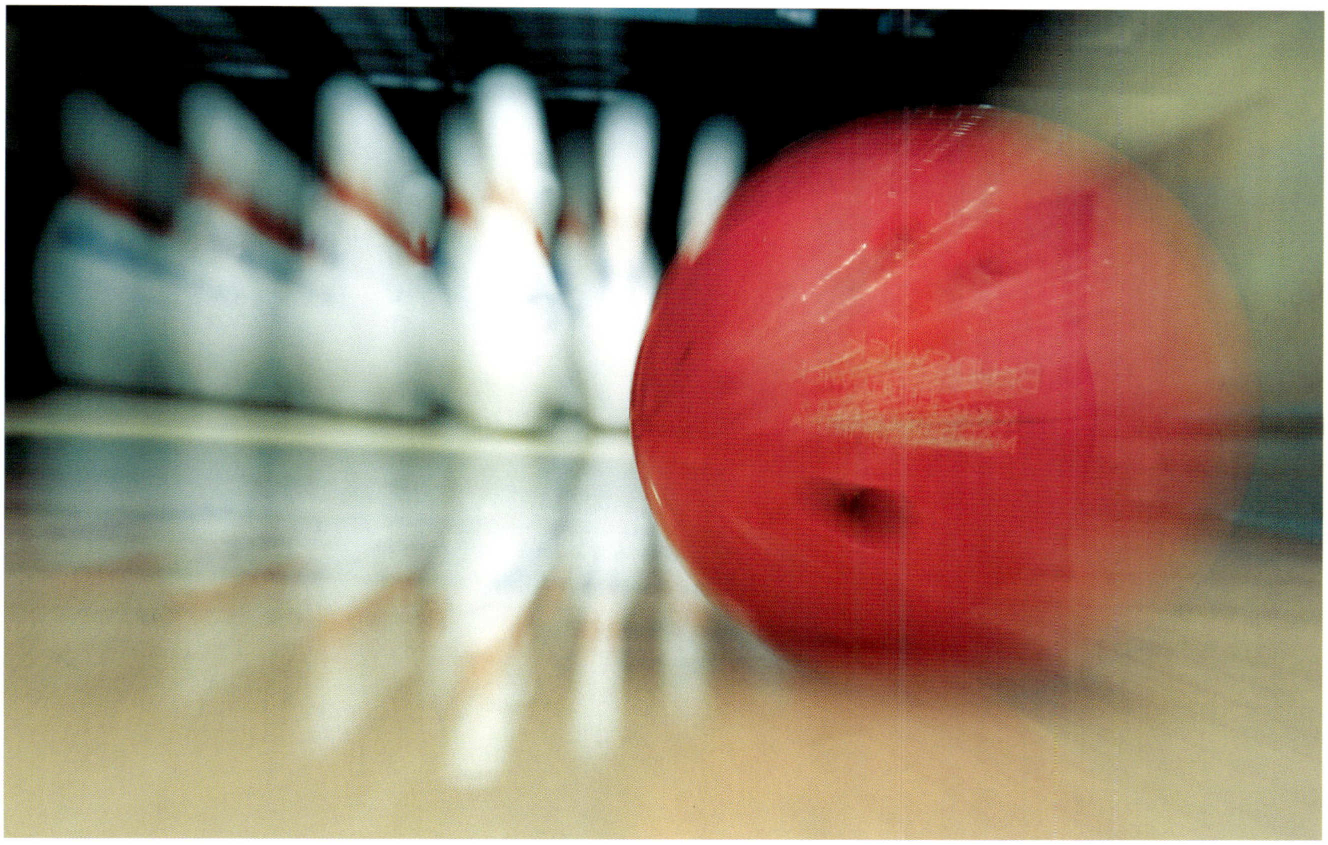

◄◄ ◄ ▲ At Thunder Bowl, 20 bowling lanes, air-conditioned video games and a pizza stand afford a relaxing family getaway from the heat and seriousness of life on the outside. While *Dubai 24 hours* was being filmed, two children were questioned about their game. One had achieved a remarkable (professional-level) score of more than 230. The 10-year old evidently bowled every night. When asked whether he didn't worry about recent scientific data suggesting young people who bowled frequently lose some of their brainpower, just like mountaineers at high altitude, he knew the question was made-up, quickly gobbled down his pizza, and returned to his favourite lane. *Photos by Joe Sassine.*

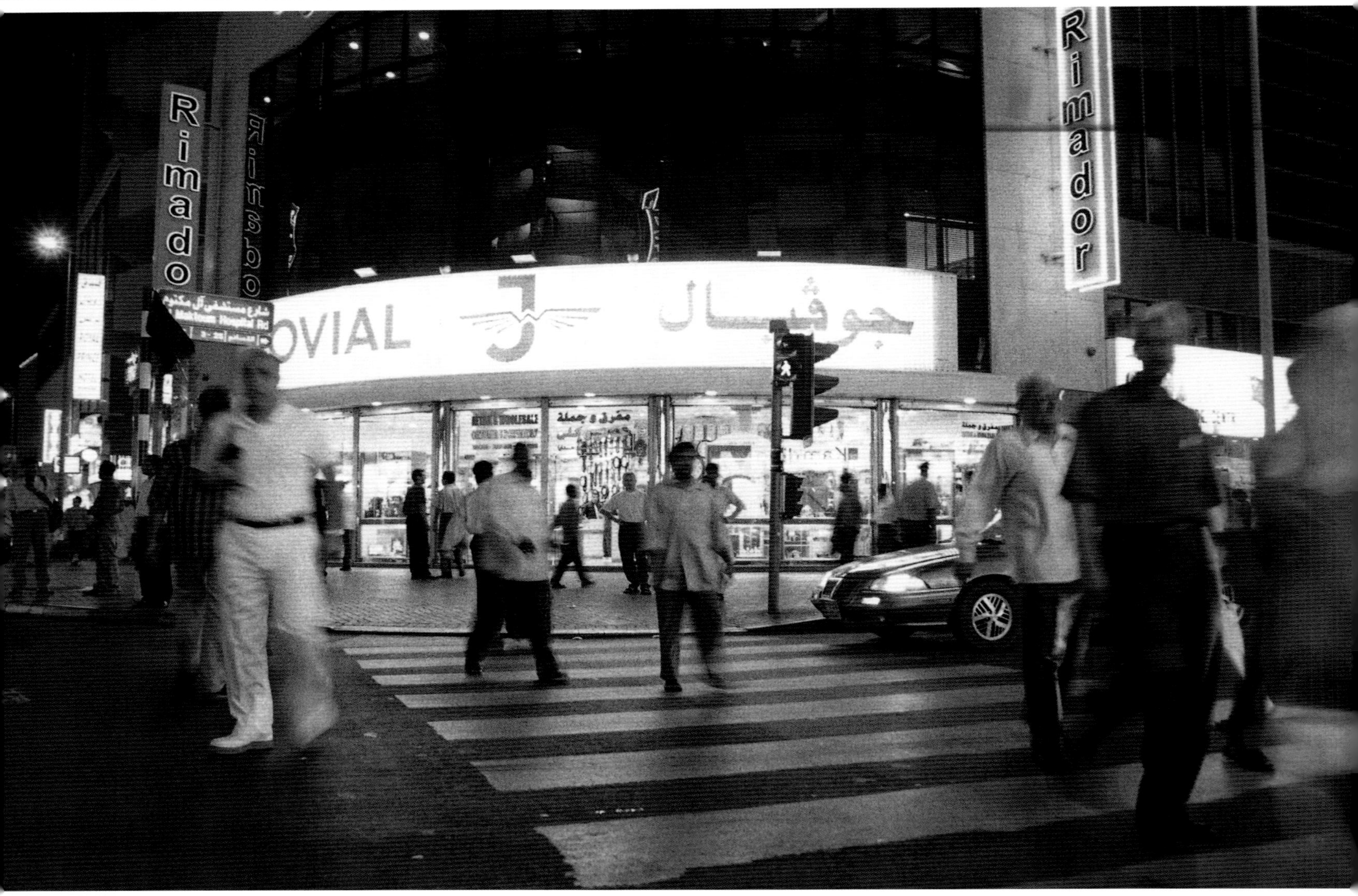

▲ ▶ When the camera crew followed Souheil Semaan into the Sabkha district one night, they had no idea that he's probably the most gregarious Lebanese photographer in the world, certainly in Dubai. The Sabkha features wide boulevards, flamboyant, Las Vegas-like neon, and thousands of lively little shops hosting an ever-streaming blend of casual visitors.

▶▶ Al Taj Studio's Nepalese photographer, Krishna Rao, prepares to photograph *Dubai 24 hours* photographer, Souheil Semaan, in the teeming Sabkha neighbourhood. "Business is good!" says 32-year old Rao, echoing the thoughts of many others. *Photos by Souheil Semaan.*

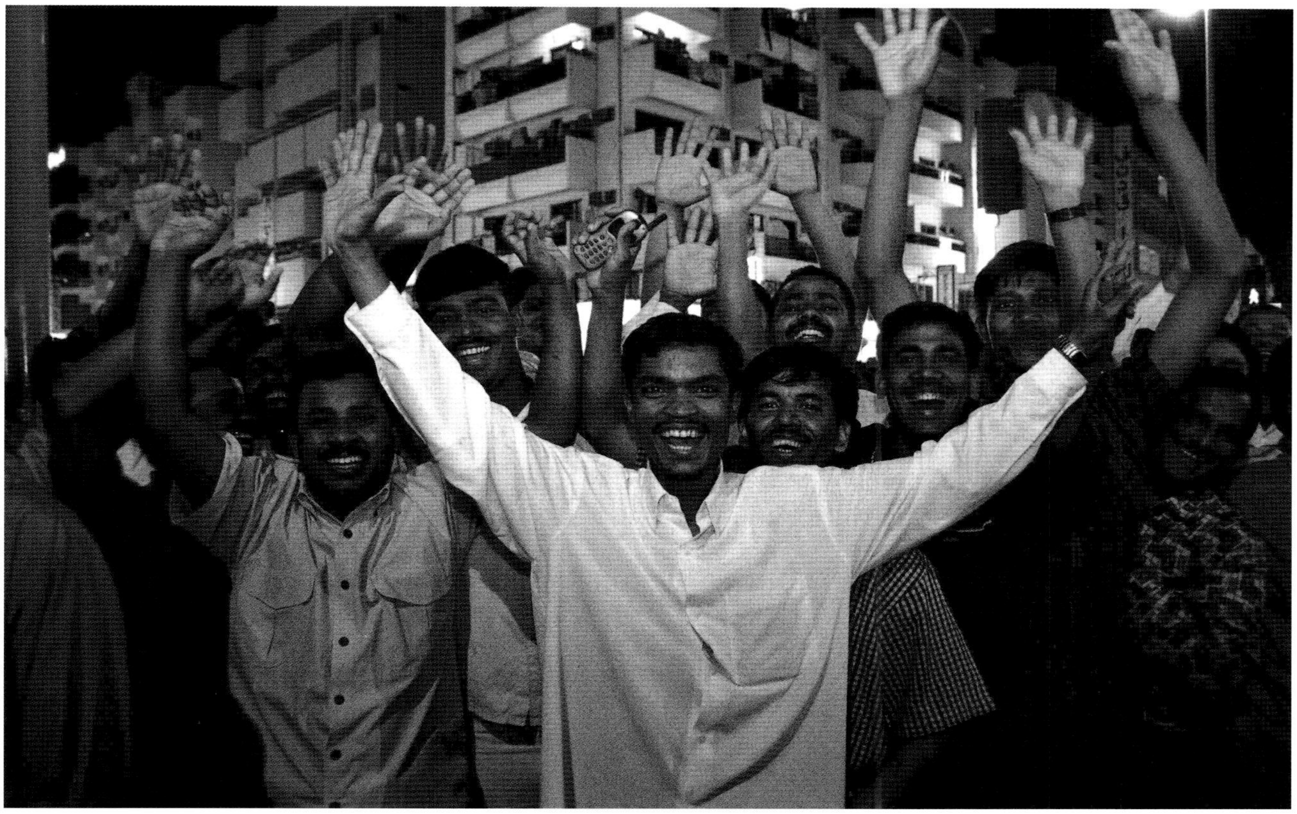

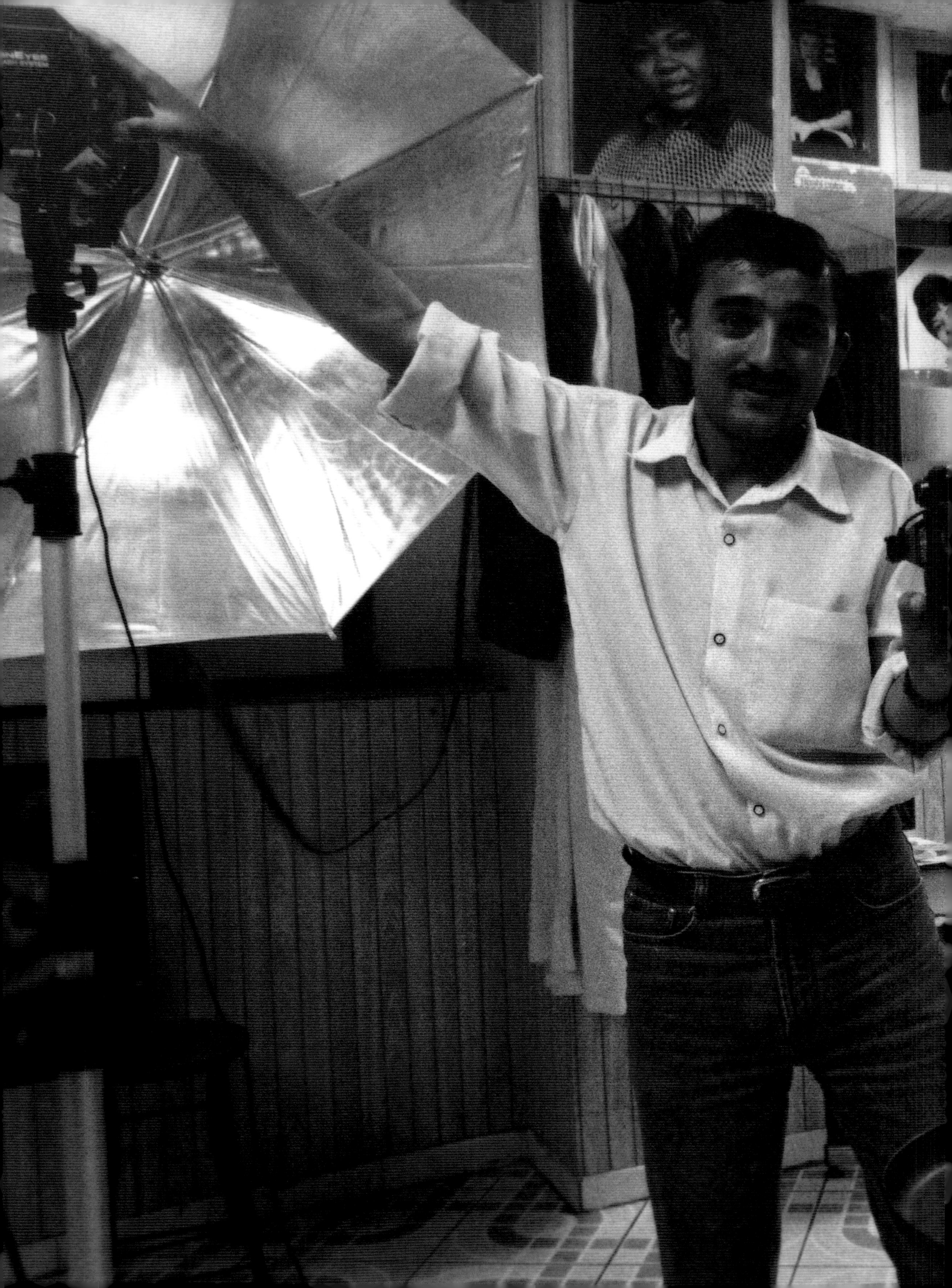

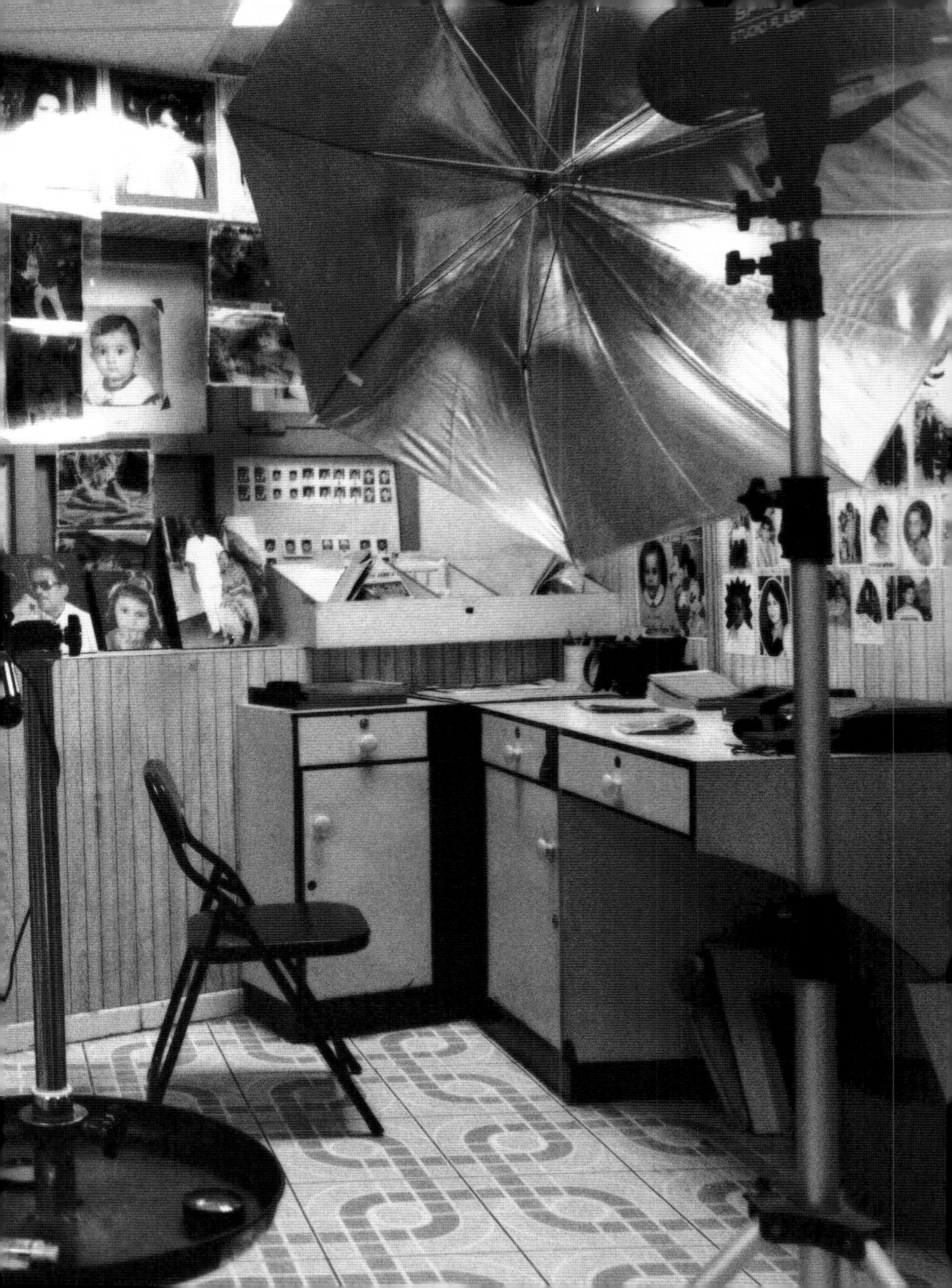

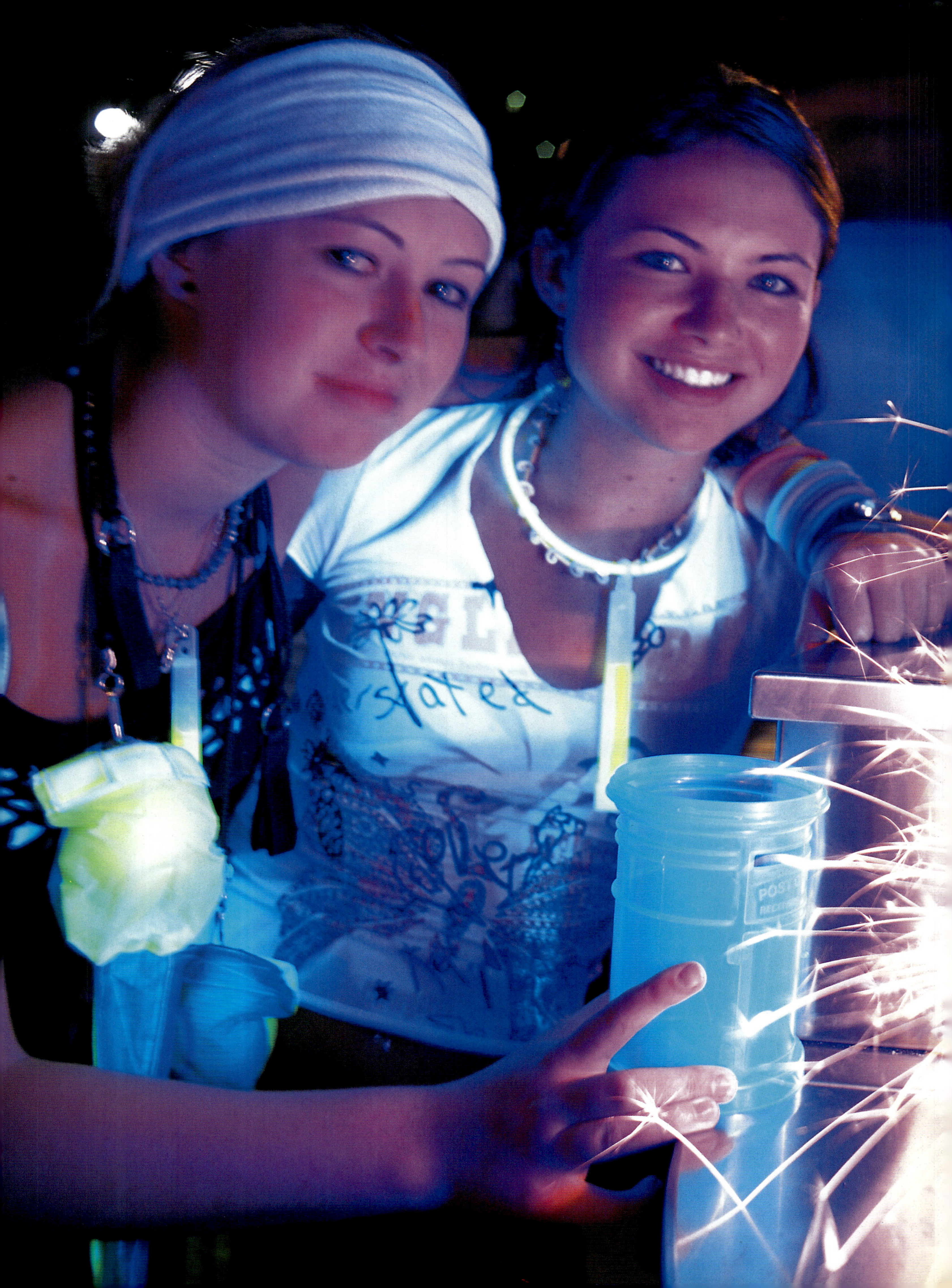

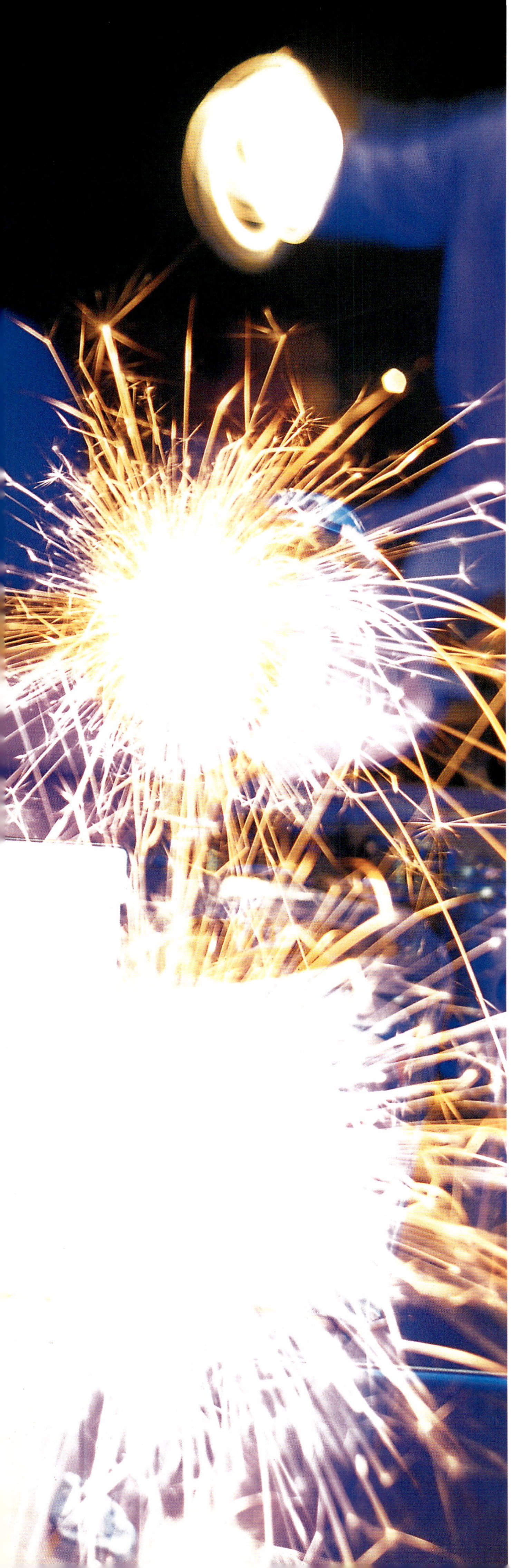

◄ ►► DUBAI, WITHOUT DOUBT, IS A SEA OF RICHES WHEN it comes to nightlife. Discos, late-night reveries, taverns and beach parties (such as the Mina Moon Beach gathering, viewed by sparklers, rather than the moon) have all become part of the culture. In Dubai, most nationalities freely blend and dance together. Darkness only accentuates the true social and ethnic integration that's occurred here and is, by all accounts, something rare and quite special. While some might shy away from such emphatic displays of abandonment, the simple truth is there for anyone to see: "girls (and boys) just want to have fun!" *Photos by Joe Sassine.*

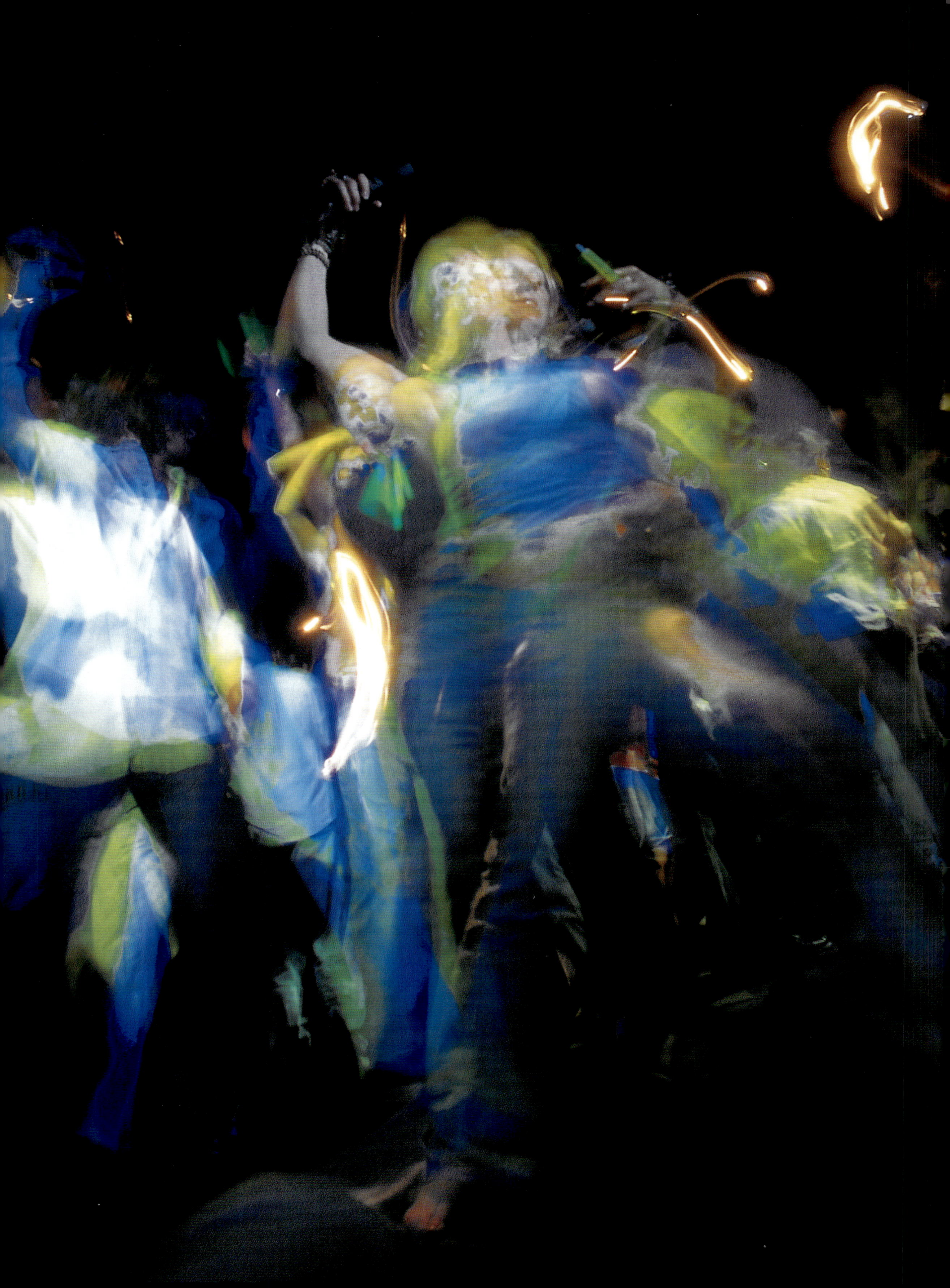

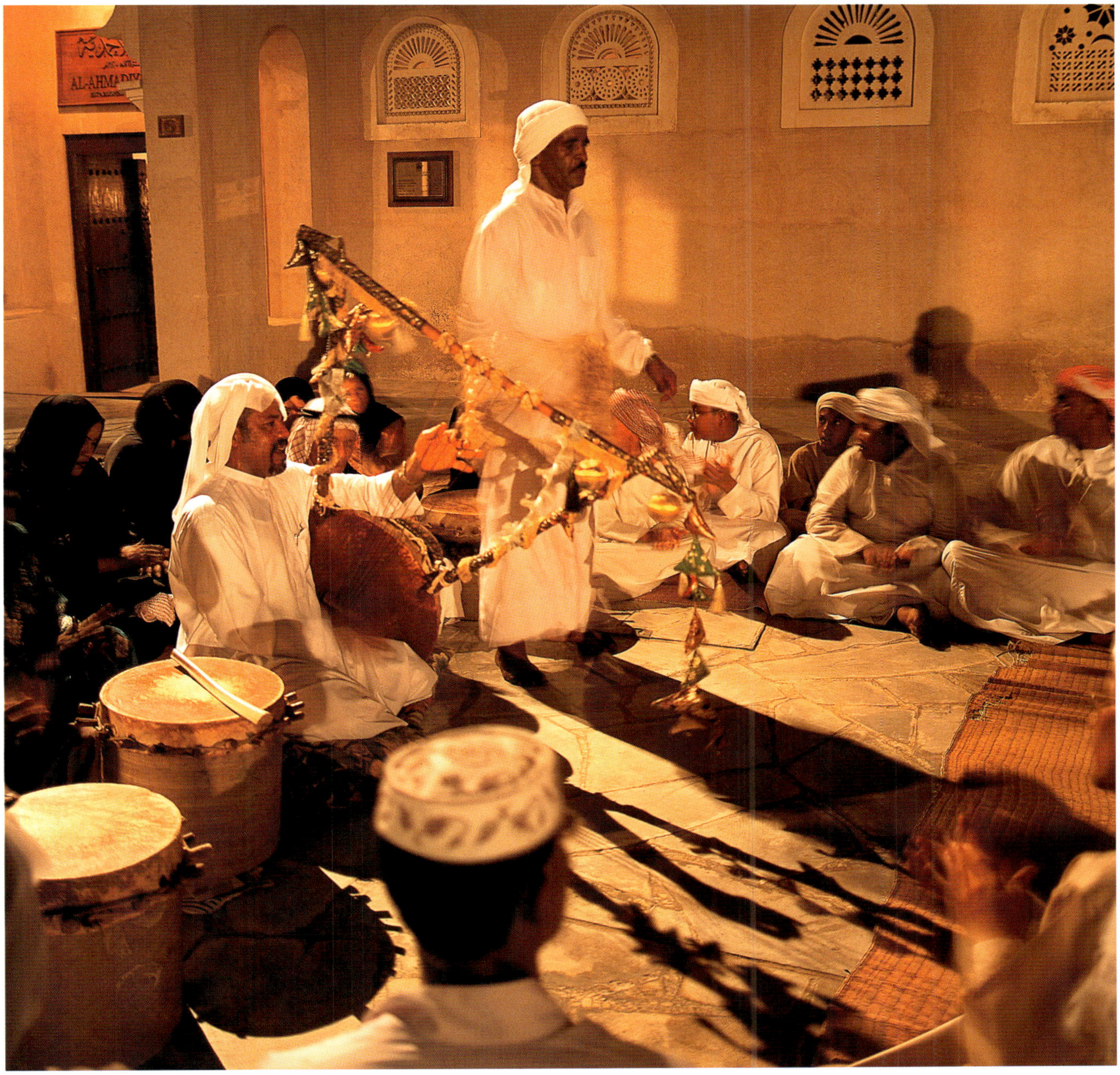

▲ SOMETIMES – WHETHER YOU'RE A VISITOR FOR A holiday in the sun, a business traveller, or a resident of whatever nationality – it might seem as though Dubai never sleeps and there's always something exciting to see or do. Here, Nubans perform a traditional dance with African roots akin to the pentatonic scale.

▶▶ AL MAKTOUM BRIDGE SYMBOLISES THE HEART OF THE Dubai waterway which, in turn, suggests a history of trade along the winding 14-kilometre Creek. The Creek is an integral part of Dubai's role as a major re-export centre, a role which is at the heart of Dubai's modern success story. *Photos by Katarina Premfors.*

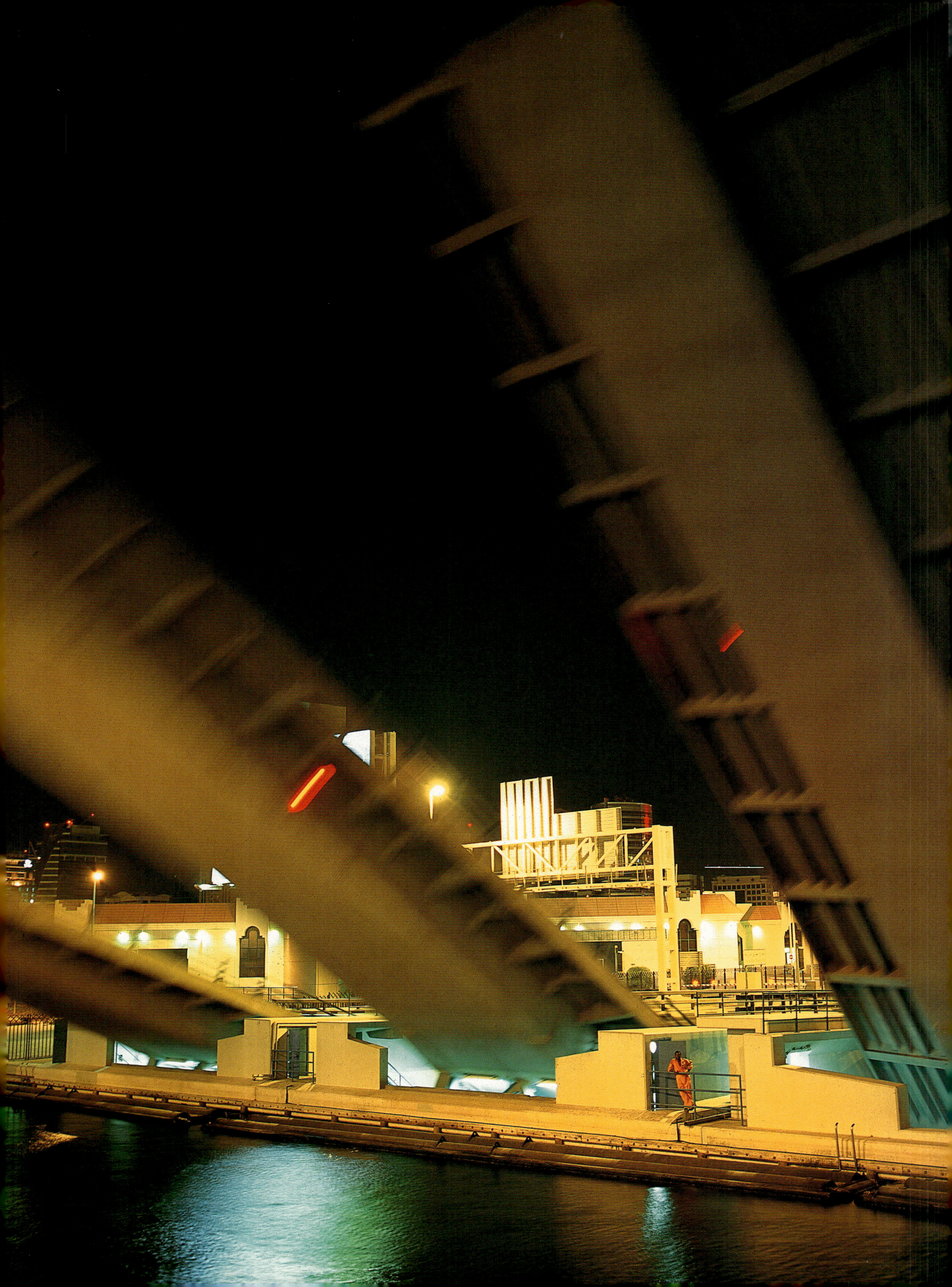

Alarabiya Productions

Alarabiya Productions is a high-profile player in the field of regional and international entertainment. Committed to providing high-end television content that will add a new dimension to the Pan-Arab media industry, Alarabiya has the expertise and infrastructure to produce, market and distribute world-class film and television content.

Constantly setting new standards and benchmarks in the world of media and entertainment, Alarabiya's previous productions include an international classic, *The Last Cavalier*, based on the poetry of Dubai Crown Prince HH Sheikh Mohammed bin Rashid Al Maktoum, and *Arab World Direct*, produced for BBC World.

The documentary film *Dubai 24 hours* is aimed at a worldwide TV audience, its mission to shed true glimpses of the emirate of the 21st century.

With its extensive know-how in Middle East production, finance and distribution, and its vision of international marketing, Alarabiya offers international partners blue-chip co-production opportunities in drama, documentaries, current affairs and a variety of other program genres.

Paramount in all the company's activities is truthfully reflecting Dubai as a world-class city of excellence and professionalism.

Dubai 2003

Dubai 2003 was created as the government organisation to facilitate the successful implementation of the Annual Meetings of the Boards of Governors of the World Bank Group and IMF, held in Dubai in September 2003.

The United Arab Emirates' hosting of this event marks the first time the biggest annual gathering of the global financial community was held in an Arab city. Hosting an event of this magnitude has significantly enhanced the international reputation of the United Arab Emirates as a financial and business hub.

Becoming the financial capital of the world for a two-week period has given this vibrant, dynamic and culturally diverse city and emirate – as well as the United Arab Emirates that it is a part of – the perfect springboard to help attract future inward investment and deliver a positive message to the international community about the Arab world.

THE PHOTOGRAPHERS

NASSER AL SHAIBA

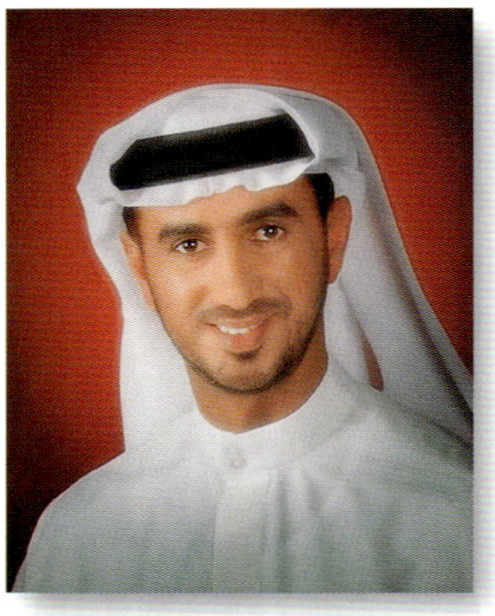

For the past 10 years the life of UAE National, Nasser Al Shaiba, has revolved around diving and the marine environment. He was previously Marine Supervisor at the Department of Environment of the Dubai Municipality. In addition to diving and underwater videography and photography, Nasser's interests include computers, travelling and keeping abreast of new developments in research, the marine environment and underwater technology.

ALIA AL SHAMSI

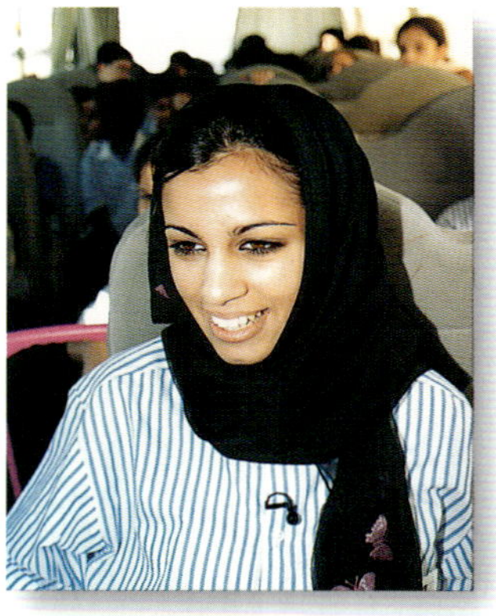

Alia Al Shamsi was born in Dubai in 1982 and discovered photography at a very early age. In 2000 she enrolled in the Visual Communications program at the American University of Dubai, where she fell passionately in love with photography. A chance to study abroad came three years later and she was admitted into Griffith University in Brisbane, Australia. Alia's dream is to complete her degree and enter the world of advertising as a successful commercial photographer.

ASMA HAMAD AL SHAMSI

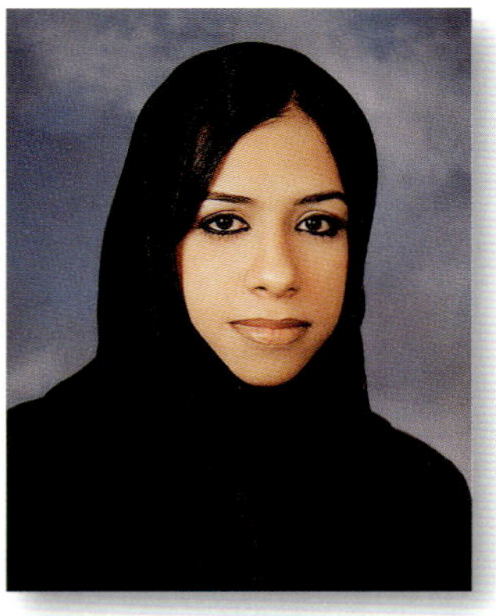

Currently working as a Multimedia Designer at the Gulf Research Centre, Asma Hamad Al Shamsi graduated from the Art and Design College at Zayed University. *Dubai 24 hours* was her first opportunity to work as a photographer and a useful and excititng experience.

TARIQ AL SHARIEF

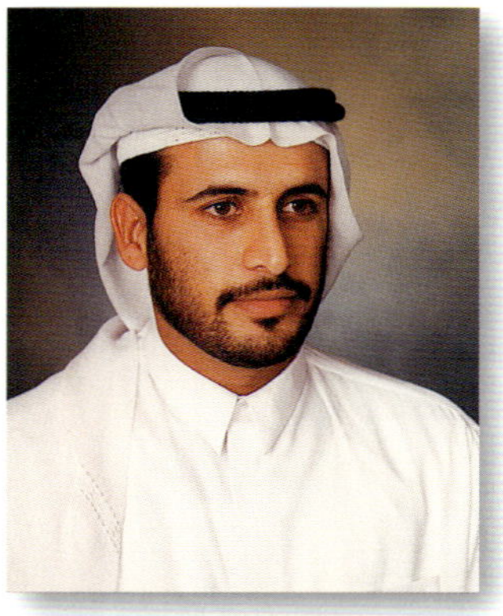

Tariq Al Sharief is a UAE National who's worked for the Coast Guard for 12 years. During the past decade he's also been a specialist marine and topside photographer. His passion for marine photography has taken him far and wide and won him numerous awards in international competitions. Tariq has worked closely with visiting international television and photographic crews and, in doing so, has made a major contribution to the knowledge of the local marine environment.

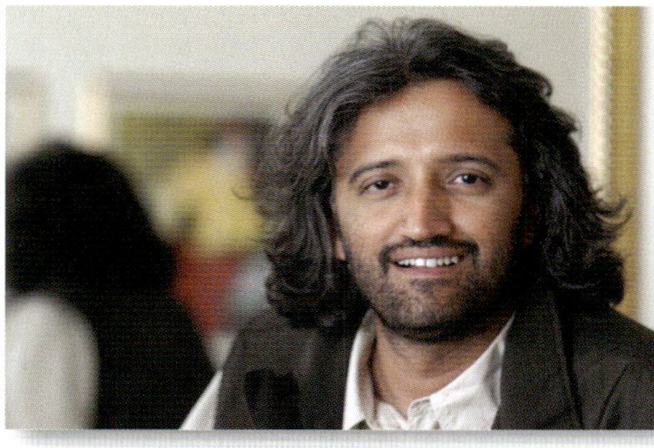

Samar S Jodha

Moving beyond the sphere of commercial photography, Samar S Jodha has taken photography to a different level. An education and apprenticeship with some of the world's renowned schools and studios led to his work being internationally acclaimed and appearing in books and publications such as *USA Today*, *Elle* and *Conde Nast Traveler*. Parallel to his editorial and social-communication work, Samar enjoys a full-time career on the international circuit for advertising and corporate photography.

Paul MacLeod

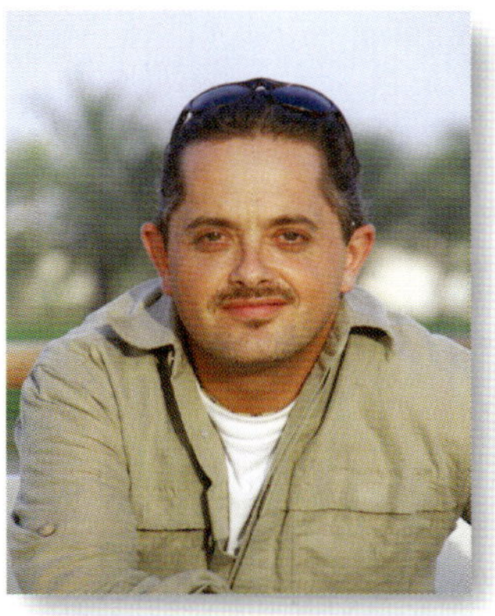

Edinburgh-born Paul MacLeod is qualified in such divergent skills as ski-instruction and clinical hypnotherapy and was an "international nomad" before deciding to turn his photographic hobby into a career. "Few places have such an alluring mix of cosmopolitan culture, ancient history and breathtaking modernity, all bound together by genuine warmth and friendship," he says, after five years behind the viewfinder in Dubai. "For me, Dubai is Aladdin's Cave and Disneyland rolled into one."

Lucy Monro

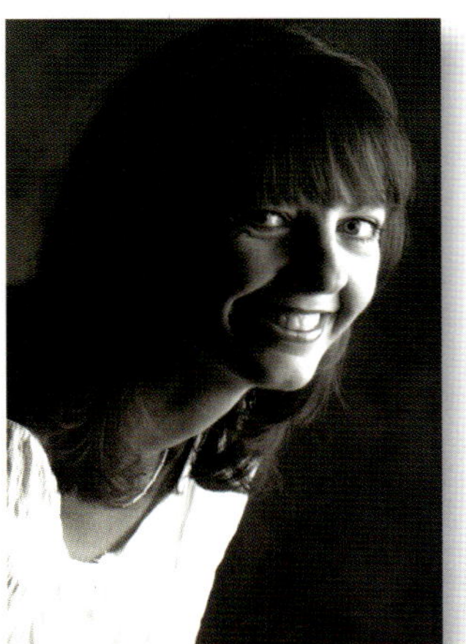

In addition to magazine and newspaper work, British photojournalist Lucy Monro specialises in equestrian photography and ranks among the world's leading photographers of Arabian horses. She's widely published in her adopted home, the UAE, and abroad. Her knowledge of the subject is extensive and she's a qualified riding instructor and veteran international competitor. Ignoring the saying "never work with children or animals" Lucy is also known for her work depicting children in the Third World.

Sara Masinaei

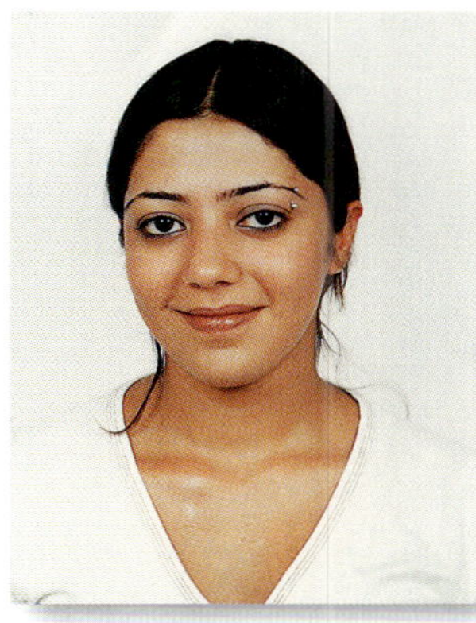

Born in Iran in 1982, Sara Masinaei has lived in Dubai since 1991 and is currently a Visual Communications/ Photography senior student at the American University of Dubai.

Katarina Premfors

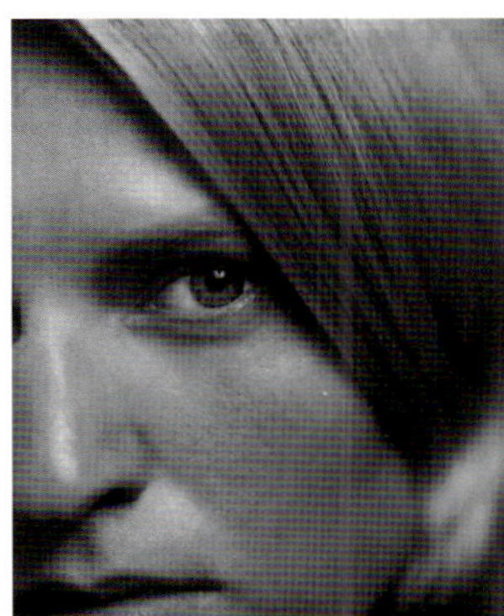

Born in Sweden, Katarina Premfors's interest in photography first showed at the age of 11 when she moved to Pakistan. Since then she's lived and travelled all round the world but has been based in Dubai for 10 years. Her passion for photography most recently took her to remote parts of Afghanistan where she shot images for a series of essays on behalf of UNICEF. In Dubai, Katarina specialises mainly in advertising and design photography.

JOE SASSINE

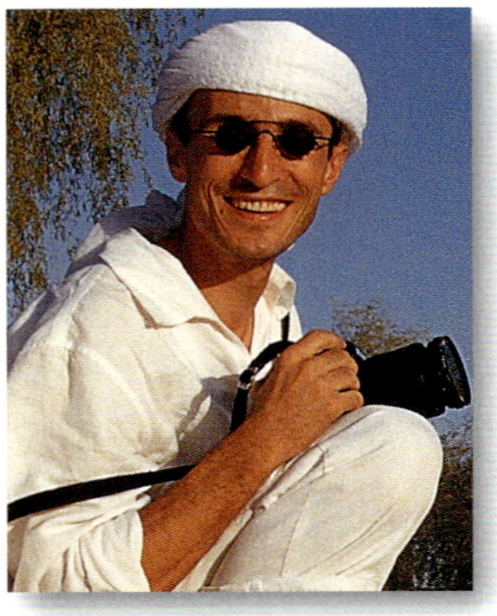

A graduate of the Professional Photographic University in Lebanon, Joe Sassine has worked for 16 years as a professional advertising and commercial photographer. He's a member and licentiate of a number of professional photographic organisations and associations, including the prestigious British Institute of Professional Photography, has won a number of major awards (notably in the annual London International Advertising Awards) and has spoken on professional photography at a number of important photographic conventions.

RAMESH SHUKLA

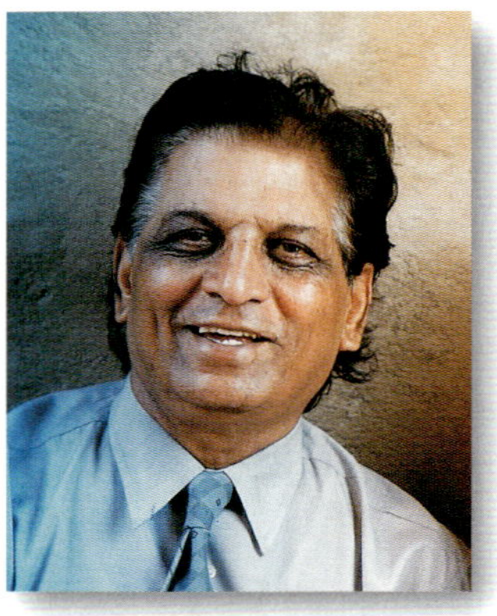

Veteran photographer and artist, Ramesh Shukla, first visited Dubai in 1965 and became a resident and a pioneer in the city's art and photographic scene shortly thereafter. He established Dubai's first art galley in 1970 and currently heads three galleries, including the largest in the Gulf. Ramesh has a comprehensive collection of historical photographs of the UAE and has never lost his passion for photography, focussing nowadays on life, nature and the advances taking place around him.

SOUHEIL SEMAAN

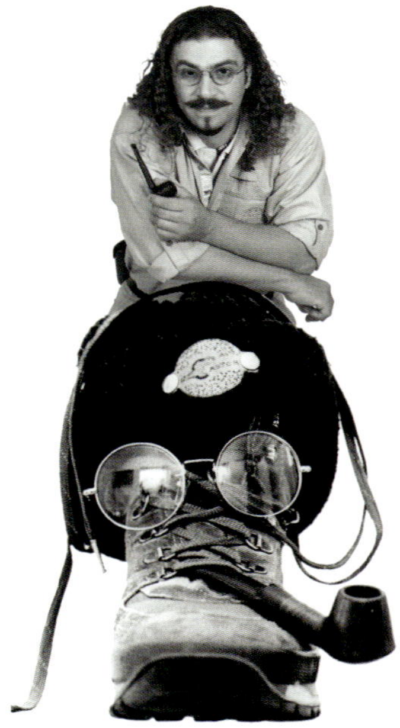

Souheil Semaan is a photographer who probes the depth of his art. Born and brought up in the Lebanon, Souheil developed a love of photography that blossomed in the midst of the strife that struck his motherland. He studied photography in Paris and photographed the Lebanese war and Balkan conflict before moving to Dubai in 1992 to set up his own studio and model agency. He lectures at universities across the Middle East, North Africa and Europe and frequently holds private seminars for professional photographers.

DARIUSH ZANDI

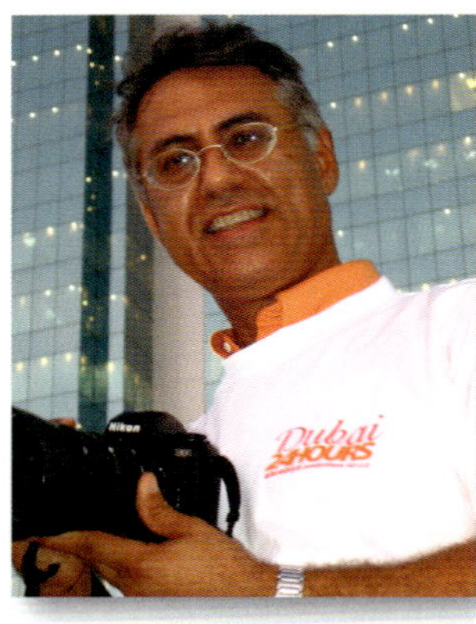

Iranian Dariush Zandi is a freelance photographer with more than 40 years experience. He's also a successful architect, town planner and a writer. He studied photography and film in New York and California and has taught several courses in various institutions in Dubai. Dariush has photographed extensively in different continents and specialises in stock photography of the Middle East. He has contributed to several books and produced four books of his own.

Alarabiya Productions

DUBAI 24 HOURS

Executive in Charge of Alarabiya Productions
Nasib Bitar
Executive Producer and Project Director
Ramzi Rassi
Producer
Tariq Syed
Film Editor
Hussein Younis
Written and Directed by
Michael Tobias

Dubai 2003 Team
Ferakh Baig
Manish Das
Mashael Al Naimi
Lama Salman
Alarabiya Executive in charge of Publishing
Naji Kitmitto
Alarabiya Executive in charge of Marketing
Dr Imam Obeid
Marketing & Promotions
Lilia Abalhasan

Project Finance
Khalil Sharawneh
Project Accountant
Adham Hashem
IT Support
Samir Abdennur
George K George
Alarabiya Office Assistants
Nicholas D'Sousa
Saleem Siddibapa
AMSS Kumar
Mohamad Rafi
Production Assistants
Lennie Aguirre
Sunu Susan
Transcriptions
Buthainah Al Sayed

Photographers
Dariush Zandi
Lucy Monro
Souheil Semaan
Paul MacLeod
Katarina Premfors
Ramesh Shukla
Nasser Al Shaiba
Samar S Jodha
Joe Sassine
Alia Al Shamsi

Additional Photographers
Asma Hamad Al Shamsi
Sara Masinaei
Tariq Al Sharief

***Dubai 24 hours* (Production)**
Segment Producer
Shehab Mahmoud
Segment Directors
Michael Tobias
Shehab Mahmoud
Tariq Syed
Ramzi Rassi

Segment Production
Animation Art Productions
Senior Segment Research
Aline Irani
Segment Research Assistants
Reham Salim
Aziz Hmeid
Tarek El Araidi
Winnie Pasion
Field Producers – Animation Art
Jovan Gill
Rachita

Cameramen
Craig Secker
Peter Davies
Additional Cameramen
John A Ward
Janah Kanj
Maher Abu Drawi
Fuad Dumar
Joseph Al Hindi
Rashed Rehan
Anthony Smythe

Camera Assistants/Behind the Scenes Cameramen
Mario Fernandes
Rashid Rehan
Location Sound Engineers
Ron Bagnulo
Mark Schofield
Crew Drivers and General Assistance
KT Ahmed
K Abdul Sattar
Usman Khan
Permits and Logistics Manager
Akbar Usman Khan

***Dubai 24 hours* (Post-Production)**
Audio Facilities
Barry Kirsch Studios
Dubbing Engineer
Mathew Faddy
Post Production Facilities
Rajtaru Videosonics, Dubai
Smoke Operators
Tarun Agarawal
Rajiv Agarawal
Manasvi Gosalia
Graphics
Murtuza Zakir

***Dubai 24 hours* (Book)**
Publishers
Motivate Publishing, Group Editor and Managing Partner,
Ian Fairservice
Written by
Michael Tobias
Book Editor
David Steele
Book Research
Tariq Syed
Alarabiya Editorial Co-ordinator
Naji Kitmitto
Editorial Assistant
Zelda Pinto
Book Designer
Johnson Machado

Photographic Stock
Supplied by
KODAK

ACKNOWLEDGEMENTS

FOR THEIR ASSISTANCE IN THE MAKING OF *Dubai 24 hours*, our sincere thanks go to:

Khalid Al Naboodah (Naboodah Farms, Awir)
Abdullah Dalmook (Diving and Heritage Village)
Adnan Mohammed Al Marzooqi (UAE family)
Abdullatif Al Sayegh (Arabian Radio Network)
Mohammed Yanis (Arabian Radio Network)
Mohammed Hilal Bin Taraf and David le Mesurier (Nad Al Sheba Avian Reproduction Research Centre)
Khalid Mohammed Ahmed, Editor in Chief (*Al Bayan* newspaper)
Hana Ezzeddine, Administration Secretary (*Al Bayan* newspaper)
Tony Williams (Al Maha Resorts)
Dubai Police
GIS Centre/Space Imaging (Dubai Municipality)
Public Relations Department (Dubai Municipality)
Rana Al Sayyed
Mary McLaughlin (Jumeirah International)
Lance De Masi (American University of Dubai)
Al Mawakeb School
Nad Al Sheba Club
Green Art Gallery
Anita Mehra Humayun (Department of Civil Aviation)
Dr Salah Al Qasim (Rashid Hospital)
Rashid Hospital
Dr Essam Duhair (Genetic & Thalassemia Center, Al Wasl Hospital)
Ahmad Said Al Gaoud (Dubai Television)
The Heritage House
Al Ahmadia School
Ibrahim Juma'a
Raju Nagrajan
Philip Bajaly
Grace Yakoub
Gail Roland
Dr AJ Racy (UCLA)
Raghida Haddad
Major Ali Saqr Al Suwedi (EMEG)
Michel Costandi (MBC)
Badr Abdullah, Bashir Fairuz, Massoud Al Marzouqi, Salem Abdul Rahman, Eisa Ali (Marine Biology and Pearl Divers)
Omar Maleh
Department of Tourism and Commerce Marketing
Dubai Chamber of Commerce & Industry

In fond memory of
Ranita Mascaranhas and Leslie Pope

And all those who provided kind assistance, knowledge and encouragement

Photographic Stock supplied with thanks by

DUBAI 24 HOURS

Written and Directed by
Michael Tobias

www.Dubai24hours.com
Alarabiya Productions FZ LLC, 2003
PO Box 32915, Dubai Media City, Dubai, UAE
Building 7, Suite 215, Dubai Media City, Dubai, UAE
info@alarabiya.com